Mary Lucille Sullivan is a feminist activist and member of the Australian branch of the Coalition Against Trafficking in Women. She lives in Melbourne surrounded by her five daughters and is passionate about creating a space for women to live their lives free of violence and oppression. With her daughters she has run a bookshop in inner Melbourne. She has a PhD in Political Science from the University of Melbourne and is the author of *What Happens When Prostitution Becomes Work: An update on legalised prostitution in Australia* (2006). She has written two other books on social justice issues, *An Australian Pilgrimage: Muslims in Australia from the Seventeenth Century to the Present* (1993) and *Colony to Community* (1997). She is also a co[...] *Sale: Feminists Resisting Prostitution and Po[...]*

MAKING SEX WORK

A FAILED EXPERIMENT WITH LEGALISED PROSTITUTION

MARY LUCILLE SULLIVAN

Spinifex Press Pty Ltd
504 Queensberry Street
North Melbourne, Vic. 3051
Australia
women@spinifexpress.com.au
http://www.spinifexpress.com.au

First published by Spinifex Press, 2007

Typeset in AGaramond by Claire Warren
Cover design by Deb Snibson

Printed and bound by McPherson's Printing Group

National Library of Australia
Cataloguing-in-Publication data:
Sullivan, Mary Lucille, 1950– .
  Making sex work: a failed experiment with legalised prostitution.
  Bibliography.
  Includes index.
  ISBN 9781876756604 (pbk.).
  ISBN 1 876756 60 8 (pbk.).
  1. Sex-oriented businesses. 2. Crime – Sociological aspects. 3. Sex crimes. I. Title.

381.4536344

Contents

CONTENTS

Acknowledgements

It would be difficult for me to adequately thank all those who have helped me with this book, but I would at least like to name a few. I want to particularly express my gratitude to Renate Klein and Susan Hawthorne, whose feminist activism and theoretical writings have inspired me in my own work. I have been exceptionally fortunate to have these two amazing women as my publishers. My appreciation too goes out to Belinda Morris for her patient and thorough editing of my manuscript and to my dearest friend Carole Moschetti for her perceptive and uplifting discussions throughout the writing process.

My special thanks also go to Gunilla Eckberg, Sweden's Special Advisor on issues of prostitution and trafficking; Melissa Farley, feminist psychologist and researcher who works closely with survivors of prostitution; Janice Raymond, feminist theorist and Co-Executive Director of the international organisation, the Coalition Against Trafficking in Women; and Catharine MacKinnon, feminist legal theorist and author of extensive works on women's human rights. Each of these women has provided personal encouragement and insight to me. As well I would like to acknowledge Sheila Jeffreys, feminist activist and academic, whose international writings on prostitution have been valuable to my work.

Finally, I would like to convey my warmest appreciation to my family for their interest and support throughout the long process of completing this book – to Paul and to our daughters, Sarah, Melissa, Emily, Rebecca and Beth.

My hope in writing *Making Sex Work* is that it may contribute to eliminating violence against women and to creating a world where women and girls are free to reach their full potential as human beings.

CHAPTER ONE

Setting the Framework: Prostitution in the 21st Century

Every movement and community for social justice does or should have an interest in recognizing and combating sexual exploitation. Systems of prostitution draw strength from the economic, social and physical vulnerability of girls and women, and reinforce the belief that girls and women are sexual objects . . . Sexual exploitation exists because people are willing to exploit or use others, and because societies allow it to happen.

STANDING AGAINST GLOBAL EXPLOITATION (SAGE 2005) – A
PROSTITUTION SURVIVOR-CENTRED HUMAN RIGHTS ORGANISATION.

In 1984 the Australian State of Victoria legalised prostitution, the first of four Australian states and territories to legitimise sex as work.[1] A decade later, the Victorian Government was acclaiming its success in creating a 'highly regulated, profitable, professional and incredibly well patronised sex industry' (Victoria 1997a, p. 1147). Today this commodification of women and girls for sex, and profit, continues to escalate.[2] At the

---

1. The Australian Federal Government does not implement prostitution industry legislation on a national level. Each state and territory develops its own legislation. The Australian Capital Territory (ACT) legalised prostitution in 1992, the State of New South Wales (NSW) in 1995 and the State of Queensland (QLD) in 1999. The Federal Government has authority over international relations, which takes in sex trafficking.
2. I use the term women and girls as they represent over 90 per cent of victims of prostitution and sex trafficking. However, throughout my book my analysis relates equally to all those entrapped in systems of sexual exploitation.

beginning of the twenty-first century, prostitution is no longer simply a legally accepted industry in Victoria. 'Sexual services' ranks highest of all personal service industries in terms of revenue (reaching as high as 80 per cent), and drives the overall growth of this economic sector in general. Further, sex-based industries in Australia are the financial equals of the 50 top-ranking publicly traded companies, with the industry growing at 5.2 per cent annually between 1999/2000 and 2004/2005, and as high as 7.4 per cent between 2003/2004 and 2004/2005. This is significantly higher than the Gross Domestic Product.[3]

What underpins a government's decision to institutionalise prostitution as work? What impact does this have on women and girls in prostitution? And how do we, as a society committed to women's right to equality and safety, come to terms with a culture where the prostitution industry is influential, pervasive and most of all, considered acceptable? In *Making Sex Work*, I address these questions. I begin by situating Victoria's experience of legalised prostitution as part of the rising global trend to legitimise prostitution as work. I expose the Victorian Government's endorsement of the sex trade as a failed social experiment that harms women and girls in prostitution and ultimately affects the civil status of all women. This book's dominant theme is that the normalisation of prostitution as work gravely undermines women's workplace equality and contradicts other avowed government policies designed to protect the human rights of women. Victoria's legalised prostitution system assists

---

3. The Australian and New Zealand Standard Industrial Classification (ANZSIC) lists 'sexual services' as 'personal services' similar to businesses such as domestic services, babysitting services and weight reduction services. I based my statistical data on information provided by IBISWorld Pty Ltd reports, *Personal Services in Australia* (1998–October 2005); *Sexual Services in Australia* (May 2006) and ABS (2006) *Gross Domestic Product*, ABS CAT NO: 52060, June 2006, 2.3GDP. See also Victoria (1999), pp. 963 and 967.

in maintaining male dominance, the sexual objectification of women, and the cultural approval of violence against women.

In the first sections of this book, I map out the social forces and ideologies that underline Victoria's shift from treating prostitution as a deviant and illegal practice, to recognising it as a 'sexual service' and a legitimate commercial activity. I then move on to examine the implications of this conversion in thinking and practice, for the State, for the pimps and buyers who now have a 'lawful' supply of women for their sexual use, and for the increasing number of individuals who have become highly saleable commodities in the marketplace. I outline the evolution of legalisation with its initial emphasis on containment and tolerance. Next I focus on more recent justifications – sexual liberalism and the rationale that prostitution is 'just a job'. This latter view fits easily with a neo-liberal vision of a *laissez-faire* economic system and the freeing up of the market place where women and girls are just another sought-after consumer good.

As I discuss further in this chapter, feminists have been divided in their approach to prostitution. At one end of the spectrum are liberal feminists who argue that prostitution should be normalised as work. This thinking differs significantly from the radical perspective that analyses prostitution through an anti-violence lens and locates it along a continuum that includes rape, sexual harassment, violence perpetrated by intimate partners, incest and child sexual abuse. The feminist perspectives that were particularly influential in the Victorian debates on legalisation reflected a libertarian outlook which assimilated with the views of the alleged prostitutes' rights movement and with the economic and political priorities of the State. These liberal feminist discourses equate the right to be prostituted with concepts of women's rights to self-determination, economic power and sexual autonomy – a woman's body, a woman's right. That the health and well-being of women oppressed in a system of prostitution was never a central concern for these feminists, nor of the State's legislators or of pro-prostitution advocates, becomes clearly apparent as Victoria progresses along its path towards making sex work.

From the outset, the liberalisation of the State's prostitution laws was based on a harm minimisation approach, a position which accepts the inevitability of prostitution. The Victorian Government hoped that making the trade in women and girls a regulated sector of the mainstream workforce would contain the highly visible and expanding massage parlour industry as well as street prostitution. Equally critical was the desire to eliminate the industry's criminal elements. Among prostitutes' rights activists there was also some belief that legalising prostitution would alleviate most of the worst abuses within the industry.

But legalisation not only does not control prostitution's harms, it produces many of its own making. State endorsement intensifies the commodification of women's bodies and greatly expands the illegal, as well as legal, sectors of the industry. Other consequences of legalisation include the encroachment of prostitution on public life, its integration into state tourism and the growing role of Australian financial institutions in supporting the industry.

The later sections of this book in particular dispel many of the myths associated with legalisation and its purported benefits for women. I shed light on the fallacy of legalisation as promoting self-employment for women, allowing for a cottage-type industry and the lack of exit programs for women who want to leave prostitution. A further fiction that I challenge is that the prostitution industry can be neatly categorised into a well-regulated business that operates similar to other legitimate commercial activities, and clandestine operations which law enforcers now have the capability to deal with. Criminal behaviour and involvement is a feature of both sectors. Sex exploiters indiscriminately traffic women for commercial sexual exploitation, into both legal and illegal brothels, the former often a safe entrepôt for the illicit trade. The increased tolerance of prostitution in Victoria, in effect, requires a steady flow of women and girls to meet the demands of the vastly expanded and lucrative market. And sex business entrepreneurs devise numerous ways to sexually exploit women to make profits and meet consumer demands. The Government must continually introduce catch-up legislation in an attempt to deal with the myriad of unforeseen problems that stem from the State's liberalised prostitution regime. Lastly, street prostitution, despite its continued illegality, increases commensurate with the industry as a whole.

One of the more compelling claims for treating prostitution as work is the theory that this will protect those within the industry from exploitation and violence. Victoria's legal prostitution system notionally provides the most optimal conditions for creating a safe place and system of work. The State, in fact, purports to be at the forefront of implementing occupational health and safety standards (OHS) for the prostitution industry. However these OHS measures, when applied to the everyday reality of women in prostitution, show the unworkability of this proposition. Far from alleviating its harms, any government's attempts to treat prostitution businesses as similar to other mainstream workplaces obscure the intrinsic violence of prostitution – violence that is entrenched in everyday 'work' practices and the 'work' environment. Sexual harassment and rape are indistinguishable from the sex the buyers purchase. That legalisation might make the pathologies of prostitution worse has been asserted in theoretical and critical literature. In *Making Sex Work*, my intention is to make this case with evidence.

Prostitution as 'work' in a global context: an overview

The shift towards viewing prostitution as work materialised in the context of the global industrialisation of what is now a multibillion-dollar sex industry. From the 1980s onwards, we have seen the emergence of commercial sex on an extensive and unprecedented scale. This immense commodity production entails the proliferation of prostitution and prostitution-like activities that include organised prostitution in brothels, massage parlours and escort services, street prostitution, internet prostitution, strip clubs, telephone sex and sex trade shows. It services military forces, sex tourism, a mass pornography trade and marriage bureaus. The media, airlines, hotel chains, tourist industries, international communication and banks all play a part in facilitating its business operations.[4]

An intrinsic component of this new world sex market is the trafficking of millions of people, mainly women and girls, for commercial sexual exploitation. Most countries are involved or affected. While profit estimates vary because trafficking is an illegal and cross-border issue, the US Government has intimated that after drug dealing, trafficking of humans is becoming tied with arms dealing as the second largest criminal industry in the world, and is the fastest growing (US Department of Health and Human Services 2006). In its report *Forced Labor and Human Trafficking: Estimating the Profits*, the International Labor Organisation (ILO), the principal human rights instrument that deals with workers' rights and labour regulations, suggests that global profits made specifically from trafficking for commercial sexual exploitation are worth US $27.8 billion. This figure takes into account intra-country trafficking. Almost half of the profits are derived from trafficking into or within industrialised countries (Belsar, 2005 p. 15).[5]

---

4. For more information on global prostitution see The Coalition Against Trafficking in Women. http://catwinternational.org

Sex trafficking generally involves movement from poorer countries with struggling economies to relatively richer ones, or domestically, from impoverished regions to major industrial centres. It affects almost all countries and reaps enormous profits for agents who provide transport or cross borders, and for brothel owners and pimps who exploit victims in the place of destination. Trafficking thus has a strong race and class component as it involves a big demand and a steady supply of women who are made vulnerable to sex traffickers through inequalities, lack of employment opportunities, violence, abuse, discrimination and poverty (Economic and Social Commission for Asia and the Pacific 2005). However Janice Raymond, feminist theorist and co-executive director of the international organisation the Coalition Against Trafficking in Women (CATW), makes the critical point that, while human trafficking itself is not new, 'What is new is the global sophistication, complexity and control of how women and children are trafficked from/to/in all parts of the globe' (Raymond 2003, p. 1). Trafficking is a huge, organised and largely international industry. The number of women and children trafficked between countries for commercial sexual exploitation is estimated to be between 700,000 and two million each year (2003, p. 1). However as Raymond argues, these estimates are preliminary.[6] The USA's 2006 *Trafficking in Persons Report* found that 'approximately 80 per cent of trafficked victims are women and girls, and up to 50 percent are minors' (Office to Monitor and Combat Trafficking in Persons 2006, p. 1). A further finding is that the majority are trafficked into com-

---

5. It is important to realise that these estimates only account for sex trafficked victims where some form of overt coercion was present that is 'forced' sexual exploitation. I discuss the serious limitations in making any distinction between forced and free sexual exploitation further in this chapter.

6. In Chapter Six, I explain how differing definitions of sex trafficking lead to differences in researchers' estimates of the phenomenon as well as differences between official statistics and non-government organisations.

mercial sexual exploitation. However the report stressed that 'With a focus on transnational trafficking in persons . . . these numbers do not include millions of victims around the world who are trafficked within their own borders' (Office to Monitor and Combat Trafficking in Persons 2006, p. 1).

Most international strategies to eliminate sex trafficking have been shaped by contemporary dialogue around prostitution and by the legal approaches to the industry. In the late twentieth and early twenty-first centuries, there exist four primary legislative methods for dealing with prostitution. These are criminalisation, legalisation, decriminalisation and a human rights legal paradigm. Criminalisation means prostitution and related activities are an illegal and criminal act, punishable by some form of sanction, either fines or imprisonment. Legalisation normally results in the state recognising some forms of prostitution as a lawful activity, while others continue to be included in the criminal code. The state then establishes a regulatory regime to ensure sex businesses do not impinge on public health and safety. Most commonly prostituted women although not buyers, are required to have mandatory health checks.

With decriminalisation states pass legislation to the effect that prostitution is no longer defined as criminal behaviour. Prostitution is then dealt with similarly to other legitimate commercial activities with no specific industry-based regulations. But importantly, both legalisation and decriminalisation permit prostitution to be recognised as legitimate work, and pimps and brothel owners as legitimate business operators. As will become progressively obvious, the efficacy of these legal paradigms for eliminating the violence, exploitation and trafficking that is intrinsic to prostitution is minimal as they fail to recognise the crucial role of buyers in perpetuating the human rights violations that distinguish the prostitution industry from others.

Women and human rights

'Human rights' is founded on the principle of equal rights for all people and the understanding that governments have a responsibility to protect and promote this principle. According to legal theorists Hilary Charlesworth and Christine Chinkin, 'The right of women to equal treatment and non-discrimination on the basis of sex is part of the traditional canon of human rights' (2000, p. 214). At the Vienna World Conference on Human Rights in 1993, the international community formally recognised that the human rights of women were 'an inalienable, integral and indivisible part of human rights' and 'that gender-specific violations of human rights were part of the human rights agenda' (Charlesworth and Chinkin 2000, p. 247).[7] Similarly at the Fourth World Conference on Women, held in Beijing in 1995, governments affirmed their commitment to respect, protect, promote and enforce the human rights of women through the full implementation of all human rights instruments, especially the Convention on the Elimination of All Forms of Discrimination Against Women (CEDAW) (United Nations 1995, p. 2).

Violence against women constitutes a violation of the human rights and fundamental freedoms of women, impairing or nulli-fying their enjoyment of those rights and freedoms (OHCHR 2006, p. 1). It is important to highlight that violence against women is not specific to any group of women or political or economic culture, but transcends class, race, religion and age. The common thread is that:

---

7. Among feminists there is debate about the usefulness of using a human rights approach for ameliorating harms to women. Some argue that its narrow individualistic language does not reflect women's experience. However international law, although limited, is proving to be an important tactic for women as it offers a framework for debate over basic values and conceptions of a good society. See Charlesworth and Chinkin for an excellent discussion of these points (pp. 201–222).

The victims suffer because of their sex and gender . . . violence against women is neither random nor circumstantial. Rather it is a structural problem, directly connected to the manifold expression of imbalance between men that can be found all around the globe (Charlesworth and Chinkin 2000, pp. 12–13).

Worldwide, millions of women each year are the victims of assaults, rape, torture, intimidation and humiliation. Violence however takes many forms. As Charlesworth and Chinkin suggest, violence 'includes such acts as abortions of fetuses because they are female, female infanticide, sterilisation and compulsory child-bearing, inadequate nutrition, wife-murder . . . "dowry deaths", practices such as sati (where a widow is burned on her husband's funeral pyre) and genital mutilation' (2000, p. 12). As I discuss further, while radical feminists have always understood prostitution to be a manifestation of male violence this is now increasingly recognised within the international community.

If prostitution is a violence against women the most advanced legal model for addressing the problem is Sweden's human rights legislative approach that defines the practice as 'a form of sexualised violence by men against women' (Winberg 2002, p. 1). The Government's prostitution legislation forms part of the country's 1999 *Violence Against Women Act*, a component of its gender equality national program. The Act criminalises the buying of sexual services and introduced penalties including a gaol sentence of up to six months and fines linked to the buyer's salary. As prostituted women and children are harmed by prostitution and seen as victims, they do not risk criminalisation or other legal repercussions (Swedish Government Offices 2001). Gunilla Ekberg, Sweden's Special Advisor of prostitution and trafficking in human beings, explains why this pro-women policy is the most effective means for eliminating sex trafficking. Her point is that:

One of the cornerstones of Swedish policies against prostitution and trafficking in human beings is the focus on the root cause, the recognition that without men's demand for and use of women and girls for sexual exploitation, the global prostitution industry would not be able to flourish and expand (Ekberg 2004, p. 1189).

In contrast to either State tolerance or State endorsement of the prostitution industry, the Swedish Government also takes responsibility for assisting women exposed to violence. Sweden's legislative model recognises that poverty and oppression make women and children vulnerable to pimps and traffickers. Thus it requires the State to introduce real strategies to allow victims of prostitution and sex trafficking to alter their situation of exploitation – through counselling, education and job training implemented at a municipal level (Swedish Government Offices 2001).

Mainstreaming prostitution

Traditionally the most common approach to prostitution is criminalisation. However in reality, most countries tolerate some forms of prostitution and adopt a policy of control and containment rather than complete prohibition. Often prostitution itself is not illegal, but related activities such as soliciting, advertising, brothel keeping, living off the earnings, and prostituting minors, are all criminal offences. In practice the law targets women in prostitution and the more overt forms of prostitution like the street trade and sex trafficking. In contrast, male buyers and pimps are seldom criminalised or prosecuted. As Australian feminist historian, Meg Arnot, makes clear, this has the effect of isolating 'the most blatant forms of prostitution' and validating the 'more discreet forms of prostitution and allowing them to flourish'. And the 'casualties have been the women' (1988, p. 42).

A unique feature of prostitution in the contemporary world is the increasing legitimisation and normalisation of the trade as an acceptable commercial practice. More and more we are seeing the integration of prostitution into the public sector economy by way of either legalisation or decriminalisation. In combination with this mainstreaming, prostituted women and men are recognised as part of the formal labour market. Sex is treated as no different from other forms of economic exchange in capitalism which is determined by supply and demand. Victoria has now experienced more than two decades of the ideology of prostitution as work. The legalisation option has recently been adopted by the Netherlands and Germany. The legalisation of prostitution was also on the agenda of the *Second Pan-European Conference – Standing Group on EU Politics* held in Bologna, June 2004. In July of the same year a major US online political forum – American Debate – asked the question 'Should We Legalize Prostitution?' The issue is rated as one of the website's top 25 viewed discussions. The United Kingdom's Home Office, after reviewing its major report, *Paying the Price: A Consultation on Prostitution* (2004) has made the decision to introduce mini-brothels where one or two people can work, although large-scale brothels and street prostitution remain illegal (Ford 2006, p. 1).

While western nations have been at the forefront in treating prostitution as work, a similar trend is now emerging in developing nations. In May 2005, the Kolkata-based Dura Mahila Samanay Committee (DMSC), made a public demand for the decriminalisation of all aspects of prostitution, the culmination of ten years of aggressive campaigning to legitimise the prostitution trade. The collective, which promotes itself as a prostitutes' rights group, consists of mostly women pimps who advocate liberalising prostitution laws while simultaneously controlling a multi-brothel prostitution/trafficking complex that houses 60,000 women and girls in Kolkata. For most women in prostitution pimping is the only means of ending their exploitation. The DMSC is itself under the control of criminal gangs which organise prostitution throughout India (Farley 2005, p. 4). I suggest there is a clear conflict of interests between the Collective which will profit from legalising prostitution as work and the thousands of prostituted women and girls it is supposed to represent. One report published on the DMSC in New York's *The Independent* magazine commented on the lack of exit programs for the many who want to leave prostitution. The organisation's bid for legalisation also does nothing to eliminate the child prostitution visible on the streets that surround the DMSC's main centre in Sonagachi, where one third of the 9,000 people in prostitution are under 18 (Stuteville and Stonehill 2006, p. 3). These realities speak volumes about the lack of initiative taken by either the State or the Dura Mahila Samanay Committee to address the socio-economic forces that lead and then entrap women and girls in prostitution.

The immediate catalyst for the DMSC's protest was the United States' *Leadership Against HIV/AIDS Tuberculosis and Malaria Act (Global AIDS Act)*, which came into effect in June 2005 (Dhar 2005, pp. 1–2). The US Government made known its intention to adopt a strong position against any endorsement of prostitution in December 2002 in its National Security Presidential Directive. Its policy was supported by evidence that the practice is inherently harmful and dehumanising, and that legitimising the industry facilitates trafficking and new forms of sexual exploitation (The White House 2003). The decision gained official support from over 100 women's health and policy organisations, as well as physicians and feminists (Medical News Today 2005). The legislation was to bring into sharp focus the debate over the most appropriate strategies for addressing prostitution and sex trafficking of women and children. It also drew attention to the increasing relationship between public programs to address the AIDS crisis, and decriminalising or legalising prostitution.

This connection between AIDS prevention and the liberalisation of prostitution laws was clearly articulated by the United Nations (UN) Programme on HIV/AIDS (UNAIDS). The Programme's international guidelines *HIV/AIDS and Human Rights* (2003), issued in conjunction with the Office of the High Commissioner for Human Rights (OHCHR), states, for example:

> With regard to adult sex work that involves no victimization criminal law should be reviewed with the aim of decriminalizing, then legally regulating occupational health and safety conditions to protect sex workers and their clients, including support for safe sex during work. Criminal law should not impede provision of HIV/AIDS prevention and care services to sex workers and their clients (United Nations Programme on HIV/AIDS 2003, p. 18).[8]

Given such official approval for the decriminalisation of prostitution as part of a global AIDS preventative strategy it is inevitable that much criticism of the US's *Global AIDS Act* focused on a controversial clause which set terms and conditions for its funding to non-government organisations (NGOs) working with AIDS and trafficking victims. These included assurances that their policies would not support the prostitution industry and sex trafficking.[9] Opponents argued that this stipulation would impede AIDS intervention programs as those within the prostitution industry are considered to be what epidemiologists call 'core transmitters' of HIV (Kaiser Daily HIV/AIDS Report 2005, p. 1). The Government of Brazil, in an unprecedented decision, refused 40 million dollars (US) from the US International Development Fund on this basis (Boseley and Goldenberg 2005, p. 1).

Brazil has a vast and well-established prostitution industry, including a thriving sex tourism trade. Although brothel

---

8. The Guidelines were originally produced in 1998. They were revised and reprinted in March 2003.

9. The 2003 *Trafficking Victims Protection Reauthorization Act* mandated this for foreign organisations. The 2005 *Global AIDS Act* related to US organisations.

prostitution is illegal, prostitution is allowed for those over 18 years. Endemic problems associated with the country's prostitution industry include high levels of child prostitution and sex trafficking. Brazil is officially recognised as both a source and destination country for women, men and children trafficked for sexual exploitation (Office to Monitor and Combat Trafficking in Persons, 2005). Conservative estimates of the number of children in prostitution is around 500,000, many trafficked internally as part of the sex tourism industry (International Network Against Child Prostitution and Abuse 1998).

Brazil's AIDS program, which is promoted as a model for developing nations, is based on 'harm minimisation' and includes safe sex education programs and free condom distribution (AIDS Conference 2005).[10] Increasingly, pro-prostitution prostitutes' rights organisations worldwide are given a role as sexual health educators in this context.[11] The DMSC collective in India, for example, receives millions of dollars a year for AIDS prevention from the Bill Gates Foundation (Farley 2005, p. 4). Decriminalisation advocates imply that liberalising prostitution laws would allow those within the industry 'the opportunity to develop expertise and specific negotiating skills for safe sex with clients . . . thus educating the wider community who access their services' (DeMaere 2005, p. 14). AIDS prevention, public health and decriminalisation of prostitution are thus intrinsically linked.

All women have the right to have access to prophylactics to protect their reproductive health. However the provision of condoms to women made vulnerable to sexual exploitation through poverty, racism and gender disparity is seriously limited as a means of protecting them from contracting the HIV virus.

---

10. The Government is currently stockpiling one billion condoms for distribution in 2006 and a new condom plant is to open in Acre State, northern Brazil.
11. In Chapter Three I trace the development of the Prostitutes' Collective of Victoria as a sexual health provider under government sponsorship.

At the beginning of the twenty-first century it is estimated that nearly 40 million people are living with HIV. Globally just under half of these are female and the proportion is continuing to grow particularly in Eastern Europe, Asia and Latin America (Global Coalition on Women and AIDS 2004). There is also evidence of the feminisation of the AIDS pandemic in industrialised countries in Western Europe and North America, where about one quarter of people living with HIV are women and where HIV has become increasingly lodged among women who belong to marginalised sections of the populations, including minorities, immigrants and refugees (Global Coalition on Women and AIDS 2004). The root cause of this development is sex inequality.

Violence against women that includes sexual violence, physical assault and emotional abuse is now recognised as a primary risk factor in contracting the HIV virus (García-Moreno and Watts 2000; Maman et al. 2000; Osotimehin 2005; Farley 2005). Men tend to have more sexual partners than women, and women may not be able to insist that men use condoms or abstain from sex, which are the only two widely available means to prevent HIV transmission. Babatunde Osotimehin, chairperson of the National Action Committee on AIDS in Nigeria, recently drew attention to the fact that neither abstinence nor getting their partners to use condoms is an option for adolescent girls in Nigeria and in many other countries. As she says, 'Many girls fall prey to sexual violence and coercion and many others are married off very young, as young as thirteen or fourteen, before they are psychologically or physically ready' (Osotimehin 2005). Women and girls' vulnerability to HIV is even further exacerbated through the need for many to resort to prostitution.

Susan Hawthorne in her powerful critique of global western culture maintains that 'The poorest of the poor are women, children, refugees (mostly women), landless (mostly women) and indigenous people (where women are less likely to be a part of the cash economy)' (2002, p. 124).[12] The UN *Millennium Development Goals Report* 2005 similarly explains that:

> Women's access to paid employment is lower than men's in most of the developing world . . . Women are less likely than men to hold paid and regular jobs and more often work in the informal economy, which provides little financial security (UN 2005, pp. 15–16).

However when women do earn income for themselves and their dependants, as poor, they belong to a group 'with no surplus income' (Hawthorne 2002, p. 126). In contrast men have the buying power. H. Patricia Hynes in her groundbreaking research on the impact of consumption on the environment exposed a marked difference in consumption patterns between men and women. Hynes concluded that 'women consume less, proportional to income, than men' as well as spending differently to men. Men, she says, spend 'on luxury items for themselves, such as business junkets, golf courses, gambling, alcohol, tobacco and sex ([A]LUXURY)'. Alternatively women spend 'more on necessities for their families and households, such as food, clothing, and health care ([A]SURVIVAL) (1999, p. 60).[13]

For millions of the world's women sex is their only currency. The ILO has pointed out that 'When sex becomes the means for a woman's economic survival, she is highly exposed to the risk of HIV' (2004). The power differentiation between women without other resources, who are forced to rely on their bodies for a livelihood, and the male buyer, means that their right to refuse sex or negotiate condoms is negated. Thus resorting to interim, crisis-driven strategies (such as safe sex programs) to

---

12. The United Nations Development Fund for Women (UNIFEM) has estimated that 'Of the 1.3 billion people in poverty, 70 per cent are women' (cited in Hawthorne 2002, p. 124).

13. [A] refers to consumption.

Morals

: women and girls' risk of HIV in reality suggests a
ice of protection that does not exist. However after
: pressure from an international coalition of pro-
prostitution organisations who continue to link AIDS prevention
with legitimising prostitution the US Government has lessened
its anti-prostitution policy so that organisations do not have to
specifically state that they are opposed to the trade (Human
Rights Watch 2005, p. 1).

The morality debate

A further, and perhaps more wide-reaching criticism of the US
anti-prostitution legislation, is that its underlying philosophy is
ideologically driven. Brazil claimed that the anti-prostitution
legislation reflects America's propensity to link its foreign aid
programs with conservative politics and the religious right (Bugge
2005). The pro-prostitution prostitutes' rights organisation, the
Empower Foundation Chiang Mai made a similar accusation,
opposing a US $1,000,000 grant to the International Justice
Mission for anti-trafficking work (2005, p. 25). Such beliefs
mirror the thinking that underlies much of the international
dialogue on prostitution and trafficking where debate is narrowly
framed as a contest between competing moral values. On one end
of the spectrum, 'the moral majority' condemns prostitution as
an attack on family values and frequently castigates prostituted
women as immoral and 'purveyors of disease'. Alternatively
socially progressive sexual liberals, perceive themselves as resisting
a range of impositions on civil liberties, unquestioningly
equating gay rights and abortion rights with the right to be
prostituted. The radical feminist movement and other social
justice activists that understand the prostitution industry as violent
and discriminatory, and prostitution as an extreme form of sexual
violence, are marginalised within this framework.

A final and critical perspective that feeds into Brazil's, and other contesters' opposition to the US anti-prostitution legislation, deals with the international trade in women and girls as multi-layered. Thus while some forms of prostitution are recognised as sexually and economically exploitative, the practice simultaneously is promoted as 'sex work' and a dynamic career opportunity based on choice. This view attempts to establish a distinction between trafficked and non-trafficked individuals, between child and adult victims of commercial sexual exploitation. It also takes out of the picture the mass male consumption of commercial sex and the expansion of the prostitution industry, which preys on the vulnerability of women and children globally.

The forced-free distinction

Internationally pro-prostitution advocates since the mid-1980s have been pressing human rights bodies and governments worldwide to make a distinction between trafficking for prostitution and prostitution *per se*. The Global Alliance Against Traffic in Women (GAATW), an international association of non-government organisations, leads this movement. GAATW and its followers situate prostitution as part of the informal labour force, alongside domestic labour. They claim that prostituted women are subjected to exploitation and abuse which are similar in nature to that experienced by others working in low status jobs in the informal sector such as the garment industry or agriculture labour.

GAATW's website provides insights into the organisation's core arguments. These begin with *a priori* assertion that prostitution is only a problem when it involves 'forced labour' or 'forced migration'. Its demands for decriminalisation rely heavily on terms such as 'adult prostitution' 'individual decision' and 'consenting adults'. This channels dialogue on sex trafficking towards determining the extent women 'volunteer' or 'choose' to

19

enter and stay in prostitution. Sex trafficking then becomes a problem to do with 'migratory movements' and 'labour violations' (Global Alliance Against Traffic in Women 2004), unrelated to women's oppression and indeed prostitution. Effectively, GAATW vanishes the word prostitution from its rhetoric entirely, substituting it with 'forced prostitution', 'sex work' and most recently 'migrant sex worker'.

Sex business interests in countries where prostitution is already established as work are well situated to advance GAATW's position. This is so within Australia. The Eros Foundation, the major lobby for the national sex industry, has challenged the Federal Government to recognise the advantages of treating people trafficked into Australia for commercial sexual exploitation as willing immigrant workers. Its chief political lobbyist, Robbie Swan, put the proposition that the sex trade in other countries would be prevented from getting a toehold in Australia 'if sex workers can legally apply to come to this country and work' (2003, p. 1). Once in Australia, these 'contract workers', would 'pay taxes [and] operate under state and territory law'. And, as genuine business entrepreneurs, 'brothel owners could act as legitimate sponsors' for trafficked women (Swan 2003, p. 1). Swan's position suggests that Australia's arbitrary federal immigration laws prevent 'migrant sex workers' from doing what Australian-born women in prostitution can legally and legitimately do under various state and territory prostitution laws.

The Scarlet Alliance, Australia's peak pro-prostitution prostitutes' rights organisation, equally promotes the view that sex trafficking is basically a problem about crossing national borders. Julie Futol, the Alliance's representative before the Australian Crimes Commission's 2003–2004 hearings on sex trafficking, took this position. Her perspective is that trafficked people are not victims of sexual exploitation, but rather 'transnational citizens in a world that is particularly globalised' (Commonwealth of Australia 2003, p. 74).

The reality of globalisation readily dispels such quixotic notions put forward by organisations like the Eros Foundation and the Scarlet Alliance. Globalisation, or more specifically global capitalist practice, has resulted in the ongoing feminisation of poverty as indigenous communities and economies are dismantled or appropriated by dominant cultures.[14] As suggested earlier being poor makes people especially vulnerable to exploitation. In their struggle to escape poverty or political and social insecurity, women and children frequently only have recourse to prostitution. Others caught up in a cycle of irregular migration are trafficked into the prostitution industry. Prostitution is thus a 'choice' based on lack of survival options.

Prostitution survivor groups have been particularly articulate in opposing the idea of opportunistic prostitution and the use of jargonised terms to dissuade people from recognising that prostitution is not something women freely choose. The San Francisco prostitution survivor organization, SAGE, describes some of the mechanisms through which women are channeled into systems of sexual exploitation:

> As military bases and western industries establish a foothold in more and more regions, women and children are increasingly recruited into systems of prostitution, and more men are encouraged to use pornography and prostitution. 'Sex tourism' is a massive industry in itself, with dramatic and destructive impacts on local cultures, economies, and individual bodies. Essentially, prostitution is one of the weapons, consequences, and foundations of global economic exploitation (SAGE 2005).

---

14. Susan Hawthorne provides an in depth analysis of this process in *Wild Politics* (2002). Another earlier and excellent source is Maria Mies and Vandana Shiva, *Ecofeminism* (1988).

Yet in countries where prostitution is already accepted as work, organisations like SAGE find it difficult to gain legitimacy and a voice. Prostitution is legal, legitimate and mostly decriminalised.

Sustaining the myth of 'choice'

The pro-prostitution, pro-'sex work' position has gained credibility with support from such diverse genus as male sexologists, human rights agencies and strands of the feminist movement. The concept of 'sex as a service' was introduced by early twentieth century sexologists who considered prostitution a valid means of meeting men's sexual needs (Ellis 1946; Benjamin and Masters 1965; Comfort 1979). Benjamin and Masters, together with other mainstream sexologists, were already popularising the idea of prostitution as a 'sexual service' in the 1960s. In *Prostitution and Morality*, for example, Benjamin and Masters strongly advocated that the trade be professionalised. They reduced all opposition to prostitution as outdated and moralistic, making a case that 'in an intelligent society, the service of sex can find a useful and beneficial place' (1965, p. 3). For these practitioners, there even existed a particular class of women who are 'physically and emotionally equipped to fulfil the prostitute's role' (Benjamin and Masters 1965, p. 437), a view that is indicative of continuing social norms on gender and sexuality.

Feminists who work within a social constructionist framework[15] have critiqued treatises written in sexology as well as other masculine systems of thought such as sociology, psychology, historiography and the law. These disciplines have been important

---

15. Stevi Jackson who, in the late 1970s, developed a feminist theory of social constructionism conceptualises 'the relationship between society and sexuality in terms of the latter being socially constructed through the process of learning to fit in with the current institutions, ideology and morality of that society' (1979, p. 72). Some feminists do argue that women have an innate sexuality that is repressed or suppressed within patriarchal society (see for example, Mitchell 1974).

producers of many of the patriarchal assumptions that remain constant in discourses around prostitution in contemporary society. Feminist sociologists Stevi Jackson and Sue Scott's writings on sexuality make clear how treatises in these disciplines mainly consider prostitution as a 'biological and psychological phenomenon often draw[ing] on a medical model which regarded difference from a narrowly defined heterosexual norm as pathological' (1996, p. 2).[16] For prostituted women, this has meant that their behaviour was pathologised, that is, in some way their supposed 'natural' sexuality has been distorted. Yet conversely, men's use of women in prostitution is commonly measured as a functional response to male sexual needs: a 'natural' biological phenomenon.

Feminists have been critical of this 'essentialist', 'natural' or 'hydraulic' model of sexuality, as it is alternatively called, because it conceptualises sexuality simply as an instinct or drive that exists independent of the social context in which male and female relations are played out. As Jackson and Scott argue, from this minimalist perspective sexuality is 'dependent on internal, biological factors such as hormones' directed at the opposite sex (1996, p. 70). Diane Richardson, writing from a radical feminist perspective, expands on this description. She says that in essentialist models 'sexuality is, ultimately [seen as] a reproductive function, with vaginal intercourse *the sex act*' (1997, p. 155). Men are the actors – 'dominant' or 'active' and women are the acted upon 'submissive' or 'passive' (Richardson 1997, p. 161).

Psychologists, Melissa Farley and Vanessa Kelly (2000), offer one of the more recent and extensive reviews of the medical and social sciences approach to prostitution. They demonstrate how these disciplines normalise prostitution through labelling and blaming the victims of sexual exploitation. Their findings

---

16. The quote refers specifically to sexuality, but as the authors qualify, debates around prostitution mirror those around sexuality (1996, p. 20).

indicate how it is still generally 'assumed that victimized prostituted women have personality characteristics which lead to their victimization' – 'inherent masochism', 'maternal deprivation', 'anal desires of the child' and 'drug addiction' (2000, pp. 10–12). Farley and Kelly also point out how the view that prostituted women are purveyors of disease is seldom challenged with 'addicted prostitutes seen as the source of danger to the john, rather than the john's posing a threat to the women in prostitution' (2000, p. 11). Thus as these authors conclude, current usage of these theories by health professionals and other supposed 'experts' on prostitution, promotes the invisibility of prostitution harm, as well as ignoring poverty as 'the one precondition' for women entering the industry, 'in addition to female gender' (2000, p. 11).

A good enough job for poor women

The pro-prostitution position that suggests that prostitution is work becomes exceedingly seductive, nonetheless, when considered in conjunction with the strong international movement towards state sanctioning of prostitution for economic reasons, especially in developing nations. By 1988 the United Nations World Health Organisation (WHO) was providing considerable currency to these arguments, portraying prostitution as 'dynamic and adaptive sex work, involving a transaction between seller and buyer of a sexual service' (cited in Scrambler and Scrambler 1997, p. 18). The ILO also has, at times, been a major advocate of the idea that prostitution is fundamentally an economic transaction from which both nations and individuals can receive extensive benefits.

In 1998 the ILO released its controversial report, *The Sex Sector: The Economic and Social Bases of Prostitution in Southeast Asia*. In this, prostitution is defined as an economic activity that should be officially recognised because of the extent and scope of the trade. Its author, Lin Lean Lim, justified this position in several ways. Firstly she drew attention to the reality that, in South East Asia, prostitution accounts for between two and 14 per cent of regional economies. On this basis, she argued, not only should prostitution be included in the Gross Domestic Product, but also countries could extend their 'taxation net to cover many of the lucrative activities allied with the trade' (Lim 1998, p. 12). Lim does concede that coercion, exploitation and violence are inherent in prostitution, but similar to GAATW, takes the stance that there is a distinction between forced and free prostitution, a problem that can be overcome through the application of proper labour standards. Lim makes the final point that for women, marginalised through poverty and lack of education, prostitution is indeed an 'economic opportunity' (1998, p. 13).

A more recent example of the ILO's acceptance of the forced-free binary appears in the 2004 International Labour Conference proceedings *Towards a Fair Deal for Migrant Workers in the Global Economy* (2004). As did Lim, the proceedings employed the terms 'sex work' and 'forced prostitution' throughout, accepting that prostitution is just another form of migrant labour that can be protected through the implementation of industrial rights protocols.

Much recent academic work on prostitution also adopts the lexis that reflects the pervasive influence of the pro-prostitution, pro-'sex work' bias. Like Lim and others, Paul Monzini's 2005 study, *Sex Traffic: Prostitution, Crime and Exploitation*, implies that for some, prostitution is a well-sought-after career opportunity. Monzini, who has worked in association with the United Nations Interregional Crime and Justice Research Institute (UNICRI), takes a perspective which, in his words, moves beyond the 'victim/slavedriver' polarity. He sets up a contextual framework which situates prostitution as part of the spread of the market economy worldwide, 'where the search for sex' is met by a 'readiness to offer sex for payment'. The differences between women trafficked for sex and 'skilled professionals' is all about economics, with victims of sex trafficking merely having 'less contractual power' (Monzini 2005, p. 21). Moreover Monzini goes to great lengths to espouse the attributes of his 'skilled professionals', describing them as 'attractive, enterprising women who engage in well-paid ongoing activity from a position of independence and seek to minimize the risks of the trade' (2005, p. 43). Monzini wants us to accept that for many women prostitution as a practice is all right. But in this discussion of freedom and prostitution, the asymmetry in power relations between men and women is dismissed just as the asymmetry between employer and employee is ignored in contemporary Industrial Relations law with its focus on individual contracts. The difference is that in contrast to prostitutes' rights advocates no socialist would pretend that employer-employee relations are equal.

Feminist perspectives on prostitution

In 1979 radical feminist, Kathleen Barry, published the classic *Female Sexual Slavery*, in which she demonstrated that prostitution was a form of sexual exploitation and was not an experience women freely chose. She defines sexual slavery as:

> Present in all situations where women or girls cannot change the immediate conditions of their existence; where regardless of how they got into those conditions they cannot get out; and where they are subject to sexual violence (1979, p. 9).

Barry's analysis of prostitution leads to the realisation that 'the only distinction that can be made between traffic in women and street prostitution is that the former involves crossing international borders' (1979, p. 9). She aims to show us that we must understand prostituted women 'not as a group set apart, which is a misogynist construction, but as women whose experience of sexual exploitation is consonant with that of all women's experience of sexual exploitation' (1979, p. 9).

However as previously indicated the question of whether prostitution should be recognised as sexual exploitation, and a form of sexual violence, has been a point of contention within contemporary feminism: between pro-prostitution feminists who accept the forced-free distinction and radical feminists who reject any such division. As suggested by Barry, the latter group understands prostitution as sexual exploitation, connected to human rights violations and dehumanisation. This feminist knowledge nullifies any possibility of distinguishing between forced and free prostitution as the experience of prostitution is itself inimical to women's health and well-being as well.[17]

The pro-prostitution position

Implicit in the statements of pro-prostitution feminists is the conviction that both historical and contemporary constructions of prostitution as deviant sexual behaviour have enforced a set of social and legal conditions that deny prostituted women their full human and labour rights. In a similar way to pro-prostitution advocates, this stream of thinking does not consider prostitution *per se* as the problem. They suggest it is the legal frameworks and the social stigma that is attached to prostitution that infringe upon the freedoms of those within the industry.[18]

Australian lawyer Marcia Neave writes from the above standpoint. She maintains that the 'whore' identity is founded on the 'distinction between the "innocent victim" who deserves pity and

---

17. I offer more extensive analyses of these feminist debates in my PhD which formed the basis for this book. See *Making Sex Work: The experience of legalised prostitution in Victoria, Australia,* The University of Melbourne, 2004.
18. Authors advocating these ideas include Bell 1994; Bindman 1997; Jeness 1993; Kempadoo and Doezema 1998; Overs and Longo 1997; Pheterson 1989, 1993; Outshoorn 2004 and Walkovitz 1996, 1999.

the punishment of those who have criminally abused her, and the willing "whore" who lacks innocence' (1988, p. 205). Neave explains that:

> Within dominant male ideology, women who make their sexuality available to everyone suggest a moral ambiguity, or the possession of power or agency, which implies that they have a choice to do so or not. As such, these women, who are distinguished from the 'virtuous woman' by the stigma of 'whore', are no longer entitled to social protection (1988, p. 205).

Legal theorist, Catharine MacKinnon, writing from a radical feminist perspective explicates the implications of this mythology in the law of rape. She says such views legitimise the idea that:

> A promiscuous woman is more likely to consent to sex on a particular occasion, that failure to pay does not make a sex act for money non-consensual, that women who have sex with many men cannot be believed, that women who have sex with many men are not harmed by being forced to have sex with one man, or the rape of a prostitute is a contradiction in terms (2001, p. 1400).

But while most feminist theorists agree that prohibition adversely affects prostituted women, those who support the idea of prostitution as work, imply that both prostitution, and attitudes towards it, can be reformed.

Jo Bindman summarises the pro-prostitution arguments in *Redefining Prostitution as Sex Work on the International Agenda* (1997), a synthesis of the views of the pro-prostitution group Anti-Slavery International and the Network of Sex Work Projects, two principal prostitution advocacy organisations. Bindman rationalises the institutionalisation of prostitution as work, by arguing that it is 'The marginal position of sex workers in society [that] excludes them from the international, national and customary protection afforded to others as citizens, workers or women' (1997, p. 3). She makes the further point that prostituted women's vulnerability 'to human and labour rights violations is greater than that of others because of the stigma and criminal charges widely attached to sex work' (1997, p. 3). This analysis of course makes invisible the critical role of the buyer in perpetuating prostitution abuse. But it allows Bindman to rationalise that normalising 'commercial sex as work' offers prostituted women protection under existing international human rights instruments. The appeal here is to draw the flawed connection between the recognition of the legal status of prostitution as work and the attainment of prostituted women's human and labour rights and the rights of all women to sexual autonomy.

Prostitution and the language of equality

Rights discourses that surround the pro-prostitution position are strongly influenced by liberal individualism, which has its roots in libertarian philosophy also known as classical liberalism. This system of beliefs advocates free will and the right of the individual and, by extension, individual property rights, natural rights and the need for constitutional limitations on government to safeguard personal liberty. Liberals generally agree that society should have very limited interests in the private behaviour of its citizens, chiefly in the areas of free speech, personal conscience or religious principles, political associations, and private sexual relations. When talking about prostitution, feminists who support its legitimisation as work utilise the language of liberal individualism to promote prostitutes' rights campaigns as a struggle for self-determination and economic and sexual freedom.[19]

---

19. Delacoste and Alexander 1988; Bell 1994; Segal 1997; Sullivan 1997; Lumby 1998; O'Connell Davison 1998; Chapkis 2000 exemplify those authors who employ this language.

A key argument that pro-prostitution theorists make is that the 'choice' to be prostituted may be a reasonable decision given that all women's lives are constrained. Philosopher, Debra Satz, sees that prostitution may be a 'rational choice for "poor" women in particular as a means of "improving their conditions"' (1995, pp. 66, 83). This idea that to be prostituted may be a form of agency for women in oppressed conditions, in part, reflects socialist feminist theorising around prostitution that began to emerge in the mid-1970s.[20]

Towards an economic analysis

Socialist feminists consider prostitution as resulting from the unequal economic and social power of men and women under capitalism and patriarchy. This involves both the exploitation of women's sexuality and their labour. Control over women's sexuality essentially parallels male control over women in other areas of their life such as work and the family. Prostitution is sustained by men's dominant economic position and purchasing power in the capitalist market. Thus sex and economic power are enmeshed.

Australian feminist historian, Kay Daniels, draws attention to the fact however, that this continuity in women's lives mainly goes unnoticed. She suggests that, 'The monetary exchange that exists in prostitution obscures the continuities between commercial sex [and] the degree of exploitation which is present in much of the work done by women' (1984, p. 1). Especially she draws parallels with marriage, since marriage traditionally gave men conjugal rights over their wives in exchange for maintenance. According to Daniels, it is only that the cash nexus in prostitution 'has masked the sexual trade-off which occurs

---

20. Some examples of feminists who offer a socialist orientation on prostitution include Scutt 1977; Aitkin 1978; Morgan and Russell 1978; Jackson and Otto 1979; Overall 1992.

within marriage and the price of unpaid sexual services women routinely provide for men' (1984, p. 1). Yet socialist feminists generally agree that prostitution embodies women's subordinate condition.

Christine Overall in 'What's Wrong with Prostitution' succinctly summarises the main points of the socialist feminist argument. She says:

> Prostitution epitomizes men's dominance: it is a practice that is constructed by and reinforces male supremacy, which both creates and legitimizes the 'needs' that prostitution appears to satisfy as well as it perpetuates the systems and practices that permit sex work to flourish under capitalism (1992, p. 705).

This perspective leaves no avenue for reform of the industry, but only for the elimination of the circumstances that compel women's involvement in prostitution. As Overall concludes, under capitalist patriarchy, 'dominance and submission, oppression and victimization are necessarily built into the practice' (1992, p. 722). During the 1990s this view was to change radically as pro-prostitution advocates more and more promoted prostitution as a paradigm for women's sexual freedom.

The concept that prostitution parallels other forms of women's work within a capitalist patriarchal system was nonetheless a critical phase towards legitimising prostitution as work. Working from the standpoint of Marxist socialist practice, socialist feminists did not seek a legal remedy for its elimination. As the cause of prostitution is based in concrete social and economic structures which subordinate women to men, it requires long term solutions. Eliminating prostitution meant targeting family, work organisation and the global economy. In practice however, some interim and immediate strategies were needed as prostituted women were experiencing violence on a daily basis. In addition they continue to be targeted by law enforcers for criminal activities while the buyers' prostitution behaviour remained beyond the law.

Indeed from a feminist perspective, if prostitution was sexual exploitation then criminalising women's prostitution behaviour was unthinkable. That prostitution was seen not to be qualitatively different from other areas of work in which women were devalued and paid poorly opened the way for developing a feminist concept of prostitution as a form of women's labour that should be protected by industrial relations. In practice though, any analysis that helps legitimise prostitution as work, even though based on an agenda that seeks to empower women, by default, institutionalises their commodification. Socialist feminists thus implicitly endorsed the way to legalisation.

The 'right' to be prostituted

The conviction that one has the right to 'choose' to be prostituted draws above all on liberal contract theory. The proponents of this theory hold that all individuals have the right to alienate their bodily property and can choose the way in which this occurs. Pro-prostitution theorists argue that this right extends to the right of women to freely contract their body out for payment (Almodovar 1999, p. 75). This contextualisation leads to an understanding that it is not the women themselves that men purchase, but simply a service, similar to other personal services.

In *The Sexual Contract* (1988), political scientist Carole Pateman, clarifies how the liberal concept of 'choice' is based on a view that an individual's sex can be separated from their personhood without harm to the self, a belief she strongly disputes. Pateman agrees that the body of a woman and sexual access to that body is the subject of contract (1988, p. 203), but she wholly rejects the notion that prostitution can be understood as a clearly negotiated contract between two equal parties for a service. The body is not a neutral object that men purchase.

Prostitution, she says, is nothing less than 'the unilateral use of a woman's body by a man in exchange for money' (1988, p. 199). As a prostituted woman sells her womanhood, she sells something that is integral to her identity and self.

Offering women sexual freedom

In addition to contract theory, pro-prostitution theorists employ sexual libertarian concepts when speaking of prostitution as work. The principle that sexual experience is the right of every human being and should be entirely a matter of free choice and personal preference is fundamental to sexual libertarianism. Sexual liberty is complex for women because sexuality is understood to be both a domain of restriction, repression and danger as well as a domain of exploration, pleasure and agency. Stevi Jackson and Sue Scott have pointed out that there has long been a tension in feminist thinking about sexuality, between the potentially pleasurable aspects of sex and its dangers. They maintain that 'heterosexuality has always been risky for women, whether in the terms of double standards and fears of loss of "reputation" or of pregnancy, disease, violence and coercion'. At the same time, 'there has been a concern with pleasure and the lack of it' (1996, p. 17).

The influence of sexual libertarian discourse on feminism became particularly arrant in the US in the 1970s and 1980s where as Diane Richardson explains, 'a search for women's sexual satisfaction [became] an important feminist goal' (1997, p. 162). Such ideas were mainstreamed at a controversial 1982 feminist conference on the politics of sexuality at Barnard College, New York, and in a follow-up edited collection entitled *Pleasure and Danger: Exploring Female Sexuality* (Vance 1984). But while feminists more generally were debating the issue of sexual pleasure throughout the 1980s – popularised as the 'Sex Wars' – pro-prostitution feminists took the debate one step further by equating prostitution with women's sexual emancipation. This outlook sought to create a feminist discourse with 'whore' at the centre of dialogue around women's sexual liberation.

Roberta Perkins, writing in the Australian context, exemplifies the way in which pro-prostitution theorists appropriate the liberal notion of sexual autonomy to create a dialogue on prostitution that promotes the industry as nothing less than a paradigm for women's freedom. She argues that the abolition of all laws relating to prostitution is a positive and necessary strategy, as only decriminalisation will remove the 'punitive threat' to those 'who aspire to freedom of sexual choice' (1991, p. 29). The work of American pro-prostitution advocate, Priscilla Alexander, follows a similar line. In the collection *Sex Work: Writings by Women in the Sex Industry*, which she co-edited with Frederique Delacoste, the assumption that 'prostitutes enjoy sex and have no qualms about enjoying sex as work' is uncritically advanced (1988, p. 16). Women in prostitution, for example, have the opportunity 'of exploring a positive sexuality' (1988, p. 142). Another common topic is the pleasure and power of sado-masochism – to be sexually aroused by 'tying a man up', 'whipping him raw' and 'fucking him with a dildo', a process we are told which uncovered some 'innate' sexuality that the author had 'forgotten about herself' (1988, p. 50).

Diane Richardson makes the point that the sexual libertarian perspective sees sexuality 'as regulated not only through prohibition [that is by law] but produced through definition and categorization' (1997, p. 158) or, in Foucauldian terms, through discourses on sexuality. Radical feminist, Dorchen Leidholdt, in her critique of sexual libertarianism, explains that proponents believe that there exists 'a plethora of sexual preferences and practices which profoundly violate societal restrictions' (1990, p. 126). These 'restricted sexual activities' in the contemporary climate encompass 'cross generational sex (to use their euphemism for child sexual abuse), fetishism, sadomasochism, and the making and use of pornography' while practitioners are portrayed as courageous transgressors (1990, p. 126). Leidholdt goes on to explain how sexual libertarians locate prostituted women within this group and suggest their oppression stems from their daring to step outside of patriarchal laws that privilege heterosexuality, marriage and procreation.

From the sexual libertarian perspective, as inferred earlier, the struggle for the right to be prostituted is then a conflict over the morality of prostitution and not about the sexual exploitation of women and children by the men who buy and sell them. The right to be prostituted becomes undifferentiated from the right of women to 'speak out against men who abuse them', to be 'visible lesbians, demonstrators in abortion rights, women resistors against dictatorial regimes', or 'unveiled women', a view put by Gail Pheterson from the Netherlands (Pheterson 1996, pp. 11–12). The difference between sexual exploitation and sexual autonomy is disappeared.

Increasingly the pro-prostitution analyses, which Alexander and Pheterson stand for, show the influence of postmodernism with its emphasis on difference between women, subjective definitions of oppression and individual solutions to oppression. In the 1990s post-modernism and 'queer theory' strengthened the notion that prostitution is a form of sexual expression. These theoretical perspectives provided an analytical framework for prostitution to become just one aspect of the continuum of human sexual relations and arrangements, where prostituted women experience oppression in a similar way to others who are categorised, according to their class, race, or sexual orientation.

This tendency to focus on notions of sexual freedom and choice at the expense of feminist analysis of power and gender depoliticises prostitution. Once prostitution was defined as 'choice' the next logical phase in the struggle for the prostitutes' rights was to accept the existing social, economic and normative structures of politics, and seek to ameliorate problems associated with those structures. This is precisely what happened.

Redefining prostitution as 'sex work'

From the early 1980s onwards discourses on prostitution spoke of the harms of prostitution more and more in relation to prostituted women's legal status, the environment in which prostitution took place and the limited options for women of colour, or those oppressed by class. This was initially spelt out in the *World Charter for Prostitutes' Rights* produced by the pro-prostitution International Committee for Prostitutes' Rights (ICPR) in the mid-1980s (1985). Pheterson writes that the ICPR maintained that 'Prostitutes' lives depend upon healthy, safe and economically viable work conditions for adults and true protection from child abuse, deceit, force and violence' (Pheterson 1989, p. 18). In turn, strategies to protect those within the industry were seen as 'meaningless without rights to work, and the right to reside, travel and participate in social security programs' (1989, p. 18). The redefinition of prostitution as 'sex work' thus became a preliminary condition for the enjoyment by prostituted women of their full human and labour rights. From this perspective, as Pheterson would later argue, those suppressing prostitution were in fact guilty of human rights violations and that 'the very principle of restricting the sex industry' should be challenged 'under criminal law' (1996, p. 8).

Catharine MacKinnon has exposed the serious limitation of claims that imply women's sex equality can be served by making sex 'work'. As she maintains:

> Sex equality challenges to laws against prostitution . . . have not challenged the sex inequality of the institution of prostitution itself, nor have they questioned, as a violation of equal protection of the laws, the criminalization of something mainly women do that is

heavily marked by gender inequality and subordinates women in a sex-unequal society (2001, p. 1437).

The salient point here is that MacKinnon recognises the core inequality and subordination underpinning prostitution.

Critiques of 'choice'

Despite the momentum gained by the pro-prostitution collective, internationally there has been a parallel movement among feminists that contests the liberal concept of choice and self-determination (including MacKinnon 1987; Pateman 1988; Leidholdt 1990; Rowland and Klein 1996; Jeffreys 1997; Stark and Whisnant 2004). These theorists look at liberal ideas of freedom in the context of hetero-reality and a male supremacist society. Pateman, in her critique of liberal contract theory, draws attention to the fact that the liberal emphasis on 'individualistic initiative (or choice) assumes that each member of society is a self-reliant and inherently discrete unit' (1988, p. 208). But as MacKinnon has argued, choice or consent is inconsequential given the 'predominant social arrangement' constructed around 'male dominance and female submissiveness' (1987, p. 7). Discourses which promote the forced-free distinction take no account of the gender power dynamic that is intrinsic to prostitution. In the pro-prostitution dialogue around sex trafficking coercion or forced prostitution takes place when a person or persons compels another individual into prostitution by implying violence or reprisal. This is the only coercive relationship of power recognised. Thus as MacKinnon explains, 'unequal power relations and dominance of one group over another are not essentially [seen as] coercion' (1987, p. 7).

Evelina Giobbe, the founder of the US-based prostitution survivor group WHISPER (Women Hurt In Systems of Prostitution), stresses that the concept of choice is nullified for prostituted women because their social and economic status ensures submission and compliance. In *Prostitution: Buying the Right to Rape*, Giobbe describes how:

> [C]hoice implies the chance, right, or power to choose, usually by the free exercise of one's judgment. . . In order for choice to be made freely there must be an absence of coercion or violence. The function of the institution of prostitution is to allow males unconditional sexual access to females, limited solely by their ability to pay. Culturally supported tactics of power and control facilitate the recruitment or coercion of women and children into prostitution and effectively impede their escape (1991, p. 144).

Thus while a woman may enter a contract to be prostituted, this does not mean that she does so of her own free will.

One of the more insidious consequences of the forced-free distinction is that it promotes the idea that prostitution *per se* is harmless and that it is only a problem under specific sets of conditions. As Janice Raymond argues, this paradigm is 'used to make some forms of prostitution acceptable and legitimate, revising the harm that is done to women in prostitution into a consenting act and excluding prostitution from the category of violence against women' (1998a, p. 1).

Applying feminist workplace equality theory to prostitution

Some feminists have also critiqued the idea of prostitution as work on the grounds that it is in direct opposition to women's strides towards achieving equality in the workplace. Since the 1970s, feminist struggles around women's work have focused on the right of women to sex equality in the workplace that includes the fundamental right to dignified work. Feminist theorists such as Catharine MacKinnon, insist that discriminatory sex-based practices within the workplace 'cumulatively and systematically shape access to human dignity, respect, resources, physical security, and credibility, membership in community, speech and power' (1992, p. 47). She goes on to say that discriminatory practices include unequal pay, allocation to less prestigious tasks and sexual harassment. Women's advocacy organisations have lobbied to gain recognition of these abuses through such mechanisms as sex discrimination legislation.

An aspect of the labour force that workplace equality theorists argue is particularly detrimental to women is occupational segregation by sex,[21] an inherent feature of prostitution. Labour feminist Lisa Adkins makes just this point. Adkins' research into the hotel and leisure industries led her to conclude that occupational sex segregation in the service industries implicitly involves sexual appropriation and thus inherently perpetuates gender inequality. Adkins' focal point is the relationship between workplace sexual relations and the organisation and structure of the labour market. She highlights two significant inter-relating points. Firstly, that in the focus industries there is an overt gender segregation of roles due to the nature of jobs in the service industry. Secondly in the predominantly male labour areas, work is valued according to economic criteria. In the areas occupied largely by females, the value of woman's physical image and socially determined feminine qualities are fundamental features of the work, that is, the work demands that women are positioned as sexed bodies (1995, pp. 45–50).

The full implications of what happens when women are positioned as sexed bodies in sex segregated workforces is taken up in *Gender and Jobs* (1998), an ILO report that examines workplace sex segregation within the current global economy. Its author, Robert Anker, found that occupational sex segregation was not just of concern because of equity issues, but because it:

---

21. Female occupational segregation occurs where, at present, women tend to have lower paying and lower status jobs and where work in female-dominated occupations is similar to activities women perform at home (Anker 1998, p. 6).

Has an important negative effect on how women see themselves by reinforcing and perpetuating gender stereotypes. This, in turn, negatively affects women's status and empowerment and consequently has an adverse effect on many social variables, such as morality and morbidity, poverty and income inequality (1998, p. 6).

The idea that human rights agencies and some feminists are joining with pro-prostitution advocates to promote opportunistic prostitution in developing nations, undisputedly segregates 'poor' women as a class set apart for sexual servitude as Janice Raymond says (1998, p. 5). If prostituted women need to escape the cycle of poverty that necessitates their sexual exploitation, then women 'need to be brought into the economic mainstream, not to have prostitution mainstreamed as legitimate work' (1998, p. 22).

Prostitution as violence against women

Several feminist theorists have recognised that in work situations where women are reduced to the sexual body, the workplace becomes an environment in which sexual harassment and sexual violence are not just conceivable, but inevitable. Radical feminist, Liz Kelly, found in one study of 60 British women that 'the frequency and form of harassment at work depended, to some extent, on how far women's work role was sexualized' (1996, p. 194). Kelly highlighted how 'the experience of six women who had worked as barmaids suggests that this job sits uneasily between display and sexploitation'. According to Kelly the women 'felt that sexual harassment was part of the job. Male customers and co-workers assumed the right to make sexual remarks and sexual advances' (1996, p. 195). What does this mean for prostitution where the workplaces are wholly sexualised?

One of the most incontestable arguments against the institutionalisation of prostitution as work is that violence is an intrinsic part of the lives of women and girls in prostitution. The liberal position that considers choice as central to the prostitution debate does not recognise how the prostituted woman herself experiences prostitution. There is a growing body of feminist research that documents prostituted women and girls' experience of violence – the violence that is commonly a precursor to women entering prostitution, as well as the abuse they undergo routinely while in prostitution (for example, Giobbe 1991; Hoigard and Finstad 1992; Vanwesenbeeck 1994; Dworkin 1997; Altink 1995; Farley 2004; Stark and Whisnant 2004).

Feminist psychologist Melissa Farley's research (1998, 1998a, 2004) offers some of the most comprehensive and descriptive analyses of the cruelty and inhumanity of prostitution. In a study of prostitution in five countries, Farley and others found 'that violence [physical assault and rape] and post traumatic stress disorder (PTSD) were widely prevalent among [the] 475 prostituted people' interviewed. Sixty-seven per cent met the criteria for PTSD. Significantly there were no differences in the incidence in four of the five countries, which as the authors conclude, 'suggests that the harm of prostitution is not a culture-bound phenomenon' (Farley, M., I. Baral, et al. 1998, p. 405).

The study did note differences in the incidence of childhood sexual and physical abuse that frequently acted as a precondition for prostitution. Nonetheless the conclusion reached by Farley and colleagues was that despite these differences in current and past violence, 'the experience of prostitution itself caused acute psychological distress and symptoms of PTSD' (1998, p. 405). An equally relevant finding was that there existed 'no difference in the incidence of PTSD' between women in street prostitution as compared to women in brothel prostitution (1998, p. 406). This discovery strengthened the authors' earlier research that psychological trauma is intrinsic to the act of prostitution. As Farley and others conclude:

For the vast majority of the world's women, prostitution is the experience of being hunted, being dominated, being sexually assaulted, and being physically and verbally battered. Intrinsic to prostitution are numerous violations of human rights: sexual harassment, economic servitude, educational deprivation, job discrimination, domestic violence, racism, classism (being treated as if you are worthless because you are poor), vulnerability to frequent physical and sexual assault, and being subjected to body invasions which are equivalent to torture (1998, p. 405).

This injury to the self and the resulting disassociation practised by women and girls in prostitution has been described by many survivors of prostitution. Andrea Dworkin says that prostitution:

is the use of a woman's body for sex, by a man . . . It is the mouth, the vagina, the rectum, penetrated usually by a penis, sometimes hands, sometimes objects, by one man and then another and then another and then another (1992, p. 5).

Evelina Giobbe, in a similar way, reflects that:

[W]hen a 'john' uses a juvenile prostitute for his own sexual gratification he is committing the crime of child sexual abuse. When he demands that a prostitute allow him to use her in sadomasochistic sex scenes, he is battering her. When a john compels a woman to submit to his sexual demands as a condition of 'employment', he is guilty of both sexual harassment and rape (1991, p. 146).

When prostitution is compared in this way to other forms of violent sexual abuse it allows us to see and define the ordinary acts of prostitution as violence against women. We come to understand that the way women and girls in prostitution disassociate is the way all women cope with the violence. As anti-violence theorists have claimed, the violence and dehumanisation that is inherent in prostitution alone, makes men's practice in prosti-

tution 'gross violence against prostitutes' (Hoigard and Fi
1992, p. 115).

Placing prostitution in a human rights framework

Radical feminists locate prostitution on a continuum of sexual
exploitation and violence against women, wherein sex is regulated
through violence, and where sex is a dehumanising experience.
As Janice Raymond says:

> It is the exchange of money in prostitution that serves to transform
> what is actually sexual harassment, sexual abuse, and sexual violence
> into a 'job' known as 'commercial sex work', a 'job' performed
> primarily by racially and economically disadvantaged women in the
> so-called first and third worlds and by overwhelming numbers of
> women and children who have been the victims of childhood sexual
> abuse (1998a, p. 3).

If prostitution is violence against women, then as radical feminists
argue, prostitution is never a 'choice'. As MacKinnon says,
feminists have 'challenged the patriarchal legal treatment of sexual
violence where violence and harm are determined by the victim,
specifically her consent to the act' (1989 p. 177).

If prostitution is not a choice but a form of violence against
women, then it must be recognised as a civil and human rights
abuse. Human rights theory, as Kathleen Mahoney explains,
'invoke[s] the state's intervention and assistance because
individuals in their capacity as members of groups are
disadvantaged for arbitrary reasons' (1993, p. 774). Catharine
MacKinnon makes clear that prostituted women, as members
of a sex class, are seriously disadvantaged:

> Women in prostitution are denied every imaginable civil right in
> every imaginable and unimaginable way, such that it makes sense
> to understand prostitution as consisting in the denial of women's
> humanity, no matter how humanity is defined. It is denied both

through the social definition and condition of prostitutes and through the meaning of some civil rights (1987, p. 13).

From this perspective, where prostitution *per se* is a serious human rights violation against women, it is nonsensical to attempt to create the false distinction between 'forced' and 'free' prostitution. Radical feminists indeed consider sex trafficking as a precursor to prostitution.

Connecting prostitution and sex trafficking

Dorchen Leidholdt provides one of the clearest and most concise conceptualisations of the relationship between prostitution and sex trafficking. Leidholdt's principal argument is that 'sex trafficking is nothing more or less than globalized prostitution' as the ultimate purpose of sex trafficking is prostitution (2003, p. 7). She supports her premise by outlining the ways sex trafficking and prostitution overlap. She identifies the key characteristics of people targeted for all forms of sexual exploitation to be 'poverty, youth, minority status in the countries of exploitation, histories of abuse, and little family support'. In contrast to the victims of sexual exploitation, 'The bulk of the sex industry involves pimps and other sex industry entrepreneurs controlling women and girls'. On the demand side, the buyers 'exploit trafficked and prostituted women interchangeably, for identical purposes' (2003, p. 7).

Leidholdt's comparison between prostitution and sex trafficking is extensive. She makes obvious how 'sex industry businesses in which trafficked and prostituted women and girls are exploited are often one and the same' (2003, p. 8). As she says, trafficked people are destined for the same brothels and stripclubs that exploit local women. The harm experienced by prostituted and trafficked women is also identical: 'post-traumatic stress disorder, severe depression, damage to reproductive systems, damage from sexual assault and beatings, and sexually transmitted diseases' (2003, p. 8). Leidholdt draws the inevitable conclusion that while sex trafficking 'intensifies the dynamics of power and control that characterise domestic prostitution,' the common-alities between the two 'far overshadow their differences' (2003, p. 8).

The limitations of legitimising prostitution on the basis of consent is recognised in the *Protocol to the United Nations Convention Against Transnational Organized Crime – to Prevent, Suppress and Punish Trafficking In Persons, Especially Women and Children*, the principal human rights instrument for dealing with global trafficking. Janice Raymond, who in her capacity as co-executive director of the Coalition Against Trafficking in Women, took part in the consultation process in the development of the protocol. She says that the UN document 'is a wide-ranging international agreement to address the crime of trafficking persons, especially women and children, on a transnational level' (2001, p. 1). The protocol states:

'Trafficking in persons' shall mean the recruitment, transportation, transfers, harbouring or receipt of persons, by means of the threat or use of force or other forms of coercion, of abduction, of fraud, of deception, of the abuse of power or of a position of vulnerability or of the giving or receiving of payments or benefits to achieve the consent of a person having control over another person for the reason of exploitation, forced labour or services, slavery or practices similar to slavery, servitude or the removal of organs (United Nations 2000, Article 3 [a]).

Thus as Raymond explains, 'the definition provides a compre-hensive coverage of criminal means by which trafficking takes place, including not only force, coercion, abduction, deception or abuse of power, but also less explicit means such as abuse of a victim's vulnerability' (2001, p. 4). However the protocol extends this definition even further, to ensure that all victims of trafficking are protected.

Part (b) of the trafficking protocol states: 'The consent of a victim of trafficking persons to the intended exploitation set forth in subparagraph (a) of this article shall be irrelevant where any of the means set forth in subparagraph (a) have been used' (United Nations 2000, Article 3 [b]). This last section is critical for victims of trafficking as it means that they will not bear the burden of proof. The key element in the document therefore is the exploitative purpose for which women are trafficked.

The most recent radical feminist thinking on prostitution goes even further in demanding prostitution be recognised as a human rights abuse. As Farley writes:

> Normalized in most cultures, prostitution is nonetheless what might well be described as a 'harmful traditional cultural practice', a term applied internationally to female genital mutilation that refers to customs that are 'based on the idea of the inferiority of either of the sexes or on stereotyped roles for men and women' (2004, p. xiv).[22]

Conclusion

Misinformation on the prostitution industry is pervasive and makes invisible the harm experienced by women and girls caught up in systems of commercial sexual exploitation. Prostitution is normalised as natural, inevitable and even a great boon for domestic economies. Simultaneously it is promoted as exemplary of women's sexual autonomy, an economic opportunity for disadvantaged women, or alternatively a dynamic career opportunity for those in more advanced nations. The people who

---

22. Discussion on the application of this term 'harmful traditional cultural practice' to prostitution is extended in Catharine A. MacKinnon (2001) *Sex Equality* and Bronwyn Winter, Denise Thompson and Sheila Jeffreys (2002) 'The UN Approach to Harmful Traditional Practices'.

sustain and benefit most from these claims are the sex entrepreneurs who derive more and more profits from the expansion of global prostitution, and by extension, sex trafficking. These discourses also protect men's 'rights' to purchase women's and girls' bodies for their own pleasure. Women and girls in systems of sexual exploitation, as I have shown throughout this chapter, are indisputably the losers in these dynamics. However pro-prostitution advocates are powerful persuaders who normalise sexual exploitation both within the community and to the women and girls who are drawn into the prostitution industry. The pace at which this is happening makes it critical to dispel the falsehoods that surround prostitution.

CHAPTER TWO

Institutionalising Men's Rights to Women's Bodies: Legalisation (1982–1997)

The prostitution industry is often misconceived. It is an industry about which most people know little. In the 1990s prostitution no longer involves tawdry, unkempt small rooms off laneways frequented by desperates wearing raincoats who seek sexual gratification . . . Of course, it operates differently in other parts of the world where it is not subject to the level of scrutiny and regulation that applies in Australia. Many of the critics of the sex industry are people who know the least about it, yet criticise it on moral or populist grounds. I have no problem with people having moral opinions about the industry, but we should look at the flip side of the coin. One person's view may be different from another's, and freedom of speech and opinion is important in democracies.

BLAIR CAMERON BOARDMAN, LIBERAL MEMBER
FOR CHELSEA (VICTORIA 1997A, P. 1147).

Introduction

The far-reaching step to legalise prostitution in Victoria was introduced by the State Premier, John Cain, after the Labor Government came to power in 1982 following 27 years of a conservative Liberal Government.[1] Victoria's reframing of prosti-

---

1. Australia is characterised by a competitive party system. However the dominance of the two major political parties, the conservative Liberal (continued next page)

tution law throughout the 1980s and 1990s reflected a shift away from prohibition and criminality – and moral concerns – towards the regulation of prostitution as 'sex work' and as a legitimate employment choice. The Government's imprimatur on the industry in turn acted to transform the public's consciousness on prostitution. Legalisation created an environment in which the commodification of women's bodies and sexuality could be treated as an acceptable commercial practice.

No change exists in a vacuum. Municipal councils, community activists, strands of the feminist movement, prostitutes' rights organisations, sex industry lobbyists, civil libertarians and religious spokespeople were among the major stakeholders propelling Victoria's prostitution 'law reform'. These interest groups represented a diversity of political and ideological perspectives as they campaigned to affect legislative outcomes on prostitution. Conservative, liberal and feminist values, in all their various expressions, were identifiable in public debate on whether the Government should introduce legalisation. Nonetheless, overall these stakeholders demonstrated a singular concern to overcome the inconsistencies of prohibition in the face of contemporary practice.

Historically Victoria's prohibitive prostitution laws had failed to contain the increasing visibility of an illegal massage parlour trade (a euphemism for brothels) and street prostitution, eliminate criminal involvement, or address the violence and exploitation which were endemic in the industry. Inevitably though, the wide spectrum of interests represented ensured a range of competing, and at times conflicting, models of what new prostitution laws should embody. At best, these various hypotheses only

---

(cont.) Party and the Labor Party (a mass party formed on the left which has a formal affiliation with the trade union movement), means that the party system operates as a two-party system at both Federal and State and Territory levels.

superficially took account of the human rights abuses that women in prostitution experienced on a daily basis.

Liberalism with its basic concerns for the development of individual freedom and social progress was the dominant discourse in Victoria's political debates on prostitution. This dominance facilitated the State legislators' treatment of prostitution principally as a private sexual activity that should not be criminalised because prostitution involved a commercial transaction. The contemporary pre-eminence given to the neo-liberal economic goal of free trade also fed into the Government's reframing of prostitution by allowing women to be reconstructed as just another trade commodity. Pro-prostitution advocates and their supporters in State parliament uncritically argued that prohibitive legislation restricted what was in reality simply a form of economic exchange that responded accordingly to supply and demand.

Socialist and liberal feminists who entered the debate on Victoria's prostitution law reform attempted to create an analysis of prostitution within this liberal and neo-liberal agenda. However Victoria's prostitution legalisation was always about men's sexual rights and business interests, and feminists' efforts to work within such boundaries faced difficulties from the start. Feminist influence within the debates reflected firstly the limitations of socialist feminist thought. As I outlined in the previous chapter, socialist feminists hoped that making prostitution 'work' would protect those within the industry from the worst abuses of the trade, although they neither wished to encourage nor institutionalise the industry. Victoria's experience shows, their efforts to give legitimacy to prostituted women as workers equally gave legitimacy to the buyers and sex business interests, and lawmakers were not concerned with even attempting to make the doubtful distinction between the two. In addition some feminists, without criticism, accepted the rhetoric of sexual and economic liberalism.

Liberal feminists focused on the potential of prostitution as work and portrayed the harm experienced by women within the industry as individual experience that could be rectified by stronger application of laws against a few aberrant 'clients' who displayed violent behaviour. The radical feminist anti-violence perspective was given no voice in the State's prostitution dialogue as it challenged the very premise that prostitution could be made acceptable under any conditions.

Background to 'reform'

The legalisation of prostitution emerged as a political issue in Victoria in the late 1970s in response to the social and commercial reality of a state-wide prostitution industry that was unregulated and mainly illegal. In 1982, the newly elected Labor Premier, John Cain, made prostitution legislative reform a policy priority of his government (Gorjanicyn 1992, p. 127). This commitment was underpinned by a belief that new legislation, rather than the clarification of the former Liberal Government's existing prohibitive prostitution law, was the only solution to the unwieldy industry. Labor's approach to prostitution was not just a pragmatic solution to the existence of this clandestine trade. Cain's agenda on prostitution reform was to parallel the party's wider political platform, which pledged to uphold the principles of a liberal democratic society (Shamsullah 1992, pp. 11–24). This encompassed the illegitimacy of state interference into what was commonly perceived as strictly private sexual activities.

Victoria's policy of containment and tolerance

For many Victorians prostitution was not a discreet interaction between two consenting adults, but something very public. The illegal prostitution industry was highly visible in the State's major urban centres throughout the 1970s. In the 1979 state election it became an issue for the ruling Liberal Government. Government statistics combined with approximations obtained from journalistic investigative reports, provide an indication of the extent to which the industry was encroaching on the community. One media report suggested that in the Melbourne metropolitan area, around 2000 women were involved in prostitution in massage parlours and on suburban streets (Dunstan 1979, p. 28). Research undertaken within the Department of Planning and the Environment between 1973 and 1983, estimated that the number of massage parlours increased from 25 to 149 during this period (Working Party to the Minister for Planning and the Environment 1983, p. 5). Local councils suggested that the number was as high as 200 (Victoria 1980, p. 2275).

Parlours included both private and public premises. The latter were typified by bright advertising signs and strong lighting, and were usually located in industrial or commercial areas, or on main roads. Employing up to 20 people, they operated between 10 a.m. and midnight, with some establishments open 24 hours (Working Party to the Minister for Planning and the Environment 1983, pp. 3–7). These parlours were frequently concentrated in one particular area, thus creating a red-light district. In Eton Place in St Kilda Road, Melbourne, for example, there were 30 to 40 parlours in three adjacent buildings (Working Party to the Minister for Planning and the Environment 1983, p. 20). 'Private home' parlours were often found in medium density residential areas, usually in terrace houses in the inner suburbs. These were less discernible than public brothels, smaller operations 'discreetly worked' by one or two women (Working Party to the Minister for Planning and the Environment 1983, p. 6). That most of these small parlours would remain illegal after the State legalised prostitution suggests that the government's agenda in legitimising prostitution favoured big business interests.

Critics of the Liberal Government's handling of prostitution within Victoria cited the existing legal framework as the major determinant for the expansion of the massage and street prostitution trade. The law was ambiguous, discriminatory and ultimately ineffectual in containing prostitution growth. Victoria's prostitution legislation was modelled on the English legal paradigm, which meant that while prostitution itself was not illegal, associated activities were criminalised (Hancock 1992, p. 166). When Labor came to power in 1982, a range of heterogeneous laws existed to deal with prostitution in the State. The major acts in operation were the *Vagrancy Act 1966*, the *Summary Offences Act 1966* and the *Crimes (Sexual Offences) Act 1981* (see Chart 1, p. 54). In effect these laws rendered prostitution illegal through a series of statutes that related to contagious disease, procuring, vagrancy, soliciting, and brothel keeping (see Neave 1994, pp. 65–67).

Protecting men's sexual rights

The laws criminalising prostitution have been defended on a number of grounds. Feminist lawyer, Marcia Neave, who became a significant influence in shaping Victoria's current prostitution legislation, considers that the most common pro-criminalisation arguments were that the laws prevented public offence and protected neighbouring landowners from nuisance. Neave further suggests that these laws were also intended to guard against sexual exploitation of prostituted women and reflect the 'social condemnation of the "pimp" or "bludger"' (1988, p. 205). In practice however, the Liberal Government's selective enforcement policies during the 1970s had worked to suppress only the more visible and exploitative forms of prostitution.

Neither in the past, nor today, have Victoria's prostitution laws targeted prostitution *per se*. Jane Inglis, writing in the context of the Liberal Government's legal harassment of prostituted women in the late 1970s, points out that the workings of the law in fact reflected the essentialist assumption that 'Prostitutes provide a

Chart 1

Acts in operation: Year	Pre-1984	1984	1986	1994
ACT	a) *Summary Offences Act 1966* b) *Vagrancy Act 1966* c) *Crimes (Sexual Offences) Act 1981*	*The Planning (Brothels) Act* (PBA)	*Health (Amendment) Act* *Prostitution Regulation Act* (PRA)	*Prostitution Control Act* (PCA)
BROTHEL PROSTITUTION	Habitual prostitution an offence under *Vagrancy Act 1966*	Remained an offence under *Vagrancy Act 1966* except where brothels have town-planning permit (PBA ss. 9[13])	Becomes an offence under the new Act (PRA s.15)	An offence to work except in licensed brothels or small owner-operated (exempt) brothels (PCA ss. 23.24)
STREET PROSTITUTION	Loitering and Soliciting for prostitution an offence under the *Summary Offences Act 1966*		Becomes an offence under the new Act (PRA s.5 [1])	Soliciting and Loitering (PCA ss. 12.13) Exemption where acts occur in licensed brothel or escort agency (PCA s.14)
LIVING OFF THE EARNINGS	An offence under *Vagrancy Act 1966*	Remained an offence under *Vagrancy Act 1966*, except where payment is made to brothels have town-planning permit (PBA ss. 9[13])	Becomes an offence under the new Act except where payment is made to brothels having a town-planning permit (PRA s.12)	An offence except where payment is to licensed brothels or escort agencies (PCA ss. 9.10)
PROCURING	An offence under *Crimes (Sexual Offences) Act 1981* where force or violence is used to keep a person in prostitution		Becomes an offence under the new Act (PRA ss. 10.11)	An offence except where brothels are licensed. The Act extended service providers to include escort agency businesses and small owner-operated businesses (PCA ss.22.23)

BROTHEL KEEPING	An offence for owner, manager or lessor under *Vagrancy Act 1966*	Remained an offence under *Vagrancy Act 1966*, except where brothels have town-planning permit (PBA ss. 9[13])	Becomes an offence under the new Act (PRA s. 12)	An offence to induce, threaten, intimidate, supply drugs or through false representation, to force a person to remain in prostitution (PCA s. 8)
CHILD PROSTITUTION	Inducing a child into prostitution an offence under *Crimes (Sexual Offences) Act 1981*		Becomes an offence under the new Act to induce, allow, or profit from child prostitution (PRA s. 6 [1].7[1].9[1])	An offence for inducing, allowing, or profiting from child prostitution (PCA ss. 5.6.7.11)
ADVERTISING	An offence under *Crimes Act 1958* to advertise employment in a brothel		Becomes an offence under the new Act to advertise prostitution services, or for employment in brothels (PCA ss. 14[1]–[3])	The Government places controls on advertising; for prostitution and for employment. For example, advertisements cannot describe service offered (PCA s. 18)
HEALTH ASPECTS			Medical professionals prohibited from providing certificate signifying or implying freedom from STDs to be used to promote prostitution	Person infected with STI prohibited from working in prostitution. Any person who manages a business providing sexual services is prohibited from allowing person with STI from working in prostitution (PCA s. 19 [1] a.b.)
'CLIENT' OFFENCES	An offence under *Summary Offences Act 1966* for the buyer to go to a public place to seek prostitution services		Becomes an offence for a buyer to go to a public place to seek prostitution services (PRA s. 5 [2]). Offence removed from 1966 Act. An offence for using the services of a child under 18 for prostitution (PRA s. 7 [1])	An offence for a buyer to go to a public place to seek prostitution services (PCA s. 12 [1.2]) Person(s) presumed to know of infection unless prostituted person undergoing regular health tests for STIs (PCA s. 19 [2] a.b.) An offence for inducing a child to provide prostitution services (PCA s. 5 [1]) Being in, entering or leaving unlicensed brothel (PCA s. 15)

safety valve for men . . . men can vent their brutish appetites and warped fantasies on these "sub-culture creatures", thus saving "decent women" from such humiliation and violation as sexual assault and rape' (1984, p. 17). This acceptance that men had a right to prostituted women ensured that the demand for prostitution remained unchallenged. A further impetus for a continued prostitution industry, of course, was the reality that prostitution is a highly lucrative commercial enterprise which benefits individual sexual exploiters or pimps and organised crime alike.

Massage parlours were concentrated in certain areas in Victoria, mostly around the Melbourne suburbs of St Kilda and South Melbourne. Historically, St Kilda in particular was connected with 'night life and prostitutes' in the public mind. The suburb accounted for 80 per cent of Victoria's street prostitution trade (Jackson and Otto 1979, p. 12). There is a case that initially the St Kilda Council facilitated its prostitution boom by promoting the municipality as 'the great entertainment centre of the Southern Hemisphere' (Jackson and Otto 1979, p. 12). This situation foreshadowed later developments in Victoria where the benefits that the state can derive from a thriving prostitution industry are openly acknowledged. By the late 1960s however, the Council was withdrawing its tolerance of prostitution, as St Kilda, similar to other inner Melbourne suburbs, was undergoing gentrification in parallel with a shift in its demographic composition. Resident activists' groups emerged during this urban transition to become one of the main stayers in Victoria's prostitution law reform debates.

The emergence of residents' activism

Predictably a community response to the encroachment of the prostitution industry on public life first emerged in the St Kilda area. From its beginnings, residents' activism was opposed to the visibility of prostitution, rather than prostitution *per se*. Its political rhetoric, as with state policy towards the industry, reflected an acceptance of the inevitability of prostitution and the male biological imperative. Residents' interest groups' core concerns were to minimise the impact of the prostitution trade on local amenities and, to an extent, the regional retail trade.

Community activism became formalised in the late 1970s with the formation of an anti-prostitution residents' group calling itself West Action. Feminists Sue Jackson and Dianne Otto examined the organisation's beginnings. They found that the impetus for the group came from local homeowners 'who were apprehensive about property values and the general "moral tone" of the area' (Jackson and Otto 1979, p. 12). This seems probable as in the two year period between 1976 and 1978, St Kilda property values declined by 30 per cent (Council Will Curb Massage Parlours 1978, p. 1). Moreover West Action stated that its activism was uncompromisingly targeted at 'cleaning up the streets' for 'decent citizens' (Groups Seek Government Action 1978, p. 7).

Residents' activism, as it emerged, reflected an odd mix of acceptance and disapproval of the prostitution industry, although sidestepping the issue of whether prostitution was inherently harmful. Significantly West Action's chairman Colin Bell, made clear that he did not consider the issue under discussion a 'moral' one. The problem as he defined it, was that 'Prostitution will always be there but we say it should not be allowed to continue in residential areas' (Council Will Curb Massage Parlours 1978, p. 1). Taking a similar position, the then Mayor of St Kilda, Councillor Brian Zouch, also told the local media that 'The council was not concerned with the moral aspect of prostitution [but the trade] must be somewhere that it does not affect decent people' (Mayor Calls for Brothel Laws 1978, p. 1). Essentially West Action's agenda was to get the Government to act. In a deputation to the State's Chief Secretary, Joe Rafferty, they stated that the problems that St Kilda was experiencing were due solely to 'the manner by which the [prostitution] laws of Victoria [were] drafted, administered or exercised' ('Groups Seek Government Action' 1978, p. 7).

Thus in the early debates about legalisation of prostitution in Victoria, community groups which advocated prostitution law reform did not want to legitimise prostitution but wanted to lessen its impact on their neighbourhood. This is an important point because their activism emerged from lack of police and government prioritising or enforcement of former anti-pimping and anti-brothel laws and not from the fact that these laws did not work, an argument that pro-prostitution advocates would increasingly propose throughout the 1980s and after.

Legitimising the massage parlour trade

The State Liberal Government was reactive in responding to ongoing public concern over the prostitution industry's incursion into suburban environments. In the hope of curtailing prostitution expansion it introduced interim planning controls, a type of quasi legalisation which in operation became a boon to the massage parlour trade. In 1975 Liberals directed the Melbourne Metropolitan Planning Scheme Authority to allow massage parlour operators to apply for a town-planning permit in a similar way to other businesses.[2] Thus massage parlours became a recognised legitimate land use, the only restriction being that operators must comply with local zoning laws.

Prostitution could flourish in these circumstances as massage parlours were defined as premises 'used for the purpose of body massage by a person other than a person registered [as a physio-therapist] whether or not it is used solely for that purpose'. This

2. This was introduced through an amendment to the *Town and Country Planning Act 1961*.

meant that brothels could operate lawfully as a business if they operated under the pseudonym 'massage parlours', irrespective of whether professional massage or prostitution was being conducted on the premises (Victoria 1985a, p. 4).

The granting of permits to massage parlours merely added a further complexity to the State's prostitution laws. Police had minimal power to close the parlours as the legalisation meant that parlours had the same rights as other businesses operating legitimately.[3] This ludicrous situation was exacerbated by the Government's failure to address prostitution operations outside of the brothel trade. Private parlours, with virtually no capital overheads, were both mobile and flexible and therefore remained almost totally beyond the law (Working Party to the Minister for Planning and the Environment 1983, p. 7). Escort agencies were partially legal as most businesses claimed their function was to provide an escort, not prostitution.[4] Women involved in street prostitution continued to be targeted by the police for soliciting under the *Summary Offences Act* which, as has been suggested previously, was discriminatory and ineffective in restricting the practice. Thus from every perspective, the Liberal Government's planning scheme was inherently flawed. However the Liberal Government's strategy foreshadowed the practice that later State Governments would adopt wherein they treated prostitution principally as a planning issue.

Before the Liberal Government and the electorate were to openly accept commercial sex on the same legal basis as other

---

3. The police were required to provide three days notice before entering a premises to ascertain if it was operating as a brothel, enabling brothel managers or owners time to cease prostitution activities (Social Questions Committee 1990, p. 2).

4. An escort agency is legally defined as a business providing or facilitating the provision of prostitution to persons at premises not made available by the agency (*Prostitution Control Act 1994*, Part 1. s. 3[3]). In contrast to prostitution, the provision of escorts had no restrictions against advertising in telephone and hotel directories.

businesses, a case had to be made to justify legal prostitution. The Liberal Government's quasi-legalisation forestalled this debate. The failure of the Liberal Government's stop-gap legislation provided the fulcrum for prostitution to become an electoral issue in the 1978 Victorian state election. Residents and public administrators in the areas most affected by prostitution were particularly virulent in their opposition to the massage parlour trade as well as to street prostitution (Bennett 1992, p. 19). In November 1978 the St Kilda Council, at the instigation of West Action, organised a public forum on prostitution, drugs and crimes. This local political agitation, which I return to in the following chapter in relation to the evolution of Victoria's prostitutes' rights organisation, provided a springboard for both state and national debate on the issue of whether prostitution should be legalised.

The open forum provided the context for a range of legal responses to prostitution to be debated, opening the way for a reframing of prostitution in the public mind. Australia's national broadcasting television program *Monday Conference* televised the event ('Mayor Calls for Brothel Laws' 1978, p. 1). The legal alternatives presented for community consultation by the Liberal Minister for Social Welfare, Brian Dixon, included prohibition or suppression, regulation or legalisation, and decriminalisation (Jackson and Otto 1979, p. 11). However the final parliamentary session prior to the 1979 election, demonstrated that the Government remained committed to the *status quo*. An amendment to Section 18 of the *Summary Offences Act* introduced further penalties for the offences of loitering and soliciting[5] (Jackson and Otto 1979, p. 14). In defence of the

---

5. Section 18 of the Act stated that 'any person in a public place or [who] loiters in a public place with the intention of committing a crime shall be guilty of an offence'. The legislation was intended to target both homosexuals and those involved in the street prostitution trade, although not their 'clients'.

amendment, government spokespeople cast residents as victims. They stressed that the change in the legislation was a response to local municipalities' concerns with the increasingly visible 'massage parlour' trade and the harm of street prostitution and associated crimes (Jackson and Otto 1979, p. 14). The message that the government was receiving was that the affected communities wanted prostitution hidden not mainstreamed.

The period between 1979 and the 1982 Victorian state election in which the Australian Labor Party (ALP) won government exposed further problems within the prostitution industry which made it difficult for any government to continue with the status quo. In 1980, the Victorian Parliament opened debate on the overt link between the drug trade, then estimated to be between A$1 and A$1.6 billion dollars, police corruption and prostitution (Victoria 1980, pp. 76–77). The massage parlour trade was recognised as an easy conduit for criminals to 'launder' monies received from drug trafficking (Victoria 1980, p. 77). Some parliamentarians also expressed concern that 'tax evasion' by criminals involved in prostitution rackets was as significant a problem as the actual operation of the brothels (Victoria 1980, p. 77). In this context, the Premier John Cain's decision to liberalise Victoria's prostitution laws began to be seen as a viable way to regulate the illicit trade.

Cain's blueprint for reform

John Cain's approach to prostitution was to prove markedly distinct from his predecessors. Labor's policy fully endorsed the decriminalisation of prostitution in contrast to the former Liberal Government's strategy of tolerance and containment although both policies in theory permitted prostitution. Soliciting, the principal criminal offence linked to street prostitution, was a crime only if it created a public nuisance. Brothels were to be recognised as legitimate businesses. Council planning by-laws and health and safety regulations applied as they did to other businesses but there were to be no industry-specific regulations (Working Party to the Minister for Planning and the Environment 1983, p. 39). Hence the new legislation was intended to end the legal hypocrisy which permitted a thriving massage parlour to exist, but denied that the parlour's business was prostitution.

However Labor's vision that prostitution be treated as a legitimate industry was compromised from the beginning. The industry is endemically exploitative and violent and regulations had to take account of this reality. Prescriptive aspects of proposed prostitution legislation related to protecting minors and living off the earnings of prostitution (Working Party to the Minister for Planning and the Environment 1983, p. 39). Thus Labor adopted the position that child prostitution and adult prostitution were two different phenomena. In a similar way women who were coerced into prostitution and women who 'chose' sexual exploitation were seen to belong to two distinct categories, the former a victim, the latter exercising her right to sexual and economic autonomy. In effect, although not stated, Labor used a forced and free distinction in formulating its new prostitution laws.[6]

Sexual liberalism and Labor's policy

Liberal individualism with all its limitations for ending the harm of prostitution underpinned Labor's prostitution reform legislation. The Premier argued that 'it should not be a criminal activity to engage in what are characterised as offences relating to prostitution simply because money changed hands' (Victoria 1982, p. 355). Political scientist and liberal feminist, Barbara

---

6. The term 'forced' and 'free prostitution' was first used within state parliament during debates on the *Justice Legislation (Sexual Offences and Bail) Act* 2004, examined in Chapter Seven.

Sullivan, has suggested that Cain was among a growing number of Australian parliamentarians who considered the decriminalisation of prostitution as part of an overall political strategy that aimed at the elimination of legal sanctions on all private consensual matters between adults (1997, p. 86).[7] Such strategies gained considerable credibility with the release of the 1957 English Wolfenden Report (*The Report on Homosexual Offences and Prostitution*). The report, which Sullivan contends became the standard for liberal reform, provided a re-conceptualisation of the nature and obligation of sexual relationships. In particular, she says, it stressed that private sexual behaviour between consenting adults was not an appropriate concern of the law (1997, pp. 92–108). In this context prostitution, thrown together with homosexuality, was redefined as a 'victimless' crime.

Within Australia traditional concepts of sexuality were also being re-evaluated and would have influenced Cain's thinking. The 1977 *Royal Commission on Human Relationships*, chaired by Justice Elizabeth Evatt, was groundbreaking in its search to understand social relationships, specifically male-female interactions that included sexual relations. Its recommendation, considered controversial at the time, addressed such topics as the rights of children, the age of consent, homosexuality, incest, contraception, family violence, abortion and rape (1977, p. 37). The Commission's ultimate finding was that traditional sociosexual roles were disintegrating with new emerging paradigms that placed emphasis on 'sexual intimacy, pleasure and experimentation', for both men and women (*Royal Commission on Human Relationships* 1977, p. 86). The Evatt Commission, as

---

7. The only caveat related to 'nuisance or annoyance' caused to other people. This reflected the trend in human rights jurisprudence in the 1980s and 1990s. As legal theorist, Simon Bronitt, explains, this has tended towards 'a broad construction of fundamental rights that is then qualified by those restrictions which are necessary in a democratic society' (1994, p. 4).

had the Wolfenden inquiry around 20 years earlier, thus provided a new dialogue on sexuality that provided the context for prostitution to be considered as an issue of private morality rather than a concern of public law.

Feminists endorse prostitution as 'work'

In parallel with this rethinking on traditional sexual mores, Australian feminists were creating their own analyses of prostitution. In the mid-1970s the radical perspective was a decisive influence on feminist prostitution politics within Victoria. The St Kilda Women's Liberation Group collective, for example, produced its pamphlet 'The Alternative to Illegal Prostitution is not Legal Prostitution' (c.1975, p. 1). The Group advocated that legalising prostitution was discriminatory and harmful to all women. The collective reasoned that, 'Every argument in favour of legalising prostitution presupposes that in order to cure male problems and crimes, women are to be used as the victims, and that male needs are paramount' (St Kilda Women's Liberation Group c.1975, p. 1). Thus from this perspective, any legal solution that facilitated the continuance of the illicit trade – in any semblance – had to be rejected.

By the late 1970s, socialist and liberal feminist analyses and practices began to dominate prostitution politics as the right to women's workplace equality became central to feminist struggles within Australia. As Barbara Sullivan has pointed out, 'feminist analysis of prostitution as work (particularly women's work) was widely adopted at this time because it was 'compatible with both the "laborist" orientation of the ALP and the [liberal] feminism of the Women's Electoral Lobby' (1992, p. 12). At the 1978 Women and Labour Conference, Jan Aitkin in her paper *The Prostitute as Worker* (1978), was already putting the proposition that 'prostitution is hard work and that its practitioners have few of the rights of other workers' (1978, p. 10). In terms of political strategy, Aitkin called for the Women's Liberation Movement to support prostituted women's struggles as workers and as women.

In a similar way, and in a similar timeframe, the Victorian branch of the ALP's Status of Women Policy Committee also introduced the notion that prostitution was work. Its proposal that the State Government should remove '"all" laws on prostitution' was supported by the controversial claim 'that marriage was, in many cases, a poorly paid form of prostitution' (Reid 1978, p. 20). Foreshadowing views that would be mainstreamed over the next two decades, the Committee made the case that decriminalisation would empower women in the industry by providing them with access to the industrial rights that were available to other workers. These rights included 'the right to set oneself up in business, subject to normal business laws, and to form a union, elect delegates to the Trades Hall and fight for better working conditions' (Reid 1978, pp. 20–21).

Essentially the Committee's aim was to secure good working conditions for prostituted women. While during the late 1970s this was indeed considered revolutionary, the idea in practice supported the *status quo*. As the radical elements in the St Kilda Women's Liberation Movement had earlier pointed out, legitimising prostitution as work tolerates that 'women are to be used as the victims, and that male needs are paramount' (c.1975, p. 1). This radical view however, was at odds with a Government committed to establishing the legitimacy of prostitution.

Labor stakes out parameters for new prostitution law

The Labor Government's first initiative in transforming its election policy on prostitution into workable legislation was to establish a working party within the Department of Planning and Environment. Its terms of reference were to determine the best location for massage parlours and how to restrict their encroachment on Melbourne's suburban and inner-suburban living. The working party's membership comprised State and local council officials and prostitution industry representatives (brothel owners) who were concerned only with how and where prostitution could operate (Working Party to the Minister for Planning and the Environment 1983, p. 21). This narrow focus on planning worked successfully to set the parameters of future prostitution law reform debate by establishing *a priori* assumptions that prostitution was a legitimate land use.

Undoubtedly the State Government attempted to present itself as unbiased in its handling of the prostitution issue. The Government justified the inquiry's restricted terms of reference by arguing that it was not its task 'to make moral or social judgements' that is to become caught up in the so-called morality debate around prostitution (Working Party to the Minister for Planning and the Environment 1983, p. 3). The Working Party's final report was far from value neutral. Uncritically, it accepted the biological determinist argument that as 'brothels have existed for some considerable time and are likely to continue to exist, irrespective of laws, [it was] appropriate to openly acknowledge their presence' (Working Party to the Minister for Planning and the Environment 1983, p. 3). The working party equally succumbed to the belief that women and girls were just another commodity in the market place. Its principal recommendation was that if brothels were recognised as a legal use of land, they would then respond to market forces. This would result in a regular distribution throughout the metropolitan area, similar to other land uses for which there is more or less universal demand (Working Party to the Minister for Planning and the Environment 1983, p. 21). In practice, this *laissez-faire* economic approach meant that every municipality would be available to organisers of the brothel industry.

The Planning (Brothels) Act 1984 **and its opponents**

Victoria's *The Planning (Brothels) Act 1984* was a direct outcome of Cain's inquiry into the location of the State's massage parlours.[8] The new Act recognised brothels as a legal land use that would be subject to the same town planning regulations that applied to other legitimate businesses under the Melbourne Metropolitan Planning Scheme. The Government's discarding of the term 'massage parlours' in preference to brothels ended the ambiguity that existed in former legislation. The change in terminology equally indicated the Government's determination to normalise the prostitution trade. There was no suggestion however, in the new law that the Government had considered the harms of prostitution for women and girls involved in the exploitative trade. The public and parliamentary debate around the new legislation was to provide the forum for such debate as well as allowing the exposure of perspectives that had been previously marginalised by the Government's determination to make planning the central focus of its prostitution reform agenda.

Among the major criticisms of *The Planning (Brothels) Act* was the Government's failure to provide for a safe and non-exploitative prostitution 'workplace', assist women in street prostitution and establish exit programs for the many women who wanted to leave the industry, problems that two decades of legalised prostitution still cannot solve. Many of these criticisms originated from Victoria's evolving prostitutes' rights organisation – the Australian Prostitutes' Collective (APC), the predecessor of the Prostitutes' Collective of Victoria.[9] The APC's primary message was that 'prostitutes have chosen this work, and attempts to stop them would be an infringement of their normal

---

8. *The Massage Parlour (Planning) Bill* when passed became *The Brothel (Planning) Act*.

9. The APC was part of a coalition which formed in 1983 in Melbourne with a similar group in Sydney.

rights' (Victoria 1984, p. 2534). This analysis was one of the strongest articulations of the liberal concept of 'choice' that had emerged in the public dialogue around prostitution in the State.

In its advocacy for further liberalisation of the State's prostitution law the APC would stress that exploitation and violence was endemic in the industry. But having accepted that prostitution was a 'choice' it defined these harms within a framework of 'labour exploitation'. Thus their political demands focused on further decriminalisation of the trade so that women in the industry could achieve more autonomy in their working lives. APC representative, Sheryl Dobinson explained, for example, that women in prostitution faced diminished economic returns within the new legalised system, as brothel owners demanded up to 50 per cent of takings. Managers were also free to set fines and bonds for breaches of 'house rules'. Legalisation moreover, did not deter brothel operators and buyers from continuing to physically and sexually harass women under their control (Dobinson 1992, p. 120). In addition there was the reality that women on 'methadone, stereotypical drug users, non-competitive workers and older workers' often had little option but to work illegally (Dobinson 1992, p. 118). That Victoria's *Planning (Brothels) Act* had not considered the harm experienced by women and girls in street prostitution was thus simply a further indication that the Government had little concern for the welfare of prostituted women.

The then Shadow Attorney-General, Bruce Chamberlain, drew on the APC's views to support the Liberal Opposition Party's case that the new Act had been introduced prematurely.[10]

---

10. In the mid-1980s the Victorian Liberal Party was opposed to the decriminalisation of prostitution, although it generally accepted that some form of regulation was required to contain the industry. As will become obvious in Part III, the Liberal Government became more *laissez-faire* and accepting of prostitution with the increasing normalisation of prostitution throughout the 1990s.

Chamberlain made reference to APC's demand for strategies to 'encourage those women who want to get out of the game to be able to do so' (Victoria 1984, p. 2534). Chamberlain also argued that a planning approach to prostitution offered 'no way to assess the number of under-age prostitutes, or the rate of disease or drug use' in the industry (Victoria 1984, p. 2534). He further queried whether there were to be restrictions for employment in brothels in Commonwealth Employment Services or School Vocational Offices (Victoria 1984b, p. 2304). This was among the few public statements that attempted to examine the implications of what negative impact normalising prostitution would have on Victorian women.

Confronted with the practicalities of treating prostitution as no different from other forms of legitimate industries, Labor withdrew its unconditional support for decriminalisation of the trade. In its place it opted for a harm minimisation strategy. This harm minimising strategy is premised on the assumption that prostitution is a harmful activity, but that, as people would continue to participate in the practice, the role of legislation was to minimise the harmful effects on those that the prostitution industry impacted upon: prostituted women, male buyers and the community. Speaking in parliament in defence of the *Planning (Brothels) Act*, Labor's Evan Walker, then Minister for Planning and the Environment, maintained that 'The Government is trying to deal with the worst aspects of the situation . . . [and while it] . . . recognised that prostitution exists . . . [I]t in no way condones or promotes the activity of prostitution' (Victoria 1984, p. 2574).

Twelve months after the passing of Labor's legislation the Government was forced to admit its failure. Victoria's prostitution industry was escalating and remained still largely unregulated. The Liberal Opposition called for an amendment to the Act, exposing a further critical oversight in Labor's legislation. There existed no provision within the 1984 Act to prevent multi-ownership of brothels. Potentially a single investor could buy up numerous brothel premises and operate a chain of brothels legally as long as each held a planning permit, thus ultimately allowing a monopolisation of the whole brothel industry (Victoria 1985a, p. 2657). In sum, Labor's legislation failed to achieve even its minimal aim of using planning codes to contain the brothel trade.

Media coverage of the Act's failure to bring the prostitution industry under control also exposed how treating prostitution as a planning issue ignored a significant part of the trade. *The Age* 'Good Weekend' magazine, for example, provided coverage of the 'booming industry' under the title 'Walker's Law: A license for Mr Big to make a killing in brothels', written by investigative journalist Bob Bottom (1985). Bottom illustrated how the 'most lucrative and booming side' of Victoria's prostitution industry – the escort services – continued to remain unchecked by either municipal council planning authorities or law enforcers. He claimed that tourist literature was dominated by ads for escorts. *The Truth* newspaper, the traditional marketplace for prostitution advertising, was said to have '9 out of 10 advertisements for escort agencies, with few of the licensed brothels rating a mention' (1985, p. 38). Making prostitution legal appeared to have actually proved a boon for escort agencies. It was against this antagonistic backdrop that the Labor Government commissioned Victoria's *Inquiry into Prostitution* (1985), known as the Neave Inquiry. Marcia Neave's[11] recommendations would become the foundation for Victoria's prostitution law.

---

11. Marcia Neave, Chairperson of the Victorian Law Reform Commission, had worked on social justice issues affecting women prior to heading the Prostitution Inquiry in the early 1980s.

The Neave Inquiry

The Neave Inquiry provided the context for a feminist analysis of prostitution to influence how Victoria's prostitution law would be shaped. The Government's terms of reference made room for a far more comprehensive analysis of the prostitution industry than its former inquiry that focused solely on the location of brothels. Neave was given the freedom to take account of the social, legal and health aspects of prostitution 'in all its forms' (Victoria 1985a, p. 1). This wider focus allowed many of the concerns raised in the ongoing dialogue around prostitution in Victoria over the last decade (including those of feminists) to be incorporated in Neave's recommendations for new prostitution legislation.[12]

A women-centred analysis

From a feminist perspective, what distinguished Neave's analysis of Victoria's prostitution industry from many of the discourses that had dominated public forums and government thinking in the state, was that she made prostituted women central to the inquiry. Neave estimated that there were between 3000 to 4000 people involved in the state's prostitution industry, predominantly women (Victoria 1985a, p. 2). This suggests a significant increase in prostitution under Labor's more liberal regime as the number of prostituted women at the end of the 1970s was considered to be around 2000. Neave recognised that prostitution was indisputably an industry based on occupational segregation by sex – where men were the buyers and women the bought.

The 1985 inquiry adopted as a starting point that prostitution was an exploitative practice that should be minimised, not encouraged or institutionalised as an occupation. Neave stressed that:

---

12. *Victoria's Inquiry into Prostitution: Final Report* (the Neave Report) (1985).

[T]he prime cause of prostitution is the economic and sexual inequality of women and that the business will continue to exist until women are able to control their own sexuality and men abandon the view that they are entitled to sexual release at all costs. It will finish only when desirability to men ceases to be the only real form of power exercised by many women (1988, p. 207).

In support of her position, Neave made reference to the strategy proposed by the 1949 United Nations *Convention for the Suppression of Traffic in Persons and the Exploitation of the Prostitution of Others* that supported the removal of these inequalities, resulting in a society in which men and women do not find prostitution a necessary or desirable activity (Victoria 1985a, p. 11).

What is particularly significant about Neave's approach to the inquiry was that her views contradicted the Labor Government's main argument for decriminalisation: that prostitution is primarily a private activity between consenting adults. However Neave's analysis, while reflecting a concern for women in the industry, reflected the same quandary that confronted socialist feminists, that is how to support prostituted women without demonstrating an approval of prostitution. Neave accepted the inevitability of prostitution even if only in the short term. By not considering criminalising buyers' prostitution behaviour and thus targeting the demand for prostitution, she limited herself to either returning to prohibition or decriminalisation. In the *Final Report* of the inquiry Neave recommended decriminalisation with appropriate government controls. An alternative form of decriminalisation as I discussed in Chapter One, is Sweden's pro-women policy. This human rights based strategy decriminalises prostitution for women and girls, but criminalises the buyers and the pimps, and creates opportunities for women to leave the industry.

One of Neave's strongest arguments in support of decriminalisation was that criminalising women in prostitution drove the industry underground and encouraged criminal involvement and the exploitation of prostituted women. In the *Final Report* of the inquiry, Neave argued for the legalisation of brothels, decriminalisation of paired or single women working from their homes, and the decriminalisation of street prostitution in specific areas. Minimal controls would relate to where prostitution activities impacted on town planning, were considered a public nuisance, affected traffic control or involved the molestation of people. In some instances, such as town planning restraints and traffic control, these were restrictions that pertain to any other legitimate business (Victoria 1985a, pp. 11–13).

The contradiction in Neave's approach, from a radical feminist perspective, is clear when we examine the implication of her recommendation to establish a specialist licensing board. Neave considered this critical if the negative trends toward multi-ownership and criminal involvement that were occurring in Victoria were to be prevented. She envisioned that the board would have the power to vet brothel applicants to ensure they did not have a criminal record and also to investigate individuals behind the operations. Equally vital was that the board would have the power to override local decision-making and therefore end any embargo on brothels by municipalities (Victoria 1985a, p. 18). According to Neave this last jurisdiction was necessary because if every council were allowed to prohibit brothels, illegal brothels would flourish. Disturbingly she did not recognise that conversely, forcing every municipality to accept brothels as legitimate commercial enterprises, encouraged and facilitated the normalisation of prostitution. More challenging still is Neave's primary recommendation to decriminalise prostitution for the industry as a whole. 'Full' decriminalisation gives legal recognition to the prostitution industry, and thus continues to legitimise men's rights to buy, sell and profit from women's and girls' exploitation.

The *Prostitution Regulation Act 1986*: its aims and deficiencies

In 1985 Labor's Minister for Planning and the Environment, Evan Walker, presented its plan to update Victoria's prostitution legislation with the introduction of the *Prostitution Regulation Bill* into parliament. The framing of the proposed Act reflected the influence of Neave's recommendations. The intended Act provided for the decriminalisation of prostitution-related activities and established a legal framework around the industry, with licensed brothels subject to public health and employment regulations. Neave's recommendation for a licensing board to regulate the industry was also accepted (Victoria 1987, p. 726). Fundamentally Victoria was going forward with a harm minimisation approach to prostitution. That the Act's major objectives included the need to 'protect young people from sexual exploitation' (*Prostitution Regulation Act 1986*, s. 4 [a]) and 'adult prostitutes from violence and intimidation' (*Prostitution Regulation Act 1986*, s. 4[b]), also indicate that the Government remained committed to its belief in a forced and free distinction.

Major opposition to the Bill being passed related again to the impact on local amenities rather than to the exploitative nature of prostitution. The Liberal Opposition-controlled Legislative Council introduced these objections into parliamentary debate. Most of the concerns articulated in parliament related to small owner-operators. The Opposition argued that the new Act concentrated on the licensing of large brothels, but that the overall decriminalisation of prostitution meant that brothels consisting of one or two people , were free to operate in suburban environments unhindered by any regulations (Victoria 1987, p. 740).

The issue of municipal control of brothels through planning[13] also remained highly controversial. Local councils argued that while they were required to accept full responsibility for regulating brothels, they had no power to prohibit them. Moreover councils had neither right of entry nor expertise in policing of illegal activities (Gorjanicyn 1992, p. 139). In all, the Opposition put some 55 amendments forward; the principal amendments had the effect that small (one or two people) operations and street prostitution remained illegal (Neave 1994, pp. 84–87). Also Neave's proposal for a specialist licensing board was dismissed. As a consequence, as had been the case in most of Victoria's history, the *Prostitution Regulation Act 1986* enabled certain forms of prostitution to exist, while prohibiting other prostitution activities. Thus the new law on prostitution would continue to disadvantage and discriminate against women, while men's sexual rights remained unchallenged.

That the Opposition promised to pass the *Prostitution Regulation Bill* on the condition that its amendments were adopted again demonstrates the unworkability of attempting to treat the prostitution industry as an unproblematic commercial enterprise. The Labor Government accepted the revisions but then refused to proclaim those that were inconsistent with the original intent of the Act (Victoria 1987, p. 733). The new legislation as it stood meant that the planning laws alone would control brothels.

The *Prostitution Regulation Act 1986* provided a further context in which socialist feminists and Victoria's major prostitutes' rights organisation, the Prostitutes' Collective of Victoria (PCV),[14] found themselves in opposition to the Labor

---

13. This was achieved through regulations introduced under an amendment to the *Planning and the Environment Act 1987* which regulated how and where brothels could be located.

14. The PCV was formed in 1988 evolving out of the Victorian branch of the APC.

Government. Neave, in a critique of the 1986 legislation, condemned the Government's failure to set up an 'instrument to control brothel management' encouraging 'large brothels, multi-ownership and the domination of the sex industry by businessmen' (1988, p. 210). She cited a further failure as the prohibition of women working in small owner-operated businesses. This, she said, channelled women into escort agencies or street prostitution, or forced them to work in exploitative conditions in the highly visible brothels run by big business (1988, pp. 210–212). The PCV similarly argued that under Labor's new Act 'many of the State's 4500 prostitutes [were forced] to work in uncontrolled escort agencies or on the street' (Pinto et al. 1990, p. 4). As Neave points out, Victoria had 'the ironic situation where multi-storey brothels flourish in Flinders Lane, but discrete prostitution is not permitted in one's own home' (1988a, p. 210).

Neave's evaluation of the overall implications of Victoria's *Prostitution Regulation Act* provide a succinct summary of its failure to assist women and girls involved in Victoria's prostitution trade. As she makes clear, while *Victoria's Inquiry into Prostitution* was intended to empower prostituted women, 'the manner in which its recommendations had been implemented seemed to have the opposite effect' (1988a, p. 54). Victoria's prostitution policy, in effect, remained one of containment and tolerance. However Neave's alternative legislative approach, which entailed full decriminalisation of prostitution, rather than legalisation, remains unacceptable. As indicated above, decriminalisation for pimps and buyers, similar to legalisation, facilitates the normalisation of the prostitution industry; an industry which Neave herself recognised as constructed upon 'the economic and sexual inequality of women (1988, p. 207).

In 1990 Joan Kirner was elected to the leadership of the Victorian Labor Party after the Premier John Cain resigned.

Kirner, an unswerving feminist who played a leading role in promoting women's involvement in Australian politics,[15] did not challenge her Government's commitment to the legalisation of prostitution. She too supported the view that decriminalisation was the only feasible alternative to prohibition.

Law Reform under a new Liberal Government

The 1992 Victorian state elections brought the Liberal Party back into power after an absence from government of ten years. A further attempt was made to effectively place some order and control over the partially regulated prostitution industry. Similar to the former Labor Government, the newly elected government, under Premier Jeff Kennett, committed itself to a non-criminalisation approach to prostitution. The Liberals' *Prostitution Control Act*, which came into effect in 1994, was designed 'to control prostitution in Victoria, through legalisation as opposed to decriminalisation of the industry' (Part 1 s. 1).

From its earliest days the Liberal Government, in contrast to its predecessor, did not promote prostitution as an occupation, whether 'desirable' or 'undesirable'. During the passage of its prostitution legislation through parliament, Attorney-General, Jan Wade, distanced the Government from the more liberal stance taken over the previous decade. The Attorney-General stressed that the introduction of the *Prostitution Control Act* did not imply Government support for prostitution. 'On the contrary' she stated, 'this Government is opposed to prostitution in all its forms' (Victoria 1994a, p. 1453). Even so Wade accepted, as had her predecessors, both the inevitability of prostitution and the inadequacy of prohibition to either contain or eradicate the prostitution industry (Victoria 1994a, p. 1453). The Liberals too would adopt a harm minimisation approach to prostitution.

---

15. Joan Kirner has been strongly involved in the Australian affiliate of Emily's List, an organisation which supports women's political careers.

Rewriting Labor's prostitution laws

The Liberal Government justified its anti-prohibition stance with reference to the Fitzgerald Report (Queensland 1989),[16] a landmark in Australia's criminal history. Fitzgerald exposed the high level of police corruption in Queensland in relation to the illegal prostitution industry and provided substantial evidence that outlawing prostitution entrenched organised crime and corruption (Victoria 1994a, p. 1453). The stated aims of the new legislation were to ensure that criminals were not involved in the prostitution industry, to minimise its 'impact on the community and community amenities' and to 'ensure that brothels are not located in residential areas or in areas frequented by children' (*Prostitution Control Act 1994*, s. 4.[a][b][c]). As will become increasingly apparent, Liberal's legislation, which became Victoria's principal prostitution law, would, like its predecessor, fail in these objectives.

The *Prostitution Control Act 1994* contained many of the provisions of Labor's 1986 Act, a mixture of tolerance and control (refer to Chart 1). The Liberals continued to use planning as a principal means of regulating the industry requiring brothels to obtain a town planning permit. This ongoing recognition of brothels as a legitimate land use, however, would in practice only facilitate their legitimacy and expansion. Conversely, street prostitution remained a criminal offence, as well as living off the earnings of those in prostitution.

Significant new clauses in the legislation involved child exploitation and the exploitation of migrants, with criminal procedures against those who forced a person to remain in prostitution, or forced a child into prostitution. A child was legally defined as someone under the age of 18. These clauses were

16. Report of the Commission of Inquiry into Possible Illegal Activities and Associated Police Misconduct

extended to include paedophiles and agents who organised sex tours involving the prostitution of minors (Victoria 1994a, p. 1453). In line with the State's focus on control rather than legitimisation of prostitution, the 1994 Act increased police powers by giving them the automatic right of entry to suspected illegal brothels (*Prostitution Control Act 1994*, s. 62).

Victoria's focus within its new Act on the more overtly coercive aspects of the industry paralleled legislative develop-ments at a federal level as well as mirroring legislative changes in other states and territories. In 1994 the Federal Government passed its *(Child Sex Tourism) Amendment Act*, which introduced harsh sanctions against Australians who had sex with children when travelling overseas (B. Sullivan 1997, p. 200). Similarly, most Australian states were in the process of legislating against both child sexual assault and child pornography. During the passage of the 1994 legislation through the Victorian parliament, the Attorney-General, Jan Wade, similarly emphasised that her government would offer no leniency to those convicted of any form of child sexual exploitation. As she stated:

> This government will never tolerate child prostitution. The bill retains harsh criminal sanctions against those who involve themselves with child prostitution. . . . The new offences in this bill [the *Prostitution Control Bill 1994*] . . . will operate to reinforce the commonwealth legislation, which expressly saves any similar state legislation (Victoria 1994a, p. 1454).

However the consensus that existed on the issue of children in prostitution did not transfer to human rights abuses against women in prostitution who were assumed to 'choose' their abuse. The new powers given to the police, ironically empowered them to arrest, without a warrant, women trafficked into illegal brothels as illegal immigrants. As will be discussed further in Chapter Five, this police power is potentially threatening to victims of sex trafficking as they have no victim status and are consequently deported.

The Liberal Government's intention to make control a feature of its new legislation was perhaps best illustrated by its provision for a specialist board to control licensing, a critical strategy that the Neave Inquiry had recommended to the former Labor Government. The newly formed Prostitution Control Board was responsible for licensing operators 'prostitution provider' businesses. A further stipulation within the Act was that licensees could operate one brothel business only (*Prostitution Control Act 1994*, Part 3, div. 1 s. 22 and s. 23). In addition the board's brief was to include both brothels and escort agencies (Part 1. s. 3). But the inclusion of escort agencies within the legal definition of what now constituted the prostitution industry, created further legitimacy for the trade by allowing a wider range of prostitution activities to be treated as lawful commercial practices.

One of the more entrenched problems that had confronted both the Labor and Liberal Governments was which body would take responsibility for overseeing the industry. As well as setting up its licensing board, the 1994 Act provided for the setting-up of its *Prostitution Control Act* Advisory Committee to advise the relevant Minister. The eleven member committee represented Government, industry and community interests (*Prostitution Control Act 1994*, Part 3, div. 10, s. 67). However as Melba Marginson, Chairwoman of the Victorian Immigrant and Refugee Women's Coalition and a committee member, pointed out, the real responsibility for overseeing the prostitution industry remained with local councils. The Committee brief as Marginson reflected was 'very limited'. As she says, 'their terms of reference are about monitoring legal brothels and the involvement of minors in the industry, [while] nothing in their [terms of reference] talks about trafficking or illegal brothels' (Commonwealth of Australia 2003, p. 62). This suggests that the Government naively believed that these systemic problems would disappear once a framework was created for prostitution to operate legitimately.

Evaluating the *Prostitution Control Act*

Ongoing debate in the Victorian Parliament surrounding the 1994 *Prostitution Control Act* again provided circumstances in which various stakeholders could enter into dialogue on the State's prostitution laws. The intensity of the criticism directed against the Liberal Government's legislation demonstrates that legalisation of the prostitution industry was proving as problematic as prohibition. The PCV was the strongest opponent of the 1994 Act, primarily because of its failure to address street prostitution. Statistics provided by the PCV revealed that those within the industry were assaulted nightly and on average were raped twice. The Collective also brought attention to the fact that in the last year two prostituted women had been murdered (Victoria 1994b, p. 1876). A summary of the PCV's criticisms of Victoria's prostitution legislation were distributed throughout the State under the title *Ten Point Plan for Decriminalisation* (1994). Its principal criticism was that the State's past and present approach to prostitution did not work. Instead the PCV offered a pro-active strategy which demanded further decriminalisation of the trade. This it argued would allow 'sympathetic' planning initiatives, prevent violence, be cost-effective as it eliminates the legal costs of policing and prosecuting prostitution offences, increase the effectiveness of outreach programs for drug addiction, aid in uncovering poverty and street prostitution, assist the families of those in prostitution and thus decrease child protection costs, and would dramatically decrease the instance of street prostitution in five years (Prostitutes' Collective of Victoria c.1994). In summary the PCV maintained that decriminalisation would create an environment which protected prostituted women's health and safety, their economic independence and end the stigmatisation experienced by those within the industry.

Several women's and social justice groups were persuaded by the PCV's arguments in the context of the increasing evidence of violence experienced by women and girls in prostitution under Victoria's current legislative regime. These organisations included the Civil Liberty Society, the Women's Electoral Lobby (WEL), the Women's Refuge Referral Centre, elements of the Catholic Church and the Salvation Army (Victoria 1994b, p. 1876). WEL Victoria, for example, put out the statement that it:

> [S]trongly agrees with the arguments put forward for decrimi-nalisation by the Prostitutes' Collective of Victoria, the more so because the collective is committed to exit programs. Women on low incomes or addicted to drugs often resort to street prostitution rather than work in licensed brothels because they see it as casual or temporary work. They frequently find themselves in a trap that cannot be sprung because recourse to helping agencies may expose them to criminal charges. For the same reason, some suffer violence because they avoid contact with police when under threat (Victoria 1994b, p. 1876).

While supporting the PCV, WEL's acknowledgement of the need for exit programs suggests that the organisation was well aware that inequitable social conditions are the preconditions for women entering prostitution as well as the major cause of them remaining entrapped in the industry. However while the organi-sation argued that it was the illegality of sectors of the trade that created problems for victims of prostitution, it did not consider that decriminalisation may make access to health agencies easier but not change the exploitative conditions that forced women to seek their aid.

Within parliament members of the now Labor Opposition became major spokespersons for the pro-decriminalisation lobby and the PCV. Labor Member of Parliament, Michael Cole, when speaking on the 1994 Bill in the State's Upper House, referred to the PCV's *Ten Point Plan* to illustrate the inconsistencies in the Liberals' agenda. Moving away from the idea that decriminalisation was simply an acknowledgement that prostitution was a private sexual act between two consenting adults that should not be the province of the State, Cole argued that women's interests would be served by further liberalisation of Victoria's prostitution laws. Similar to the arguments proffered by sexual libertarians the PCV had argued that it was the law as opposed to prostitution *per se* that operated against the interests of prostituted women.

The crucial difference between the Opposition and the Government during debates on the 1994 Act was the failure of the latter to address the problems of violence and exploitation in street prostitution (Victoria 1994b, pp. 1851–1860). Cole highlighted the limitations of the legislation: that among its critical objectives was the intention to eliminate criminal activity and industrial abuses in legal brothels, but it ignored other sectors of the industry. Street prostitution remained illegal, which Cole argued had a high level of underage prostitution (Victoria 1994b, p. 1852). Further opposition to the Liberals' prohibition of street prostitution paradoxically emerged from the St Kilda Street Prostitution Strategy Committee, which represented the interests of local residents and traders.

The inclusion of this Committee within the pro-decriminalisation collective demonstrated a realignment of stakeholders, as resident activists for the first time supported prostituted women. As reported in parliament, residents considered that 'a large majority of these men who prowl our streets do not come here to actually engage a sex worker, they come to exercise male power over women with violent physical and verbal abuse from cars' (Victoria 1994b, p. 1869). In this context street prostituted women were construed as victims, not criminals, which made it difficult to argue for continuing prohibition.

Labor's Jean McLean offered one of the strongest feminist analyses of the 1994 *Prostitution Control Act*, wherein she recognised the extreme harm of prostitution. McLean began her critique of the Liberal Government's new Act with the proclamation that the debate about the prostitution industry had always been surrounded by 'cant and hypocrisy' and this was exemplified by the new Act. McLean made connections between the Liberals' regulatory regime and other state institutions that institutionalise the sexual exploitation of women. In supporting her proposition, she linked Victoria's treatment of prostituted women with that of the military's, identifying them both as patriarchal institutions that perpetuated the sexual and economic exploitation of prostituted women. As McLean argued, 'The right of members . . . of the forces to look after their need, as it is so coyly put, by payment or force, is all part of the acceptable macho image of the military game' (Victoria 1994c, p. 1264).

McLean made particular mention of the Victorian Government's requirement under the 1994 Act, that prostituted women must undergo mandatory testing for sexually transmitted infections (STIs). She argued that this requirement harmed women working in Victoria's prostitution industry in the same way as mandatory testing harmed 'the thousands of women recruited around United States bases', specifically Subic Bay and the Clark Air Force Base in the Philippines. Women were infected with sexually transmitted diseases and HIV as a result of their contact with the US forces. As she put it, 'While servicemen brought disease, women were blamed' (Victoria 1994c, p. 1264). McLean's major contention was that the State collaborated with men in giving them access to women's bodies, thus upholding the paradigm that prostitution, although not desirable, was essential because of man's 'natural' instinct and biological need for heterosexual sex. As a socialist feminist McLean, however, continued to support the idea that decriminalisation of the prostitution was the most feasible solution to ameliorating the harm experienced by prostituted women in their working lives.

The core of Labor's opposition to the Liberal Government's legislation was that decriminalisation, rather than a strict regulatory regime, would allow sympathetic planning initiatives and prevent violence by providing prostituted women with industrial rights. Labor portrayed the Liberal Government's intentions as 'punitive' and argued that the legislation 'simply made money for brothel owners' by forcing women to work illegally or in unfavourable industrial conditions (Victoria 1994c, p. 1264). Significantly the Liberals (in their role as Opposition during Cain's Premiership) had earlier made this charge against Labor. Moreover both sides of the floor claimed to be following the recommendations of the Neave Report.

In practice then, the Liberal Government (like the Labor Government before it) was unable to come to terms with the competing elements at play on the issue of prostitution law reform. As the Opinion Editor of *The Age* newspaper commented, 'middle-class thinking and middle-class inhibitions marred the Kennett Government's plan to come to grips with prostitution. The result is a mixture of soundly based prescriptions and unrealistic proscriptions' (Forell 1994, p. 13). The ultimate outcome of the 1994 *Prostitution Control Act* was that irrespective of whether the Liberal Government disapproved of prostitution, like the Labor Government, it too had given its official imprimatur to the industry by recognising some sectors as legitimate commercial practices. Moreover it left unchallenged buyers' behaviour by legitimising them as 'clients'.

The rhetoric of commerce

The legal recognition of brothel prostitution and escort agencies continued to be sustained by a new discourse on prostitution formulated around the language of commerce. Political scientist, Barbara Sullivan, suggests that by the 1990s neo-liberalism, with its 'confidence in wealth creation and its use of the language of commerce', became a pervasive force in Australian prostitution policy and legislation (1997, p. 217), a trend that I introduced in Chapter One. That the State of Victoria accepted the legitimacy of the marketplace to determine the appropriateness of prostitution, was demonstrated by successive State Governments' official recognition of brothels as a legal town planning and land issue and the provision of prostitution through escort services as a legitimate occupation.

The gender-neutral and commercial terminology adopted within the Liberal Government's 1994 legislation demonstrated that the commercial credentials of prostitution were being mainstreamed as an idea. Prostitution was understood as the 'provision of sexual services', 'the provision by one person to or for another person (whether of or not of a different sex) of sexual services in return for payment or reward' (*Prostitution Control Act 1994*, Part 1. div. 3. s. 3). Brothel owners and former 'pimps' were identified as 'service providers' (*Prostitution Control Act 1994*, Part 1. div. 3. s. 3). Parliamentarians and stakeholders increasingly employed the term 'sex worker'[17] as an alternative to the commonly used, pejorative term 'prostitute', and the prostitution trade was officially recognised as the 'sex industry' (Victoria 1994b, p. 1851). By 1998 brothel keeping, escort agency services, and prostitution services were defined under *The Australian Standard Industry Classification System* as a 'Personal Service' similar to

---

17. The first instance of the use of the term 'sex work' or 'sex worker' in parliamentary debate took place during the second reading of the *Therapeutic Goods (Victoria) Bill* (Victoria, 1994c, p. 1322).

babysitting services, marriage celebrants and weight-reducing services (IBIS Business Information 1998, p. 3). Even in the case where the sexual exploitation of children is involved a new vocabulary was developed. The prostitution abuse of young people became interchangeable with 'sex for favours' (see for example, Department of Family and Community Services 2000).

Women's voices

Women's voices were not totally dismissed by Victoria's law makers. However those women who remained prominent in the State's prostitution debates mostly became apologists for male sexual rights and men's business interests. Pru Goward, who between 1997 and 2004 headed the Federal women's advisory unit – the Office of the Status of Women – was prominent within this group. In an article written a year prior to her taking office, Goward described prostitution as 'an essential service for randy men' and 'a necessary market solution to a fundamental difference between men and women: the nature of their sexual desires' (1996, p. 18). Goward told the media that she had given her husband permission to use the 'prostitution solution' while overseas (1996, p. 18). Both the Liberal Government and the Labor Opposition underpinned the soundness of legitimising prostitution as a 'bona fide' business by reference to Goward's expertise as an advocate of women's rights (Victoria 1997, p. 1621). Within parliament Goward was described as 'progressive', 'honest' and 'able to speak her mind'; 'admirable qualities for someone representing Australian women in the 1990s' (Victoria 1997, p. 1621). This acclaim I would suggest was because Goward supported the male sexual prerogative and represented the liberal feminist position which considered prostitution *per se* as unproblematic.

However the socialist feminist perspective that opposed the institutionalisation of prostitution could offer no feasible alternative to the liberal feminist position articulated by Goward. The 1995 Australian Council of Trade Unions's *Working Women's Policy* (Australian Council of Trade Unions 1995) continued to reflect the feminist dilemma of how to support prostituted women, while simultaneously seeking to legalise the prostitution industry. As its policy stated:

> [C]ongress condemns in the strongest terms the recent trends in service industries such as retail, hairdressing and hospitality to promote sales and services through the employment of topless and scantily clad staff. Such developments encourage the perpetuation of sexist attitudes towards women. Unions taking action against employers who engage in such activities will receive the support of the entire trade union movement (Australian Council of Trade Unions, 1995, Clause 4.2).

Conversely the same policy stresses that:

> While recognising differing moral views of prostitution, Congress supports prostitution law reform which will enable this group of overwhelmingly female workers, who will continue to work in the community, to organise; obtain regulated wages and working conditions; and obtain OH&S and worker's compensation coverage (Australian Council of Trade Unions, 1995, Clause 3.6).

Moreover while a socialist feminist economic analysis provided the context for some feminists to support the decriminalisation of prostitution, and argue for the rights of prostituted women as workers, in practice any concern for the rights and conditions of female victims was diminished under the liberal corporate model.

While radical feminism was mainly excluded from the more public debate on prostitution law reform, the formation in the mid-1990s of the Coalition Against Trafficking in Women (CATW), Australia has allowed some scope for challenging the pro-prostitution position. CATW is part of an international feminist organisation made up of autonomous networks in each world region aimed at combating all forms of sexual exploitation. The Coalition focuses on the connections between human trafficking and prostitution and maintains that women are not involved in prostitution through choice but because of inequitable resource allocation and the lack of gender equality globally. It evolved out of a 1987 United States conference organised by the Women Against Pornography Movement and the prostitution survivor group WHISPER. Dorchen Leidholdt, CATW's current co-executive director, says that 'the organizers understood trafficking in women as a broad, umbrella concept that encompassed all practices of buying and selling women's and children's bodies' (Leidholdt 2003, p. 4). At the beginning of the twenty-first century, CATW, which has Category II Consultative Status with the United Nations Economic and Social Council, has established affiliated groups in the Asia-Pacific, Latin America, Africa, North America and Europe (Raymond 2003, p. 1). The major struggle for CATW Australia and a radical feminist voice is to have an abolitionist message heard in circumstances where prostitution is accepted as inevitable and institutionalised as work. The only debates the State's decision-makers appear to engage in are those related to how, and to what extent, prostitution should be regulated or decriminalised.

Conclusion

The catalyst for Victoria's prostitution law reform beginning with the Planning (Brothels) Act 1984 was the unworkability of its existing legislation. Ostensibly, the later 1994 laws were responsive to the diverse interest groups that made up the Victorian electorate as well as overcoming some of the practicalities experienced by the former Labor Government in treating prostitution as an industry similar to other legitimate businesses. However at best, the evolution of the State's prostitution laws could be viewed as an uneasy negotiation between pro and anti-decriminalisation advocates. In practice, successive Victorian Governments adopted a harm minimisation approach that was mainly a response to male sex rights combined with the demands of community interests to lessen the encroachment of highly visible prostitution trade on public life and community amenities.

Feminists – both socialists and liberals – attempted to fit themselves into this legal framework. However they unwittingly found themselves in an alliance with either conservatives or sexual libertarians and economic rationalists. The ideologies that underpinned these camps reinforced gender inequalities and women's oppression. The compromise which socialist and liberal feminists adopted, ostensibly as a means to end prostituted women's experience of sexual exploitation, was to promote the liberalisation of Victoria's prostitution laws. To all intents and purposes this necessitated the acceptance of prostitution as work. Liberal feminists' support for prostituted women, as 'workers', was in reality indistinguishable from support for prostitution *per se*. Socialist feminists, who sought to ameliorate the harm of prostitution through industrial rights mechanisms, in practice, would find it impossible to maintain the quasi distinction between supporting prostituted women's rights as workers, and facilitating the normalisation and legitimisation of prostitution. Once the industry was legitimate, sex entrepreneurs and big business could readily tap into the profits to be made from merchandising women and girls to male buyers for sex.

CHAPTER THREE

From Prostitutes' Rights to Sex Industry Advocates: The History of the Prostitutes' Collective of Victoria

Sure we have an entire program dedicated to concentrating on issues for male prostitution, but the Collective as a whole sees prostitution as, essentially, a women's issue as it is based on patriarchal control. Just because some women join the oppressors (i.e. Thatcher) and some men join the oppressed (i.e. working boys), this fundamental political truth does not alter.

BRETT MCMILLAN, PROSTITUTES' COLLECTIVE OF VICTORIA PROJECT WORKER, *WORKING GIRL* (OCTOBER 1988, P. 13).

As a male hooker, I can subvert gender roles . . . I am the adult embodiment of what Freud called the 'polymorphous perverse infant.' I see this as the goal of an evolving concept of sexuality, and as a whore I see it as my goal to assist individuals to develop and grow in this direction.

JUSTINE, 'FROM STRIPPER TO WHORE', IN *WORKING GIRL/WORKING BOY* (1997, P. 14).

Introduction

The pro-'sex work'/pro-women theme was an ongoing and ostensibly compelling argument that sustained the State of Victoria's shift from prohibition to treating prostitution as work. The Prostitutes' Collective of Victoria (PCV), allegedly representing prostituted women within the State, emerged as one of the strongest advocates for the decriminalisation of the prostitution trade based on this connection. While the Collective's social roots were in the Women's Liberation Movement of the 1970s, and its initial aims were to campaign for the rights of prostituted women as women's rights, mainly within a socialist feminist framework, over the next two decades this gradually changed. Throughout the 1990s, the PCV became explicitly anti-feminist.

The relationship between prostitutes' rights organisations and feminism as I have previously suggested was always tenuous. However as the PCV matured, other social forces and ideologies apart from feminism came to dominate the Collective's internal perceptions, its aims and its organisation. The most decisive of these developments was the AIDS crisis, which emerged in the mid-1980s. The increasing normalisation of the prostitution industry, which the PCV itself had a major role in establishing, proved a further stimulus for change. Each of these events provided an opportunity for the organisation to shift from being a marginalised representative of a still largely stigmatised group within society, to a mainstream pressure group with potential union power. The irony was that once the Collective's viability as an organisation became dependent on State funding for HIV/AIDS preventative programs and the legitimisation of the industry, its focus became linked with those of sex business interests, male buyers and the Victorian Government's public health programs. The aims of these various stakeholders would contradict the initial feminist orientated goals which had underpinned the PCV in its earliest days. In its later guise, the Collective promoted the rhetoric of sexual libertarianism and economic rationalism. Prostitution was no longer considered a form of women's oppression but a legitimate profession, freely chosen and sexually liberating. From the 1990s onwards the

PCV's struggle for 'prostitutes' rights' progressively would come to mean 'the right to be prostituted' and include the overt celebration of prostitution as a form of sexual freedom.

The political beginnings of a prostitutes' rights collective

Australian pro-prostitution activist Roberta Perkins, a transsexual who attempts to define prostituted women as belonging to an oppressed sexual minority, says that 'social attitudes and legal reflections of them have long been a source of outrage to prostitutes' (1991, p. 9). An organisational response by prostituted women to legal and social control, however, is a comparatively new phenomenon that was stimulated by group identity politics and the rights discourses of the 1960s and 1970s. Victoria's first prostitutes' rights organisation, the Prostitutes' Action Group (PAG) had its beginnings, although in a relatively unstructured form, in the late 1970s. The group's formation was a direct response to the intense public debate over the growing visibility of prostitution, the setting up of formal anti-prostitution residents' activist groups, and these organisations' demands for the governing Victorian Liberal Party to contain the prostitution industry through effective legislation.

'Decent women' and 'prostitutes'

In November 1978 the City of St Kilda, which had a high concentration of brothels as well as street prostitution, held a public forum on 'Vice, Drugs and Prostitution'. The forum provided the immediate circumstances wherein prostituted women within the State took their first tentative steps towards political mobilisation by forming the PAG (Prostitutes' Collective of Victoria 1990, p. 1). Throughout the 1970s and 1980s, local councils, encouraged by newly created residents' activist groups demonstrated an overt hostility to women in prostitution. Feminists Sue Jackson and Dianne Otto, writing in the aftermath of the forum, reported that the women were being targeted along with single mothers, homosexuals, the unemployed, tenant and low-income earners, all of whom were believed to 'threaten the respectability that West Action [residents' group] desires for its community' (1979, p. 12). Thus the general view was that prostituted women belonged with other perceived social sub-cultures or 'social misfits', which threatened the social order.

The more virulent residents' anti-prostitution campaigns openly employed the 'whore' stigma turning any idea that prostituted women were victims of either sexual or economic exploitation on its head. Rather, it was residents and society as a whole which were victimised. The local Liberal member for the Melbourne suburb of Syndal, for example, claimed that the elimination of prostitution was essential 'to protect women and children and to support the institution of the family and marriage' (Victoria 1978, p. 2353). In a similar vein the St Kilda Mayor, Brian Zouch, asserted that prostitution 'must be some-where that it does not affect decent people' ('Council Will Curb Massage Parlours' 1978, p. 1). Inevitably the labelling of prosti-tuted women as some sort of social evil underpinned the St Kilda forum. Their marginalisation was further demonstrated by their exclusion from the list of invited speakers which according to the local media included the Minister for Social Welfare, Brian Dixon; a West Action representative, Graham Bradbury; Coun-cillor Helen Halliday; and the Chief Commissioner of Police ('Mayor Calls for Brothel Laws' 1978, p. 1). Jackson and Otto commented that during the forum those women who turned up as representatives of prostituted women in the area were 'met with hostility and outright hatred from the majority of people in attendance' (1979, p. 12).

However prostituted women's alienation from the majority of those present at the forum was, in part, a consequence of the lack of any grassroots organisation. Jackson and Otto suggest that as prostituted women are 'not immune to the contempt with which society regards them' many women simply 'feared to come out' (Jackson and Otto 1979, p. 12). As they explain, 'once labelled, prostitutes fear police victimisation and loss of legal status [typically] in rape or custody trials' (1979, p. 12). Indeed the day prior to the forum the St Kilda police conducted a 'blitz' against women involved in the street prostitution trade ('Mayor Calls for Brothel Laws' 1978, p. 1). This action strongly suggests that law enforcers used harassment as a means to control the women as well as demonstrating to the community that something was being done to eliminate the polluting influences of the prostitution trade.

Making alliances with Victoria's women's movement

Pro-prostitution advocates such as Roberta Perkins have stated that 'From an early period in the feminist movement it was obvious to most sex workers that they were going to get no support from that quarter' (1991, p. 122). That the PAG from its first days was linked with Victorian women's organisations, contradicts this belief. Its beginnings trace back to a feminist organised seminar held at the University of Melbourne on Prostitution and the Law. The group remained very much linked with Women Behind Bars and the St Kilda Women's Liberation Group (Johnson 1984, pp. 338–359) and feminist theory and practice influenced its political activism. It recognised that its political potential lay in its ability to create solidarity and support for women in prostitution. Its initial objectives included maintaining 'a support group for prostitutes' and facilitating 'the formation of a prostitutes' organisation' (Prostitutes' Collective of Victoria c.1996, p. 1). One of its first strategies involved asking women in the industry about their working conditions, police harassment, motivation for being in prostitution and its effect on their lives (Jackson and Otto 1979, p. 13).

Consciousness-raising groups were critical to the Women's Liberation Movement, because they allowed women to tell of their experience of rape and abortion, for example. Equally important, as radical feminist theorist Kathleen Barry says, 'these group meetings of women found commonality in their experiences of subordination; and from a feminist critique of power, they produced the critical awareness that "the personal is political"' (1995, p. 85).

Aligning with gay rights activists

Victoria's 'clean up the street' campaigns perhaps inevitably also created a potential for an alliance between prostituted women and other marginalised groups within St Kilda, specifically the more politically active homosexual community.[1] For instance, the Prostitutes' Action Group worked with the Homosexual Law Reform Commission (HLRC) in forming a delegation to oppose the Amendment to Section 18 of the 1966 *Summary Offences Act*[2] which had allowed for an increase in penalties against any person loitering in a public place. But while the Liberal Government's legislation created a context for the fledgling prostitutes' rights organisation to politically align with gay rights activists, this relationship was temporary. It would be the AIDS crisis in the mid-1980s which created stronger alliances between the homosexual community and Victoria's prostitutes' rights movement, an association that became even stronger when queer politics began to permeate the Prostitutes' Collective of Victoria in the 1990s.

---

1. In this context I use the term 'homosexual' to refer to males who have same sex relationships. It was mainly homosexuals who were involved in the Homosexual Law Reform Commission (Jackson and Otto 1979, p. 14). Throughout this book I define female same sex relationships as lesbian.
2. Assented to on 19 December 1979. *Summary Offences (Amendment) Act*.

The PAG, in the aftermath of the St Kilda Forum, changed its name to Hetairae[3] because many of its members did not want to be identified as 'prostitutes'. The group was dissolved in the early 1980s. Unlike the gay community, there existed little sense of solidarity among prostituted women within Victoria and minimal incentive to begin the first steps to 'speaking out' as prostituted women. At this point in time few women saw themselves as belonging to a specific workforce or considered prostitution a long term 'career choice'. Moreover there was no potential for any alliance between industry representatives and those exploited within the trade. Indeed, local brothel owners had refused to allow PAG representatives to contact women working in their parlours (Jackson and Otto 1979, p. 15).

Ultimately it was the international Prostitutes' Rights Movement which became strong in the 1980s that provided both an impetus and a model for the establishment of successive Victorian State-based prostitutes' rights organisations – the Australian Prostitutes' Collective (APC) and the PCV.[4] However this influence would broaden the focus of the Victorian movement so that it became a vehicle for servicing the industry as a whole rather than the women which it purported to represent. Disturbingly, the inherent contradiction between the competing interests of sex businesses and prostituted women

---

3. Hetairae was a Greek name for courtesans in classical Athens (Prostitutes' Collective of Victoria, 1990, p. 1). The idea was that the association with supposedly more empowered women would help overcome the stigmatisation experienced by prostituted women.

4. Several authors have documented the history of the International Prostitutes' Rights Movement (Jaget 1980; Inglis 1984; Delacoste and Alexander 1988; Bell 1994; Nagle 1997). These authors argue that the Movement gave rise to a public awareness of prostitution problems both at a local and international level. It encouraged the formation of new collectives and solidified those already established. Within Britain and Europe, in particular, the Prostitutes' Rights Movement was linked to the Women's Liberation Movement. For an excellent critique of this Movement see Jeffreys 1997.

would be glossed over, as the PCV in the 1990s extended its 'client base' to include brothel owners and procurers, as the Collective struggled to ensure its organisational survival.

Consolidating Victoria's prostitutes' rights organisations

In 1983 the APC established itself as Victoria's new prostitutes' collective initially deriving its membership from the now defunct PAG, encompassing both prostituted women and 'women not on the game' (Inglis 1984, p. 17). From its first days the APC sought to create a wide network with similarly orientated organisations and in 1984, formed a coalition with the Sydney based Collective of Australian Prostitutes in the State of New South Wales. As well, it established substantial links with socialist-based prostitutes' rights groups in Europe and the US. In particular it affiliated with the English Collective of Prostitutes (ECP) adopting its economic analysis of prostitution as well as reflecting its tendency to interact strongly with the socialist part of the Women's Movement (Hunter 1992, p. 112).

The Prostitutes' Rights Movement unilaterally made a demand for 'decriminalisation of prostitution' central to their language of protest.[5] The common perception within the Movement at that time was that legalising brothel prostitution would simply exchange legal harassment for commercial exploitation (Jaget 1980, pp. 18–19). The ECP, for example, argued that it opposed legalisation as this would institutionalise prostitution and simply make the State the pimp (1977, p. 2). Socialist feminist, Jan Inglis, suggests it was precisely this thinking that shaped the APC's political strategies. As she says, the APC's main goal 'was to establish acceptable ground-rules

---

5. The term was first used in relation to prostitution in 1973 when the American National Organisation of Women (NOW), a women's equal rights group, made the abolition of all laws related to prostitution its platform (Pheterson 1989, p. xix).

for the industry allowing working women a form of self-management – freedom from the pimping style control of the state, police and pimps themselves' (Inglis 1984, p. 18).

To begin with the APC met at the Fitzroy Legal Service, located in an inner Melbourne suburb. Its agenda was to determine the implications of Victoria's proposed *Brothels (Planning) Act 1984* (Prostitutes' Collective of Victoria 1990, p. 1), the first substantial piece of State legislation worldwide to legitimise prostitution as work. In March of the same year, the collective participated in a Sydney-based Task Force On Prostitution, established to negotiate with the New South Wales Select Committee Upon Prostitution [1983–1984]. Bebe Loff, Marianne Phillips and Cheryl Overs, all from Victoria, appeared as witnesses before the Committee in July 1984 (in Perkins 1991, p. 15).

Cheryl Overs later commented that 'Sheer fury at the anti-prostitution laws' provided the motivation for APC's adversarial stance throughout the Committee hearing, a position that was in line with the ECP and similar socialist based collectives' struggles (in Perkins 1991, p. 72). Overs, in the 1990s, became a key participant in the national prostitutes' rights organisation, the Scarlet Alliance, formed in 1989, and the international United Kingdom's Network of Sex Work Projects. Both groups promoted a pro-prostitution position and were equally opposed to socialist feminists' and radical feminists' analyses of prostitution (Overs and Longo 1997). The extent to which Overs changed her political allegiance in line with her new status as an international player in the pro-choice prostitutes' movement is reflected in her 1998 interview by Jo Doezema from the Network of Sex Work Projects. Overs' reframed perspective was that:

> [T]he women's movement is no longer the home of the sex workers rights' movement. The happiest time for me was the late eighties

and early nineties when HIV/AIDS brought new links with gay men, and Madonna rose and rose. Our small band of sex worker rights' activists suddenly had a new political family. Once a pro-sex feminist theory was articulated we even had new supporters from the women's movement who were listening to sex workers for the first time (Doezema 1998, p. 204).

Clearly there is some indication that the APC, more than its predecessor, was aware of the considerable advantages that could be achieved by aligning itself with the gay community. This is particularly suggested by the inclusion of the gay youth organisation, Twenty-Ten, in its Task Force On Prostitution. In the US, the pro-prostitution group, COYOTE, an acronym for Call off Your Old Tired Ethics, had successfully demonstrated the political leverage that could be achieved in prostituted women situating themselves as part of a 'beleaguered minority group'. Valerie Jeness, who recorded COYOTE's history, explains how the pro-prostitution movement that the organisation represented, used the 'discursive themes of the gay and lesbian movements' to identify those in prostitution as belonging to a 'victim class' (1993, p. 21). This identification was based on the construction that the prostitutes' rights movement was ultimately part of a struggle for sexual autonomy, with COYOTE and similar organisations defining themselves as 'a self-identified movement' (Kempadoo and Doezema 1998, p. 19).[6]

The notion that the pro-prostitution prostitutes' rights movement was in effect a sexual liberation movement was particularly spelt out by the International Committee of

---

6. COYOTE claimed legitimacy based on its assertion that it was constituted around prostituted women's self-representation, thus more representative of a 'grass roots' organisation than other socialist feminist orientated collectives (Pheterson 1996, pp.xvii). However COYOTE's membership consisted of women and men in prostitution as well as 'students, clients of prostitutes, politicians, media personnel, activists, and representatives from other advocacy organisations' (Jeness 1993, p. 43).

Prostitutes' Rights (ICPR), formed in 1985 by COYOTE's Margo St James with Gael Pheterson. The ICPR's central tenet was that to deny a woman the option to be prostituted, 'under conditions of her own choosing', was to restrict women's 'sexual choice, economic security, free speech and erotic pleasure' (Pheterson 1989, p. 18). From this perspective, the ICPR urged governments to 'Decriminalize all aspects of adult prostitution resulting from individual decision' (1985, p. 1). In the Australian context, Andrew Hunter, from the Scarlet Alliance, agreed. He too saw:

> government controls on sex work and sex workers . . . [as] part of a broader issue of the state attempting to set moral limits by criminalising certain consensual sexual acts. Sex workers are discriminated against in a similar way to other people who do not fit into the narrow, accepted sex roles tolerated in our society (Hunter 1992, p. 13).

However as radical feminist Sheila Jeffreys points out 'the often repeated assertion that lesbian and gay rights and prostitutes' rights are intertwined is based on the erroneous view that the Prostitutes' Rights Movement is one of sexual liberation' (1997, p. 69). The notion nonetheless successfully helped to shift the struggle for prostitutes' rights from being about women's rights and define it as a liberation movement, concerned with both sexual and economic self-determination (Jeffreys 1997, p. 69).

The APC's political philosophy

For the most part, the APC's principal affiliation did remain with the socialist-based British ECP. There was minimal evidence in the APC's political rhetoric to suggest that those within the industry freely 'chose' prostitution as a career option or indeed celebrated it as a form of sexual liberation. Spokesperson, Ros

Nelson, a former massage parlour 'worker', self-identified feminist and a founding member of the APC, was uncompromising in her view that prostitution must be considered a 'women's rights issue' (in Inglis 1984, 17). She promoted the political importance of a 'united movement' between feminists and prostitutes' rights organisations and stressed that women work in prostitution 'because there are no alternatives' (in Inglis 1984, p. 17). 'The demand remains . . .' she says, '[A]nd that won't change until patriarchal attitudes to . . . and perceptions of heterosexuality and women change radically' (1984, p. 18). Thus the prostitutes' rights struggle was indisputably seen here as the struggle of all women to be free of capitalist-patriarchy. What is most significant about Nelson's statements was that in 1984, the APC was expressing a view that the problem with prostitution was male demand, an analysis consistent with radical feminism, which they later refuted.

The APC also strongly supported the need for exit programs for the many women who wanted to leave prostitution. This too was central to the ECP's platform. In its collection of essays *Prostitute Women and AIDS* (1988), the British collective consistently advocated that Governments should introduce measures that would prevent women entering into prostitution or assist them to leave the industry. This translated into demands for adequate welfare and resources for women to escape poverty traps (Lopez-Jones and English Collective of Prostitutes 1988/1993). However the ECP's and the APC's struggle to have prostitution recognised as 'women's work', and thus a struggle for labour rights, in effect meant that the collectives had a vested interest in establishing prostituted women as legitimate employees entitled to industrial rights and conditions. As I have previously suggested, in practice, this approach facilitates the recognition of prostitution as similar to other valid occupations, a circumstance that makes it difficult to oppose the interests of buyers and 'legitimate' sex businesses.

'Women's rights' versus 'workers' rights'

The *Planning (Brothels) Act 1984*, which had introduced the legal reality of brothel prostitution as a legitimate business, created an acceptable context for prostitutes' rights to be spoken of in terms of 'workers' rights' and 'industrial rights', in addition to 'women's rights'. By the mid-1980s, the idea of prostitution as a form of labour was dominating the APC's public education exercises. Its *Working Girl* publication was specifically created to distribute information on 'workers' rights'.[7] Similarly, the Collective's weekly program on Melbourne's community radio station, 3CR, promoted the message that the APC was 'establishing a public voice for the most oppressed workers and people were beginning to listen to what [it] had to say' (Prostitutes' Collective of Victoria 1990, p. 3).

The APC's tendency to normalise prostitution as 'just work', was buttressed by its official identification with the ICPR in 1987 following its formal association. This alliance exposed the Collective more and more to the influence of the pro-prostitution ideology that was associated with COYOTE, the ICPR and its followers. Progressively, the APC's ideological foundations wavered between socialist feminism and the pro-prostitution position. This ambiguous position was starkly obvious in the Collective's newly created constitution. It took the position that:

[W]hilst the [organisation] will not encourage anyone to adopt prostitution as a job option nor encourage the idea of prostitution as a profession or career, it will recognize and offer support to anyone who freely chooses to adopt prostitution as a job and who

---

7. The first issue of *Working Girl* was published in June 1984.

considers this to be his/her profession (Australian Prostitutes' Collective 1987, p. 1).

Thus while the Collective did not support the institutionalisation of prostitution, it did nevertheless, endorse the concept of a forced and free distinction. By the late 1980s the contention that some people 'freely' choose to be prostituted, and that prostitution could be recognised as a legitimate profession, had permeated the organisation's political philosophy.

State cooption of Victoria's prostitutes' rights organisation

A further catalyst which encouraged the APC to recast its views on prostitution was an increasing reliance on government financial assistance to sustain the organisation. In 1987 the Collective received a grant from the Labor State Government subject to the organisation becoming formally associated.[8] This was the first phase in successive Victorian Governments' cooption of the State's prostitutes' rights organizations – the APC and later the PCV – to assist them in regulating and controlling the prostitution industry. The funds made the collectives viable but it also meant that their agendas were influenced by what the Government prioritised as important for the prostitution industry. The funding would continue as long as the collectives' and the State's interests coincided.

Similar to what was happening in other Australian workplaces in the 1980s, this first grant was to be used by the collectives to assist women in the legal sector to obtain equity in their 'workplaces'. The money was meant to provide assistance for childcare, increase access to legal services to deal with breaches under existing industrial laws and provide ongoing dialogue about workers' rights in general (Inglis 1984, pp. 17–18). This 'ongoing dialogue' consisted of prioritising tax issues, work cover

8. The Department of Community Services Victoria provided the grant.

schemes, income securing loans and equal opportunity, themes that were picked up repetitively in the APC magazine. The APC's energies were therefore drawn to acting as a work support group for the now legalised prostitution industry which, as discussed in the previous chapter, had its beginnings with the introduction of the *Planning (Brothels) Act 1984*. This new role diminished the Collective's function as an advocacy group for prostituted women faced with legal discrimination and which had supported women in both the legal and illegal sectors of the industry.

Roberta Perkins maintains that the cooperation between the Labor Victorian Government and the APC inspired the formation of other State and Territory prostitutes' rights organisations (1991, p. 14). This view is justified to an extent as prostitutes' rights collectives were subsequently established in Western Australia, the Australian Capital Territory and the Northern Territory (1991, p. 14). That the Victorian Collective was adapting itself to become a significant stakeholder in Victorian prostitution politics, however is particularly indicated by its decision in 1987 to change its name to the Prostitutes' Collective of Victoria (PCV). This followed its formal separation from the New South Wales branch of the organisation (Prostitutes' Collective of Victoria 1990, p. 2).

The new style Collective suggested a 'professionalism' that paralleled its mounting acceptance of the idea of prostitution as work. In fact, its management committee described the organisation as consisting of a new 'breed of worker' that welcomes the opportunity to talk about AIDS, brothel regulations and tax (Overs 1988, p. 2). Such rhetoric undoubtedly reflected the mainstreaming of the Collective, but it also implied an increasing stratification among women in prostitution. Women working in the legal prostitution industry were now referred to as 'brothel workers' or 'career prostitutes'.

In contrast to these 'professionals', there was the 'young or itinerant worker who drifts through the industry' (Overs 1988, p. 2). This supposed specialisation, and the distinction between 'career prostitutes' and 'other workers', would intensify as the PCV evolved into a dominant stakeholder in prostitution law over the next decade and a half. However it would be the AIDS crisis in the mid-1980s that would ultimately prove to be the most critical and ongoing influence in determining the PCV's organisational culture. This would see it cast aside its socialist feminist's roots and become a body servicing the State, sex business interests and the buyers.

Creating an identity as 'sexual health educators'

The AIDS phenomenon of the mid-1980s was fundamental to creating an ongoing interdependence between Victoria's prostitutes' rights movement and the Victorian State Government. Reflecting what was occurring internationally, Australian governments hoped to enlist prostitutes' rights organisations to educate prostituted women and, in turn, the buyers, on issues of sexual health. Their definitive plan was to create the façade that the State could control the threat of AIDS to the wider heterosexual community (wives and partners), created through male use of prostituted women. As I discuss in Chapter Six, this was in fact an unworkable strategy because it did not take account of the reality that a legalised prostitution system does little to alter the power imbalance between the male buyer and women in prostitution, and men's continued demand for 'unsafe sex'. Nonetheless, in Victoria, this State agenda did enable the PCV to move from the margins to the centre of public policy around prostitution, as the Collective more and more promoted itself as a service provider for sexual health. Thus, in contrast to the changes effected by either the influence of the international pro-prostitution movement or the normalisation of prostitution within Victoria, the emergence of AIDS ushered in a total transformation in the make-up and the thinking of the PCV.

The links between the prostitution industry, STIs and public health became a continuing theme in public debate around AIDS and associated treatises on sexually transmitted diseases (STDs) in the latter part of the 1980s. Globally the epidemic brought to the forefront public concern about the relationship between prostitution and the high incidence of the disease. Several authors have suggested that the public's anxiety about AIDS resulted in an intensification of the legal, moral and social censure of prostituted women.[9] Academic Paul Sendziuk, in his analysis of the impact of the AIDS crisis in Australia, says that the first case of AIDS was reported in the *Medical Journal of Australia* in May 1983 (2003, p. 1). According to Sendziuk, a 1986 opinion poll found that 25 per cent of Australians 'favoured the quarantine of infected individuals'. Twelve months later this figure had risen to 50 per cent. Sendziuk considered that '[A]n even greater number supported mandatory testing of "high risk" groups, such as gay men, injecting drug users and sex workers' (2003, p. 1).

Feminists have been particularly critical of mandatory testing of prostituted women for STIs, considering this an abuse of civil liberties and reflective of the double standard of morality that pertains to a male supremacist society, an argument I will examine in depth in Chapter Six. However it was the more organised gay anti-AIDS communities that provided the most immediate and strongest resistance to the imminent threat against high-risk, HIV-positive groups. These communities emerged spontaneously out of existing gay organisations, setting up programs on AIDS prevention as well as caring for the sick,

---

9. Some of the authors who present this view include Alexander 1988; Brock 1989; Bastow 1996; Scrambler and Scrambler 1997; Sendziuk 2003.

to deal with the immediacy of the crisis[10] (Carr 1992, pp. 15–17). Sendziuk maintains that gay AIDS activists were able to gain both private and public funding as well as align themselves with sympathetic medical professionals, ultimately creating 'a key role for themselves in defining public policy on AIDS' (Sendziuk 2003, p. 3). Gay organisations were particularly represented on strategic committees such as the 1985–1988 National Advisory Committee on AIDS (NACAIDS), and later the Australian National Council on AIDS (ANCA) (see Altman 2001, p. 56).

The PCV's political strategy to counteract the AIDS 'scare' was modelled on gay rights activism around the pandemic and thus proved a catalyst for strengthening alliances between the two groups. While this association smoothed the progress of PCV towards legitimacy, the Collective subsequently became dependent on public health discourses in its campaigns for the decriminalisation of prostitution. Victoria's prostitutes' rights organisations promoted themselves as well situated to become proactive on AIDS prevention. As early as 1985, the APC produced the booklet *Facts on AIDS for Working Girls* (Australian Prostitutes' Collective 1985, p. 1). The material focused on 'peer education' and 'harm reduction', concepts that would later become central to the PCV's strategies for containing AIDS and other STIs. A critical rethinking around AIDS within the wider public, however, was a prerequisite if the prostitutes' rights groups were to successfully assume the role they hoped to play as a sexual health service provider.

Australian prostitutes' rights organisations generally advanced the idea that AIDS was a generalised epidemic. More significantly

---

10. One of the more prominent of these groups was the Victorian AIDS Action Committee (VAAC), which was established in July 1983 and evolved out of the ALSO Foundation, Victoria's largest gay and lesbian welfare organisation (Carr 1992, p. 18).

they promoted the idea that women in prostitution had a critical role to play in containing the spread of the virus (Banach and Metzenrath 2000). The APC too argued that its intention was to educate the community. The Collective publicised the fact that its 'safe sex endorsement' was not just about the sexual health of women in prostitution, but was designed 'to demonstrate to the community that it had a serious role in prevention' (Overs 1988a, p. 2). This focus meant that in addition to being a support and representative group for women in the industry, APC was already forced to direct its energies towards, 'management and clients'. Certainly, the Collective emphasised that 'working girls' were among the most aware societal groups on the AIDS issue as it was in their own interest to be informed about their health and safety (Australian Prostitutes' Collective 1985, p. 1).

The PCV, throughout the 1990s, would progressively extend its 'client base' to include the buyers and sex business interests. Indeed the Collective promoted itself as the lynch pin for anti-AIDS intervention strategies in the State arguing that, 'The reality [was] that sex workers have been almost solely responsible for the safe sex education and personal counselling of hetero-sexual men in this country' (Prostitutes' Collective of Victoria 1992–1993, p. 17). In addition to recasting its image, the organisation also sought to establish its relevancy directly with the pivotal government bodies concerned with sexual health. Among these initiatives was its submissions to the Victorian Department of Human Services consultation on the new infectious diseases legislation, which in due course became incorporated into the *Victorian Health (Brothels) Regulations 1990* (Prostitutes' Collective of Victoria 1990a, p. 15).

The PCV's interaction with Government public health bodies was extended to other mainstream organisations dealing with AIDS, as well as the gay community. But it was the APC's association with NACAIDS, the principal Australian body researching AIDS, which opened the way for it, and later the PCV, to become integrated into the mainstream health system. Sendziuk explains how NACAIDS' ideological outlook on AIDS prevention can be summarised by its commitment 'to trust and empower gay men, sex workers and injecting drug users to care for themselves and for others' (Sendziuk 2003, p. 8). At a practical level, NACAIDS funded the 'Sex Industry and the AIDS Debate', Australia's first national conference for those within the prostitution industry, organised by the newly formed PCV in 1988. The proceedings from the national conference are considered by pro-prostitution advocates to be a 'milestone' in the international Prostitutes' Rights Movement (Nengeh, Allman et al. 2000, p. 2).

In the aftermath of the conference, the PCV claimed that the exercise reflected the co-operative approach that was part of Australia's national agenda around AIDS. Cheryl Overs suggests that the conference brought together representatives of state and territory prostitutes' rights organisations, AIDS organisations, government spokespeople and medical experts (1989, p. 6). Themes for discussion included legal frameworks for prostitution which hindered or assisted in AIDS treatment as well as the ethical and human rights issues raised by the experience of being prostituted (1989, pp. 4–7). Roberta Perkins contradicts the PCV's positive assessment when he states that the conference 'seemed more beneficial to government officials and bureaucrats' as these 'considerably outnumbered prostitutes attending from the various states' (1991, p. 14). This view further highlights the increasing interdependence of Government agencies and the Collective. The crucial subtext was that prostitution needed to be treated as work, which matched the priorities of prostitutes' rights organisations, whether or not they were opposed to the State's suggested takeover of how this was to occur.

The Conference Report and associated papers demonstrated a consensus that continued reform of Australia's prostitution law was required to promote optimum conditions for the practice of safe sex within the prostitution industry. Many speakers highlighted that a primary obstacle to health care for women in prostitution was the fear of disclosure and the inevitable criminal proceedings which meant they did not access health professionals. Delegates argued that prostituted women who were HIV positive were particularly isolated from Australia's health care system. The Conference's principal recommendation, relating to prostitution and AIDS, was that the industry must be regulated like any other commercial activity and all sexually transmitted infections treated as an occupational health and safety (OHS) issue (Overs 1988, pp. 108–10). These conclusions thus necessitated the decriminalisation of prostitution and the legitimisation of prostitution as 'sex work' as a pivotal strategy for AIDS prevention.

That the Conference was instrumental in mainstreaming the PCV as a sexual health provider became immediately apparent through the appointment of the organisation's representative, Julie Bates, to ANCA,[11] the major committee on AIDS in the country (Overs 1988, pp. 108–10). The Australian Federation of AIDS Organisations (AFAO), the peak non-government organisation representing Australia's community-based response to AIDS also provided funding to the PCV to be used in relation to AIDS education. The funding allowed the PCV to have a representative on the committee of the newly formed Scarlet Alliance, the umbrella group for Australian prostitutes' rights organisations (Blakey 1991, p. 4).

The Scarlet Alliance, in its mission statement for the years 1993–1996, defined its purpose solely in terms of facilitating

---

11. ANCA replaced NACAIDS in 1989.

safe sex for the prostitution industry. As the organisation maintained:

> [T]here is a consensus amongst the member organisations that the role of the Scarlet Alliance as a national sex worker organisation is to strengthen the position of member organisations to allow them to provide better representation for, and HIV/AIDS service delivery to sex industry workers (c.2000, p. 1).

The Scarlet Alliance, in line with the thinking that emerged from the 1988 National Sex Industry Conference, campaigned strongly to have STIs recognised as an OHS concern that should be treated within an industrial relations framework. Its major study – *National Consultation on the Issue and Needs of HIV Positive Sex Workers* (Overs 1991) – was intended to sway Government policy towards decriminalisation of prostitution by purporting that law reform was critical to the containment of STIs. The report was released in conjunction with the 1991 Legal Working Party of the Intergovernmental Party on AIDS, whose agenda was to determine the role of state and territory governments in minimising the spread of STIs and HIV within the prostitution industry.

In support of its position, the Alliance drew on a case study of two HIV positive women in Victoria's prostitution industry. The women had been charged with 'conduct endangering life' (Hunter 1991, p. 31). Its central argument was that people involved in prostitution were discriminatorily 'singled out from others with HIV'. The study's general findings were that criminalising prostitution as a strategy failed 'to prevent the spread of HIV and only creates an inaccessible underclass of sex workers' (Hunter 1991, p. 31). Reiterating most of the recommendations of the 1988 National Conference on AIDS the Alliance called for the recognition of those within the industry as 'workers' and

STIs as a work consequence. Thus STIs and AIDS were to be treated within the context of OHS.

That the PCV saw itself as very much caught up with this thinking is suggested by its involvement in the Scarlet Alliance 1991 workshop on 'HIV Prevention and Support for Young People Involved in Sex Work'. This was a cooperative training program that involved various Australian prostitutes' rights organisations, including Sex Industry Employees Rights Association (SIERA), Sex Workers Outreach Project (SWOP), Workers in Self Employment (WISE) (Blakey 1991, p. 4). As reported in *Working Girl*, the PCV considered that this was the major initiative it had undertaken in that year (Blakey 1991, p. 4). The inclusion of 'Transsexual Youth Issues' and 'Young Male and Female Sex Workers Issues' workshops was indicative of the increasing diversity of the groups the Collective was now targeting with its health programs,[12] groups who considered their struggle for prostitutes' rights was a struggle for sexual rights rather than to be free of male oppression and exploitation.

The PCV adopts the State's public health agenda

By the mid-1990s, 50 per cent of the PCV's involvement with other committees and forums were AIDS and sexual health related (Prostitutes' Collective of Victoria 1996, p. 22). The avenue for community consultation on AIDS was a direct outcome of Australia's national response to the epidemic. Federal, State and Territory Governments were adopting a dual model to deal with the impending health crisis – mandatory testing and community liaison. Mandatory testing as I have already

---

12. Other projects developing around peer education on safe sex involved Victoria's major medical centres working with AIDS and other STIs. These were the Centre for the Study of Sexually Transmitted Diseases at La Trobe University, the Venereology Section of Monash Medical Centre, and Fairfield Hospital's HIV/AIDS Unit (*Working Girl* 1994, p. 19).

suggested, is discriminatory and relatively ineffectual in inhibiting the transmission of STIs and AIDS. Partnerships between communities most affected by AIDS and government and medical experts, potentially are a more workable and less discriminatory approach to the pandemic.[13] As Sendziuk explains, most 'state and federal governments . . . liaised with community groups in order to gain their expertise in communicating with, and educating, people at risk' (Sendziuk 2003, p. 3).

The PCV benefited directly from this interaction as it provided the opportunity to have input into Victoria's evolving prostitution 'reform' regulation as well as receiving financial support from Governments for its sexual health programs. Jocelyn Snow, the PCV's STIs advisor in the early 1990s, makes the point that 'with the AIDS crisis . . . the Health Department . . . actually assisted us to get funding' (Sullivan 1999c). From this perspective, both Governments and the PCV had a stake in ensuring the success of the Collective in its role as a sexual health service provider.

One of the first joint initiatives was the PCV's *Working Girl* video (1988). It was designed to fit in with the Federal Government's OHS video *Work Safe Play Safe* (Overs 1989, p. 5). The co-production was significant for several reasons. Firstly both the Federal Government and the PCV were promoting STIs as a workplace issue, a further move towards the normalisation of prostitution as a legitimate occupation. Secondly, the PCV clearly put the message out that its knowledge of STIs was 'as good and usually more advanced' than that of other groups

---

13. The 1989 World Health Organisation's (WHO), *Global Programme on AIDS and Programme of STD* reinforced the idea that prostitutes' rights organisations had a critical role in AIDS prevention. Its recommendations were for 'appropriate representation from the international legal and civil rights communities to address issues such as laws that impinge on social, economic, and legal rights' of people with STDs (*Global Programme on AIDS and Programme of STD* 1989, p. 1).

involved in AIDS prevention programs, thus bolstering its role as a sexual health provider. The video includes extensive focus shots of the Collective's safe sex programs, peer education workshops and its needle exchange operation, which Cheryl Overs claimed was the first and largest exchange in Australia (Prostitutes' Collective of Victoria 1989). This message also worked to counteract the idea that those within the industry were 'purveyors of disease'. The community in fact was told to look to the PCV for guidance and education around the issue of 'safe sex'. By 1994, the Commonwealth Health Department had provided the PCV with A$70,000 to produce safe sex literature. A further A$150,000 was specifically designated to produce materials for those within the industry who came from Non-English Speaking Backgrounds (NESB) (Prostitutes' Collective of Victoria 1990a, p. 15). That Government funding was critical to the very existence of the Collective is indicated by the fact that in 1993, its net profit was a minimal A$1481 (Prostitutes' Collective of Victoria 1992–1993, p. 31).

The PCV's success in gaining public recognition as a sexual health provider was reflected in the Victorian Government's increasing recognition of the Collective as a significant stakeholder in the State's prostitution law reform. Labor Senator Caroline Hogg, during debate on the *Prostitution Control Bill 1994*, extolled the positive results of her Government's support to 'high-risk groups' while it had been in office. She praised the PCV for the 'Tough measures its members put in place to try to ensure that safe sex is practised' and argued that it had created 'a barrier preventing the spread of HIV/AIDS into the heterosexual community' (Victoria 1994, p. 106). The Liberal Government's invitation to the PCV to take up membership on both the Prostitution Control Board and the *Prostitution Control Act* Advisory Committee, contrasted sharply with the earlier experience of the APC which had been excluded from the

St Kilda Council's forum on 'Vice, Drugs and Prostitution' in the late 1970s.

In 1998, the PCV's income from federal and state funding for AIDS strategies was $A350,000 (Prostitutes' Collective of Victoria 1998, p. 42). This equals approximately a 60 per cent increase of funds within five years. Jocelyn Snow, who worked as a Project Manager for the Collective during this period, explains how the PCV by the end of the decade defined its role solely in relation to STI prevention. She stressed the point that while 'a lot of people think we are a union . . . we are not'. According to Snow, its main role was 'to educate sex workers about sexually transmitted diseases' (M. Sullivan 1999c).

By the beginning of the 21st century, the message emanating from prostitutes' rights organisations Australia-wide was that 'responsible' sexual health management and the legitimisation of prostitution as work were intricately linked. The Scarlet Alliance in its *Guide to Best Practice*, an OHS manual for the prostitution industry, stressed how:

> Displaying a commitment to recognised legitimate business practices and systems strengthens the prostitution industry's image as a well-managed, legitimate section of the business community. It also assists in gaining recognition from existing legislative bodies such as the Worker's Compensation Tribunal and Occupational Health and Safety Authorities (Elder 2000, p. 2).

Professionalising the PCV

The mainstreaming of the PCV that resulted from its recast image as a sexual health provider was paralleled by a shift in its organisational culture. This was characterised by the Collective's increasing bureaucratisation. In addition, it not only put aside its socialist-feminist roots, but more generally, it cast off its grass-roots foundations. In 1992, the PCV's Management Committee was upgraded to a Board of Management which appointed an administrator to liaise between the Board and staff members (Prostitutes' Collective of Victoria 1992, p. 12). The new board subsequently announced that its client base was the legal prostitution industry and prostituted women were now not just 'sex workers' but 'sexual service providers' (1992, p. 12). This restructuring fitted well with the State's agenda to regulate the prostitution industry and co-opt the Collective to educate prostituted women to be providers of 'safe sex'. Since the State Liberal Government had adopted the term 'service provider' when it introduced its principal 1994 prostitution legislation, the PCV's use of the term was predictable.

Throughout the 1990s, the PCV progressively argued that the State Government's focus should be on obtaining workers' rights for women in prostitution, rather than on how to control the industry. Similarly the Collective exhibited an increasing tendency to indiscriminately promote women's sexual servicing of men as totally acceptable. As a member of the 1994 Coalition for the Regulation of Sexually Explicit Entertainment, the Collective argued that tabletop dancing, a phenomenon I discuss in depth in Chapter Five, should be recognised as a legitimate sector of the prostitution industry. But the Collective went further than merely defining sexually explicit work as a valid occupation. Indeed, it advocated that tabletop dancing 'can and will, if used correctly, provide [a woman] with a future including independence, strong self-esteem, freedom from financial worries, and the chance to materialise your dreams' (Prostitutes' Collective of Victoria 1994, p. 7).

The PCV's attempt to unionise the prostitution industry in the mid-1990s was perhaps the most overt demonstration that it had wholly accepted the position that prostitution was simply a job like any other. Maryanne Phoenix, the first paid union organiser for the PCV, believed that the step towards unionisation demonstrated that the PCV had gone past its 'victim stage' (Walsh 1996, p. 50). The Collective had worked with the Australian Liquor, Hospitality and Miscellaneous Workers Union (ALHMWU) to unionise those in legal prostitution. It targeted 'workers' in Victoria and the Australian Capital Territory (ACT), which legalised brothel and escort prostitution in 1992. ALHMWU representative, Ruth Frenzell, defended the highly controversial initiative having wholly accepted the proposition that prostitution differed in no way from other occupations. 'These workers', she argued, 'are entitled to the same conditions as any of our other members working in any other area we cover' (in Walsh 1996, p. 50). From this perspective, the human rights violations experienced by prostituted women were labour abuses, nothing to do with gender violence or male power. Both Frenzel and Phoenix in fact stressed that the exploitative nature of prostitution 'will be eradicated when society views sex work as an industry' (in Walsh 1996, p. 50).

In all, only 150 women applied for union membership. This minimal number meant that there were insufficient funds to meet the required union membership fees.[14] The PCV's analysis of the prostitution labour force's failure to unionise was that many women 'feared to disclose themselves as sex workers' (Hanuschack 1997). An alternative view was put by Jocelyn Snow. She believed that most women in prostitution saw their 'work' as transient, and not as a career (Sullivan 1999c). I consider that the latter explanation is the more feasible. According to a PCV survey conducted just prior to its attempt at unionisation, 64.2 per cent of prostituted women wanted to leave prostitution (Noske and Deacon 1996, pp. 9–10).

---

14. In 1997 union membership fees were set by the Australian Commission of Trade Unions and based on a one per cent rate of Full-Time Adult Weekly Ordinary Time Earnings (AWOTE).

Fitting women in with their exploiters

As suggested previously in this chapter, the early socialist feminist orientated collectives considered that there existed no common ground between prostituted women and sex business interests. Indeed this belief was a driving force underpinning the PCV's bid for unionisation. The Collective's position was that while, 'There are employers who are broadly supportive of the concept [of union-isation] . . . when push comes to shove, we are going to end up with a huge fight in the Industrial Relations Commission' (Walsh 1996, p. 50). A fundamental and ongoing problem between pros-tituted women and business interest would be that, as the PCV itself recognised, 'employers [were] desperately trying to make sex workers look like contractors, not employees' (Walsh 1996, p. 50). But as I have suggested throughout this book, in arguing for labour rights and the right of prostituted women to be recognised as legitimate 'workers', the PCV equally legitimised their exploiters (brothel owners and other sex business operators) as well as buyers.

The PCV's *Working Girl* magazine is a useful vehicle for tracing the way in which the Collective increasingly broadened its 'client base' to include sex business interests together with women in prostitution. As early as 1990, the Collective was offering advice to escort agencies and brothel management on 'legal issues, police matters . . . and safety' (Prostitutes' Collective of Victoria 1990c, p. 17). A later issue encouraged 'workers' to 'talk to the boss as his interests are the same as yours and the clients' (Prostitutes' Collective of Victoria 1993a, p. 14). That the PCV increasingly assumed that prostituted women and business entre-preneurs shared common interests is equally apparent by its asso-ciation with major industry lobby groups. In 1993 for example it liaised with the Australian Adult Entertainment Industry,[15]

---

15. The Australian Adult Entertainment Industry is the parent organisation of the Eros Foundation, the major lobby group for the Australian Sex industry now operating as a corporation.

Australia's foremost sex industry representative group, on a joint submission to the Victorian Department of Justice (Prostitutes' Collective of Victoria 1993, p. 5). By 1994 the PCV was 'available to male, female and tranny sex workers, prostitution industry clients, owners and managers, people thinking about working as an option and services and businesses who have contact with sex workers' (Prostitutes' Collective of Victoria 1994).

The dissipation of women's rights

The AIDS phenomenon indisputably facilitated the PCV's assimilation into Victoria's mainstream health care system. Despite the inherent conflict that existed between prostituted women and sex business interests, the PCV's new role as a sexual health provider demanded a broadening of its client base to include sex businesses. The AIDS pandemic also saw the Collective aligning itself more and more with gay AIDS activists, strengthening the conviction that prostituted women were a distinct sexual group stigmatised because of their sexual choice, an analysis already established within the pro-prostitution ICPR. Throughout the 1990s the ideological shift within the Collective that resulted because of these changes was sustained by recourse to queer theory, a theoretical perspective that reiterated the concepts of sexual liberalism. Sexual liberalism conveniently blurred the boundaries between sexual exploitation, sexual expression and sexual freedom. At a more subliminal level, the queering of the PCV signalled a marked antagonism towards the inclusion of all streams of feminist theory and practice within the Collective.

The queering of the PCV

Feminist academic, Sheila Jeffreys, explains that a perspective on prostitution drawn from gay male theory began to be influential in the 1990s. In critiquing the work of Andrew Hunter from the Scarlet Alliance, whom she considers an advocate of queer theory, Jeffreys highlights the way in which he criticises the economic approach of the socialist feminist orientated collectives, including the APC. As Jeffreys says, this is because Hunter sees prostitution as an expression of sexuality – 'an expression which in itself is good' (1997, p. 76). This belief, she maintains, 'is allied to queer politics of the 1990s which could be seen as "out and proud" and confrontationist rather than assimilationist' (1997, p. 76). Her central point is that 'gay male proponents of prostitution have been influential in constructing a pro-prostitution position, based on the experience of gay male prostitution which is significantly different from the situation of women in many ways' (1997, p. 76).

In Jeffreys' contemporary critique – *Unpacking Queer Politics* (2003) – she argues that from the late 1970s onwards a powerful male gay culture developed which rejected 'the gay liberation project of dismantling gender hierarchy and chose "manhood" as its goal'. As she explains 'Through sadomasochism, gay male pornography, sexual practices of public sex and prostitution that celebrated masculine privilege, dominant areas of gay male culture created a hypermasculinity and said this was gayness, and this was good.' (2003, pp. 1–2). Gay proponents of this sexual libertarian movement drew on queer theory and in particular Focauldian ideas of 'transgression' to justify their position (see Chapter One). Queer theory allowed for a 'coalition politics based on the acceptance of anyone with unusual sexuality or practice' (Jeffreys 2003, p. 37). Queer gay activists indeed celebrated and included in their ranks 'gay men who wear drag, transvestism, transsexuals, butch/femme role-players and all those who don the character-istics of clothing usually assigned to the sex class other than that in which they were brought up' (2003, p. 43).

Thus as Jeffreys concludes:

the idea of revolutionary activism that might challenge the material power differences between the sexes, of which gender is simply an expression, has been replaced by the idea . . . that transgression on the level of dress and performance is revolutionary and will bring down the gender system (2003, p. 42).

What this left in place were an acceptance of patriarchal sexual values and the heterosexual equation of sex and penetration and domination and submission.

Ideas derivative of queer theory began to permeate the PCV's magazine – *Working Girl* – at the same time that 'women's issues' became marginalised. Gender and transgender became important topics for discussion. The December 1990 issue, for instance, featured a letter by 'Dana'. Dana, a transsexual, offers 'her' expertise to assist others with gender identity problems. Dana writes how 'she' is, 'happy to meet some of my sisters out there and give them some help with doctors who are sympathetic to us about things like plastic surgery or hormones' (Dana 1990, p. 16). The same issue noted a lack of services for transsexuals in Victoria.

By 1992 the PCV was celebrating its 'make-over' which included a new style cover for its magazine with the reworked title *Working Girl/Working Boy* (Prostitutes' Collective of Victoria 1992b, pp. 2–3). Its editorial stated that, 'we all know there are some essential differences between how boys and girls work. It's time boys had a space of their own in this mag' (Prostitutes' Collective of Victoria 1992b, p. 2). Features included a spread on 'Fantasy and Bondage and Discipline Workshops' intended 'to explain the dominant and submissive sexual point of views', as just one of many legitimate forms of sexual expression (1992b, p. 24). Similar themes became commonplace in the magazine. 'Lesbians: Light Up the Love Industry' where cross-dressing was promoted as 'a feature of both lesbianism and prostitution' (Vicqua 1994, p. 38) was an article typical of the emerging genre. 'Diary of a Male Street Worker' (Prostitutes' Collective of Victoria 1994c, p. 6) and 'Handy Hints for Transsexuals' (Prostitutes' Collective of Victoria 1994d, p. 45) are other typical examples.

Within a decade the PCV had not only depoliticised prostitution, but sexual practices constructed around dominant and submissive archetypes were celebrated as being at the cutting edge of sexual freedom. In 'A Worker's Guide to Fantasies', the PCV informs the reader that if we reframe the way we see prostitution, 'sexual expressions previously not imaginable or tolerated [and which] may appear to be excessive aspects of the prostitution industry' can be equally understood as 'a way in which sexuality and desire transgress boundaries and seek the erotic' (Mayson 1995, p. 28). Oppression thus becomes only a subjective experience totally devoid of material reality. In these circumstances, the abuse and violence of prostitution is trans-formed into something that occurs only in the mind of the prostituted woman. This was a clear shift away from socialist feminism materialism and the idea that patriarchal structures operating within a capitalist society create the conditions which draw and entrap women into prostitution.

In parallel with this diminishing of feminist thought within the Collective, *Working Girl/Working Boy* began to publish a distinctively anti-feminist line. Helen Vicqua's 'Feminism and Prostitution' (1994) reiterates Cheryl Overs' attack on the 'victim feminism' of the earlier feminist-influenced collectives. Vicqua claims that the idea that women in prostitution are caught up in a system of exploitation undermines 'the dignity and service of sex work and continues to commodify prostitutes as commercial sex objects by talking about them as gormless and in need of "correction"' (1994, p. 36). Indeed, she goes further by suggesting that feminists who oppose prostitution support traditional structures where 'women have been caged by an ideology of idealised female chastity, female vulnerability and the dangers of unleashing women's libido' (1994, p. 36). In contrast I argue it is Vicqua who ties prostituted women to their traditional patriarchal role.

Vicqua's understanding of prostitution relies on the essentialist biological model of male sexuality where prostitution is a valid service for meeting men's sexual needs. She says:

> [P]rostitutes are skilled in many arts that are hidden from most other women. Prostitutes handle men much more assertively than the cultural norm and use safe sex techniques. Prostitutes learn the power of play and acting and dispense more than sexual services. Clients find with prostitution a kind of power release and solace not otherwise available to them and many prostitutes perform complex support and even therapeutic roles for their patrons (1994, p. 36).

There is nothing here that is revolutionary, least of all women's continued sexual and emotional servicing of men. Nonetheless, the trend within the PCV to juxtapose prostitution 'services' with women's sexual liberation, allowed for a new spin to be put on prostitution. Prostitution would more and more be portrayed as a 'people's profession', similar to psychotherapy and similar health care services.

The 'career prostitute'

The 1990s was a period in which the Collective began to portray prostitution as a highly skilled profession and promoted the idea of the 'therapeutic power of sexuality' (WISE 1994, p. 18). The article 'Stripper to Whore' is a celebration of the 'career whore'. The author, a 'male hooker' who adopts the name 'Justine', argues that the 'good whore . . . performs a vital role in our society and culture . . . [functioning] as a healer, a therapist [and] a confessional confidante' (Justine 1997, p. 15). He promotes prostitution as economically empowering, sexually transgressive, as well as, importantly, a contract between two individuals of equal status. Justine defines prostitution as 'a two-way transaction . . . a social contract executed in private between individuals' (1997, pp. 14–15). The links between such speech and the gender-neutral equality language of liberal theory are obvious.

The idea that all forms of sexual practice were permissible progressively seeped into the Collective's thinking. Inevitably so too did the view that there should be no boundaries to the commodification of women's bodies including women's repro-ductive capacities. In the article 'The Working Mother To Be' prostituted women are encouraged to integrate pregnancy into their 'working lives' (Bronte 1999, p. 19). Breast-feeding in particular is advocated as a 'prostitution service' that can achieve good financial returns for women. As the author explains, 'a number of men find drinking breast milk either arousing or soothing' (Bronte 1999, p. 19). Women in brothels, she believes, can get the receptionist to 'push that to good advantage'. In addition, she 'may even be able to charge extra for those who choose to do so' concluding 'not a bad idea given the drain on her body's nutrients' (Bronte 1999, p. 19).

It is difficult to determine the extent to which the PCV's pro-male/pro-sex analysis of prostitution represents the views of individual members. Alison Arnot-Bradshaw, a self-identified 'sex worker' and member of the Collective, suggested that there was little common ground between men and women in the prosti-tution industry. Speaking at a 1999 Melbourne University Criminology Department seminar on 'Sex Work and the Law', Arnot-Bradshaw stressed the differences between how men and women in prostitution experience sex. She considered that while she saw prostitution as a means of making money 'for male prostitutes, it is about sex'. But as she pointed out 'these differences were ignored however, as they 'didn't fit with queer theory' (Arnot-Bradshaw 1999).

There is no conclusive comparative research on male and female experiences of prostitution. Most studies on male prostitution focus on high risk behaviour particularly around 'safe sex'.[16] Recent studies undertaken by Victoria's Centre for Sexually Transmitted Diseases have attempted to expand current conceptions of male prostitution. *Sex Work and the Accumulation of Risk: Male sex work as cultural practice*, for example, was designed to develop 'significant new theory on male sex work as cultural practice, and in particular the articulation of sex work practices with broader male sexual cultures and practices of masculinity' (Willis, Peterson et al. 2004). Some of the conclusions reached in this study are that 'many [males in prostitution] continue to work in this industry over a long period of time and do not find the work stressful' (Willis, Peterson et al. 2004, p. 6), a view which differs significantly from the PCV's finding that 64.2 per cent of women wanted to leave the industry. Yet despite such differences, as well as the significantly lower involvement of males in prostitution compared to females, as Arnot-Bradshaw indicated, 'boys' projects and issues now dominate the Collective' (Sullivan 1999a).

The dissolution of the PCV

Just as there is minimal evidence to suggest that women and men in prostitution share common interests, there is also no evidence that the majority of women who engage in prostitution for economic reasons in Victoria have a sense of themselves as professional 'sex workers'. However at the end of the twentieth

---

16. Some relevant Australian studies that examine male sex prostitution include Perkins, R., Prestage, B., Lovejoy, F., & Sharp, R. (1993), Browne, J., & Minichiello, V. (1996) and Minichiello, V., Marino, R., Browne, J., & Jamieson, M. (2003). These all take a pro-prostitution position.

century the PCV was undoubtedly recognised as a legitimate stakeholder representing those involved in prostitution in Victoria's prostitution law debates. Unquestionably this recognition was premised on its expertise as a sexual health service provider for a legal prostitution industry, a position that assimilated well with both the Federal and State governments' safe sex agenda and program to bring prostitution under their control. The alliances that were created with gay AIDS activists also saw the PCV promoting itself as an organisation concerned with the rights of a beleaguered sexual minority. This direction required a broadening of the Collective's sexual repertoire into one that celebrated prostitution and thus fitted easily with the business interests of the prostitution industry as well as the buyers. The PCV had become a prostitution industry advocate. This transition ultimately meant that the PCV lost its distinctiveness as a prostitutes' rights group, and even more so as an organisation committed to prostitutes' rights as women's rights.

The Collective's reliance on government funding had meant that in line with normative bureaucratic evaluations, performance indicators would determine its success as a sexual health provider to the prostitution industry. By 1999 the Victorian Government had indicated that a new body, which would operate completely under the auspices of the Victorian Health Department within the Public Health Protection Program, would more effectively manage this role. In June of that year, the PCV's Board of Management held an extraordinary meeting to determine the Collective's future in the context that government funding would be withdrawn (Sullivan 1999c).

Board member, Jocelyn Snow, who was supportive of the government takeover, believes that the Collective's inability to operate as a business meant that 'deregulation', was 'a good thing'. She is critical of the PCV's management style, arguing that it is 'fine for sex workers to say we want sex workers to work for sex workers, but if they don't have those skills that are required to operate a business . . . then it's been a bit of a mess . . . especially where your ability to get grants is affected' (Sullivan 1999c). Snow dismisses any political aspirations that the Collective's members may have held in the past as inappropriate. As she says, 'another organisation might prefer to be more political' but the purpose of the PCV should primarily have been that of a service provider (Sullivan 1999c). As a former brothel owner, Snow's lack of interest in prostitution politics and her acceptance that the Collective's role should have been that of a sexual health provider may reflect her association with the prostitution industry. The Government's appropriation of the PCV, however, had a far broader significance than Snow suggests. The Collective, in transitioning from a feminist-based pro-women organisation to an industry-based group coopted by the Government to assist in its regulation of State prostitution, had become just another government managerial body with no political status.

In February 2000 funding for the PCV was transferred to the Inner South Community Health Service (ISCHS). The ISCHS next set up Resourcing Health and Education in the Sex Industry (RHED) as a state-wide health service. Its task is 'To reduce the incidence of sexually communicated disease in the community by working with, and through, the prostitution industry' (Resourcing Health and Education in the Sex Industry 2000, p. 1). RHED's placement within the Southern Healthcare Network, which includes the City of Port Phillip and the St Kilda areas (the focus of Victoria's street prostitution trade), suggests that the Government remained mainly concerned with resident activists' 'clean the streets' campaigns. And in contrast to the PCV, RHED made no pretensions that its role was other than that of a sexual health provider. This point was in fact stressed in its promotional material. While RHED is currently an associate member of the national umbrella organisation, the

Scarlet Alliance, the material states that RHED was 'not a representative body for members of the sex work industry' (Resourcing Health and Education for the Sex Industry 2000, p. 1). I would argue that there is no contradiction here as both organisations' primary role is related to the promotion of safe sex for the prostitution industry.

The new health service for the prostitution industry departed from the PCV in other ways. It is interconnected with the massive international AIDS industry. RHED's website is linked to Inform Victoria which was developed by the group known as Social Workers and AIDS (SWAIDS) (Inform Victoria 2001). The latter is the umbrella organisation for various AIDS agencies under the auspices of Victoria's major hospitals and the State Department of Human Services. It is notable that Inform's website offers 'particular thanks to "Roche"' (Inform Victoria 2001). Roche is part of the transnational pharmaceutical conglomerate Hofmann-La Roche, one of the major manufacturers of AZT, the leading AIDS treatment drugs.

In the absence of any prostitutes' rights organisation in Victoria, the question arises as to whether RHED has any potential to fill the vacuum. Despite the dominance of sexual health issues, RHED, when it was created, did offer a commitment 'to supporting the rights of all people working in the prostitution industry' (RHED 2001, p. 1). A review of the first edition of its *Red* publication, 'a magazine for the sex industry' (2001, p. 1) suggests, however, that where women's voices are presented, they have become indistinct from either the sexual libertarians or business interests that make up the prostitution industry. This simply reiterates the pro-prostitution, anti-women bias that was already occurring within the PCV.

The magazine's target audiences include: those involved in prostitution (female, male and transgender), prostitution industry management, prostitution industry buyers, and friends and families of people involved in the prostitution industry. Eight out of the magazine's 36 pages are devoted to brothel and escort agency advertising, together with two and a half pages of listings of brothels, escorts and private workers (RHED 2001, p. 1). The edition features as major articles 'Behind the Scenes: Bondage Discipline Sadism Masochism' (2001, p. 23) and a review of the book *Change for Better*, 'the story of an ordinary boy who was to become an extraordinary woman' (2001, pp. 20–23). In 2006 RHED'S focus has not changed. As its web page reads, the organisation 'is committed to respecting and reflecting the needs of the sex industry': 'sex workers: female, male and transgender'; 'commercial and private partners of those associated with the sex industry'; and 'relevant service providers' (RHED 2006). Thus RHED promotes not just the Government's public health agenda, but also the pro-prostitution and business sectors of the prostitution industry.

RHED's relationship with the prostitution industry's business sectors is particularly highlighted in its association with the Australian Adult Entertainment Industry Incorporated (AAEI). The AAEI was incorporated in April 2001 as a political lobby group for registered brothels and escort agencies. RHED encouraged the AAEI to promote itself in *Red* suggesting its work could have a positive impact on the Victorian prostitution industry (RHED 2001, pp. 20–22). RHED, which followed in the path of a collective campaigning for the right of women in prostitution to be free of sexual and economic exploitation, now works in association with those who, at its beginnings, were identified as their exploiters.

Conclusion

The PCV's growth from a grass roots prostitutes' collective to a mainstream prostitutes' rights organisation, may be seen as part of the visibility of prostituted women's resistance to economic dependency on men and to sexual exploitation, violence and rape. This transition may also be understood as part of women's struggles for the right to control their own bodies and to sexual autonomy outside the norms defined by hetero-reality. But the history of the PCV reveals that within the Collective the human rights interests of prostituted women were displaced by political agendas that serviced the State, the pro-prostitution movement and ultimately benefited sex business interests and male buyers. The interests of these various stakeholders, although commonly portrayed as supportive of prostituted women, are not concerned with women's empowerment or with creating the means to end the sexual and economic exploitation and abuse that are inherent in prostitution.

From its beginnings the Prostitutes' Rights Movement in Victoria always harboured paradoxes. The moment the Collective sought to become a key player in State legislation on prostitution law reform, it was forced to synthesise ideals and pragmatic solutions. The term 'sex worker' had initially been adopted to de-stigmatise women in prostitution and end the legal harassment that was discriminatory to women in prostitution. At an analytical and rhetorical level, the PCV, and its forerunner the APC, appeared committed to the socialist feminist view. This defined prostitutes' rights as women's rights to be free of exploitation within a capitalist-patriarchal system, a perspective that was essentially anti-prostitution although in contrast to radical feminists, socialist feminists accepted the idea of prostitution as work as an expedient measure. The liberalisation of Victoria's prostitution laws from 1984 onwards created a framework in which the rights of prostituted women could be defined as 'worker's rights'. Although it never promoted itself as a union, the PCV's programs and actions increasingly focused on industrial issues. But by operating within an industrial rights framework, the PCV had no scope to attack prostitution *per se*.

The AIDS crisis which engendered enormous opportunities for the PCV to gain political legitimacy, made it even more difficult for the Collective to protest the idea that prostitution was anything other than legitimate work. Its cooption by the State to facilitate its public health agenda on AIDS, enabled the PCV to establish a credible place for itself as a sexual health service provider for the prostitution industry within Victoria. To counteract the social stigmatisation against those within the industry as a 'high risk' AIDS group, the Collective had to portray prostitution businesses as legitimate and responsible about public health. Up front it advocated that sexually transmitted diseases be recognised as an occupational health and safety issue.

Integral to this strategy was the PCV's identification of differences between women involved in the State's legal prostitution industry and others who participated intermittently in the unregulated and transitory prostitution trade. It was the former group who made up the new 'professional career prostitute' that the PCV more and more sought to represent. To establish its credibility further, the Collective broadened its 'client base' to men and transsexuals involved in prostitution, as well as buyers and prostitution business operators. This succeeded in blurring the boundaries between the oppressed and the oppressors within the industry, making any form of feminist political analysis of prostitution impossible.

The pro-prostitution sexual politics that came to dominate the PCV throughout the 1990s was an equally strong catalyst which worked to distance the Collective from its roots in the Women's Liberation Movement. Having little political legitimacy lost the PCV's effectiveness as an organisation. Inevitably the Government chose to adopt a more effective means of sexual health service delivery to the prostitution industry than the PCV could offer. RHED's priorities are certainly focused on public health and pro-prostitution politics that serve the interests of buyers and prostitution businesses. The power wielded by sex entre-preneurs in the 21st century within Victoria has resulted in the massive commodification and marketing of prostitution, making the mobilisation of any feminist opposition to prostitution exceedingly difficult.

CHAPTER FOUR

Living Off the Earnings of Prostitution: Sex Industry Expansion and Its Beneficiaries

For the guy who wants to make a profit, it's no longer a matter of owning prostitutes, but of getting his hands on the means of distribution, the means of practising prostitution, the places where prostitutes can practise . . . state control, the institutionalisation of prostitution, brings with it at the same time industrialisation of methods . . . prostitution is now planning and marketing . . . it's no longer a question of collecting a prostitute's cash at the end of the day . . . But of bringing her into a system in which she's made to pay more and more for services – hotel chains, Eros Centres, apartments. Pimping demands more big business know-how than muscle . . . The game that is being played is the recovery of profits from prostitution.

CLAUDE JAGET, AUTHOR OF *PROSTITUTES OUR LIFE* (1980, PP. 182–184).

Introduction

Victoria's prostitution law 'reform' implicitly favoured sex business interests and buyers, and the agendas of consecutive State Governments. The political goals and ideological positions of the successful stakeholders were shown in the long term to be at variance with both socialist and radical feminists' analyses, which consider prostitution as a form of economic and sexual exploitation, and, for radical feminists also a manifestation of male violence against women and an abuse of their human rights. The effects of Victoria's legitimisation of prostitution as work demonstrate only too clearly how State endorsement of prostitution, sustained from the mid-1990s onwards by economic discourses on the primacy of market forces, intensified the commodification of women's bodies.

Victoria's legalisation of prostitution was intended to contain the industry and prevent its dominance by big business interests. In reality legalisation has had the opposite effect. Making prostitution work encouraged industry expansion and its takeover by large sex operators, now legitimate business entrepreneurs. As the industry escalated so did the demand for prostitution by Victorian men. More and more women have been drawn into prostitution to feed this demand and ensure steadily rising profits. Sex business interests and the buyers (now considered a 'legitimate' consumer group) continue to be the beneficiaries of the increasing normalisation of prostitution as just another form of labour. Most prostituted women neither own nor control their 'working' lives.

I suggest that legalisation has explicitly eased the way for the commodification of women by allowing 'sexual service providers', shareholders and financial institutions, all to profit from men's purchase of women for sexual gratification. The Victorian Government also profits from prostitution through taxation, licensing fees and the promotion of prostitution tourism. The irony is that the State's lawmakers when formulating Victoria's principal prostitution legislation made it an indictable offence, with a ten year maximum sentence, for a person to 'live wholly or in part on, or derive a material benefit from, the earnings of prostitution' (*Prostitution Control Act 1994* s. 10[1]). Those who are criminalised for such behaviour are commonly the partners of women in prostitution and others who have not availed themselves of working within the legal sector which is totally sanctioned by the State.

One of the less recognised consequences of Victoria's acceptance of prostitution as work was that it now allows normal commercial marketing and lobbying techniques to be applied to the prostitution industry. Sex industry-lobbyists over the last decade have indeed played a critical role in advancing the normalisation of prostitution as no different from other occupations. Sex business interests are starkly apparent in its staging of Sexpo, an annual trade show for the 'adult'[1] sex industry, initially held in Melbourne in 1996. Sex business entrepreneurs, the Eros Foundation (the industry's predominant lobby group), and Victoria's politicians, have successfully coalesced to provide a political support structure for Sexpo, as well as for the wider trade in women's bodies.

The logic of the marketplace

When the Victorian Liberal Government introduced its principal piece of prostitution legislation – the *Prostitution Control Act 1994* – it stressed that prostitution was not to be encouraged or institutionalised as work. The then Attorney-General, Jan Wade, publicised the fact that her Government was 'opposed to prostitution in all its forms' (Victoria 1994a, p. 1453). Despite such claims, Victoria's prostitution industry under Liberal and successive Labor Governments has become a high economic growth area in terms of size, profits and of the number of male

---

1. The term 'adult' industry complies with a national classification scheme introduced under the *Classification of Publications Ordinance 1983* (Commonwealth). The Australian Law Reform Commission states that 'this legislative package was designed to affect the following principles: [that] adults are entitled to read, hear and see what they wish in private, and in public, people should not be exposed to unsolicited material offensive to children; [and that they] must be adequately protected from material likely to harm or disturb them' (*Australian Law Reform Commission Film and Literature Censorship Procedure 2003*, Clause 1.6).

buyers of prostitution services. Within five years of the passing of the 1994 Act, the work of Mark Forbes, an investigative journalist for Melbourne's *The Age* newspaper, was cited in parliament as evidence of an extensive and chaotic prostitution trade.[2] The problems with Victoria's legalised prostitution regime were encapsulated in media headlines. 'Sex Boom Fuels Super Brothel Bid' (Forbes 1999c, p. 1), 'Police Brothel Alarm' (Forbes 1999d, p. 1), and 'Prostitution Scheme Slammed' (Forbes and Marino 1999, p. 6) are typical examples. From 1984, when Victoria first introduced the concept of prostitution as work, to 2004, the number of licensed 'sexual services providers' increased from 40 to 184. Of these, 49 are brothel licenses and 34 escort agency licenses. A further 101 licenses have been granted for operating a brothel and escort agency simultaneously (Business Licensing Authority 2004a, p. 1). As I discuss in the following chapter, significantly these figures do not include the growth in illegal prostitution, estimated to be at a minimum four times the size of the regulated sector.

Of course driving the growth of the industry are the profits to be made from the sexual exploitation of women and some men, now sanctioned by the State. Financial returns available to individual brothel owners provides a gauge on just how profitable prostitution has become. Jocelyn Snow, former owner of Follies, purchased the legal brothel in 1989 for A$200,000 in South Melbourne. The business was sold within three years for $A400,000 (Sullivan 1999c). When the State's 1994 prostitution legislation was passed, brothels were changing hands for over A$1 million (Sutton et al. 1999, p. 6). That brothels are not only

---

2. Forbes' investigative report was published in *The Age* throughout February and March 1999. Parliamentarians from both political parties used his reports as evidence for further prostitution law reform during debate on the *Prostitution Control (Amendment) Act 1999*. See, for example, Victoria 1999, p. 967; Victoria 1999a, p. 1195.

legal, but continue to be highly profitable was suggested when *The Age* Business Section ran an advertisement for a 'Land Banking Opportunity' in the prestigious suburb of South Yarra for premises with a permit for a fourteen-room brothel (Business Section 2004, p. 1).

The estimate for total annual turnover of Victoria's prostitution industry five years after the passing of the *Prostitution Control Act 1994* was $A360 million per annum (Victoria 1999b, p. 963). Conservatively, industry revenue Australia-wide has increased from A$1,525 million in 1999–2000 to $1,780 million in 2004–05 representing a percentage increase of 17 per cent.[3] This trend is to continue. Economic analyst, IBIS Business Information, in its forward prediction to 2010 confirmed that the 'sexual services sector will experience growth in revenues increasing to $A2,475 million by 2010 equating to a 6.8 per cent annualised rise' fuelled by male demand (IBISWorld 2006, p. 23).

Recent research into Australia's sexual behaviour found that one in six men have paid for sex, while for women the figure is negligible (Richters and Rissel 2005, p. 100). Under Victoria's legalised prostitution regime there are approximately 3.1 million purchases of 'sexual services' per year – that is in an adult male population of around 1.8 million.[4] This means that in Victoria the number of men who have used women in prostitution could be as high as a ratio of 1.7 sexual services per adult male each year. IBIS have also forecast that, over the next five years, there will be 'strong growth in the volume of demand for sexual services' and 'continued growth in the "premium" segment . . . such as escort

3. I used IBISWorld Business Information Pty. Ltd. reports *Personal Services n.e.c. in Australia* (1998–October 2005) and *Sexual Services in Australia* (May 2006) as the basis for these statistics.
4. As the basis for these estimates, again I have used IBISWorld Business Information Pty. Ltd. *Personal Services n.e.c. in Australia* reports (1998–October 2005) and *Sexual Services in Australia* (May 2006). See also Victoria (1999a, pp. 1191–1211).

services' (IBISWorld 2006, p. 23). IBIS's most critical finding was that it is 'the size of the sector' that was the main cause of 'industry activity'. This suggests that the legal and commercial reality of prostitution has meant that Victorian men, who prior to its legalisation in 1984 may never have considered using prostitution, are now comfortable in purchasing a woman for sexual gratification. Legalisation has created an ever-increasing 'lawful' supply of women for men's use, which, as I examine later in this chapter, is heavily marketed to the male consumer.

Despite the prostitution industry's efforts to suggest that women are increasingly using 'sexual services' too, prostitution remains an explicitly sex-segregated industry. The massive expansion of prostitution in Victoria, as expected, demands a steady influx of women to 'service' male demand. There are no exact statistics on the number of women who work in Victoria's legal brothels and escort agencies. Under the State's prostitution regulations, 'prostitution service providers', that is sex business operators, must be licensed by the Business Licensing Authority (BLA). This does not apply to the women who provide 'sexual services' in legal brothels or for licensed escort (Business Licensing Authority 2004a, p. 1). The 1985 Neave Inquiry estimated that there were between 3,000 to 4,000 people involved in the industry. This covered both the legal brothels and the illegal sectors – illegal brothels, escort agencies, private workers and street prostitution (1988a, p. 202). By the mid-1990s, Victoria's Centre for the Study of Sexually Transmitted Diseases determined that there were between 1,000 and 1,400 women in the State's legal brothels alone (Pyett, Haste et al. 1996a, p. 84). Forbes' more recent research found that by the end of the decade this figure had risen to near 4,500 (Forbes 1999, p. 3).

In 2006 IBIS reported that Australia-wide in the five years from 2000 to 2005 the 'number of officially reported prostitutes' increased 27 per cent, again, as a direct result of 'the gradual easing of [prostitution] laws' (2006, p. 23). As Victoria's normalisation of prostitution as work is becoming more and more acceptable, the increasing trend in the legal exploitation of women will continue. There are no estimates of the number of women exploited in the massively expanded illegal prostitution sector.

Liberal parliamentarian, Blair Cameron Boardman, has commented positively on the fact that, 'In the 21st century the prostitution industry is booming and will increase commensurate with demand' (Victoria 2000, p. 303). He allegedly is perplexed 'that in this modern age some in the community are still looking for a scapegoat and consider the industry to be evil' (2000, p. 303). That such views are advanced at a parliamentary level, demonstrates how the normalisation and success of the prostitution industry has enabled pro-prostitution advocates within the Government to dominate debate and silence opponents. This is so, although the Liberal Government, of which Boardman was a member in 2000, had initially been adamant that it did not approve or seek to institutionalise prostitution as work.

Creating a prostitution culture

One of the Victorian Government's core justifications for legalising prostitution was that it would limit the visible and tangible impact of the industry on the community. Legalisation has, in fact, resulted in brothels and other sex businesses becoming commonplace throughout Melbourne. Although zoning laws restrict brothels from locating in residential localities, the State's planning laws allow licensed sex operations in business centres and on local shopping strips close to residential areas. The City of Yarra, which has the highest concentration of brothels in the State, has sixteen legal brothels (Commonwealth of Australia 2003, p. 2). The inner city suburbs – Southgate and South Melbourne – have ten licensed sex operations (Marino 2003, p. 5). And, as critics of Victoria's contemporary prostitution law predicted, multiple brothels now exist in seven suburban municipalities, while most suburbs have at least a single brothel.[5]

The effect of Victoria's prostitution laws in practice is that local communities and their representatives have no authority to restrict brothels if their operators hold a valid license from the Victorian Business Licensing Authority. The problem experienced by the City of Knox in the late 1990s highlights the powerlessness of many citizens to refuse sex businesses in their suburbs. As a result of the Prostitution Control Board's issue of a brothel licence to a developer in 1998, Tom Blaze, the City's Mayor, was forced to accept another brothel in his municipality. This meant that Knox now had six licensed brothels, despite community opposition (Dargan 1998, p. 18). This push by sex entrepreneurs to establish brothels throughout Melbourne is equally occurring outside the metropolitan area.

Municipal councils have the legal right to refuse applications for brothels where the population is 20,000 or less (Victoria 1997, p. 1623). Most municipal councils outside of Melbourne, like their urban counterparts, have minimal options to refuse to locate a brothel if its owner is a legitimate licensee. Indeed, several rural councils claim they have been compelled to direct considerable financial and human resources to contesting a brothel opening. Russell Savage, a National Party member for the rural district of Mildura,[6] brought this to the Government's attention during parliamentary debate on the 1997 amendments

---

5. Several members of the Victorian Parliament raised concern about their constituencies' fear that brothels would infiltrate communities particularly during the Second Reading of both the Prostitution Regulation Bill 1986 and the Prostitution Control Bill 1994. See Victorian Parliamentary Papers (Hansard).
6. The National Party and the Liberal Party in 1992 formed a conservative coalition allowing the Liberal Government to control the State Government under Premier Jeff Kennett. The National Party mainly represents rural districts.

to the State's principal prostitution legislation. The proposed legislative changes under discussion were aimed at addressing the escalation of the industry since 1994. Savage stated that although a community survey indicated that 76 per cent of his electorate did not want a brothel, whether or not 'they are controlled by an act of Parliament . . . the Government refuses to acknowledge the fact' (Victoria 1997, p. 1623). Mildura was forced to accept its first legal brothel in 1997.

In this prescriptive atmosphere it is difficult to see how the Liberal Government responsible for introducing the 1994 *Prostitution Control Act* could have purported to be opposed to prostitution *per se*.[7] Liberal Government representatives at the time publicly acknowledged that there are considerable financial gains to the State economy if new markets for prostitution can be tapped into. Gary Stocks, when acting as Deputy Register of the Prostitution Control Board, was quoted in Mildura's *Sunraysia Daily* newspaper as saying that the town 'would be a prime location for a brothel because of its itinerant population increase during harvest' (Victoria 1997, p. 1623). This tendency to promote the expansion of prostitution as enhancing either municipalities' or the State's economic interest has become a persuasive tool for pro-prostitution advocates in their quest to have prostitution normalised.

Financial benefits to the State

Currently, Victoria benefits through taxation and licensing fees from legalised prostitution. Taxation is a federal issue, but the Commonwealth Government redistributes income taxes back to the States and Territories. As early as 1991, the Commonwealth Government demonstrated that it appreciated the tax benefits that could be derived from women's exploitation by allowing a

---

7. Since 1998, Victoria has had a Labor Government, which remains committed to legalisation and regulation of the prostitution industry.

concessional tax rate to be applied to Australian sex businesses. Australian Tax Office spokesperson, Bernie Gallagher, justified this concession when speaking at the Australian Institute of Criminology Conference on 'The Sex Industry and Public Policy' (in Horin 1991, p. 1). The explanation offered was that the 'special circumstances of the work has led the department to let brothel owners apply a flat rate of tax to employees' wages'. This differs from normal taxation practice where a sliding scale is applied to Pay as You Earn (PAYE) tax. Gallagher's ultimate point, however, was that without the concession it was unlikely that tax returns would be lodged and 'the alternative [was] probably no revenue at all' (1991, p. 1).

In addition to the implied tax benefits for Governments in bringing the prostitution industry into the legitimate economic sector, Victorian Governments benefit directly from the State's prostitution licensing system. In August 2004, the annual licence fees rose from A$400 to A$2,050. Similarly, applications for new brothel licences rose from A$200 to A$3,588 and for escort agencies to A$1,794 (Business Licensing Authority 2004, p. 1). According to one financial report published in *The Age* newspaper, these increases will earn the Victorian Government A$850,000 per annum (Silkstone 2004, p. 1).

Prostitution tourism, allowable under Victoria's legalised prostitution system, potentially will prove highly lucrative for the State and can be added to its Gross Domestic Product. Socialist feminist and Labor parliamentarian, Jean McLean, highlighted the links that already existed between prostitution and State tourism during debate on Liberal's 1994 prostitution legislation. McLean who has publicly criticised the State's masculine culture and its progressive acceptance of prostitution exposed how Melbourne's casino culture and Victoria's new 'legitimate' brothel trade feed into one another. McLean highlighted how, when the State's Crown casino opened in May 1994, 'our scummy casino chips' were accepted as legal currency in local brothels (Victoria 1994c, p. 1265). She referred specifically to Melbourne's Top of the Town brothel which encouraged its 'clients' to pay for their brothel booking with casino chips as a means of cross promotion between the two businesses. Her prediction was that, 'The commodification of women would only intensify', particularly, as she believed, Australia is already 'part of a new wave of world tourism that is made up of package tours with all services supplied including prostitution' (1994c, p. 1265).

There is considerable evidence to support McLean's accusation that brothel prostitution is an acceptable part of Victoria's casino culture and associated hospitality industry. When Crown relocated into its new premises in 1997, a new prestigious brothel – The Boardroom – was set up adjacent to the gambling complex. Both are located in what was termed the city's 'new re-energised area', part of *Agenda 21*, a State-sponsored strategy to revitalise Victoria's economy (Public Affairs Branch for the Office of Major Projects 1996, p. 2). As outlined in its business plan, The Boardroom's intention was that business will flow on to the brothel from the new casino, Victoria's exhibition and convention centre, the State arts' centre precinct and Southgate (a prestige hotel and shopping mall), to form part of a big tourist trade complex (Longo 1997, p. 3). Within six months of the casino opening, six operators had applied for brothel licenses in South Melbourne in close proximity to the casino (Naidoo 1996, p. 1). The market research company, Sutherland-Smith, verified links between the Crown casino and the influx of brothels in the area (Koval 1997).

A decade after Crown's opening, prostitution 'services' are directly provided by the casino staff (mainly escorts) to gamblers and hotel guests of the casino's Crown Towers. The Australian Adult Entertainment Industry (AAEI) openly acknowledged that 'Getting sex workers for guests is certainly a service Crown offers'.

An AAEI spokesperson made the valid point that 'it is a legitimate and legal service' therefore no laws were being breached (Moor 2004, p. 1).

The connection between Victoria's tourism industry and State prostitution was strongly highlighted by IBIS Business Information's 2006 report on *Sexual Services in Australia*. It concluded that a significant contributor to the prostitution industry revenue growth was:

> The hosting of the Commonwealth Games in Melbourne (probably Australia's brothel and table dancing capital). The Games were followed immediately by the Formula 1 Grand Prix . . . Over the period, clubs have effectively marketed themselves to wide audience – companies tend to hire drive-around advertisement hoardings – which have helped normalise sexual services in the eyes of many (especially the young males they seek to attract) (IBISWorld 2006, p.17).

Living off the earnings of prostitution

Beyond the direct benefits to sex entrepreneurs and the Victorian Government, the legalisation of prostitution has opened yet another whole new area for investment for ordinary Victorian citizens. Sex entrepreneurs are free to market prostitution operations as excellent financial investments. They can readily argue that brothels are a permanent fixture of society and no longer fleeting businesses. Moreover, the high consumer demand created by buyers who are increasingly responding to the opportunity to purchase women for sexual gratification like any other marketable product, creates profits. The industry's financial potential is such that it has become both economically viable and publicly respectable for a brothel to be floated as a public company on the Australian Stock Exchange (ASX).

Multi-ownership on a large scale

Victoria hosted the world's first stock market-listed brothel, the Daily Planet Ltd, which began operating in 1975 prior to legalisation, and started trading publicly on 3 May 2003 (Australian Associated Press 2003, p. 1). The share float was a successful attempt at camouflaging sham ownership arrangements to circumvent licensing protocols, which prohibit multi-ownership of brothels. One of the major objectives of the State's introduction of a licensing system was to 'ensure no one person has at any one time an interest in more than one brothel licence or permit' (Business Licensing Authority 2004, p. 1). The Liberal Government explained its stance, arguing that:

> [L]imiting concentration of brothel ownership assists in reducing the risk of coercive or exploitative employment practices taking hold in the industry before the licensing system is able to respond, inhibits the involvement of large-scale criminal involvement in the industry and encourages small owner-operators (Victoria 1999, p. 810).

On this basis, the ASX refused the Daily Planet listing, as it considered that a share float opened the way for multi-ownership as the Business Licensing Authority would be unable to vet individual shareholders. To circumvent the Government's restriction, Daily Planet directors, John Trimble and Andrew Harris, incorporated the brothel's premises (the building) separately from its sex operations business (Paul 2003, pp. 16, 41). This meant that the owners or investors could avoid legal probity checks as they were only purchasing the property arm of the Daily Planet.

Business media provided extensive coverage of the share trade. Such coverage in itself suggests brothels now have a respectability that was noticeably absent prior to legalisation. The Daily Planet company was reported to have an annual gross profit of A$2 million per year. Its prospectus offered an 8.4 per cent return at a time when most public companies paid between seven and eight per cent. This offer was on the basis that the adult prostitution industry makes a 60 per cent profit. In its first day of trading, 6.9 million shares changed hands out of just 7.5 million shares on the market. Between May and September 2003, shares rose from A$0.5 to A$1.3, with total stock market capitalisation of A$23.5 million (Salmons 2003, p. 2).

Making pimps respectable

The greater part of the Daily Planet's non-tradeable shares are held by the brothel's original owner and the company's chairman, John Trimble. Trimble is a former pimp, who as owner and operator of an illegal brothel since 1975 was involved in criminal activities. Trimble had connections with the Australian Mafia, and is a nephew of Robert Trimbole, a prominent Mafia figure in the 1970s and early 1980s accused of murder, marijuana and heroin trafficking, police corruption and money laundering (see Bottom 1991).

Bob Bottom, who was awarded the Order of Australia[8] for investigating and reporting on organised crime, considers that criminal activity remains the norm within the industry irrespective of the legalisation in 1984 of the massage parlour trade. In 1991, Bottom wrote:

Most brothels are owned by companies, and changes in directors are hard to keep up with . . . The use of 'front men' in the company structures allows anyone to own a legal brothel, irrespective of prior convictions (1991, p. 84).

In these circumstances, Bottom says, 'police are convinced front men are acting as "owners" for criminal groups [and] money

---

8. The Order of Australia is awarded for service to Australia or humanity. Recipients are nominated by the community.

made from drug trafficking easily passes through the brothel accounts to become legitimate' (1991, p. 84).

Despite the semblance of respectability that Trimble was able to acquire as a 'legitimate' businessman of the now legal Daily Planet, Trimble himself appears to have a low opinion of Victorian law. He was reported in State Parliament as saying that legalisation had made the industry both 'boring' and 'restrictive' (Victoria 1999a, p. 1191). However legalisation means that sex entrepreneurs like Trimble are now in a position to utilise mainstream institutions to create legitimacy for themselves and their prostitution operations.

Andrew Harris, who acts a Chief Executive for the Daily Planet, believes 'an ASX listing in particular provides the brothel with a legitimate and legal image' (in Paul 2003, p. 41). At a more subtle level, former pimps and criminals have gained acceptance by ingeniously linking the industry with mainstream cultural events. Harris, for example, recognised the benefits of approaching the Australian Football League and other similar organisations with sponsorship offers (in Paul 2003, p. 41).

An equally successful strategy to mainstream sex businesses is to emphasise their professionalism. The Daily Planet's web page places great emphasis on skills and talents of those involved in the company. Its use of the language of meritocracy is particularly persuasive. Such language of course also fits easily with the current fashion for neo-liberal economics. The profile of Robert Bottazzi, a member of the company's Board of Directors, illustrates this point well. The reader learns that:

> Robert is a young entrepreneur (with fifteen years experience in the hospitality industry) whose success comes from a fresh and unique approach to conducting business. Robert has outperformed his competitors through his ability to understand the market and its future direction, implementing with planned marketing initiatives

and developing innovative strategies that successfully satisfy customer needs (Daily Planet 2003).

This self-promotion works to convince potential investors that prostitution industry entrepreneurs are not only legitimate businessmen, but highly professional individuals on the cutting edge of the commercial world.

Women as tradeable commodities

Legalisation does not alter the reality that the Daily Planet's business is marketing and selling women for men's sexual gratification and for profits. The brothel's owner, the directors of the company, and those who invest in its stock, treat women as tradeable commodities. Speaking at the first shareholders' meeting, Harris attempted to cling to the duplicity that it is not women that are being sold. 'At no stage at any time in the trading history of this business', he says, 'has money ever been taken off a working girl' (in Charles 2003, p. 35). The company's prospectus in fact reads:

> [I]nvestors wondering how to value a bordello . . . should consider it a stake in a very busy . . . hotel with revenue coming purely from room fees at $A120 an hour from each guest (2003, p. 35).

Similarly, the brothel's web page highlights how:

> [T]he Daily Planet is . . . Melbourne's only six-star hotel allowing sexual services on site. And like a six-star hotel, the Daily Planet is proud to maintain the highest standards of hygiene, safety, and customer service and customer satisfaction (Daily Planet 2003).

This use of such terms as profits and customer service delivery, or, in turn investment in the hospitality industry, obscures the fundamental nature of the Daily Planet and makes the sexual exploitation and abuse experienced by women in prostitution disappear.

There can be no doubt that the Daily Planet's business is selling women and sex. When interviewed by *The Age*'s financial expert, Sonali Paul, in 2002, Harris made it clear that 'The Daily Planet wanted to embrace adult products, table-top dancing clubs, "conservative cabarets with strippers", and large-scale restaurants with "a tinge" of adult entertainment. "Anything to do with entertaining anyone over 18 years is what we're going to go for"' (Paul 2002, p. 3). The intention plainly was to use finance provided by the Daily Planet float to buy a myriad of sex establishments allowing it to make more and more inroads into the prostitution industry. At the first shareholders' meeting, the company's Board of Directors gained approval for the A$7.4 million acquisition of the real estate and business of Melbourne's King Street tabletop dancing venue – Showgirls Bar 20 (2002, p. 3). Within twelve weeks, the Daily Planet had exceeded budget expectations by A$316,346 (Daily Planet 2003). Under its new name (Planet Platinum Limited), the new company had expanded into tabletop dancing and a chain of Showgirls Bar 20 Strip Clubs. It intends to extend the chain throughout Australia and Asia and may expand into escort services as well as sex internet web sites (Planet Platinum 2004).

The role of Australian financial institutions

The Daily Planet's new respectable image unmistakably satisfied mainstream corporate business interests. Sonali Paul reported that an ASX spokesperson had confirmed that the Exchange 'had no moral objections to listing the Daily Planet as long as it met standard listing requirements' (Paul 2002, p. 3). Harris himself maintained that the public offering 'opened a lot of doors that were closed . . . before' (Webb 2003, p. 4). That the National Australia Bank, one of Australia's key financial institutions, is alleged to have provided the bank guarantee supports Harris' view. Moreover, the bank's terms were a six per cent interest rate as opposed to sixteen per cent, the normal rate for brothel operators. The Business Section of *The Age* indeed exposed that 'Shares were now being offered as an excellent retirees' investment because they were bank guaranteed and offered a five per cent fully franked dividend' (Webb 2003, p. 4).

Given that some of Australia's major financial institutions are now facilitating prostitution industry expansion the Liberal Government's former assertion that the legalisation of prostitution was not intended to 'encourage' or 'institutionalise prostitution' is nonsensical. Moreover no legislative body has recognised, and therefore addressed, the challenge of multi-ownership that is created through managed share portfolios, where clients' funds may be invested in prostitution businesses. The idea of brothels being offered as part of a shareholder's portfolio is in direct contradiction to the State's principal prostitution legislation that prohibits multi-ownership.

The ASX in its decision to adopt a value-neutral approach to the prostitution industry, and to consider only legality and financial stability as relevant, sets a precedent within the business community. Management funds' directors, in meeting their obligation to their clients, work to attain the best possible return on investments. This may include investments in the prostitution industry. Similarly if institutions such as banks and superannuation funds purchase brothel company shares, we will have a situation where ordinary investors in these institutions may well be benefiting from profits generated by prostitution, whether they are aware of the fact or not. The financial stability of many investors in the Australian financial market will become inherently connected with the survival of a profitable and expanding prostitution industry.

Women's economic disempowerment

One of the seemingly more compelling arguments underpinning legalisation of prostitution is that women have more control over their working lives once prostitution is no longer criminalised. Victoria's legal system has in fact delivered the reverse. Industry profits have generally remained with large operators, as suggested by the history of the Daily Planet. In real terms, prostituted women are financially worse off while their options to choose their own working conditions are severely limited by legal restrictions on how and where they can work. From the 1990s onwards these problems have been exacerbated by decentralisation of the labour market and the increasing role of enterprise bargaining.

Who owns Victoria's 'sexual services'?

The *Prostitution Control Act 1994*, as suggested in the previous chapter, had its detractors. The Prostitutes' Collective of Victoria (PCV) was one of the strongest critics of the way in which the new laws worked to consolidate the position of big business. PCV spokesperson, Deborah Mayson, alleged at the time that 'the regulations will put the three big brothels, Daily Planet, Top of the Town and California Club in an unassailable position' (in Rollins 1995, p. 11). Prostitution regulations, she believed, would impact specifically on private workers, 'those who do not fit the criteria, those who find it difficult to get a permit, those who do not have the cashflow' (1995, p. 11). Mayson also argued that if the large brothels could also get escort agency licences, they would be able to offer a huge range of services.[9] Such predictions were based on the reality that women in prostitution were economically incapable of competing against these larger operations

---

9. As I indicated previously, the number of dual licenses the Business Licensing Authority issued in 2004 is 101. In 2001, 70 dual licenses were issued (Murray 2001, p. 17).

and indeed legalisation has only exacerbated the difference between prostituted women and former pimps and brothel owners.

Prostituted women face significant barriers to establishing their own businesses. Victoria Roberts, a prostitution industry representative on the Prostitution Control Board, maintains that, 'Generally, it's not the nature of women in this industry to build up a large capital base . . . most women who come into the industry are in immediate financial difficulty' (in Lacy 1996, p. 43). She estimated that women owned only seven per cent of Victoria's licensed brothels, although they make up the majority of the workforce.[10] Two significant reports produced in association with the PCV support Roberts' assessment. The reports – *A Profile of Workers in the Sex Industry* (Pyett, Haste et al. 1996b) and *Off Our Backs: A Report into the Exit and Retraining Needs of Victorian Sex Workers* (Noske and Deacon 1996) – confirmed that 'economics' is the primary determinant as to why women in the State 'chose' prostitution, irrespective of legalisation.

Ironically Roberts' solution to addressing the economic disparity between prostituted women and those who own and operate prostitution businesses is to call for a more independent type of women to enter prostitution. She argues that if the Government would eliminate all restrictions on the industry, this would encourage others besides those who 'use prostitution as a means of survival' into the business (in Lacy 1996, p. 43). Roberts' thinking clearly parallels the ideas that came to dominate the PCV in the late 1990s. By this stage the Collective was making a clear distinction between 'career prostitutes' and 'itinerant workers'. Additionally such thinking reflects sex business interests' continuing push for the Government to allow

---

10. Australian privacy laws mean that the personal history of brothel operators/owners is not available. There is no information therefore about whether or not these women were formerly involved in prostitution.

ideas of free trade and the efficiency of the market to shape the industry – a market in which women's bodies are a highly profitable commodity. Roberts herself had investments in brothels (in Lacy 1996, p. 43).

The failure of Victoria's licensing system

Sex entrepreneurs' dominance within Victoria's prostitution industry was undoubtedly assisted by the Prostitution Control Board's ineffective management of licensing procedures. Prior to the passing of Liberal's 1994 prostitution legislation, Peter Richardson, proprietor of Top of the Town brothel, and chairman of the Australian Adult Entertainment Industry Association (AAEI), provided evidence that the Liberal Government would smooth the progress of established sex entrepreneurs into its new legal system. Richardson acknowledged that brothel owners operating with a valid land permit prior to the new law would automatically be 'given an identical renewal of the original licence' (Eros Foundation 1993a, p. 2). This applied to Richardson himself. This automatic renewal meant that many operators avoided 'the strict proprietary checks' required under the 1994 Act.

One of the principal purposes of the Governments' licensing procedures was to prevent a person with a history of criminality from operating a sex business. The 1994 Act specifically stipulates that the Board must refuse an application where a person 'is not of good repute, having regard to character, honesty, and integrity' (*Prostitution Control Act 1994* s. 4[a]). As had been the case with John Trimble, Peter Richardson's history of illegal prostitution would theoretically disqualify him. In 1992 *The Age* reported that Richardson had formerly managed seven illegal brothels under a company called Caroll Consultancy (Robinson 1993, p. 9). Additionally the paper disclosed that the Brunswick Magistrate's Court had found him guilty of having an under-aged girl on the premises of his Top of the Town legal brothel (1993, p. 9). However not only did the Board permit people with a questionable reputation to be licensed as a 'sexual service provider', but it also failed to make any serious inroads against ownership of multiple brothels.

Mark Forbes' 1999 'Insight Series' for *The Age* on the prostitution industry, exposed the Prostitution Control Board's ineffectiveness in preventing 'sham operations'. Forbes, for example, uncovered how one major player used a network of front people and bogus documents to build a sex business conglomerate connected to five of the State's brothels (Forbes 1999, p. 3). Such networks led to demands from the Office of Public Prosecutions 'to close loopholes hampering operators hiding behind fake documents and bogus companies' (1999, p. 3). The police acknowledged that there were at least six multiple operators.

The 1999 *Prostitution Control (Amendment) Act* was an attempt by the Liberal Government to tighten licensing procedures in response to the obvious failure of its licensing board. The Act introduced the provision for probity checks to be applied to associates of body corporates as well as individuals who operate premises. It also made it an offence to own more than one permit or license (Victoria 1999a, p. 1195). However, the Government's transference of the Prostitution Control Board's role to the State's Business Licensing Authority (BLA) in July 1998 (*Business Licensing Authority Act 1998*, 6[a]) demonstrates that any concern to ensure strict licensing procedures and thus protect women against exploitation has disappeared, even at a rhetorical level.

The Prostitution Control Board was a seven-member specialist authority. In contrast the BLA has a broad-based portfolio and is responsible for administering the licensing and registration provisions of a number of Acts. The process for issuing prostitution licenses is now similar to that of car sales agents, travel agents, credit providers and real estate agents (Victoria 1999b, p. 966). We must conclude that the Liberal Government takes no responsibility for regulating or determining how the prostitution industry will function within the State other than through normal regulatory procedures that apply to other commercial transactions. Successive State Labor Governments have not reverted to the former specialist board. But without a specialist authority, it is difficult to determine how any government will ensure that large operators and former 'disreputable' brothel owners are kept out of the prostitution industry. As I will examine in the next chapter, local council authorities now have the major responsibility for policing the legal industry, without adequate powers or qualifications to carry out this task.

The fallacy of a cottage industry

The one legal avenue for women within Victoria's prostitution industry to become self-employed is to operate an 'exempt brothel'. Under the 1994 *Prostitution Control Act*, the Government allowed for one or two women to set up as 'sexual service providers' without having to obtain the normal license and the accompanying probity check that is required for larger prostitution operations. Nonetheless these small exempt brothels must register their 'prescribed particulars' with the BLA and they must comply with local zoning (Business Licensing Authority 2004, p. 1). The Government restrictions that exist around these small owner-operator prostitution businesses in effect make it almost impossible for women to take up this option. Brothel planning regulations mean that women cannot 'work' from home, as sex businesses must be situated 100 metres from the nearest residence and 200 metres from the nearest church, school, hospital, playground, or anywhere where children frequent. In these circumstances, prostituted women ultimately find themselves competing unsuccessfully with the established players who control the industry.

Jocelyn Snow, reflecting on her experience of working with women through the PCV, commented that there were so few places available that met local planning requirements that, 'it turned out to be an absolute nightmare for sex workers' (Sullivan 1999c). She said an additional problem for women is that the law requires 'exempt providers' to inform their landlord in writing that they are conducting a prostitution business and gain their permission. According to Snow the regulations have in fact resulted in some prostituted women paying exorbitant rents to landlords. As Snow says, when women found suitable premises 'once they informed the landlord of their intention to operate as an exempt brothel, that actually would triple the rent' (Sullivan 1999c).

The main option for self-employment for women who wish to work legally is to find premises in industrial areas or dock-lands. This leaves already vulnerable women open to further violence, fear and isolation. It is thus predictable that only five of the 1958 women who registered in 2004 as exempt brothel operators with the Victorian Business Licensing Authority run their own prostitution business. The remaining women continue to 'work' for a third party, mainly for escort agencies (Business Licensing Authority 2004a, p. 2).

The power dimensions of employer-employee relations

Women working in Australia's legal prostitution industry are entitled to have their rights as workers protected by the State. This argument is examined fully in Chapter Six. My focus here is to highlight how, despite Victoria's regulation of the prostitution industry, the working conditions for prostituted women in legal brothels and licensed escort agencies are largely determined by the dominant position of employers and the market place.

In the mid-1980s the Australian Prostitutes' Collective was already raising awareness of 'worker discrimination' within the industry. The most critical problem was the question: Are prostituted women workers or contractors?[11] The APC argued that identifying prostituted women as contractors was the strongest example of 'worker discrimination' (Prostitutes' Collective of Victoria 1987, p. 2). At an APC seminar held in 1987, Denis Nelthoppe from the Consumer Credit Legal Service, exposed that many brothel owners defined prostituted women as contractors, not employees, as a means to avoid paying a Work Care[12] levy and group tax. It took a decade for a test case to be run. In October 1996, one woman did win an unfair dismissal claim against a brothel in the Victorian Industrial Court. The court's ruling, that the prostituted woman was an employee of the brothel (rather than an independent contractor), was significant (IBIS Business Information Pty Ltd 1998, p. 10). However such hard-fought successes are limited because the onus on establishing that a woman is an employee rather than a contractor remains with the prostituted woman who is seriously disadvantaged in employment negotiations in general. As I discuss further, this is becoming increasingly harder with the introduction of the Federal Government's new industrial relations system based on Australian Workplace Agreements (AWAs).

Historically most employment awards in Australia were established by the Australian Industrial Relations Commission (AIRC)

---

11. A contractor is a person who can choose whom they work for and when they work. They can organise someone else to do their work. However they do not receive employee benefits such as holiday pay, superannuation entitlements or work cover insurance.

12. A Work Care levy [or Work Cover as it is more commonly called] refers to insurance employers must legally take out against employees' injuries at work. This ensures injured employees continue to receive salaries until they are able to return to work.

or State and Territory Commissions. These awards were designed to protect all the workers in an industry by establishing minimal terms and conditions for that industry. The various Commissions are responsible for setting minimum wages, hearing test cases to alter awards and arbitrating disputes. As prostituted women lack union power, and most in reality are still struggling to have brothel owners recognise them as employees not contractors, it is inevitable that no awards have been set for the prostitution industry.

In the absence of employment awards, women in the industry are covered to a degree by the 1996 Federal *Workplace Relations Act*. However the legislation weakened the employment entitlements of the majority of workers covered by the Act and offered prostituted women little in the way of equitable pay and working conditions. The Federal Liberal Government, when it introduced the 1996 Act, began a process of replacing Australia's centralised system of awards worked out by the AIRC with a system based on enterprise bargaining and individual work contracts (AWAs) (Catanzariti and Baragwanath 1997, p. 1). The Australian Council of Trade Unions (ACTU) has consistently argued that 'for employees working in a large organisation with strong union representation', the new system allows 'for the negotiation of better pay and working conditions'. In contrast, 'for other employees perhaps disadvantaged by small workplaces, low union representation and poor negotiation skills, the laws pose a very real threat to hard won rights and conditions' (Australian Council of Trade Unions 2004, p. 1).

Under the above criteria prostituted women would certainly be categorised as 'marginalised workers'. But they are even further disadvantaged as 'women workers'. The United Nation's 1997 CEDAW Committee report on Australia, concluded that the status of women had gone backwards with the introduction of the 1996 Federal *Workplace Relations Act*. It revealed that the legislation was 'placing the burden on individual women of recognising and enforcing on an individual basis and at their own expense their employment rights at a time when legal aid funding is being cut' (Capital Women 1997, p. 7). Australian industrial relations expert David Peetz from Queensland's Griffith University supports this view. He argues that women's struggles for workplace equality have been diminished by AWAs illustrating his point with the fact that 'women on AWAs had hourly earnings some 11 per cent less than women on registered collective agreements' (Peetz 2005, p. 11). Moreover 'the gender gap was worse' as women under collective agreements received 90 per cent of men's wages while on AWAs this figure fell to 80 per cent (2005, p. 11). Despite such criticism the Australian Government remains firmly committed to establishing an industrial relations system based on individual rather than collective bargaining.

In March 2006 the Federal Liberal Government put into action a new national workplace relations scheme which the ACTU predicted to be even more harmful to women, youth and other marginal workers, and by default, women in prostitution. The Government's agenda is to have most workplace relations (up to 85 per cent) based on AWAs. Its position is that a 'statutory form of non-union individual employment contracts [is] . . . preferred over and above collective agreements'.[13] Under the new system Australian Industrial Commissions (both Federal and State) are to be abolished.[14] Moreover unions are to lose their

---

13. My discussion of the AIRC system is based on information provided by the Australian Federal Government's website *Work Choices: A New Workplace Relations System*, https://www.workchoices.gov.au/ourplan/ and an overview presented by *The Australian* in a major feature article 'Howard's Workplace Revolution' (26 March 2006, p. 1).

14. In the mid-1990s, the Victorian Liberal Government under Premier Jeff Kennett dismantled the State's industrial relations system. It is the only State or Territory to have handed the State's power to negotiate employment relations over to the Federal Government.

power of collective bargaining as employees renegotiating an AWA award are denied the right to be protected by strike action. Ironically the Federal Government promotes its 'new package' as 'a better way to reward effort, increase wages and balance work and family life'.

Jenny Macklin, Deputy Leader of the Federal Labor Opposition, is among those critics who have highlighted the serious implications of the AWA system, especially for women. As she states:

> It is already the case that women are paid less than men in individual contracts . . . The vast majority of women working casual or part-time don't have a strong position of negotiation. It's very difficult for women to negotiate as individuals with employers to improve their wages. The only way they can seek to improve their position is through collective agreements where they can work together with their union (2005, p. 1).

The already inequitable relationship between 'employer' and 'employee' within the prostitution industry that has resulted from Australia's current push for individual workplace agreements is intensified because of the high level of competition among prostituted women for 'work'. While legalisation has seen a substantial increase in demand for prostitution and a boost in total revenue, this has occurred in parallel with an oversupply of sexual services, and so women must compete for buyers. At the end of the 1990s IBIS Business Information Services reported that fees charged by prostituted women had not changed significantly over the previous ten years. Women on average earned between A$400 to A$500 per week, did not receive holiday pay or sick leave, and worked around four ten-hour shifts per week (1998, p. 9). Five years later the situation deteriorated further. As sex businesses recruit more and more women to service Victoria's thriving prostitution trade, competition for buyers has increased. Thus while sex businesses benefit exceedingly from rising demand for 'sexual services', in real unit prices, that is the money women take home, their earnings have dropped significantly (IBIS Business Information 2005, p. 18).

Alison Arnot-Bradshaw, in her role as PCV project worker in the late 1990s, provides some further insights into the cold reality of deteriorating economic returns for women under Victoria's legalised prostitution system. She maintains that, subsequent to the failure of the unionisation of the prostitution industry in 1997, 'a lot of women are working a shift for A$100 to A$200 with an average shift being eight to twelve hours' (Sullivan 1999a). The problem is exacerbated, she also believes, because of the lack of a specialist board to deal with the particularly exploitative nature of the industry. As she says, 'there is no avenue of complaint for sex workers about management . . . unless they do that as a Statutory Declaration and most [women] won't do it and so there is no one to complain to' (Sullivan 1999a). According to Arnot, overall 'owners and managers have increased the level of control over workers by determining services to be offered, fees to be charged and clothes to be worn' (Arnot 2002, p. 1).

In the above circumstances, the only viable option for women is to leave the exploitative prostitution workplace. But this again ignores the reality that the primary reason for becoming involved in prostitution is often because of a lack of other viable options to economically survive. This point was succinctly made by the Darebin Community Legal Centre and the Advocacy Program for Women in Prison in its submission to the Senate Community Affairs Inquiry into Poverty in Australia (2003). The group who work closely with many prostituted women stressed the point that:

[W]omen, simply by being women, are automatically employable as prostitutes. This makes prostitution among the most accessible jobs for economically disadvantaged women who do not have a level of social security that allows them to consistently and effectively acquire and maintain skills in order to be more widely employable . . . Recent increases in higher education and training costs exacerbate the problem. Many women who are determined to increase their employment options through education support themselves during this process by working in prostitution (2003, p. 8).

The myth of exit programs

The provision of exit programs for women who want to leave prostitution was recognised as a primary consideration when Victoria legalised prostitution. In 1994 the Liberal Government specifically stated that:

[A] function of the Prostitution Control Board will be to assist organisations involved in helping prostitutes leave prostitution and to disseminate information about the dangers of prostitution, including health dangers, especially in the case of street prostitution (Victoria 1994b, p. 1874).

Such programs were to be financed through brothel and escort agencies' licensing fees (*Prostitution Control Act 1994*, s. 67[1A] [e]).[15] Between 1995 and 1998, the Prostitution Control Board collected A$991,000 through licensing (Forbes 1999a, p. 3). One must question in the first place the warped logic of a government employing monies derived from the exploitation of women to assist them to escape their exploitation. But it is particularly disturbing that despite the Victorian Government's clear legal responsibility as outlined in its own State legislation to sponsor exit programs, no such programs were ever created.

---

15. The section was amended by No. 44/1999 s. 24(1)(f) which took account of the fact that the BLA was now responsible for the licensing of prostitution service providers.

In 2001 during debate on *Prostitution Control (Proscribed Brothels) Act 2001*, the then State Deputy Leader of the Liberal Opposition, Andrea Coote, used the opportunity of the amended legislation to express unease that funding for exit programs had been lost or diverted. She expressed particular concern over the PCV's becoming part of the Southern Health Care Network as this placed 'a greater focus on the problem in St Kilda' and 'on just one area [sexual health] rather than the overall problem' of prostitution. She argued that 'the services that need to be looked at carefully for these women include exit programs and other programs that will address the issues that cause them to turn to prostitution' (Victoria, 2001, p. 639). I suggest that it was unlikely that the current Victorian Labor Government would reaffirm a commitment to exit programs in circumstances where prostitution is increasingly normalised as 'just work' and a valid 'career option'.

Prostitution: just another job

The acceptance of prostitution as just work is disturbingly highlighted by the trend for students in Australia's tertiary institutions to take up prostitution. The issue of student prostitution has been ongoing for over a decade. The media did an exposé of the problem in 1998 when the University of Melbourne Students' Union set up a support group for students 'working' in prostitution. The student welfare officer at the time, Catherine Lawrence, was reported as saying that 'students were turning to the sex industry to supplement their Federal Government benefits' (in Brady 1998, p. 3). Sarah Lantz in her PhD, *Sex work and study: students, identities and work in the 21st century* (2003), supports these claims. Lantz's research uncovered that increasing numbers of both Australian-born and international students were becoming involved in prostitution. This, she argued, was directly related to the fact that students attending Victorian universities found it difficult to obtain employment that was permanent and sufficiently well-paid for them to complete their academic studies. International students had particular difficulty in accessing economically viable work because of restrictions to their student visas (2003, pp. 320–328).

To date neither Labor nor Liberal Parties when they have been in office have addressed the problem of students working in the State's prostitution industry. However Jenny Macklin, the Federal Australian Labor Party Shadow Minister for Education, raised the topic in 2002 in her criticism of the Federal Coalition Government's refusal to release its report on student poverty.[16] Macklin, using data from New South Wales' prostitutes' rights organisation, Sex Workers Outreach Program (SWOP), stated that up to ten per cent of those within the industry were university students (2002, p. 1). But for Macklin and others like her who see this development as a dangerous trend, there is really not much they can do. If the students are over 18 and involved in legal prostitution this is deemed acceptable. The Office of the then Federal Education Minister, Brendan Nelson, used just this argument to sidestep Macklin's disapproval. Macklin was reportedly told that '"People make individual choices about the sorts of work they do" and that the issue of on-campus recruitment by sex industry operators was "up to the universities to govern"' (2002, p. 1). By 2004, the Student Union of the Royal Melbourne Institute of Technology, one of the State's prominent tertiary educational institutions, had created a web page for students involved in prostitution under the heading 'Your Work, Your Rights'. This included a somewhat sanitary description of what prostitution involves, what forms of prostitution are legal within Victoria, and what occupational health and safety standards apply to the industry (RMITunion 2004, p. 1).

16. The Melbourne University Higher Education Studies (Victoria) completed the report in mid-2002 confirming a high level of student poverty throughout Australia.

The new respectability of the prostitution industry

Another way prostitution has become normalised is through the power of the prostitution industry's lobbyists and their public relations exercises. These are designed to advance sex entrepreneurs' values and practices into the mainstream. The model for this image making is the United States pornography industry. Sheila Jeffreys analyses their tactics in *Beauty and Misogyny* (2005) which examines the connections between contemporary beauty practices and prostitution. As Jeffreys explains:

> The US industry went to great efforts to gain acceptance. It hired lobbyists, participated in charity and campaigned for condom use to prevent HIV infection . . . The American porn industry created sex industry exhibitions . . . [and] invented the awards ceremony . . . (2005 p. 68).

Jeffreys concludes, as does the US pornography industry, that these strategies considerably raised the profile of the pornography trade both throughout the United States and globally (2005, p. 68).

Similarly in Australia, the Eros Foundation, the national lobby group for the Australian 'adult' prostitution industry, has created considerable political momentum for normalising prostitution in most States and Territories. Eros started in 1992 as a pornography organisation under the umbrella of the National Adult Entertainment Association (NAEA), and then expanded into brothels. Its agenda has been to coordinate and integrate the disparate elements that make up the Australian prostitution industry into a relatively homogeneous group. Indisputably as a single but numerically strong entity, the prostitution industry is in a more favourable position to raise its public profile than fragmented into different sex trades. The Foundation claims to represent 75 per cent of industry participants, encompassing all interest groups. Sex businesses such as brothels, tabletop dancing venues, adult shops, adult media, professional industry associations and 'workers', all come under its umbrella. The Eros Foundation also claims to represent the industry's ancillary workers – brothel receptionists or drivers for escort services (Eros Foundation 1997a, p. 2).

In parallel to the PCV's emergence as a sexual health provider (see Chapter Three), the Eros Foundation has created a specialist role for itself as a professional lobby group championing sexual and economic liberalism. The organisation advocates the removal of all restrictions on the sale of sexual services or goods for adults, by adults. In its call for 'logical law reform' it is careful to maintain a distinction between child and adult sex products, suggesting that there is a respectable and legitimate industry, distinct from coercive practices and criminality that is linked to child pornography for example, which should be banned (Eros Foundation c.1998, p. 2).

Eros couches its promotional rhetoric in terms of a moral crusade. It indiscriminately groups together 'conservative politicians and separatist feminist groups' claiming that in joining Eros, a member 'will assist in this battle against the rising tide of moralist and anti sex campaigners' (1994, p. 1). The Foundation has received explicit support from both the Australian Young Liberal Party and the Australian Democrats Party.[17] In its formative days it won support from both the Australian Capital Territory (ACT) and the Victorian branches of the Young Liberals, for its campaign to end the Federal Government's traditional X-rated category for pornographic videos and replace it with a NVE (Non Violent Erotica) (1993, p. 1). By July 1998, the Democrats were also publicly supporting the Eros

---

17. The Australian Democrats are a small political party which from the late 1990s until the October 2004 Federal election held the balance of power in the Australian Senate. The Australian Greens Party has replaced the former party as a political power broker.

Foundation and its bid for decriminalisation of prostitution (South Australia 1998, p. 910). More recently the Australian Greens Party has since come out openly in support of legalising prostitution (Australian Greens 2006, p. 4). This means that most main Australian political parties, in effect, adopt a pro-prostitution position.[18]

The Australian Democrats Party's particularly close links with Eros were highlighted in 2001 when John Davey, Eros's chief executive at the time, ran for pre-selection for the Australian Democrats for the seat of Molongolo in the ACT. Although defeated, Davey continued to act as political advisor to the Democrats (Clack 2004, p. 6). Newspaper reports alleged that Eros had covertly infiltrated the ACT branch and that 11 of the 18 nominations for ACT executive elections later in the year were aligned with Eros (Clack 2004, p. 6). The Democrats' financial disclosures for 2001 showed that both Eros and the Hill Group of Companies (the umbrella company for the Club X porno-graphic video chain, Australia's largest porn distributor), had made contributions to the Party (Australian Democrats 2001). Company director Eric Hill was elected Vice-President of the Foundation in 1995 (Eros Foundation 1995, p. 8). In the same year the Democrats became the only political party to have an attendance at Sexpo, a trade show for Australia's prostitution industry co-sponsored by Eros and Club X. As a special Sexpo offer visitors to the stand could receive half price membership to the Party.

But it was the legal context in which the prostitution industry operated in Victoria for two decades – and at a later date in New South Wales, the ACT and the State of Queensland – which was critical to Eros's credibility as a professional lobby group. Legalisation allows the Foundation to portray itself as similar to

---

18. In 2006 the conservative Family First Party has emerged as one of the few political groups opposing the legalisation of prostitution.

other professional associations and it has access to the same marketing tools as legitimate industry groups. As its prospectus makes clear:

In the same way that the National Farmers Federation represents farmers and the rural sector and the Metal Trades Industry Association represents traders in metal products, so the Eros Foundation represents those who have chosen to make a business from trading in adult or sexual goods and services (1997a, p. 1).

Undoubtedly Eros has worked effectively to further the interests of its various stakeholders. Between 1994 and 1997, Fiona Patten, as president, participated in the ACT AIDS Council and the ACT Prostitution Industry Advisory Group, a statutory body with industry, legal and police members, which has been consulted by State and Territory governments on proposed brothel legislation (1997a, p. 1). However as with other pro-prostitution advocate groups, the Foundation has particularly promoted itself as an organisation that is women-centred.

The minutes of Eros's first Annual General Meeting in 1993, exposed that its members from the first days recognised the importance of diluting the fact that the organisation primarily reflected the interests of those who financially benefited from the exploitation of women. The minutes noted it should be 'a woman' who represents the industry to the public. Moreover its promotional campaign should be specifically targeted at introducing 'women to the industry [to] make them feel comfortable with its services' (Eros Foundation 1993, p. 3). Within a year Patten had taken part in the ACT Student Law Association 'Women and Safe Sex Forum', a NSW 'Women in Film and Television Forum' and the International Women's Day Committee (Patten 1994, p. 3). Referring to the latter event, Patten acknowledged that it was the prostitution industry's growing respectability that made the presence of a prostitution industry lobbyist acceptable. As she recognised:

> In the past it would not have been seen as politically correct to ask Eros to be involved in such an event. This year the majority of the organisation meetings took place in our office and I myself signed all letters to politicians (1994, p. 3).

By 1997, Patten was profiled in the liberal feminist journal *Capital Women* (Eros Foundation 1997, p. 1).

Sexpo: a trade show for the prostitution industry

Nowhere is Eros' success as evident as in its staging of Sexpo, first staged in Melbourne in 1996. Sexpo demonstrates the Foundation's extraordinary achievement as a public relations organisation. It also exposes how the prostitution industry's major stakeholders – the industry's commercial enterprises, the male consumers (the buyers) and to an extent, the Victorian Government – all coalesce to make prostitution, as well as other sex-based products, legitimate and popular commodities, that all Australians could, and should, have the right to purchase.

Sexpo is a trade show in the traditional sense, a stage-setting event where prostitution businesses and other sex-based industries show and compare products and ideas for the benefit of potential buyers – in this instance, the general public. Pornography, private lap dances, brothel and escort agencies and sado-masochist 'services' are promoted – all acceptable forms of sexual exploitation under a legal prostitution industry. Child pornography, which is prohibited by both Federal and State legislation, appears to be among the small number of industry products not available.[19]

---

19. Child pornography is prohibited under the *Classification of Publications Ordinance 1983* (ACT) and *Commonwealth Classification (Publications, Films and Computer Games) Act 1995*.

Once inside the exhibition space, crowds attending the event have access to an array of pornography – in the flesh and on video – such as stallholders marketing 'Full Nude Shows' at bars and internet sites. Images of oversized vulvas and breasts flash from screens, which are then transmitted via the Internet around the world. Stage shows are ongoing. Typical performances involve women pretending to orgasm, while in the open stands men sit with their faces between women's thighs. These men pay between A\$20 and A\$35 for a personal lap dance, the price depending on whether a woman wears a G-string or is nude. Sexpo offers phone sex at a price of A\$4.95 per minute. This cross marketing of sex products is what American pro-pornography campaigner Laurence O'Toole describes in his contemporary account of the pornography industry (*Pornocopia*) as 'the future of adult retail' (1998, p. 28).

The exhibition has much in common with the American Adult Video News Awards, a highly successful vehicle for mainstreaming pornography which was started in 1983. The US industry in 2002 celebrated how:

> [W]ith more and more mainstream media attention focused on the Awards Show every year, the extravaganza has also served to considerably raise the profile of the industry throughout the nation and indeed, the world . . . a Best Film or Best Video Feature statuette can significantly boost that production's sales and rentals (*Adult Video News* 2000 in Jeffreys 2005, p. 68).

The Eros Foundation similarly conceived Sexpo to further the interest of Australian sex businesses and raise the sex industry's profile (Eros Foundation 1995, p. 3).

Making Sexpo legitimate

Despite Eros' readiness to employ contemporary marketing strategies to sell prostitution, its organisers do work 'to soften the 'image' to increase the level of community support for the event (Exhibition and Event Association of Australia 2002). Sexpo's website goes as far as stressing that the trade show is 'not about sex' just as the Government says it is not in favour of prostitution. Its organisers work hard to persuade the public that Sexpo offers frank and accurate information on all aspects of 'health, adult entertainment, sexuality, and adult lifestyles' (ClubXSexpo 2005). Language is pivotal in constructing this mythology. Promotional material seldom refers to the 'prostitution industry', but to 'adult' products and services. Other common terms include 'choice', 'sex between consenting adults', 'privacy', 'celebrating sexual differences' and 'lighten up – sex is fun': all libertarian notions that work to make invisible the power relations inherent in the exploitative and violent sex that Sexpo advocates.

To sustain the idea that Sexpo is not a trade show about prostitution, its organisers progressively try to broaden the base of exhibits to include what it terms 'non core (adult industry) traders'. Scattered among stands selling sex there is the odd exhibit promoting aviation, wine tasting, electronic home entertainment systems, holiday resorts and spa pools (Exhibition and Event Association of Australia 2002). But Sexpo's cooption of health professionals to help sell the prostitution industry's products is perhaps the most insidious strategy adopted by the event's organisers.

The Sexual Health and Relationship Education (SHARE) exhibition became a feature of Sexpo in 1998. Dr Feelgood (a pseudonym) who was the original convenor is a registered medical doctor. SHARE exhibits comprise a range of mainstream health and medical stands, which are offered to exhibitors free of charge. In 2003 organisations changed the health oriented section of the exhibition to Sexual Health Exhibition (SHE). Several health care participants, including the Australian Research Centre in Sex, Health and Society and the MacFarlane Burnett Institute, have a demonstrated pro-prostitution position and are closely linked with the industry through their research on STIs. Melanie Nasarczyk, fundraiser for the Muscular Dystrophy Association (MDA), sums up the appeal for other health organisations. Her point is that the MDA 'could use the exposure and [it] wants to generate income through Sexpo' (ClubXSexpo 2004a). For many organisations seeking public funding, their involvement in the exhibition is simply about economics and Sexpo's organisers have been quick to feed into this need.

SHARE's impact on the exhibition in terms of health professions' physical presence is minimal. Their participation rate averages around ten stands out of some 300 Sexpo exhibitors, and these are physically located on the fringe of the trade show. Nonetheless health professions' participation, even if minimal, permits Sexpo's organisers to promote the trade show as 'an important and expensive public service' educating the wider community about sexual health (ClubXSexpo 2004).

Health professionals' participation in Sexpo has further assisted the prostitution industry to extend its market as it has allowed sex entrepreneurs to mainstream the idea that prostitution is therapeutic. This functional spin on prostitution mirrors theories developed by 20th century sexologists, ideas which have progressively been taken up by pro-prostitution advocates.[20] A developing 'niche market' is sex therapy for disabled men as illustrated by a 2005 article in *Marie Claire* entitled 'Prostitution Gives Me Power'. Its by-line reads 'here's how they're using their bodies to foster trust, compassion and happiness in the world'. A further caption reads 'prostitution is like social work' (Blume 2005, pp. 108–111).

In Victoria the PCV was already promoting such ideas by the mid-1990s. In 'Sex and Disability', an article that appeared in

---

20. I discuss sexologists' views and their appropriation by the prostitution industry in earlier chapters.

a 1994 edition of *Working Girl/Working Boy*, we were told, for example, that 'teaching sexuality to the intellectually disabled' is a vital service that prostituted women offer (WISE 1994, p. 18). Moreover, prostituted women are seen to have 'a key role in teaching about correct condom use, sexual health and bedroom etiquette' (1994, p. 18). Indeed it considered that prostituted women were better placed than 'some well meaning carers from getting down to the nitty gritty' because 'we deal with the practicalities of sex day after day' (1994, p. 18).

The presence of Accsex/Access Plus at Sexpo is associated with its bid to have the idea that prostitution should be offered as a 'health service' to disabled people accepted within the wider community. The organisation is a lobby group representing people with disabilities and receives financial support from the Federal Health Department (Accsex/Access Plus 2001, p. 1).[21] Its spokesperson, George Taleporos, who was born with spinal muscular atrophy, sees Sexpo as a vehicle for promoting the sexual rights of disabled people. In an interview with *The Age* Taleporos put the case that 'What we want is access to really loving intimate relationships first. While that isn't happening we want access to facilities or venues where we can meet people or express our sexuality as adults' (in Crawford 2001, p. 3). Predictably Melbourne's Sexpo readily promotes brothels and escort agencies specialising in 'servicing' people with special needs. The 2001 trade show, for example, orchestrated a special promotion of the Pink Palace, which claimed to be the first Victorian brothel to offer facilities specifically designed for people with disabilities (The Pink Palace 2003, p. 1), although 'people with disabilities' seems to be restricted to men here. This juxtaposition of the rights

---

21. ACCSEX's webpage defines its organisation as a community development project based in Melbourne, made up of people with disabilities and interested organisations who work together to address issues of access, training and research in sexuality, disability and human relationships.

of the disabled with the right to have access to 'sexual services' successfully masks that what is being demanded is the male sex right to use women for men's sexual gratification.

Touching Base is the major Australian advocates group connecting the rights of people with disabilities with the right of men to prostitute women.[22] It states its aim as facilitating 'links between people with disability, their support organisations and the Sex Industry'. The New South Wales prostitution industry was instrumental in the creation of the organisation which evolved out of a forum held in 2001, co-hosted by Sex Workers Outreach Project (SWOP) and People with Disabilities (PWD). Like Sexpo, Touching Base has drawn support from mainstream health professional services in its bid for legitimacy. FPA Health (formerly Family Planning NSW), Access Plus, ParaQuad, Royal North Shore Hospital, Spinal Care Unit, Headway (acquired brain injury support) and the Council for Disability have all been represented on its committee.

Touching Base unreservedly promotes prostituted women as 'sex therapists'. Indeed it makes the argument that those within the industry have unique skills that allow them to service buyers' special needs, specifically 'people with disabilities' and 'adults recovering from sexual abuse'. Touching Base has even created a Professional Disability Awareness Training program developed by SWOP targeted at both brothel and private 'workers'. While the program has neither an assessment process nor competency standards that would allow it to be recognised by the Australian National Training Authority, undoubtedly it helps to encourage the myth that the industry is a valuable asset to Australia's public health system.

---

22. The primary resource I used for my discussion on Touching Base was the group's web page which contains fact sheets, mission statement and related articles (http://www.touchingbase.org/about.html).

Another strategy that Touching Base adopts to further prostitution business interests is to advocate for disability and also aged care facilities to assist buyers have access to prostituted women and pornography' or what it terms 'delivery and receipt of sex services'. Touching Base identified that a major hurdle for men with disabilities accessing prostituted women is to identify who was responsible for providing 'the personal care that is directly assisting a Service User accessing a sexual service'. Its solution included that organisations should introduce the funded role of a Sexuality Lifestyle Assistant to provide 'transport, dressing, undressing, personal hygiene, transferring positioning etc, but does not include assisting with any sexual activity'. Alternatively, organisations could adopt an Attendant Care model which uses an external agency to provide similar assistance. I find it disturbing that in the context where no funding is available for exit programs for prostituted women, it is acceptable that funds are made available so that men are not restricted in accessing 'prostitution services'.

The legal implications for disability service providers, policy officers and carers who do not facilitate disabled men's demands for prostitution are equally unsettling. Touching Base's committee has argued that:

> there is a clear need for our training project, to provide education for providers and carers, assisting them to fulfil their legal obligations to assist people with disabilities to follow the sexual lifestyle options of their choice, including non-heterosexual lifestyles.

Correctly under the Disability Service Act service providers have an obligation to support sexual lifestyles of people with disabilities. Where prostitution is accepted as a legitimate occupation, this duty of care may extend to 'delivery and receipt of sex services'. Thus organisations which reject Touching Base's proposition to assist in the prostitution of women may be open to discrimination for failing to fulfil their 'legal and ethical responsibilities'.

In the 21st century the idea that access to prostituted women is a disability rights issue was mainstreamed in the Victorian parliament. In April 2000 Labor Parliamentarian Christine Fyffe introduced the topic into discussion on the *Prostitution Control (Planning) Act 2000*. Her views supported the pro-prostitution lobby's push to extend its market by seeking to eliminate all legal barriers to prostitution. Fyffe's central point is that as prostitution is a social service it should be accessible not only to the 'mentally and physically handicapped', but also to the 'socially disadvantaged' (Victoria 2000a, p. 859). 'Parents', she says, 'see it as a way of helping their [disadvantaged] children meet their needs without threatening anyone else in society'. Fyffe concluded that without access to brothels and the 'sexual relief' they provide, those belonging to disadvantaged groups 'could cause tremendous social problems for the rest of society' (2000a, p. 859).

The obvious inference to be made from Fyffe's comments is that there are classes of people in this society – the 'mentally or physically handicapped' or otherwise 'socially disadvantaged' – who if denied access to prostituted women will commit rape to relieve their sexual frustration. Fyffe's beliefs are clearly discriminatory and reinforce particular stereotypes which imply that individuals who do not conform to mainstream physical and sexual norms, are incapable of forming 'really loving relationships'. Moreover if their 'biological urges' are thwarted it is assumed they will turn to violence. Fyffe and those who hold similar views undermine rather than support the right of disabled individuals to integrity and self-worth. They unwittingly narrow sexuality issues for disadvantaged groups down to a fundamentalist belief in the male biological imperative for sexual release, which has always been the justification for prostitution. Ultimately this supports sex business interests and their drive to expand the prostitution market. Disturbingly Fyffe does not concern herself with women's rights to be free of violence and exploitation, nor does she acknowledge that prostitution does not prevent rape of women.

Australian crime statistics on sexual assault over the last decade signify that the national shift towards legalised prostitution does not prevent rape and sexual assault.[23] According to the Australian Bureau of Statistics (ABS), Australia-wide sexual assaults have increased by an average of 0.1 per cent each month since 1995. The Bureau considers this trend statistically significant. The ABS uses offence based crime statistics derived from police reporting. Sexual assault includes rape, sexual assault, sodomy, buggery, oral sex, incest, carnal knowledge, unlawful sexual intercourse, indecent assault, and assault with intent to rape.[24] The ABS further reports that 'victims include proportionately more females, particularly young women, while perpetrators for whom information is available include proportionately more males, particularly young to middle-aged males' (ABS 2004, p. 13). This indicates that rape in Victoria remains a crime of male sexual violence.

As shown in Chart 2, prevalence rates for female victims of sexual assault in Victoria remained relatively constant between 1993 and 2002 (with some increase in 1995). Thus, rather than falling, sexual assault in Victoria grew in line with, or slightly higher than, population growth.

---

23. Comparative figures before 1993 for crime statistics are not useful because a different reportage system was used.

24. Offence based statistics, however, are likely to be lower than the actual incidence of sexual assualt as victims face both personal and institutional barriers to reporting (for further discussion of this point see ABS 2004, pp. 15–17).

Chart 2: Female Victims of Sexual Assault

Year	1993	1995	1998	2002
Prevalence Rate*	0.4	0.7	0.3	0.5
* Number of victims relative to total adult population				

(Source: ABS, *Crime and Safety, Australia*, April 2002 (cat. no. 4509.0) Table 15)

The most recent statistics available for Victoria are Police Crime Statistics, which distinguish between rape and sexual assault. These reveal that, while overall crime rates fell within the State, rape rose 11 per cent and other sexual assaults were up 1.2 per cent between 2002/03 and 2003/04 (see Chart 3).

The above analysis indicates that Victoria's legalisation of prostitution has not lessened the extent of rape. But an even more insidious problem with the idea that it may do so, means that the State is prepared to allocate a class of women (prostituted women) to be accessed by potentially violent men to prevent 'decent' women from becoming victims of rape. However as Victoria's experience of legalisation demonstrates, legitimising prostitution in reality has little to do with preventing sexual violence against women either inside or outside of the industry.

Selling Sexpo as pro-women

One of the most disturbing and successful ploys of the prostitution industry to gain legitimacy has been to portray prostitution as an issue of women's sexual liberation. Sexpo's organisers have similarly adopted this strategy. Contrary to the reality that Sexpo was conceived to further the interests of prostitution businesses, its webpage claims that the trade show's aim is to assist women to explore their sexuality, 'a comfortable environment for women to purchase sex toys and erotica' in what was previously a 'male domain' (ClubXSexpo 2004c). A 'Ladies Day', male strippers, a

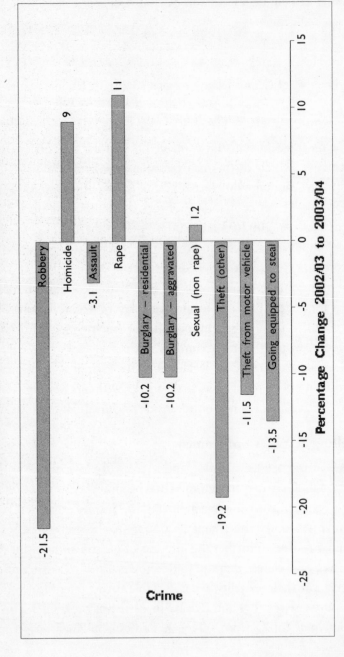

Chart 3: Crime Rates Victoria 2002/03 to 2003/04

Crime

Percentage Change 2002/03 to 2003/04

Robbery -21.5
Homicide 9
Assault -3.1
Rape 11
Burglary – residential -10.2
Burglary – aggravated -10.2
Sexual (non rape) 1.2
Theft (other) -19.2
Theft from motor vehicle -11.5
Going equipped to steal -13.5

Source: Victorian Police (2004). Victorian Crime Statistics http://www.police.vic.gov.au

free dildo and an on-site crèche are now regular program items.[25]

The organisers go to great lengths to convince the wider public that Sexpo is indeed all about women's empowerment. Dr Cindy Pan, the convenor of SHE's 2004 exhibits, describes female visitors as 'confident and open-minded about sex' (ClubXSexpo 2004c). And, 'For those attending with a partner', she says, 'the woman is quite often the instigator and/or decision-maker when it comes to buying adult products' (ClubXSexpo 2004c). If indeed, as the trade show's organisers suggest, 40 per cent of those attending SEXPO are women, then its advertising propaganda is successful.

Such promotions differ from *The Age* journalist Andrew Masterson's perspective on the exhibition. As he says:

> For all of its purported democratisation and openness, much that the sex industry presents at Sexpo still evinces the values of a 19th century freak show. It's not about sexuality, much less sensuality, but about the profitable objectification of women and the exploitation of men. It offers, not freedom, but commercial exchange, and in the ribbed, knobbed, rotating, vibrating, expanding, brutally penetrative apparatus of sex 'play', a sadism all the more deceitful because of its guise of pleasure-giving (Masterson 1998, p. 2).

Masterson's view unravels much that is wrong about Sexpo. However, I argue that men who have the economic and social power over prostituted women cannot be considered to be exploited, or, as I have demonstrated throughout this book, prostitution is hardly a 'commercial economic exchange'.

Adult products available at most exhibits conform again to stereotypical ideas of women's sexuality as defined through pornography – large dildos supposed to enhance 'sex play' or a

---

25. The crèche was a response to parents who took Sexpo organisers to the Victorian Equal Opportunity Commission in 1997 for refusing them entry because their children accompanied them (Conrad 1997, p. 5).

video screening of two women (one with her nipples chained together) – whose sexual interaction consists of one woman inserting a metal instrument into the other woman's vagina. Brazilian waxing, which consists of hot wax poured around a woman's genitals, followed by piercing of the labia were among the beauty practices particularly marketed during Melbourne's 2005 exhibition.[26] Many of the ancillary products work to normalise prostitution and pornography practices into the lives of all women, thus making prostitution the paradigm for all sexuality. Male strippers who performed at the exhibition adopted dominant stances. Typically, a woman is placed on a massive central stage floor and the male stripper lowers himself on top of her and simulates intercourse, finishing by kneading her breasts, or opening her legs and simulating cunnilingus.

That Sexpo has been a successful marketing tool for the sex industry is indisputable. Within two years, the industry's exposition of its products had undergone a rapid transition from a relatively insignificant event held at Melbourne's Carlton Crest Hotel, to a mainstream public production. The 1996 Melbourne event displayed twenty-four exhibits and attracted 15,000 people (National Adult Entertainment Industry 1996, p. 1). The following year Sexpo was staged in Sydney and Melbourne, with an estimated 40,000 visitors attending the Melbourne exhibition (ClubXSexpo 2002). By 1998 the Australian business newspaper, *The Financial Review* gave major coverage to Sexpo, alongside a profile of Australia's sex industry economic value, which it conservatively estimated as having an annual turnover of $A1.2 billion Australia-wide (Newton 1997, pp. 3–4). In 2006, Sexpo will be opening in three to four major cities and is reported to have reached its one-millionth visitor. Sexpo organisers

---

26. The descriptions of Sexpo's products and performances are based on personal observations made during my attendance at various shows from 1997–2005.

estimate that a record 70,000 people will attend the Melbourne tradeshow held in November 2006 (ClubXSexpo 2006).

Sexpo's success, however, has been largely dependent on the implicit endorsement of Governments. The ability of Sexpo to deliver its message via the Internet means that it is the perfect marketing tool to offer the Australian prostitution industry's services internationally. In the Australian *Adult Industry Review*, Sexpo organiser, David Ross, promoted the idea that the 'live stage performances . . . to be seen around the world [were] . . . likely to encourage tourism' (Eros Foundation 1998a, p. 21). That Melbourne's Convention and Marketing Bureau (formerly the Melbourne Tourist Authority) lists Sexpo as an associated business makes it difficult for any Victorian Government to protest that it is not ready to enjoy the profits that can be made from the State's prostitution tourist economy.

However Sexpo's carefully orchestrated image became seriously discredited when Paul Anthony Hatzakortzian admitted to 80 counts of trafficking and conspiring to traffic a drug of dependence in Melbourne Magistrates' Court on 6 October 2006. He was one of seven people arrested. Hatzakortzian, a member of Victoria's Police Sexual Offences and Child Abuse Unit, was alleged to have taken leave to work as a promoter for Sexpo in Melbourne, Sydney and Perth where he trafficked drugs to friends and associates (Medew 2006, p. 3).

Conclusion

Conclusively State-sanctioned prostitution in the State of Victoria is big business in the 21st century. Prostitution is a major economic activity that is legitimised not only by the State Government, but also by financial institutions and health professions. Successive governments, in institutionalising sexual exploitation of women as legitimate work, turning former pimps and brothel owners into respectable businesspeople, and brothels into an acceptable use of land under local planning laws, encouraged an unprecedented demand for 'sexual services'.

In Victoria's tolerant climate, sex business entrepreneurs are free to market their products, thus fostering an ever-escalating sexual consumerism. Their marketing campaigns employ concepts of economic individualism, sexual freedom, and even claim that prostitution is a valuable social service. Most disturbingly making prostitution work is promoted as being critical to women's right to self-determination. Such libertarian discourses easily suit the prostitution industry's business interests and profits whose growth depends on the continuing expansion of prostitution services. The major agenda of the prostitution industry is to eliminate all barriers to preventing prostitution from operating in a free market economy. However as I have made clear, women working in the State of Victoria's legal industry have not benefited economically and their so-called sexual empowerment consists of 'choosing' to remain in a system of sexual exploitation that continues to service men.

CHAPTER FIVE

Unregulated and Illegal: Clandestine Prostitution Under Victoria's 'Model Legislation'

Prostitution and sex trafficking are the same human rights catastrophe, whether in local or global guise. Both are part of a system of gender-based domination that makes violence against women and girls profitable to a mind-boggling extreme. Both prey on women and girls made vulnerable by poverty, discrimination, and violence and leave them traumatized, sick, and impoverished. Both reward predators sexually and financially, strengthening both the demand and criminal operations that ensure the supply. The concerted effort by some NGO's and governments to disconnect trafficking from prostitution – to treat them as distinct and unrelated phenomena – is nothing less than a deliberate political strategy aimed at legitimizing the sex industry and protecting its growth and profitability.

DORCHEN LEIDHOLDT, CO-EXECUTIVE DIRECTOR OF THE COALITION AGAINST TRAFFICKING IN WOMEN INTERNATIONAL (2003, P. 13)

Introduction

The Victorian Government's increasing tolerance, and at times promotion, of prostitution over the following twenty years, encouraged both profiteering and rising demand as sex entrepreneurs reaped the benefits from the relatively unrestricted commodification of women's bodies. The ongoing existence of a vast unregulated sector and continued criminal involvement in the trade though, demonstrates explicitly that prostitution cannot be regulated like any other industry. Throughout the 1990s and early 21st century, successive State Governments were compelled to introduce further legislative changes to the principal 1994 *Prostitution Control Act* in an attempt to eliminate the covert industry. But the *laissez-faire* mentality that now dominates Victoria's prostitution industry means that any such legislation remains ineffectual. Sex business interests continuously devise ways to further sexually exploit women to ensure their profits and meet the increased consumer demands. Tabletop dancing, peep shows, gentlemen's clubs, and bondage and discipline centres have all expanded in parallel with brothel prostitution and escort agency businesses. As the problems resulting from this diversification develop, the State Government has to constantly adapt its prostitution legislation to deal with commercial sex practices that operate on the periphery of the prostitution industry.

The most significant component of Victoria's unregulated prostitution sector is illegal brothel prostitution, which in terms of size is four to five times that of the legal industry. Difficulties in regulating illegal prostitution are made more complex because, in practice, the boundaries between the two sectors are blurred. Sex entrepreneurs, often associated with criminal elements, own and operate both legal and illegal brothels simultaneously. Women and girls are trafficked for sex indiscriminately between the two sectors. Child prostitution also exists across the spectrum. Victoria's 'model' legislation has been equally unsuccessful in eliminating street prostitution which has expanded in parallel with the industry as a whole, although it remains illegal. The State's response has been to flag a harm minimisation approach, a tactic that is in line with its overall acceptance that prostitution is inevitable.

Expanding the boundaries

Victoria's actual experience of legalised prostitution is that in addition to brothel and escort prostitution, there are numerous forms of sexually explicit entertainment businesses, where women are treated as sexual products for mass consumption. Strip clubs, and in particular tabletop dancing sites, are the most visible expression of this form of commercial sexual exploitation. Today's thriving tabletop dancing trade (including topless dancers and lap dancers) emerged in 1992 and has progressively involved more physical contact, as well as increased harassment and abuse of dancers. Within five years, 35 venues opened and Victoria's strip-culture quickly transgressed into a state-wide phenomenon (*Prostitution Control Act 1994* Advisory Committee 1997, pp. 4–5). The main clubs bring in around 1,000 male customers a night and offer between 60–100 dancers (Marino 2003, p. 5). Women dancers do not have an award wage. Most commonly they pay club owners for the right to perform out of tips. Management takes up to 50 per cent of their earnings (Marensky 2003).

As no State legislators had foreseen that a sexually explicit entertainment trade would burgeon in parallel with legalised brothel prostitution, tabletop dancing remained relatively unregulated throughout the 1990s. Most tabletop dancing clubs operated in hotels or bars, licensed under the Liquor Licensing Commission (LLC) to provide and sell alcohol (*Prostitution Control Act 1994* Advisory Committee 1997, pp. 4–5). The Commission required licensed operators to obtain a generalist cabaret permit which covered all forms of live entertainment, including sexually explicit entertainment. The *Crimes (Sexual Offences) Act 1981* allowed some scope for lessening the clubs' impact on the immediate vicinity as it made it an offence to behave in an 'indecent or offensive manner while in a public place' (Murray 2001, p. 20). The overall ambiguity of Victoria's legislation around the tabletop dancing trade meant, nonetheless, that most municipal councils had no legal avenue to close the clubs if they were operating legally with a cabaret permit. Chief Inspector John Ashby of the Victoria Vice Squad, commenting on the situation, stressed how Victoria's lack of adequate legislation meant that 'almost any sexual act on stage is not prosecutable' (in Forbes 1999, p. 3).

The history of Victoria's tabletop dancing trade

The State Government's failure to provide a legal framework to regulate the tabletop dancing trade became evident publicly by the mid-1990s. The Liquor Licensing Commission's (LLC) report – *King Street 1995 'Enough is Enough'* – had exposed a proliferation of 'very-late night venues' in Melbourne's King Street precinct in the city centre, including tabletop and sado-masochistic orientated nightclubs (Victoria 1995, p. 989). The report, which was tabled to the Minister for Small Business and Planning, provided evidence that 'The mixing of sex and liquor was seen to have disastrous effects'. The larger clubs reported banning 'bucks bus tours from entry because of the trouble resulting from large groups of intoxicated men' (Victoria 1995, p. 989).

Pauline Burgess, the Industrial Relations and Women's Officer for the Shop Distributors and Allied Employees Association (SDA), substantiates the LLC's finding. Burgess, who was also appointed to the Liberal State Government's *Prostitution Control Act 1994* Advisory Committee Inquiry (the Dixon Inquiry), set up in 1997 to evaluate the legalised prostitution industry, found extensive evidence that club patrons sexually harassed and abused women outside the clubs. Women informed her that men taunted them with quips like 'show us your tits' or, 'the girls in Santa Fe thought we were okay . . . if we want sex we will take it'. Anecdotal evidence suggests that in smaller rural communities the impact of the introduction of the trade was particularly devastating for residents. The Salvation Army reported that in one rural area over a period of eighteen months 'child sexual abuse went through the roof after one hotel introduced tabletop dancing' (Sullivan 1999b).

The criminal connection

The inadequacy of Victoria's prostitution legislation to take account of the tabletop dancing phenomenon was also demonstrated by media exposure of criminal involvement in the trade. By 1997, *The Age* journalist Mark Forbes reported that the LLC had confirmed 'that violence and standover tactics were used by underworld figures to grab control of a city nightclub [the Platinum Club] and turn it into a nude table-dancing venue' (1997, p. 5). The two men involved in the case had previously been disqualified from having any associations with licensed premises. Forbes also disclosed that Australia's Westpac Bank had funded the purchase (1997, p. 5). As I suggested in the previous chapter, Australia's mainstream financial institutions are prepared to adopt a value-neutral approach to prostitution treating it as no different to legitimate businesses. Westpac's backing of the Platinum Club suggests that its support went further. The bank offered financial support to sex businessmen who had a record of criminal behaviour and possible links with organised crime.

Pauline Burgess' account of her dealings with the owners and managers of tabletop dancing clubs provide further evidence of 'standover tactics' within the industry. Burgess required five months of physiotherapy after being subjected to violence and eviction from Melbourne's Santa Fe Club, while conducting investigations for the Licensing Commission in 1997. When I interviewed her, Burgess described how she 'was grabbed from behind by two males [with] another one at the side taking [her] arms'. She was 'dragged across the floor' and then pulled and dragged down the stairs. Burgess believes that it took her two years to regain her sense of personal safety (Sullivan 1999b). Still, tabletop dancing came under scrutiny mostly because of its troublesome expansion and 'the adverse off-site effects in terms of loss of amenity, perceived safety, character and image of an area' (Melbourne Planning Scheme 2000, p. 1).

Stakeholders included The Melbourne City Council, The Australian Liquor, Hospitality and Miscellaneous Union (LHMU), the Shop Distributors and Allied Employees Association (SDA) and a community group made up of the National Council of Women, the Salvation Army and the Victorian Council of Churches (Sullivan 1999b). That interested parties included the SDA and the LHMU indicates that there was some concern about the working conditions of women in the trade in addition to disquiet over its intrusion into public space. By 1997, the Liberal Government had set up the Dixon Inquiry whose terms of reference took in tabletop dancing. The Inquiry found that no specific regulations or local planning by-laws existed that dealt with this trade (*Prostitution Control Act 1994* Advisory Committee 1997, p. vii).

The Victorian Government then attempted to solve the problems associated with tabletop dancing through an amendment to its principal 1994 prostitution legislation. Its intention was to bring the trade under state regulation in a similar way to the regulation of brothel prostitution. The then Premier, Jeff Kennett, made this point clear when the 1997 Spring Session of Parliament opened. He said that while 'table-top dancing denigrated women and was not a good occupation for them, as long as there were proper controls on the industry and activities occurred in private venues it was a matter of adult choice' (Das 1997, p. 6). Like prostitution, tabletop dancing was normalised as legitimate work.

Kennett's response was a 'reasoned' position given that successive Victorian Governments put forward the same arguments in relation to prostitution. The Prostitution Control Advisory Committee in a similar way focused on whether local planning regulations were adequately dealing with the size and extent of the trade rather than whether the mainstreaming of the industry was in direct contradiction of women's rights to decent work and health and safety. A further interest was to determine whether prostitution was occurring in tabletop dancing venues, and if so, how best to regulate it in line with other prostitution services (*Prostitution Control Act 1994* Advisory Committee 1997, p. 4).

What defines prostitution?

A major problem that emerged as the State attempted to regulate the trade under its principal prostitution legislation was whether tabletop dancing was prostitution as defined by its principal 1994 prostitution legislation. Feminist psychologist Melissa Farley, and her colleagues, make the point that, 'Since the 1980s the line between prostitution and stripping has been increasingly blurred, and the amount of physical contact between exotic dancers and customers has increased, along with verbal sexual harassment and physical assault of women in strip club prostitution' (Farley et al. 2003, p. 61). By 1997 the major pro-prostitution stakeholders were arguing that the practice be accepted as a legitimate part of the prostitution industry. Both the Shop Distributors and Allied Employees Association and the Prostitutes Collective of Victoria (PCV) were making the argument that tabletop dancing should be treated as part of the legal prostitution industry as it was indeed 'borderline' prostitution (Sullivan 1999b).

There is a scarcity of research about what occurs in Victoria's tabletop dancing clubs. Feminist activist, Kelly Holsopple, a former stripper, has carried out extensive investigations into the experiences of women in strip clubs in the US. Her findings provide useful insights about whether tabletop dancing, in practice, differs from prostitution *per se* (1998). Holsopple's research describes how sexually explicit 'entertainment' commonly involves women dancing 'nude or seminude on tables or a podium and where their breasts or genitals are at eye level with their male buyer' (1998, p. 258). Alternatively women may 'straddle the man's lap and grind against him until he ejaculates in his pants'. Other behaviour includes clothed males entering a showroom with one or more women, massaging or soaping the women's bodies and private dances. Holsopple explains that private dances are located away from the main public area, providing the opportunity for men to 'masturbate openly, get hand jobs and stick their fingers inside women' and where 'women are often forced into acts of prostitution in order to earn tips' (1998, p. 259).

The experience of women in the US stripping trade has many parallels to the Victorian context. Submissions to the Dixon Inquiry suggested that 'sexually explicit entertainment' potentially provided the male audience with an environment where they could 'make offers or proposition dancers for sexual services to be provided' (*Prostitution Control Act 1994* Advisory Committee 1997, pp. 4–5). Common 'performances' involve close contact with or touching of men, double acts with other women or men (showers, oil wrestling), and personal or lap dances where the dancer sits on a man's lap 'gyrating, twisting and generally stimulating his groin area, or rubbing her breasts in the patron's face' (1997, pp. 4–5). Penetration of women with fingers, or objects that have included mobile telephones, being inserted into the dancer's vagina also occurs (Sullivan 1999b). There was also evidence provided that tabletop dancing had become more explicit since its introduction and that management frequently required dancers to provide prostitution in VIP rooms situated away from public view (*Prostitution Control Act 1994* Advisory Committee 1997, pp. 4–5). The Advisory Committee had little option but to conclude that 'live sexually explicit entertainment service providers' were providing prostitution-like services (1997, p. 5).

For Victoria's legislators, the essential problem in regulating the tabletop dancing trade was that the types of activities that occurred within Victoria's strip clubs existed in a 'grey area' between sexually explicit entertainment and the State's legal definition of prostitution. The Government therefore agreed with the Committee's principal recommendation which proposed that prostitution should be redefined in terms that took account of the clubs' activities. This in principle would allow tabletop dancing to be regulated under the *Prostitution Control Act 1994* with the same probity requirements and regulations that apply to brothels. Summing up her Government's position, then Attorney-General, the Hon. Jan Wade, stated:

> [T]he government does not seek to ban any activity from taking place or to disallow the activities. It seeks to ensure that sexual services are carried out in a controlled and regulated environment where alcohol is not served, where criminal activities are curtailed and where the health and safety of both the workers in the industry and the clients can be guaranteed (Victoria, 1999b, p. 965).

Using this justification the Victorian Liberal Government used the *Prostitution Control (Amendment) Act 1999* to broaden the definition of prostitution to encompass the various prostitution-like activities that occurred at tabletop dancing venues.

Under the new legislation the provision of 'sexual services' was now taken to include:

(a) taking part with another person in an act of sexual penetration; and

(b) masturbating another person; and

(c) permitting one or more other persons to view any of the following occurring in their presence –

(i) two or more persons taking part in an act of sexual penetration;

(ii) a person introducing (to any extent) an object or a part of their body into their own vagina or anus;

(iii) a person masturbating himself or herself or two or more persons masturbating themselves or each other or one or more of them – in circumstances in which –

(iv) there is any form of direct physical contact between any person viewing the occurrence and any person taking part in the occurrence; or

(v) any person viewing the occurrence is permitted or encouraged to masturbate himself or herself while viewing – and for the purposes of this definition, a person may be regarded as being masturbated whether or not the genital part of his or her body is clothed or the masturbation results in orgasm (*Prostitution Control (Amendment) Act 1999*, s. 4. [3]).

This new reading of the Act meant that 'service providers' who offered sexual activities that involved physical interaction and masturbation such as lap dancing and peep shows became subject to the *Prostitution Control Act 1994*. In effect such businesses were legally considered to be no different than brothels. As such most clubs should be closed as under the Act, prostitution cannot occur in premises where liquor is served (Office of the Attorney-General, 1999, p. 1). However, these added laws governing sexually explicit entertainment exhibit the same unworkability that characterised Victoria's principal prostitution legislation.

The failure of the State's tabletop dancing amendment

The 1999 Amendment Act made no significant impact on the encroachment of the tabletop dancing trade on city and suburban living. The clubs simply continued to operate. As Burgess pointed out, those areas which were the locus for tabletop dancing clubs remained 'male spaces where women avoid going' (Sullivan 1999b).

Clubs that provided sexually explicit entertainment (strip shows where no physical contact occurred) could continue to operate if they were licensed by the Liquor Licensing Authority (LLA)[1] and complied with local planning laws. Clubs operating without an Adult Entertainment Permit (AEP) were liable to a fine of A$15,000. The intention was that applicants would be required to undergo 'extensive probity checks' and 'extensive criminal history checks' similar to brothel applicants. Between April 2001 and July 2001, 34 applications were received (Department of Tourism and Trading 2002, p. 1). As I demonstrated in the previous chapter, 'probity checks' have done next to nothing to eradicate criminal elements from obtaining a brothel license or preventing multi-ownership. Moreover the legal ambiguity that surrounded the LLA's attempt to define sexually explicit entertainment meant that many sex business operators could claim that the performances their clubs offered did not fall within the Authority's definition.

The Victorian Department of Tourism and Trade is responsible for processing permit applications within the State. Its brochure concerning AEP applications for a licence highlights the uncertainty around just what the practice entails from a legal perspective. Under the heading 'Is Lap Dancing Allowable?' the following information is provided:

> If your staff or performers are wearing a g-string only, an AEP may be required given the nature of the performance. Many acts attempt to excite the audience by the entertainers threatening or appearing to remove their g-strings or other covering apparel. If exposure is evident of the genitalia, either accidentally or intentionally by the

---

1. In 1999 the LLC's function was taken over by Liquor Licensing Authority within Consumer Affairs Victoria.

performer or staff member during the provision of the entertainment or other activities at the venue, it may be safer to have a permit in place to avoid possible prosecution. If you do not hold an AEP, the performer's g-string or other apparel would have to completely cover relevant areas of the body and be sizeable enough so that no 'accidental removal' could occur (Department of Tourism and Trading 2002, p. 1).

If the LLC has difficulty defining the nature of what is permissible under its AEP, how can the State Government hope to deal with, and regulate, the prostitution industry as a whole, which is constantly expanding and changing its form?

As well as being licensed, under the Melbourne Metropolitan Planning Scheme all forms of sexually explicit entertainment, including tabletop dancing venues, were required to meet local planning laws. This meant that legally these businesses were recognised as a legitimate use of land although without the more restrictive rules that prevented brothels from locating in residential areas or near schools. The Melbourne City Council had lobbied for the clubs to be brought under local planning laws as a part of its overall *Strategy for a Safe City (2000–2002)*. The Council's agenda was to inhibit the concentration of sexually explicit entertainment venues (together with adult sex bookshops) in Melbourne's King Street and Russell Street area in the City's Business District (Melbourne Metropolitan Planning Scheme 2000, p. 2). On the other hand, municipal councils throughout Victoria have been consistent in their criticism of the scheme because as a legitimate land use tabletop dancing clubs are permitted in both 'business zones' and 'shopping centres in the middle of residential suburbs' (City of Stonnington 2003, p. 1).

The powerlessness of municipal councils to veto the tabletop dancing trade was highlighted in 2003 when Glen Eira City Council's decision to reject an application for a sexually explicit entertainment venue was overturned by the Victorian Civil and

Administrative Tribunal (VCAT). The application was for a club in the main shopping strip of the suburb of Carnegie that serviced a large residential area. The VCAT's decision was premised on the failure of the council to prove that prostitution was occurring on the premises. This is the only basis under the State's 1999 prostitution amendment legislation that allows councils to refuse a club's application (Victoria 2003, p. 1507). In practice, even if prostitution is taking place surreptitiously it is unlikely that councils would be in a position to close the clubs.

Tabletop dancing or illegal brothels?

Marissa Marensky who produced the program *Stripping* (2003) for the Australian Broadcasting Commission, interviewed several women who were involved in tabletop dancing after the new laws were enacted. They confirmed that prostitution-like practices were continuing in the clubs. As one of the interviewees claimed, while the rules in Victoria are 'no touching', men do have physical contact with dancers and 'in private rooms some girls are not afraid to do more than others' (in Marensky 2003).

A central problem in eliminating prostitution from the tabletop dancing trade was that the 1999 amendment laws provided for no workable mechanisms to detect whether or not prostitution did occur at such venues. Under the Act, admission charges to clubs constitute payment for 'sexual services' if prostitution is offered. The non-specialist Business Licensing Authority is in charge of monitoring prostitution services in the clubs in the same way it does for brothel prostitution. But as Labor parliamentarian Jean McLean pointed out during the passage of the amendment legislation through parliament, 'What qualifications will those inspectors have . . . You have to judge whether it is an actual or simulated sexual act. I wish the inspectors luck!' (Victoria 1999b, p. 967).

In addition to prostitution post the 1999 legislation, criminal involvement in tabletop dancing clubs also continues. In February 2003, journalist Selma Milovanovic reported that Nicholas Romano and three other managers of the now defunct Diamond Club were found guilty in the Melbourne Magistrates' Court of rape and assault against 24 strippers between November 1999 and September 2001 (2003, p. 4). During the court hearings, Senior Constable Scott was reported as saying that the women did not complain to police at the time of the assaults, but spoke of their ordeal when police tracked them down during an intensive investigation. According to Scott, Romano and his associates used 'fear and intimidation as a management tool'. He also pointed out that 'some victims were still having psychological treatment' (in Milovanovic, 2003, p. 4).

The introduction of the Spearmint Rhino chain into Melbourne's tabletop dancing scene in 2002 is of further concern as it indicates that criminals will remain a strong presence in the industry. The opening of Spearmint Rhino's Gentlemen's Club makes Victoria one of the locations for a global strip club conglomerate that has fifty-three franchises across Russia, Europe and North America (Murphy 2002a, p. 3). The Business Section of Melbourne's *The Age*, promoted the new club as 'Australia's Most Exclusive Venue'. The website for the new franchise operation claims it has an expansion rate of 10 new clubs per annum (Spearmint Rhino 2002). Large billboards throughout Melbourne publicise the club which is not subject to restrictions that apply to prostitution advertising.

An exposé by British investigative reporter Adrian Gatton and other journalists have disclosed a clear pattern of criminal conduct associated with John Grey, the owner of the Spearmint Rhino chain. Gatton and Chris Blackhurst found evidence that the strip business is linked to one of New York's La Cosa Nostra families (Gatton and Blackhurst 2002, p. 1). They reported that

Grey has six convictions in the US for offences ranging from possessing a concealed weapon to fraud. In 1999 the City of Los Angeles had 38 separate lawsuits against Grey or his businesses (Gatton and Blackhurst 2000, p. 1). His clubs in the UK have had their licenses revoked for being a 'front' for prostitution (Gatton and Lashmar 2002, p. 1). A pregnant woman at a Camden Club in London won £60,000 in a sex discrimination claim after she was dismissed from her waitressing job for refusing to wear a more revealing dress. During the legal hearing of the case, the woman maintained that male staff referred to dancers as 'mingers' and 'wildebeest' and negotiated among themselves about which women they would have sex with (Gatton and Blackhurst 2000, p. 1).

Tabletop dancing and the harm to women

In the public debate on tabletop dancing that has taken place in Victoria there has been little concern for the women who work in the trade. Research into the harms of prostitution established that

> prostitution is multitraumatic whether its physical location is in clubs, brothels, hotels/motels/john's homes (also called escort prostitution or high class call girl prostitution) motor vehicles or the streets. There was also no difference in the percentages of women in brothel, street, or stripclub/massage prostitution who wanted to escape prostitution (Farley et al. 2003, p. 60).

Kelly Holsopple's research into the experiences of women in strip clubs describes how men's violence and abuse of women dancers has become normalised in the tabletop dancing industry. Holsopple found in one study of 18 women strippers that they all experienced physical and sexual abuse and had been subject to verbal harassment, stalking and being propositioned for prostitution (1998, p. 252). According to Holsopple, while the buyers were the main perpetrators of this systematic violence, abuse by managers and staff also occurred (1998, p. 251). Physical violence ranged from women being spat on, having trash thrown at them, their hair or bodies yanked and their costumes ripped to being 'bitten, licked, slapped, punched and pinched' (1998, p. 262). Women also reported that buyers 'often attempt and succeed at penetrating strippers vaginally and anally with their fingers, dollar bills and bottles . . . expose their penises, rub their penises on women and masturbate in front of them' (1998, p. 263). Men employ sexual pejoratives such as 'cunt, whore, pussy, slut and bitch' to verbally harass the women and threaten them with 'ass whipping' or 'rape' (1998, p. 265).

There has been no comprehensive examination of the violence experienced by dancers in the Victorian tabletop dancing trade. Similar to the US clubs described by Holsopple, the Victorian venues do reflect what she calls, 'gendered spaces and gendered power dynamics where nude or partially nude women perform for fully clothed male buyers' (1998, p. 252). Pauline Burgess, for example, in her investigation of the tabletop dancing clubs in Victoria, found that incidents of physical and sexual violence, sexual harassment and stalking were common (Sullivan 1999b). One of the women interviewed for *Stripping* described how one dancer was physically abused and had a gun put in her mouth by a buyer who followed her into the lane adjacent to their club (Marensky 2003). That such male violence harms women is incontestable. Farley et al. in fact concluded that, 'women prostituted in stripclubs had significantly higher rates of dissociative and other psychiatric symptoms than those in street prostitution' (2003, p. 60). The problem for women involved in Victoria's tabletop dancing is that this violence remains hidden and not publicly discussed. Thus the major focus in the Government's attempt to regulate the industry is merely to prevent the clubs impacting on the wider community.

What goes equally unrecognised in the Government's strategy to incorporate tabletop dancing as an arm of the prostitution industry is that the normalisation of such abuse as 'sex work' is in direct contradiction to the right of women to workplace equality as well as feminists' struggles to desexualise the work environment. Burgess, who has campaigned extensively for women in non-union work places to prevent topless work, says that the 'Liquor trade union has always been fighting for equity and recognition in terms of [women's] skills rather than on the size of their breasts' (Sullivan 1999b). This topic was examined in depth by feminist labour historian, Diane Kirkby, in *Barmaids* (1997), a study of women's work in Australian pubs.[2] Kirkby's analysis demonstrates how gender shaped the pub culture through the interaction between female bar staff and male clientele, and traces the sexualisation of the industry. Kirkby says today, 'Young professionally trained bar attendants in the 1990s had credentials in management, accounting, public relations and labour relations' (1997, p. 212). Kirkby is naturally disturbed at the growth of the tabletop dancing trade that undermines the trend towards desexualising the hotel industry. She does, none-theless, accept that tabletop dancing is a form of work and argues that women's choice to do such work must be respected (1997, p. 212). In contrast, I suggest that the introduction of tabletop dancers into the hospitality industry must be viewed as a back-lash against feminist work in the hospitality trade to achieve workplace equality.

Illegal brothels in a legal system

The tabletop dancing trade is only one component of Victoria's prostitution industry that, in effect, operates outside of the State's regulatory system. The existence of an extensive illegal trade in

2. Pubs are the Australian equivalent of local bars or taverns.

women and girls for sex makes a farce of the Government's claim that legalising prostitution will bring the industry under its control and eliminate its criminal elements. Illegal brothel prostitution, in particular, has burgeoned to meet buyers' demands for 'cheaper' or 'unrestricted' sexual services. As has been the case with most of the problems associated with Victoria's legalised prostitution regime, the reality is that the State's prostitution legislation provides no effective mechanisms to tackle this illegal trade.

The transitory and clandestine nature of the illegal sector makes it difficult to gain a definitive understanding of the extent to which prostitution operates outside of the law. In 2003 the Parliamentary Joint Committee on the Australian Crimes Commission (PJC), a Federal Government parliamentary inquiry commissioned to examine the issue of sex trafficking into Australia, disclosed evidence of extensive illegal activity in the State of Victoria (Commonwealth of Australia 2003). Police sources at the time indicated that there were around 400 illegal brothels and predicted that the numbers would increase (Rose 2003, p. 4). The impact of the number of illegal brothels on local communities is extraordinary. The Monash City Council reported, for example, that in a two-year period between 2002 and 2004, there were 26 illegal brothels operating in the municipality (Monash City Council 2003, p. 1).

Not surprisingly, the legal sector is among the strongest critics of illegal operations because they see unlicensed brothels as unfair competition which directly threatens their profits. These 'legitimate' sex businessmen make a case that the illegal sector thrives because it operates on a more profitable level, foregoing the 'stringent regulations' planning and health regulations placed on licensed businesses (Birnbauer 2003, p. 4). I suggest that the real force fuelling the growth of the illegal sector is the increased demand for all forms of sex that followed Victoria's legalisation of prostitution. According to Ken Wolfe, from the City of Yarra, illegal brothels mostly offer buyers 'masturbation and oral sex'. They thrive, he says, because 'the prices are much lower' for these 'services' (Commonwealth of Australia 2003, p. 14).

Councils ineffective in policing role

Because legal brothels had fallen within a planning framework, the common perception was that any brothel that opens, licensed or not, was the responsibility of municipal councils. The Victorian police and the Municipal Association of Victoria (MAV) have consistently criticised the State's principal prostitution legislation for treating prostitution mainly as a planning issue. Municipal councils make the point that while they have the legislative mandate to inspect all Victorian brothels without the owners' consent, they do not have the power to arrest or prosecute those suspected of operating an illegal business (Murphy, 2003, p. 2). Ken Wolfe, when providing evidence for the PJC about illegal activity in the City of Yarra, explained how the council normally became informed about illegal brothels through complaints. It also took a proactive approach by canvassing the 'massage section' of local newspapers to identify any new clandestine operations. Once identified, the council then applies to the VCAT to have the illegal brothel closed down. The penalty for non-compliance is an A$1000 fine. But as Wolfe found, treating illegal prostitution as a planning issue means that the same operators simply open in other locations (Commonwealth of Australia, 2003, p. 14).

The Victorian Government's response to the unworkability of State prostitution legislation to regulate the industry effectively, was to again introduce minor adjustments to principal legislation. Both the *Prostitution Control (Amendment) Act 1999* and the *Prostitution Control (Proscribed Brothels) Act 2001* gave police greater entry, search and seizure powers. Under the 1999 Act police could enter a suspected illegal operation without a warrant and then apply to the VCAT to close the brothel in a similar way to local council authorities (s. 61K [1] a). In addition, the legislation contained a 'strict liability' offence (s. 8 [3] 2a). This meant that the burden of proof was on the owner of a building to prove they had no knowledge that prostitution was taking place, thus overcoming the legal loophole that had allowed illegal operators to claim that they were merely landlords. The 2001 Act was similarly intended to make it easier for police to gain a conviction as it extended the period that police have to provide evidence that a premises was being used for illegal activity from 24 hours to 14 days (4 ss 1,2,3). But while Victoria's legislators may have widened police powers the State made no real measures to move responsibility for policing illegal prostitution away from the councils.

In practice, neither the 1999 Act nor the 2001 Act changed the reality that brothel prostitution was treated mainly as a planning issue. Critics believed that the police's inability to deal with illegal brothel prostitution was exacerbated by the Victorian Gaming and Vice Squad disbandment in the mid-1990s. The MAV argued that even though the Government had widened police powers those left with the responsibility for coping with the illegal trade, were mainly local police without any specialist skills (Monash City Council 2003, p. 1). Between 2002 and 2003 police records revealed that only 4.5 per cent of offences related to illegal prostitution were for operating an illegal brothel (Holland 2003, p. 1).

That the situation in Victoria concerning illegal brothels is totally out of control is indeed evident by the fact that the MAV has resorted to using undercover people to close the clandestine businesses. Chief Executive, Brad Mathieson, reported that the Association had instructed the Melbourne law firm, Maddocks, Lonies and Chisholm, to employ private investigators to enter suspected brothels and elicit 'sexual services' (Murphy 2002, p. 1).

Such evidence, of course, is proving inadmissible under the State's prostitution legislation which makes it illegal for anybody, including private investigators, to be on the premises of an illegal brothel.

Given the confusion over who is responsible for policing illegal brothels, coupled with the ineffectiveness of most of the legislative measures to deal with the problem, the Government was forced to establish its specialist task force – Operation Pierglass. The squad, which was set up within the Police Commissioner's Office, has been given the role of determining the extent of illegal prostitution activities within the State and deciding which agency should have the ultimate responsibility for policing the illegal brothels. However the State Cabinet's Social Development Subcommittee, the body responsible for implementing the taskforce's recommendations, has not as yet been able to even decide whether to give the job of policing the brothels to the police or to the councils (Commonwealth of Australia, 2003, p. 23).

Legal versus illegal: the false distinction

Given all the problems discussed above, I would argue that the Victorian Government has indisputably failed to put in place any effective strategies to close down the illegal brothel trade. But even if the Government did treat the problem more as a police issue rather than a planning issue (providing police with further legislative power and human resources to close the trade), this would not eliminate illegal prostitution activity in the State. I suggest that the Government's focus on illegal brothels as the hub of illegal activity in Victoria is in itself a faulty strategy. 'Legitimate' sex businessmen, some with a history of criminal associations, own and operate both legal and illegal brothels concurrently. Indeed the legal brothels frequently provide vehicles for money laundering from drugs as well as illegal prostitution.

And sex businesses across the spectrum readily exploit victims of sex trafficking and underage girls to meet the increased consumer demand that has followed on from legalisation.

In 2004 the Australian Crimes Commission identified 100 organised crime cells operating nationally with 47 operating within the State of Victoria (Silvester and Munro 2004, p. 1). Many of these are involved in prostitution. The link between organised crime and Victoria's prostitution industry, and to an extent police corruption, was exposed by the Australian media in its extensive coverage of 'gangland murders' between 2003 and 2004 (see Bottom 2004 and 2004a; Bottom and Medew 2004). One case *The Age* newspaper uncovered involved the double execution of Steven Gulyas and Tina Nhonthachith Gulyas who operated an introduction agency. The business, Partner Search Australia, specialised in Russian and Asian women. According to police sources the couple employed underage Asian girls in brothels (in Silvester et al. 2003, p. 1).

Further evidence of links between organised crime and Victoria's prostitution industry surfaced during the PJC inquiry. Robert Sercomb, the Deputy Chair of the Crimes Committee, was among those who confirmed a relationship between the 'murders', 'the sex industry' and 'people who are operating in the sex industry' (Commonwealth of Australia 2003, p. 35). Ken Wolfe, speaking of his experience of working for the City of Yarra, also gave evidence that 'gangs' were 'involved in the ownership of some of [the City's] legal brothels' which they used to launder money. Their tactic, he says, is simply to 'get somebody licensed and operating' (Commonwealth of Australia, 2003, p. 18).

Sex trafficking under Victoria's model legislation

One of the most critical problems that the UN identifies as arising from criminal involvement in prostitution is sex trafficking (see Chapter One). Currently the numbers of women and children trafficked for sexual exploitation are difficult to determine. As it is a criminal activity the real extent of the problem is not easy to determine. Moreover historically few countries had non-trafficking laws which would have provided some statistical data to understand the scale of the problem. The US Department of State's annual *Trafficking in Persons Report* is a recent development aimed at providing a comprehensive analysis of the illicit trade, but five years into the program, official statistics on the crime are only beginning to emerge.[3]

Estimates of women trafficked into Australia for prostitution (taking in all states and territories) range between several hundred and a thousand women at any one time (Commonwealth of Australia 2003, p. 37). Although official statistics on the number of children trafficked for prostitution is negligible, anecdotal evidence suggests that it is also prevalent. Father Chris Riley heads an Australian-based *Youth off the Street* program, an NGO that has a high success rate in rehabilitating children involved in street prostitution. According to Riley, his work has brought him in contact with 'a large number of children from Asian countries working in the sex industry' (in Ray 2003, p. 67).

Paul Holmes, former head of Scotland Yard's vice squad and current advisor to international governments on trafficking, supports Riley's views that trafficking statistics are likely to be underestimated. Speaking at a *Stop the Trafficking* conference held in Melbourne in 2003, Holmes said that 'the real level of illegal exploitation in Australia's sex industry was probably much higher' and once 'an in-depth intelligence was conducted by law enforcement agencies and NGOs working together . . . [the

---

3. Since 2000, the Department of State has been legally required to report annually to the US Congress 'on foreign governments' efforts to eliminate severe forms of trafficking in persons'. It is aimed at raising global awareness of the problem and compelling governments to comply with a set of minimum standards to eliminate trafficking within their own borders (2005, p. 1).

figures] would mirror the experience in other countries'. As Holmes pointed out, 'once there's a deliberate targeted attempt to go out and find it [sex trafficking], you tend to find it in most of the places you look' (cited in Minchin 2003, p. 3).

Defining sex trafficking

A further, and more difficult problem in identifying the extent of sex trafficking relates to the way governments and various stakeholders define the activity. Trafficking usually implies some form of coercion as opposed to people smuggling where people willingly cross borders illegally to gain entry to a country. But the issue of consent is complex and most traffickers employ various forms of coercion and deception rather than overt force or violence. Also people may initially consent to a situation of exploitation as they are unaware of the reality of their situation. More critical is that the question of whether individuals are aware of their exploitation should be irrelevant; the reality is that victims of trafficking end up in a situation from which they cannot escape.

One of the most important documents that addresses the issue of consent in relation to sex trafficking is the UN *Protocol to the Convention Against Transnational Organised Crime – to Prevent, Suppress and Punish Trafficking In Persons, Especially Women and Children* (the Palermo Protocol). Janice Raymond, co-executive director of the Coalition Against Trafficking in Women, one of the key NGOs involved in the consultation process on the Protocol, explains how the UN document widens the definition of coercion. It specifically takes into account the less overt forms of coercion which entrap women (2001, p. 1). According to its definition 'trafficking in persons' encompasses:

> The recruitment, transportation, transfers, harbouring or receipt of persons, by means of the threat or use of force or other forms

of coercion, of abduction, of fraud, of deception, of the abuse of power or of a position of vulnerability or of the giving or receiving of payments or benefits to achieve the consent of a person having control over another person for the reason of exploitation, forced labour or services, slavery or practices similar to slavery (United Nations 2000, Article 3 [a], p. 2).

As Raymond explains, the Palermo Protocol 'provides a comprehensive coverage of criminal means by which trafficking takes place, including not only force, coercion, abduction, deception or abuse of power, but also less explicit means, such as abuse of a victim's vulnerability' (2001, p. 4).

That one of the main intentions of the UN document is to have governments recognise the insidious forces that compel women into prostitution is highlighted in Part (b) of the document. Here it is stated that 'the consent of a victim of trafficking persons to the intended exploitation . . . shall be irrelevant' (United Nations 2000, Article 3 [b], p. 2). This last section is critical as it means that victims of trafficking do not have to bear the burden of proof. The key element in the document is the exploitative purpose for which women are trafficked.

Most stakeholders interested in Australia's policy on sex trafficking accept that some women who are trafficked into the country are aware that they will be involved in prostitution (Tailby 2001, p. 3; Commonwealth of Australia 2003, p. 33). Nonetheless the Australian Government's position on victims of trafficking should be clear as we signed the Palermo Protocol in December 2002, ratifying it in September 2005. Thus we have a duty to comply with both its wording and meaning in its treatment of trafficking victims. Despite Australia's acceptance of the UN principles, debate on just who should be classified as victims of trafficking continues.

According to the Australian peak prostitutes' rights organisation, the Scarlet Alliance, the number of women trafficked into

Australia may be as few as 10 at one time. Its view is that most trafficked women 'consensually agreed to come here on contract' with few deceived, 'tricked' or kidnapped with the intention of forcing them to be prostituted (Commonwealth of Australia 2004, p. 26). In contrast, Project Respect, which has documented three hundred cases of sex trafficking, suggests that a more accurate estimate of the number of victims is around 1,000 at any time (2006, p. 1). Reflecting the principles outlined in the Palermo Protocol, the organisation focuses on the exploitative purpose for which women are trafficked.

Traffickers begin the process of exploiting women by arranging for them to be brought into the country legally, commonly on tourist visas (Tailby 2001, p. 4). Some women reported that they were smuggled out of their country of origin with inflated bank accounts, accompanied by sham family members or with fake passports to meet immigration requirements (O'Brien 2003, p. 15). Once in Australia, traffickers lodge an application on behalf of the women for a protection visa from the Federal Department of Immigration and Multiculturalism and Indigenous Affairs (DIMIA). These visas allow women to stay in Australia while their application is processed for refugee status. They also permit the trafficked women workers' rights for a period of 12 months. In these circumstances bringing criminal charges against traffickers is virtually impossible as no immigration laws have been breached. Indeed the traffickers are able to employ Australia's immigration laws to their advantage, although as I later discuss these same laws victimise trafficked women.

Within Victoria there have been few incidents of sex trafficking that have come under the Government's scrutiny since prostitution was first legalised in 1984. In the late 1980s, six Thai women were deported after police and immigration officers raided Lady Madisons, a legal brothel in the inner city suburb of Port Melbourne (Bottom 1991, p. 73). In 1988, police reported that Asian crime syndicates had trafficked 400 Thai women to work in both Sydney and Melbourne brothels (Bottom 1991, p. 74). A more publicised case implicated Gary Glazner, a local organiser of the international trafficking trade who between 1997 and 1998 illegally imported at least 40 Thai women for sexual exploitation in Melbourne brothels – both legal and illegal (Forbes 1999, p. 3).[4] In May 2004, more Thai women were found in three of Melbourne's licensed brothels, allegedly in conditions of sexual servitude. In the latter two cases the women were again put into detention to be deported (Binnie 2004, p. 6). This is consistent with Australian Government's general treatment of trafficking victims who are treated as illegal immigrants not as victims of crime.

Sexual servitude is not 'work'

The Australian Institute of Criminology, which defines slavery in accordance with international law, states that slavery is 'the condition of a person over whom any or all of the powers attaching to the right of ownership are exercised, including where such a condition results from a debt or contract made by the person' (Tailby 2001, p. 4). Sex traffickers bring women into Australia mainly to be prostituted in brothels. The conditions under which they 'work' make it nonsensical to define their experience other than as sexual slavery. They are bought and sold, their lives controlled. Sex traffickers ensure women comply with their conditions through threats of violence, isolation or through threats to their families in their country of origin.

Detective Senior Sergeant Ivan McKinney, from the Asian Squad of the Victorian Police, provided extensive detail to the PJC about how sex trafficking was operating in Australia and the conditions experienced by women once they arrive in the

---

4. Investigators believed that four to five times this many women were involved (McKinney 2001).

country. He explains that the women are indentured to pay off debts supposedly incurred in bringing them into Australia. They are kept in debt bondage, their passports are confiscated and their freedom severely restricted (Commonwealth of Australia 2004, p. 33–35).[5] McKinney reported that the Thai women involved in the Gary Glazner case were held under conditions that were tantamount to imprisonment. The women were housed in the Clifton Hotel in the Melbourne suburb of Kew, then as his business increased he moved his prostitution racket to a rented house in South Melbourne and finally operated out of two legal brothels in the same area (McKinney 2001). McKinney's description of the Clifton Hotel accommodation illustrates well the harsh conditions in which the Thai women were kept. According to McKinney they lived in the upstairs rooms of a small pub with no common room, antiquated bathrooms, and bars on the windows; 'the outer windows that faced the street had all been nailed and painted shut'. 'The conditions were grotty' and 'they were stacked in the room' (Commonwealth of Australia 2004, p. 35).

The basic indentured contract at the end of the 1990s was between A$35,000 to A$40,000 (Commonwealth of Australia 2004, p. 42). Police sources estimate that operators take about 40 per cent with the rest going to the brothel owner (Murphy 2003b, p. 1). In the case of the Thai women they would have needed to 'service' 500 buyers, working six days a week to pay off their debt. McKinney says that the women were often compelled to work seven days a week 'to earn some money for personal necessities'. McKinney made the further point that women trafficked into 'so called massage parlours' would be required to

---

5. Debt bondage means that people are illegally kept under contract and occurs where a person finds themselves contracted to work in exploitative or deceptive conditions, or where the purported debt is disproportionate to the services they must provide.

service even more men as 'the fee for service is lower' in the illegal sector (Commonwealth of Australia 2004, p. 42).

There is extensive evidence that the psychological harm to women trafficked into prostitution is so extreme that it is inconceivable that trafficked women 'choose' to remain in sexual servitude. As Dr Louise Newman, the New South Wales Chair of the Royal Australian and New Zealand College of Psychiatrists maintains, 'many [trafficked women] have suffered extremes of trauma and maltreatment for prolonged periods of time' (Bartlet 2003). The inevitable 'psychological and emotional effects of that sort of treatment' she says 'really make it impossible in many situations for women to give any sort of consent to these sorts of processes' (Bartlet 2003). And as McKinney stresses, women's compliance is certainly ensured 'through fear of retaliation' (Commonwealth of Australia 2004, p. 42). *The Age* journalist, Mark Forbes, reported that Gary Glazner had kept a loaded gun in the hotel to intimidate and coerce the women into compliance (Forbes 1999, p. 3). The women were also threatened with retaliation against their families in Thailand (Police vs. Gary Glazner and Paul Donato Mariono 1999: 48).

Sex trafficking and organised crime

Glazner, who trafficked the Thai women and then exploited them once they arrived in Australia, is undoubtedly part of a global network of criminals who exploit the vulnerability of women and children worldwide. The involvement of organised crime in the trafficking of women for prostitution into Australia, like the incidents of sex trafficking itself, is relatively undocumented. The international organisation – End Child Prostitution and Trafficking (ECPAT) – has identified 10 small crime syndicates which traffic around three hundred Thai women yearly (ECPAT 2004). However, according to the Australian Institute of Criminology almost all sex trafficking cases involve organised criminal activities. Its line of reasoning is that, 'trafficking, by its nature, involves not just irregular movement of migrants, but also subsequent exploitation for criminal purposes'. Thus traffickers require 'contacts throughout the journey and a presence in the destination country in order to exploit arriving migrants and enforce compliance' (Tailby 2001, p. 3).

The main source countries for the Australian sex trafficking trade are Thailand and China, and more recently South Korea. Project Respect also reports that women are trafficked from Japan and Russia (Commonwealth of Australia 2003, p. 48). Even now source countries are constantly changing as sex traffickers are able to tap into a worldwide market of women whose economic and social disadvantage make them vulnerable and whose countries have inadequate laws to protect them. Melba Marginson, from the Victorian Immigrant Refugee Women's Coalition, has pointed out that in the early 1990s women from the Philippines made up a significant proportion of women trafficked into Australia. She believes this has changed because the Philippine Government subsequently introduced stricter policies to combat the high incidence of Filipino women trafficked internationally, particularly for the mail-order bride trade (Commonwealth of Australia 2003, p. 64–65).

There is little dispute among policy makers that strategies designed to tackle sex trafficking must take into account the social and economic inequalities between source countries and destination countries. There is increasing recognition that the conditions which make women and children vulnerable to traffickers must be changed (see Chapter One). Even so the main profit from the trafficking of women and children for sex comes not from the trafficking of people into a country, but from the ensuing exploitation. Government sources estimate that organisers of the trafficking in women and children into the Australian brothel market make approximately A$1 million per week (Victoria 2004c, p. 755). Glazner, for example, was reported to have paid between A$15,000 and A$18,000 for the Thai women that he brought into Victoria. The ensuing 'contract' between Glazner and the women required that they each pay him back between A$35,000 and A$40,000 (McKinney 2001). As the women were forced to 'service' 500 buyers to 'work off their contract', and given that the going rate was around A$100 per service, Glazner's net profit on each individual woman would have averaged out at A$32,000. But trafficking thrives not just because of high profits but also because it is a relatively low risk activity as there are minimal laws against trafficking for sexual servitude.

Sex trafficking under Victorian law

Australia's role as a significant destination country means that despite the Government's commitment to the Palermo Protocol it is seriously failing in its duty to protect women and girls from sexual exploitation. In June 2004 the United States *Trafficking in Persons* report identified Australia as a destination country for Chinese and South-East Asian women trafficked for prostitution (Office to Monitor and Combat Trafficking in Persons 2004, p. 1). More recently, the UN Office on Drugs and Crime (UNODC) again listed Australia as a significant destination country for trafficking. In fact Australia was the only country within the Oceanic region which ranked high in the UNODC's citation index which ranged from very high to very low (2006, p. 105).[6]

As suggested above, the failure of governments globally to introduce adequate laws to effectively deal with sex trafficking

---

6. The report lists countries on a scale of very high to very low for countries of origin, transit countries and destination countries. Globally ten countries rated high as destinations while Australia was one of 19 countries which were listed in the second highest category.

greatly facilitates the global sexual exploitation of millions of women and girls. Until recently there has been no Federal or State legislation that makes trafficking of women for sexual servitude into Australia an offence.[7] The two pieces of legislation that the Victorian Government could apply to deal with traffickers were the *Prostitution Control (Amendment) Act 1997* and the Commonwealth's *Slavery and Sexual Servitude Act 1999*. The Victorian 1997 Amendment Act allowed authorities to cancel brothel licences where operators were prostituting trafficked women. On the other hand, the licences were cancelled on the basis that the brothel owners had breached the Migration Act by employing 'illegal immigrants' (Victoria 1997, p. 1614). In this context, sex trafficking is treated as an immigration problem related to Australia's border protection policies and people smuggling. Victoria's lawmakers simply invalidated any claim that trafficked women are victims brought into the country normally through some form of extreme coercion and are kept in conditions of sexual slavery to be prostituted by Australian men. Most commonly trafficked women picked up in the State's brothels are deported back to their country of origin. Moreover traffickers can operate with virtual immunity as there is no threat of a criminal conviction or threat to their financial assets.

The Commonwealth's 1999 sexual slavery legislation was Australia's first attempt at recognising trafficking for sexual servitude as a crime. The Act created an offence where trafficking involved sexual slavery or sexual servitude but with the caveat that traffickers had to use 'deceptive recruiting' methods (*Slavery and Sexual Servitude Act 1999*). This meant that irrespective of whether women found themselves kept in slave-like conditions, if they had some prior knowledge that they would be involved

---

7. Victoria's *Justice Legislation (Sexual Offences and Bail) Act 2004* and *Criminal Code Amendment (Trafficking in Persons Offences) Act (2005)* attempt to overcome the limitations of the former Acts.

in prostitution, the law does not consider them to be victims. Moreover the law is ambiguous about what 'deception' and other forms of 'duress' entail. It dismisses the reality that debt bondage, for example, is a coercive debt arrangement, and trafficked women have no freedom to end their servitude until the debt is repaid. Additionally, as pointed out by the Australian Institute of Criminology in its critique of the Commonwealth Act, ownership rights are difficult to establish, indeed an even 'more onerous burden than establishing the presence of exploitation on the basis of the various forms of duress mentioned in the [UN] Trafficking Protocol' (Tailby 2001, p. 4). For most victims, their ability to come forward to make a claim of being trafficked for sexual servitude is hampered by language barriers, fear of retribution from their traffickers and fear of authority. A further problem, of course, is that the Federal legislation does not cover women trafficked across domestic borders.

Given that Australia has lacked any strong legislation against trafficking for sexual servitude, it is inevitable that the number of criminal convictions for traffickers is negligible. In the Glazner case, the prosecution was run under the Victorian principal 1994 prostitution legislation. Glazner was convicted for operating unlicensed brothels and living off the earnings of prostitution. The charges laid carried a maximum of four and five years but Glazner received an 18 month imprisonment (which was suspended) and an A$31,000 fine (Forbes and Hemmings 2000, p. 4).[8] An initial charge of false imprisonment was dismissed despite evidence that Glazner had confiscated the women's passports and restricted their movements (Ford 2001, p. 17). Furthermore the judge's ruling on the case had included an acknowledgement that certainly Glazner was involved in trafficking 'contract girls' and

---

8. An appeal that followed public outrage at the leniency of Glazner's penalty resulted in a 30 month imprisonment (again suspended) and a A$31,000 fine (Taylor 2001, p. 6).

'the systematic manipulation of the Commonwealth immigration laws' (Queen v. Glazner, Gary 2000, p. 818).

The first jury prosecution, under the *Federal Slavery and Sexual Servitude Act 1999,* occurred in June 2006. That case involved the sexual exploitation of five women from Thailand by a Melbourne brothel owner Wei Tang, whose restrictions on the victims involved 'insidious use of control by way of fear of detection from immigration authorities' (Sentence: The Queen v. Tang, Wei 2006, p. 5). Wei Tang was one of four people charged in July 2003 with bringing the Thai women into Australia and forcing them to work as 'sex slaves'. The arrests were made after a series of brothel raids, six in Melbourne and one in Sydney, including legal brothels (Commonwealth of Australia 2003, p. 18).[9]

The complainants in the Wei Tang case knew they were to 'work' in prostitution. In Melbourne they were placed in Club 417 in Fitzroy where the women were contracted to each pay off A$45,000 which required each of them servicing up to 900 men over a period of several months. Tang confiscated their passports and return airline tickets and warned the women to avoid immigration officials as they would be deported (Sentence: The Queen v. Tang, Wei 2006, pp. 1–2). Tang was sentenced to 10 years jail (Sentence: The Queen v. Tang, Wei 2006, p. 17).[10] Such a significant sentence reflected the categorisation of the crime as one against humanity. It also importantly recognised that psychological pressure does work as a form of coercion to entrap women in sexual slavery. Judge McInerney, when handing down his sentence, stated that 'the sentencing principles of general

---

9. One of the accused pleaded guilty to 3 counts of slavery and 2 counts of slave trading and was sentenced by the Court on 12 April 2005 (Sentence: The Queen v. Tang, Wei, p. 1). At the time this book was published the other two co-accused had not pleaded guilty and they have not yet been prosecuted.

10. Wei Tang was sentenced on 10 counts of criminal behaviour. She was to serve her sentences concurrently (Sentence: The Queen v. Tang, Wei 2006, pp. 16-17).

deterrence, denunciation and just punishment assumed considerable importance in this case' (Sentence: The Queen v. Tang, Wei 2006, p. 11). However the case highlights how difficult it is to legally prove the required level of coercion to establish that the crime of slavery was committed. Wei Tang was initially brought to trial 12 months earlier but the jury could not reach a verdict.

The lawyer for the five Thai women also highlighted that they were applying for protection visas (Lauder 2006). Despite their assistance with the conviction, it continues to remain at the discretion of the Federal Government to decide whether the women who have now been freed from sexual servitude at Club 417 will be allowed to stay in Australia (Lauder 2006). This threat of deportation exists although one of the enticements which trapped these women into sexual slavery was a promise that they could work legally in Victoria's prostitution industry. No Australian government takes responsibility for the fact that Australia's acceptance of prostitution has created an easily accessible and growing market for sex trafficking victims. The irony does not stop there. While Wei Tang had her license revoked and lost her business, the brothel remains open under a new operator as the premises have a town planning permit that was not revoked.

Sex trafficking in Victoria's legal brothels

Victoria's legal system indisputably exacerbates problems that lawmakers experience when dealing with sex trafficking crimes. Within Victoria, brothel operators must be licensed by the Business Licensing Authority (BLA), but this does not apply to the women in the brothels. When McKinney presented his evidence to the PJC, he stressed that his investigations were hampered because 'there is a legal prostitution industry in Victoria'. As McKinney says, 'some of the women who were in these brothels . . . technically were here legally' (Commonwealth of Australia 2003, p. 39). In these circumstances neither council nor police have the right to interrogate women who they may suspect are trafficked into the industry. As suggested above many trafficked women are brought into Australia on travel visas, for example. McKinney pointed out, given 'the resourcing and budgets that you have to allocate to various investigations it was difficult [for his Department] to justify the expenditure' (Commonwealth of Australia 2003, p. 39).

The inherent and ongoing problem when addressing criminal activity within Victoria's prostitution industry has been that law enforcers assume that criminal activity, including sex trafficking, is associated with the illegal brothel trade. The assumption is that Government regulations mean that Victoria's legal brothels operate within the law. In contrast, Ken Wolfe argues that on an operational basis, a split between the legal sector and the illegal sector is ineffective when dealing with sex trafficking (Commonwealth of Australia 2003, p. 14). Similarly the Acting Deputy Commissioner of the Victorian Police's Legal Policy Department, says that he deals with prostitution as an industry, 'some of it is regulated, some of it is unregulated – and illegal activity cuts across both' (Commonwealth of Australia 2003, p. 15).

In addition to the problem that the law operates as if sex trafficking is a by-product of illegal brothel activity, prosecution of traffickers is ultimately hampered because the women whose travel visas lapse are normally deported once authorities discover them in brothels, irrespective of their 'victim' status. This inevitably works against victims reporting their situation to police or to immigration authorities. I maintain that an even more critical oversight in current Australian approaches to eliminating sex trafficking is our Government's failure to acknowledge the intrinsic role of demand in creating a market for trafficked women and girls.

Solutions: ignoring consumer demand

Article 9 of the UN's anti-trafficking Palermo Protocol states that all parties:

> [S]hall adopt or strengthen legislative or other measures, such as educational, social or cultural measures, including through bilateral and multilateral cooperation, to discourage the demand that fosters all forms of exploitation of persons, especially women and children, that leads to trafficking (2000 p. 4).

While the Protocol is the first international human rights instrument to address trafficking and recognise the association between demand and the exploitation of people, more and more, other UN bodies are insisting that governments worldwide address demand in their anti-trafficking policies. In 2003 for example, the Commission on Crime Prevention and Criminal Justice insisted that such policies must take account of the reality that 'the volume of trafficking has increased rapidly due to the demand for prostitution in destination countries [as well as] the poor social and economic conditions in source countries' (Makkai 2003, p. 4). A 2006 UNODC report, *Trafficking in Persons: Global Patterns*, similarly emphasised that globally, 'the main challenge [in reducing trafficking] is *to reduce demand*', (emphasis in original) (2006, p. 10). Again one of its principal recommendations was for all member states to undertake measures to discourage demand that fosters exploitation which leads to trafficking (2006, p. 12).

The Federal Government's instigation of its Crime Commission's Inquiry on sex trafficking (2003–2004) suggests that the Australian Government is committed to reducing the incidence of trafficking into the country. Other Federal initiatives included a 20 million dollar budget for programs over a five-year period that would assist in apprehending the traffickers, including setting up a police taskforce (The Federal Capital Press of

Australia Limited 2003, p. 1). Yet the Federal Government, as does the Victorian Government, side-steps the problem of demand. Both ignore that Australia's increasing normalisation of women as just another commodity fuels the market for women and girls which traffickers are more than ready to make use of.

The PJC Inquiry was mainly concerned with evaluating Australian legislative and administrative response to the increasing evidence of sex trafficking in the country (Commonwealth of Australia 2003, p. 4). The Inquiry canvassed solutions to trafficking that reflected ideas of best practice both domestically and internationally. These covered work visas, witness protection programs and applying asylum procedures (Commonwealth of Australia 2004, pp. 26, 55). What was clearly absent was any serious discussion of addressing the demand side of the trafficking phenomenon.

The pro-prostitution position was put by the Scarlet Alliance which argued for the introduction of a 'prostitution work visa', which would allow trafficked women to be treated as no different than other workers who legally immigrate to meet the demand for specific industries in the host country (Commonwealth of Australia 2004, p. 29). I suggest that, in practice, traffickers would simply apply for these visas on behalf of women as they do for tourist visas. The women would remain vulnerable to force and coercion and still end up in sexual servitude as the conditions which make people vulnerable to traffickers remain unchanged. Traffickers would be even freer to manipulate our immigration laws to ensure their high profits. By providing work visas, the Australian Government would, in effect, assist traffickers by allowing them to operate within the law.

A decisively more humanitarian approach to sex trafficking is currently developed within the United States and the European Union. The focus is on protecting victims. In Italy for example, trafficked women are given protection visas with the possibility of residency if they provide testimony against their exploiters (Commonwealth of Australia 2004, p. 26). The limitation here is that requiring sex trafficking victims to 'provide testimony' is often not feasible. Eshoe Aghatise, Director of the Italian based Association Iroke Onlus, which assists Nigerian trafficking victims, explains that women who have been trafficked through several persons and destinations, are frequently incapable of assisting police inquiries regarding their traffickers. Moreover the problem remains that many women are coerced into silence by threats to themselves or their families (Aghatise 2004).

Sheila Jeffreys, a feminist academic and member of the Australian branch of the Coalition Against Trafficking in Women, was the first to introduce the importance of focusing on consumer demand into the PJC's Inquiry. 'Male buyers', she argued, 'do not make a special demand for trafficked women to use; they simply demand to buy prostituted women' (Commonwealth of Australia 2003, p. 62). McKinney presented a similar view to the Inquiry's Committee. 'What was happening', he said, 'was that a group of people were going to legal brothels and saying: "If you are having trouble getting workers, I can supply workers. You don't pay the workers; you pay me and I'll take care of all that for you"' (Commonwealth of Australia 2003, p. 42). He agreed that ultimately the number of women depended 'on the market forces at the time and the availability of ways to get them into the country' (Commonwealth of Australia 2003, p. 50). By May 2004, a *Herald-Sun* newspaper investigation had confirmed that at least 10 Melbourne brothels admitted that they were willing 'to take imported women even if their passports were confiscated' (Binnie 2004, p. 6). Any government response to sex trafficking that ignores the pull factors within Australia, that is, male demand for women and girls, will ultimately fail to eliminate the trafficking trade.

Sexual exploitation of non-trafficked women and children

One of the most crucial factors in understanding that victims of trafficking are brought into Australia to serve a ready market of male buyers allows us to recognise that the exploiters' main concern is to ensure a supply of women to maintain their profits. To achieve this end they are equally willing to coerce and keep Australian-born women and children in conditions of sexual slavery where possible. When giving evidence before the PJC, Greg Barber, then Mayor of the City of Yarra, commented that 'It should not really matter whether [victims of sexual servitude] have been brought in from another country, although no doubt that makes them much more vulnerable' (Commonwealth of Australia 2003, p. 8). This thinking, of course, has critical implications for policies on sexual slavery. As Barber concluded,

> if you are going to start treating coercion as the crime you will no doubt be brushing up against some of the practices of even the legal Australian brothel industry and totally leaving out the immigration question (Commonwealth of Australia 2003, p. 13).

As I have illustrated, Australia's inadequate monitoring and reporting systems has meant that the extent of trafficking women and girls into the country for prostitution can only be estimated at this stage. Such statistics that are available do not consider women trafficked for sex within Australia, from one State or Territory to another. Moreover, no Government, neither Federal nor State, has an understanding of the number of women who are kept in conditions of sexual servitude in the escort agency trade or coerced into another avenue of the industry such as stripping or pornography. There is also a significant child sex trade in Australia, with only some of the children trafficked from outside the country.

Prostituting Victoria's children

One of the most compelling arguments for the introduction of Victoria's legalised prostitution system was that it would 'protect children from sexual exploitation and coercion' (*Prostitution Control Act 1994* s. 4[a]). Indeed five of the 18 offences set out in the State's principal 1994 prostitution legislation involve child prostitution.[11] But, as with other forms of prostitution, two decades of legalised prostitution within the State have not eliminated the child prostitution trade.

In 2001 an Australian national radio station presented a report on the sexual exploitation of children, in which it made the damning announcement that 'Australia's child sex industry is growing' (Jennings 2001). An ECPAT 1998 report, which currently offers the most comprehensive findings of child prostitution in Victoria, says the Victorian industry alone exploits 1800 children, the highest of all Australian States and Territories (1998, p. 57). The research, which was part of a national inquiry into the involvement of young people (under 18 years of age) in 'commercial sexual activities', found that the majority of children prostituted were aged between 16 and 17 years, although there were a number of 10 to 12-year-olds, as well as some children under 10 years of age. Both girls and boys were involved in the child trade, although 68 per cent were female (1998, p. 57). The profile of the children in the ECPAT survey reflected a history of homelessness, insufficient income and unemployment, dysfunctional family backgrounds, a history of sexual abuse and lack of self-esteem and feelings of isolation within society (1998, pp. 35–36). Its report, however, offered little evaluation of either

---

11. Provisions under the 1994 *Prostitution Control Act* dealing with children are 'Causing or inducing a child to take part in prostitution' (s. 5 [1]); 'Obtaining payment for sexual services provided by a child' (s. 6 [1]); 'Agreement for provision of sexual services by a child' (s. 7 [1]); 'Allowing a child to take part in prostitution' (s. 11 [1]) and 'A child over 18 months not to be in a brothel' (s. 11A [1]).

the sexual demand for children or, crucially, why a State that promotes itself as having the most advanced legislation for prostitution in Australia, and possibly the world, has the largest child prostitution trade in the country!

As with sex trafficking, child prostitution occurs in all sectors of the prostitution industry because it is there to meet the demand created through Victoria's tolerance of prostitution. The first conviction for offences relating to child prostitution in Victoria related to one of the State's licensed brothels – Sashas International. In 1999 the three operators were charged with a range of offences that included 'allowing a child to take part in prostitution', 'inducing a child into prostitution' 'forcing a person to remain in prostitution', and 'sexual penetration of a child between ten and sixteen years' (Forbes 1999, p. 3). Fred Lelah, one of the men charged, had already served a two-year term for having sex with minors (Johnson, 1994, p. 3). Despite this, the Victorian Government had allowed Lelah to operate a legal brothel.

Victoria's new sexual exploitation laws

In 2004 the State Labor Government introduced its *Justice Legislation (Sexual Offences and Bail) Act*, as another putative attempt to overcome the failure of Victoria's 'model' prostitution legislation to meet its objectives. The new Act was promoted as part of a social justice package that was aimed at addressing some of the humanitarian concerns that had emerged in the public debate around sex trafficking, and the wider coercion and sexual exploitation, particularly of children, that continued to characterise Victoria's prostitution industry (Victoria 2004c, p. 925). As the State Attorney-General, Robert Hulls, made clear, his Government's intention was to 'fill gaps in Victoria's existing criminal law to combat sexual servitude and to "complement" the Commonwealth's 1999 sex slavery legislation' (Victoria 2004, p. 712).

One of the more progressive aspects of Labor's legislation was its adoption of the term 'commercial sexual services'. This extended the definition of 'sexual services' as defined by the principal 1994 prostitution Act, which referred solely to physical contact and prostitution. 'Commercial sexual services' covered all 'commercial use and display of a person's body for the sexual arousal or sexual gratification of others' (*Justice Legislation (Sexual Offences and Bail) Act 2004*, s. 3 [60AB(1)]). This wider interpretation of the sexual exploitation enables law enforcers to target the previously unregulated child stripping and pornography trade.

The Act also introduced new offences for deceptive recruiting and the use of coercion to force a person to provide, or continue to provide, prostitution (2004, 60AB[2]). Thus Victorian police could use State legislation to convict operators who traffic women domestically for sexual servitude. Moreover in contrast to the Commonwealth's 1999 sexual slavery legislation, the definition of 'coercion' within the State Act is widened to more directly mirror the directives laid out in the UN's 2000 anti-trafficking Palermo Protocol. The term 'manifestly excessive' debt, for example, means that the law recognises debt bondage as a form of coercion and a criminal offence.

Despite some advancement in the State's 2004 legislation, if Victoria is serious about Australia's obligations under the UN agreement, I suggest that it must recognise the connection between trafficking and prostitution. Nevertheless, this demands a complete rethink of its policy on prostitution. As I demonstrated in the previous chapter legalisation has been critical in creating the upsurge in male demand for commercial sex and the ongoing commodification of women's bodies. I believe such a rethink is unlikely to occur. Successive Victorian Governments have remained committed to regulation and legalisation of prostitution. The industry is now a highly profitable and pervasive influence in the State, with the Victorian Government among the various stakeholders who would lose out if prostitution was not tolerated in any form, and if for example, Victoria adopted the Swedish legislative model which protects women and targets male consumers' demand for prostitution.

The Commonwealth's *Criminal Code Amendment (Trafficking in Persons Offences) Act 2005* promised to be more reflective of the principles outlined in the Palermo Protocol as the Government created the legislation as a direct response to the UN document.[12] Significantly, the Amendment Act began by creating new trafficking and debt bondage offences that included a broader definition of 'deceive' than that contained in the Commonwealth 1999 sexual slavery legislation. Under the Federal law it is now an offence to deceive 'workers' about the kinds of services they are contracted to provide or their working conditions. Mirroring Victoria's 2004 *Justice Legislation Act*, the new debt bondage offences refer to exploitative contracts that involve exploitation, impose excessive up front contract amounts which are manifestly unfair, and the confiscation of the person's travel documents (*Criminal Code Amendment (Trafficking in Persons Offences) Act 2005* ss 270.1 [1] a–e). One of the major revisions in the Amendment Act is that these offences apply to domestic trafficking as well as across national borders. The Government thus acknowledges that, unlike people smuggling, trafficking in persons is not limited to transnational operations.

My major criticism of the Federal Act is its acceptance of the forced-free distinction, that is that victims of sex trafficking choose their exploitation and choose to remain in conditions of sexual slavery. Whether women 'choose' to come to Australia or are 'forced' or 'deceived' about their exploitative 'working'

---

12. For a comprehensive overview of the legislation see *Inquiry into the Criminal Code Amendment (Trafficking in Persons Offences) Bill 2004 (The Senate Legal and Constitutional Legislation Committee* 2005).

conditions, they will be recruited, transported and controlled by organised crime networks whilst in Australia. Moreover the 2005 Act does not recognise the more subtle forms of coercion as outlined in the Palermo Protocol starting with 'the abuse of a victim's vulnerability' (United Nations 2000, Article 3 [a]). These more subliminal coercive forces compel many women from economically disadvantaged nations to be trafficked for prostitution into the richer countries. Here male buyers have both the social and economic power to buy women and girls for their sexual gratification, which most disturbingly, as is the case of Australia, is mostly sanctioned by the State.

As a consequence of Australia's continued advocacy of the notion of choice, even in its most recent anti-trafficking legislation, victims of sex trafficking are commonly treated as criminals who have flouted the country's immigration laws. Nowhere is there any mention of the Australian Government's responsibility under Article 7 of the Palermo Protocol to take legislative and other measures to provide victim support. According to the UNODC's 2006 report, at a minimum, these measures demand that governments 'provide for the physical, psychological and social recovery of victims' including 'counselling', 'housing', 'medical assistance' and 'employment and training opportunities' as well as providing for 'the physical safety of victims' (UNODC 2006, p. 13).

A potential avenue for trafficked women to gain protection under Australian law is the new visa system provided for within the Commonwealth's *Migration (Amendment) Act 1994*. This created a range of visas that included Bridging Visas and Witness Protection Visas which could be used by unlawful non-citizens to extend their stay in Australia. The first of these permits illegal immigrants to be released from detention while an application for a Criminal Justice Stay Visa is processed. If their application is successful they avoid compulsory return to their country. An applicant is considered eligible if they can substantially assist in the conviction of a criminal. As suggested above, the ability of victims of sex trafficking to provide evidence against their exploiters is often not feasible. Victims of trafficking may never be in a position to assist investigations because of language barriers, or through trauma created through their experience of sexual slavery, or fear of repercussions against their families. In contrast, the Witness Protection Visa ostensibly offers a greater degree of support to women trafficked into Australia as it provides for a two-year temporary stay followed by automatic permanency if evidence they provide to assist trafficking investigators means that they are at risk of harm if they return to their country of origin (Norberry 2005, pp. 12–13). In practice however, few trafficked women have been allowed to make use of the visa system to assist them.

There is increasing evidence that women trafficked for sexual exploitation into Australia, once picked up by authorities, are deported to their country of origin, irrespective of the consequences for victims. In January 2005, *The Australian* newspaper disclosed that a Thai sex-slave informant who was initially granted a Criminal Justice Stay Visa was deported because evidence she had provided to investigators was proven to be insufficient to gain a criminal conviction against her traffickers. This was irrespective of the fact that the woman had said that she feared reprisals if she returned to Thailand. Of the 59 women who were picked up in raids on Sydney brothels in 2005, 39 of them were transported to the Villawood Detention Centre to await deportation. Their 'employers' were simply issued with a warning (Wynhausen and O'Brien 2005).

Street prostitution

The Victorian Government's lack of concern for women is further highlighted by the continued existence of the illegal street prostitution trade at the beginning of the 21st century. In 2001, the Attorney-General, Robert Hulls, set up a Street Prostitution Advisory Group (AGSPAG) to come up with strategies to contain the highly visible trade which continued to be focused in the St Kilda area in the City of Port Phillip.[13] The AGSPAG in its *Final Report* confirmed that under the State's 'model' prostitution legislation, street prostitution had 'become significantly more prevalent' particularly 'in the past 15 years'. The numbers of women involved in the street trade had also risen, in contrast to males and transsexuals (2002, p. 44).[14] A further finding was that violence and rape had increased in parallel with these rising numbers (2002, p. 8).

When the Victorian Labor Government first introduced legalised prostitution in 1984, there were 200 women involved in street prostitution, with 30 on the street at peak periods. Currently, the numbers range between 300 and 350, with 50 on the streets at any given time (AGSPAG 2002, p. 44). This equals a 100 to 150 per cent increase over the last 20 years. The way the street operates has also changed as the trade is no longer transient. As highlighted in the AGSPAG's report:

> There are now established early morning and afternoon markets for street sex with clients, principally businessmen, tradesmen and taxi drivers travelling to or from work, or during their lunchbreaks (2002, p. 44).

In a press release, the Attorney-General, Robert Hulls, provided details of the impact that this constant trade was having on St Kilda. According to Hulls, women were prostituted 'day

---

13. Members of the Group included State Parliamentarians, Port Phillip City Councillors, residents and representatives of the St Kilda-based organisation RHED, the main sexual health service provider for Victoria's prostitution industry.

14. The public nature of street prostitution means that police have substantially more official statistics on the street trade in comparison to illegal brothel prostitution and sex trafficking.

and night' with 'street sex workers and residents, being subjected to violence, abuse and harassment, and serious damage being caused to traders and the local amenity' (Hulls 2002, p. 19). Public unease about the constant trade mirrored that of West Actions' concerns over prostitution in St Kilda in the late 1970s which was one of the significant catalysts for Victoria's shift towards legalisation. Ironically, it was hoped then that legalisation would 'clean up' street prostitution as the regulated industry would meet male demand for prostituted women.

Model legislation or legally sanctioned sexual exploitation?

One of the most striking things about Labor's current approach to street prostitution is that it has given up on trying to eliminate the trade. From its beginnings the AGSPAG was directed to develop proposals based on a harm minimisation strategy that would 'facilitate community management of street prostitution issues' (Attorney-General's Street Prostitution Advisory Group 2002, p. 8). Hulls mirrored successive Victorian Governments approaches to prostitution, when setting the parameters for the AGSPAG's inquiry. He accepted that ultimately it was a practice that went on in private between consenting adults. Thus the State should only regulate prostitution when it caused 'demonstrable harm'. As Hulls reiterated, the debate on the decriminalisation of the street-trade is a contest between progressives on the one hand, and on the other, 'prohibitionists' and 'moralists' (Attorney-General's Street Prostitution Advisory Group 2002, p. 8). When interviewed by *The Age* journalists, Hulls insisted:

> You can either bury your head in the sand over these issues and take this 1950s, white picket fence, myopic view of the world, that if you shut your eyes, street prostitution will go away . . . Or you can look at innovative solutions to minimise the harm that's occurring as a result of street prostitution (cited in Kelly and Burstin 2002, p. 1).

Thus the AGSPAG began with the *a priori* position that prostitution is inevitable and that it is not a government body's role to make a 'moral judgement' (Attorney-General's Street Prostitution Advisory Group 2002, p. 7). On the contrary, I argue that the Government has totally supported the male sex prerogative at the expense of women's right to health and safety. In my analysis of the Group's recommendations, it is clear that its proposed strategies will not create a safe environment for street prostituted women, nor will they guarantee public safety.

The AGSPAG's study focused primarily on the St Kilda area, where 97 per cent of street prostitution in Victoria takes place (2002, p. 35). Its recommendations contain two major strategies. These were to create tolerance zones and 'street worker' centres, anticipating that these would remove street prostitution from residential areas. As the AGSPAG argued, tolerance zones 'would address issues relating to the collection of street workers' while the centres provided the most strategic option for reducing 'the incidence of public sex and the risk of workers being assaulted' (2002, p. 35). Indeed, the AGSPAG promoted the centres as offering women on the streets 'safe and more secure facilities in which workers could service clients'. The model was for state-owned premises to be used for women to take their 'clients', after paying a fee for use of rooms allocated for prostitution (2002, p. 35), although as I will explain further, without the legal restrictions that apply to licensed brothels.

Red light districts

The experience of the Netherlands shows that once a designated area or tolerance zone is set up, as proposed for the St Kilda area, an upsurge in demand for prostitution will inevitably follow. Feminist activist, Julie Bindel, carried out research in the City of Utrecht which houses the country's major red light district. She published her findings in the British *Guardian* newspaper, basing her discussion on a tour taken with Jan Shoenmaker, an official responsible for policing the zone, and one of the major promoters of using the area as a best practice model for other cities (2004 pp. 4–5).

Bindel's commentary immediately exposes the lack of health provision and physical protection for women who operate in the red light district. According to Bindel, the area consists of:

[T]welve parking spaces separated by 6ft-high wooden partitions, as well as one for cyclists, or those who wish to stand up to have sex . . . The floors of the cubicles are littered with tissues, used condoms and cigarette butts. There are empty food cartons, clumps of hair and human excrement, and incongruously, torn gift-wrapping paper. In one, a pair of men's underpants lies among the debris (2004, p. 4).

The evening pick-up area, 'a stretch of road behind an industrial estate teems with women'. Bindel noted that 45 cars passed along the stretch of road in five minutes (2004, p. 5). Against this backdrop, just how did Shoenmaker defend Utrecht's decision to create its red light district?

According to Bindel, Shoenmaker saw the main benefits for the way Utrecht handled its street prostitution trade as being that it offered the women involved optimal protection against violence perpetrated by male buyers. As Shoenmaker explained, before beginning 'working' in the area women have to register with police, a strategy he argues, that assists the police when the same women disappear (2004, p. 4). Shoenmaker appears to see no incongruity that women are disappearing, despite Utrecht's pretence to be a best practice model for regulating street prostitution. Creating a red light district had also not eliminated day-to-day violence, as many women using the cubicles set aside for prostitution continue to report violent incidences. Indeed, women resorted to painting the cubicles in different colours to allow raped women to identify more easily in which cubicle the abuse had occurred (2004, p. 5). But identifying where one has been raped does not eradicate the rape itself. As well the likelihood of police being able to convict a rapist when women have to resort to this desperate strategy is almost negligible. As Shoemaker commented 'looking for DNA among all this . . . mountain of semen-soaked articles covering the ground' is impossible (2004, p. 5).

Utrecht's experience demonstrates well that a harm minimisation strategy will neither protect street-prostituted women nor eliminate street traffic. Prostitution will only be channelled into specific prostitution zones or 'red light' districts, although Victoria prefers the term 'tolerance areas' because they are to be council controlled rather than operated by sex business entrepreneurs or pimps. I maintain that the change in terminology is an attempt by the Government to convince the public that, rather than St Kilda being home to a violent and highly intrusive street prostitution trade, prostitution in the area will come under Government scrutiny, operating similar to the regulated sectors of the industry. Moreover as I discuss below, councils' operation of 'street worker' centres means that they, rather than pimps, benefit directly from women's the sexual exploitation.

'Street worker' centres or illegal brothels?

The proposal for 'street worker' centres demonstrates just how far Victorian Governments will go to ensure that men can have access to women's bodies. The supposedly stringent Victorian prostitution legislation is intended to ensure that the licensed brothels are free of criminals and are not premises where illegal activities such as drug use can take place. The AGSPAG emphatically states that its model 'does not compromise the existing effective management of the legal sex industry'. Its proposal is for a new and separate definition of 'street worker' centres under the 1994 *Prostitution Control Act*. This was intended to create 'a system of licensing and planning parallel to the existing brothel scheme, with tailored amendments as required' (2002, p. 67). However if they are to meet the needs of street prostituted women these new centres must be different from legal brothels. This will dilute current prostitution legislation, specifically in relation to health and safety regulations and the probation of criminal activities taking place in licensed brothels.

Most street prostituted women, as the Advisory Group acknowledges, have drug problems and would not be able to work in legal brothels (2002, pp. 32–33). But the AGSPAG report does not state whether drugs can be used in the proposed 'street worker' centres. In addition while much of the debate around decriminalising street prostitution has focused on facilitating women's greater access to health professionals, and in turn protect buyers' sexual health, it is easily apparent that regulating street prostitution will not achieve this. The AGSPAG proposes that trained outreach workers be employed to 'distribute harm-reduction resources (including supplying condoms, lubricant and health information) and provide referral to local support services' (2002, p. 66). There is already evidence that the Government does not provide adequate resources to allow for health inspections and HIV testing for the legal industry (Victoria 1999a, p. 1191). Are we to believe that it is willing to fund an expanded program?

A further limitation of the proposed outreach program is that there is no pressure for male buyers to undergo routine health checks even though it is widely recognised that these men come from across a wide spectrum of the community, many married, living with partners or engaging in casual sex (Victoria 1999a, p. 1147). While I will demonstrate further the incongruity of placing responsibility for public health on prostituted women and not the buyers (see Chapter Six), suffice to say here that it is immediately obvious that public health cannot be protected if male buyers are not made accountable for their prostitution behaviour.

Protecting or exploiting women on the margins?

The most critical limitation of the AGSPAG's harm minimisation approach is its failure to address the reality that street prostituted women have minimal power to negotiate safe sex practices with buyers. In 2000 the Women's Team of the Sacred Heart Mission in St Kilda, a welfare support group for women in street prostitution, produced its own report on the problems associated with the street-trade. The report, *From Exclusion to Community and Connectedness* (Mitchell 2000), was based on a survey of 65 women in the St Kilda area with whom the Women's Team had contact over a period of a month. The researchers found that most women had little employment, apart from prostitution (2000, p. 52). Thirty-five were actively involved in prostitution at the time (2000, p. 13). The main connecting factors underpinning their experience of being prostituted on the streets were a history of sexual abuse in childhood (more than 50 per cent) and a third had a childhood history of contact with child protection services (2000, p. 27).[15]

Other experiences that made the group particularly vulnerable to sexual exploitation included most having been victims of domestic violence, while 19 were directly coerced into prostitution by their partner. Twenty-four of the 35 women had been abused by male buyers. The report also disclosed that of the 15 women whose mental state was known, 13 had been diagnosed as mentally ill; nearly two-thirds of the women were currently

---

15. Most of the women in the Mission's survey were Australian born and not trafficked from overseas. This reinforces the view that many women find themselves vulnerable to sexual exploitation despite living in a first world country.

taking heroin. As well a number of women had prison histories with most of those with children having had them removed from their care. All the women experienced educational disadvantage (2000, p. 6). That the Government could assume that these women are in a position to 'negotiate' safe sex with male buyers, who have significant economic and social advantage over them, is certainly incredible.

The AGSPAG's proposal for 'street worker' centres is also faulty because it assumes that buyers will use such places. Several studies have shown that the essential nature of street prostitution is that women, who work to support a drug habit or to earn money quickly, are picked up off the street and taken in cars to unknown destinations. Their 'clients' are men who want to remain anonymous and who are sexually aroused by the illegal nature of buying a woman for sex off the street (see for example, Hoigard and Finstad 1992; Pyett, Warr and Pope 1999). The AGSPAG's psychological profile of men who use street prosti-tuted women, also reported that a specific power dichotomy exists in street prostitution negotiations. Their research showed that the primary reasons men use street prostitution include 'the power to request specific sexual acts, the thrill of sex with a variety of women, the ability to have sex with specific types of women, and the thrill and danger of illicit sex' (2002, p. 41). As well there is evidence that men who buy street prostituted women are more violent than men who use other forms of prostitution.

Another criticism I would make against the AGSPAG's harm minimisation strategy is that tolerance areas and 'street worker' centres do not eliminate the exploitation of children in the street-trade. The AGSPAG acknowledges that 'Child street sex work is unacceptable and should not be permitted in any circumstances' (2002, p. 10). In its *Final Report* it recommends that police should follow established protocols for street child prostitution 'and notify the Department of Human Services Child Protection and Care Unit' (2002, p. 10). If these processes are already in place, why are significant numbers of children still being prostituted on St Kilda's streets?

While official statistics claim that there is minimal child street prostitution, health workers in the area of St Kilda maintain that three out of 10 of those prostituted on the streets are under-age (Victoria 2001, p. 640). If child prostitution is not tolerated in St Kilda, these children and their buyers will simply move into adjacent suburbs where street prostitution will be less policed. There is already evidence that young people are engaging in prostitution in Melbourne's CBD. As most activity is generally covert, again the exact numbers are difficult to determine (Resourcing Health and Education 2003, p. 1). The AGSPAG's recommendations do nothing to address the question of why children are prostituted on the streets, nor does it eliminate male demand for children for sex.

There is also no recognition by the AGSPAG that its harm minimisation approach takes public space away from women and children not in prostitution. The AGSPAG itself found extensive evidence of buyers and sex tourists harassing women who live or work in St Kilda. Residents are angry that these men 'often proposition women and children walking in their own streets' (2002, p. 41). According to the AGSPAG's findings, the 'sex tourists' who travel into St Kilda from neighbouring suburbs to harass prostituted women, do not distinguish between them and other women they encounter in the area (2002, p. 49). International studies have described how those who are called 'sex tourist', get excited at the mere contemplation of buying a woman like a commodity (see Hoigard and Finstad 1992).

The Government in the past has made some attempts to curtail sex tourism in St Kilda. But penalties for gutter crawling which were introduced in 2001 have not deterred this overt display of harassment and hostility towards women in the area. The violent behaviour of male sex tourists, who prowl the streets, exercising their power over women through physical and verbal abuse, will only intensify as St Kilda becomes a sex tourist centre. Furthermore it is inevitable that more and more drug dealers and criminals will be drawn into the area, further encroaching on people's ability to use public space. As suggested above, those involved in street prostitution are already an established market for drug dealers. Currently substance abuse is a critical social problem within Victoria, and the Government and health professionals are grappling to deal adequately with the expansion of the drug industry. It is unlikely that the City of Port Phillip, with its current limited resources, would be able to contain further drug use or police the drug trade. If the AGSPAG's proposals are introduced, St Kilda is likely to become ghettoised within Melbourne as an area of sex and drugs.

As I have argued throughout, the AGSPAG's harm minimisation strategy is the only 'realistic response' to St Kilda's street prostitution given that the State Government accepts the commodification of women for sex. It must be seen to be able to contain and control the more overtly unpleasant aspects of the industry to ease public criticism about its failure to prevent the industry impact on community living. An alternative and a feasible solution to street prostitution was put forward by the Sacred Heart Mission. It sees the solution as beginning with Government funding for crisis accommodation, mental health services and drug rehabilitation (Jacaranda 2004, p. 3).

The 2003 Victorian state election forestalled the decision on street prostitution when residents who would have been affected if tolerance zones were created protested strongly at having them located in their neighbourhood. Media reports claimed the Government was heading off a potentially powerful community backlash in the lead up to the state election later that year

(Minchin 2003, p. 5). In contrast to Labor, the then Opposition Leader, Denis Napthine, advocated a 'zero tolerance approach'. At the same time the Port Phillip Council withdrew its endorsement of the four sites in St Kilda that had been nominated as tolerance zones. Both the Government and the Council are reported as saying that they had not given up the strategy, 'but that the location of the designated areas needed more research approach' (Minchin 2003, p. 5).

The newly elected Labor Government introduced further stop-gap measures to quell the community concern over street prostitution. Police were given new powers to 'at their discretion' issue a fine of A$100 for sex tourists that act offensively, that is verbally or physically harass, either prostituted women or the general public. Hulls stressed that 'the fines would not punish well-behaved customers of street prostitution'. In a leap of logic Hulls concluded that his statement 'should not be interpreted as condoning or legalising prostitution' (Silkstone 2004, p. 9). The Government at the same time set up specialist sessions at the Melbourne Magistrates' Court for street prostitution and related charges such as addiction abuse. The women charged were to be supported by health and welfare workers with the ultimate aim of rehabilitating them as opposed to prison sentences (Gray 2003, p. 7). As successive State Governments have continuously failed to meet their responsibility to provide exit programs for prostituted women, this new measure is meaningless.

The State's refusal to address the demand for prostitution means that street prostitution, although illegal, continues to flourish relatively unopposed. And as the Government remains committed to its harm minimisation approach to prostitution, the idea of some type of red light district is again being considered. By mid-2004, an Editorial in *The Age* reported that welfare agencies in St Kilda had confirmed violent incidents against street prostituted women were escalating. The violence culminated in the murder of Grace Illardi, the second woman murdered within two years ('Time for a rethink on street soliciting' 2004, p. 2).

Conclusion

Victoria's actual experience of prostitution shows clearly that successive State Governments' continued reliance on regulation – and legalisation – to control prostitution, is inherently flawed. Sexually explicit entertainment which differs little from prostitution, illegal brothel prostitution, trafficking for sexual slavery, child prostitution and the street prostitution trade remain relatively unregulated despite various desperate legislative attempts to reverse this situation. As municipal councils and police attempted to grapple with the increasing crime surrounding prostitution, they exposed that criminal activities were occurring across the spectrum of the State's industry, in both the legal and the unregulated sectors. But as market forces now shape how prostitution operates within Victoria, the Government is confronted with the reality that no legislative framework can ever contain its growth, or dictate how and under what circumstances prostitution occurs.

Despite the Government's continued efforts to bring the tabletop dancing trade under a stricter regulatory regime, it still mainly operates on the margins of legalised prostitution. But even defining what constitutes 'legitimate' prostitution and what constitutes illegal prostitution activities is a problem. Victoria's legislators are unable to foresee the diverse and innovative ways sex entrepreneurs market women and abuse women caught up in a state-tolerated system of sexual exploitation. Every strategy that the Government has put in place to regulate prostitution has failed. Local planning schemes are ineffective because criminal activity is made invisible through legal operations. Sex trafficking is burgeoning as Victoria's legal brothels warehouse prostituted women who are then trafficked between legal and illegal brothels' operations, both within Victoria and to other Australian States and Territories. Victoria's tolerance of prostitution means that Australia is now recognised as a destination country by traffickers, international governments and buyers alike. No regulation can alter this reality. Nor, as we have seen, can regulation and legalisation that does not address the demand for prostitution, eliminate street prostitution. In this instance even the Government is forced to admit that it is left with an insoluble problem. Indeed Amsterdam's city authorities are currently being compelled to rethink their pro-sex policies. By the end of 2006 one-third of the city's red light districts are to be closed because of the high level of criminal involvement in the area's sex trade (Castle 2006, p.1).

Irrespective of the fact that over two decades of evidence that legalising prostitution has not delivered control of the industry to the Government, it remains philosophically committed to maintaining its legalisation regime. Successive State Governments have argued that they must come at the problem from a value-neutral perspective, indeed championing their non-moralistic stance. They continue in their belief that the debate around prostitution must be couched as a struggle between conservatives and progressives, ignoring the human rights perspective that recognises that prostitution is violence against women and an abuse of their civil and human rights. As such the Government has no option but to continue to attempt to put in place some workable legislative framework or return to prohibition. In the next chapters I examine the legal prostitution industry where prostitution is regulated as work and occupational health and safety standards apply. Here I test the claim made by the Government and pro-prostitution advocates that the regulated sector of the prostitution industry provides the optimal conditions for the health and safety of prostituted women.

CHAPTER SIX

Victoria's 'Safe Sex Agenda': Occupational Health and Safety for the Sex Industry

No action will stabilize the sex industry more than legitimating prostitution through the health care system. If medical personnel are called upon to monitor women in prostitution, as part of 'occupational health safety', we will have no hope of eradicating the industry. Furthermore from a health perspective alone, it is inconceivable that medicalization of women in the industry will reduce infection and injury without concomitant medicalization of the male buyers. Thus medicalization, which is rightly viewed as a consumer protection for men rather than as a real protection for women, ultimately protects neither women nor men.

JANICE RAYMOND, CO-EXECUTIVE DIRECTOR FOR THE COALITION AGAINST TRAFFICKING IN WOMEN INTERNATIONAL (1998B, P. 5).

Introduction

Much of the pro-prostitution literature on the harms of prostitution begins with the premise that a regulated industry has the greatest potential to safeguard the health and wellbeing of those within the industry.[1] Ine Vanwesenbeeck in discussing prostitution in the Netherlands, for example, has argued that some form of regulation is 'needed to contest the power and

---

1. I have discussed this point more extensively in Chapter One.

dominance of employers over women, which remains invisible because of the illegality of their business' (1994, p. 157). Victorian Governments too, have time and again taken this position. One of the principal objectives of the *Prostitution Control Act 1994* is 'to maximise the protection of prostitutes from violence and exploitation' (s. 4 [f]). In practice, however, harmful and discriminatory practices within Victoria's legal industry not only exist, but are indeed perpetuated through the State's regulation of sex businesses, in particular health regulation.

Occupational Health and Safety (OHS) is a useful lens for looking at prostitution. OHS is an area of industrial relations that encompasses the fundamental right of employees not to have their health put at risk through the normal requirements of their work. The application of OHS to legal prostitution would eliminate the harms and hazards of the 'job'. I question whether OHS delivers the protection it promises.

The legislation and regulation that at present influences how OHS is implemented for Victoria's licensed brothels and legalised escort work is in part reflective of the State's overall approach to OHS. This is informed by both international human rights' conventions and feminist theory and practice on women's workplace equality. These are responsive to the health risks for marginalised workers as well as those in the mainstream workforce. The definition of occupational health and safety includes mental as well as physical wellness. However I argue that overall the Victorian Government prioritises the public's *sexual health* in its OHS policy on prostitution thus minimising the risks to prostituted women resulting from everyday 'work' practices and the prostitution 'work' environment. Moreover as I will discuss further, supposedly more responsive OHS models towards holistic health protection proposed by Australian prostitutes' rights organisations are similarly flawed.

Industrial relations, human rights and OHS

Prostituted women working in Victoria's licensed brothels and as escort workers have the status of legitimate workers. This standing gives them access to the same entitlements under Australia's industrial relations system as workers in other industries. The Scarlet Alliance, the national body for Australian prostitutes' rights organisations, has indeed argued this point in its OHS *Best Practice* manual for 'workers' in the industry. As it states, the basic right of all workers to health and safety applies 'no matter what industry they work in' including 'all those in the sex industry' (Elder c.2000, p. 1).

Australian industrial relations are commonly equated with employment relations and labour stability. They affect how jobs are designed, valued and rewarded, as well as how conditions in the work environment are negotiated (Dufty and Fells 1989, p. xii; Deery 1991, pp. 3–30). In addition industrial relations entail a human rights dimension which is concerned specifically with the rights of workers or employees. This includes the promise of minimum labour standards and conditions.[2] In theory this makes them particularly useful for marginal groups such as those involved in prostitution, although as I have explained, all workers' rights are being seriously diminished under Australia's current deregulated industrial relations system (see pp. 157–160).

Placing prostitution within an international industrial rights framework

The International Labour Organisation (ILO) is the major body providing a broad framework for international labour standards that specifically address injustice, hardship and privation within the workplace (Deery 1991, p. 81; Leary 1995, pp. 580–619).

---

2. For an elaboration of this point and some excellent critiques of Australian industrial relations see the work of Braham Dabscheck 1995, 1998.

Its 1998 *Declaration on Fundamental Principles and Rights at Work* is exceptionally comprehensive. The Declaration refers to a series of basic legal rights, which take account of the right to join a union; wage rates (either minimum wage, award rates, or rates as per an Enterprise Agreement); protection against discrimination (because of sex, sexual orientation, disability, marital status, career status, pregnancy, age, physical features, religion, political beliefs, membership of trade union); protection from sexual harassment, workers compensation and OHS (Clause 2[a][b][c][d]).

The ILO Declaration has been a powerful impetus for reform, because it contains a pledge that all member states are to respect, promote and realise the principles set out in the Declaration. Importantly it recognises that 'members of the ILO, even if it has not ratified the conventions in question, have an obligation to respect "in good faith and in accordance with the conventions, the principles concerning the fundamental rights which are subject to those conventions"' (Hansen 2002, p. 1).[3] The Australian Federal Government, as a signatory to 57 of the ILO's 184 binding conventions has established a sound constitutional basis for legislation that sustains a fair and equitable system of employment (International Labour Organisation 1996). In line with this commitment individual States and Territories have established legal and administrative frameworks specifically designed to establish and implement effective preventative and protective policies and programs within the workplace. Women working within Victoria's legal prostitution sector – as opposed to women who are prostituted in illegal brothels or in street prostitution – have access to these processes.

---

3. In order to ensure the implementation of these rights, 'states that have not ratified the core conventions, will be asked to submit reports on progress made in implementing the principles enshrined in them' (Hansen 2002, p. 1).

OHS in Victoria has its foundations in the international standards set out in *The Occupational Safety and Health Convention 1981*. This Convention, which promotes the establishment of safe and healthy working conditions, recognises both a state role and employer responsibility in ameliorating harmful work practices. What is and what is not harmful ideally is defined through consultation with workers. As Article 4 of the Convention states:

> Each member [State], shall in the light of national conditions and practice, and in consultation with the most representative organisations of employers and workers, formulate, implement and periodically review a coherent national policy on occupational safety, occupational health and the working environment.

The Convention's overall aim is to prevent accidents and injury to health arising out of work by minimising 'the causes of hazards inherent in the working environment' (1981, Article 4).

In Australia, and in turn in Victoria, these guiding principles have become operational through the *Federal Occupational Health and Safety Act 1985* with major parallel statutes introduced by State and Territory Governments.[4] The principal Victorian *Occupational Health and Safety Act* came into force in 1985,[5] with a new Act in 2004. In reviewing Australia's industrial relations laws, Petzall et al. explain how the principal OHS Act of each State and Territory keeps faith with the 1981 UN Convention by imposing 'a primary duty of care placed on employers to provide a safe system of work' (2002, p. 193). The Act allows for sanctions including prosecution for employers who fail to meet their responsibilities. The various Acts also recognise

---

4. Australia in 2006 had not ratified the Convention. However as a member state it is morally, if not legally bound, to implement the principles outlined in the Convention in accordance with its constitutional processes.

5. Amendments to the 1985 Act were introduced and became effective in 1990, 1992, 1993, 1996 and 1997.

the central role that should be played by workers in developing OHS guidelines. The legislations call for the creation of mechanisms in the workplace (specifically health and safety representatives and committees, and their rights and functions) for the resolution of issues, and protection for both workers and those representing them.

Thus by the beginning of the twenty-first century the occupational health and safety of Australian workers is, in theory, guaranteed through employer responsibility to facilitate a safe working environment that takes account of the nature of individual work experiences, and in particular, is responsive to how workers themselves define occupational health and safety issues. According to the Victorian WorkCover Authority (VWA), the major statutory body responsible for the State's workplace relations 'The duty of employers to consult employees is one of the most significant changes introduced by the OHS Act 2004' (Victorian WorkCover Authority 2006). Codes of practice developed through consultation with workers provide practical guidelines that reflect various work-related risks that workers face according to the specific type of work they do, as well as a number of options for eliminating harm from the workplace. While codes of practice are not themselves legally binding, they provide regulatory authorities with a standard to measure whether employers are meeting OHS responsibilities.

Making OHS applicable to the prostitution trade

Making codes of practice specific to work experiences of specific labour forces potentially offers women working in Victoria's legal prostitution industry a practical means of addressing the harms that are germane to prostitution. The work practices and work environment related to legalised prostitution find few parallels in other forms of legitimised work, as I will explain further in the following chapter. However the establishment of comprehensive

OHS codes and guidelines for the State's licensed brothels and escort agencies has been difficult. This is firstly because of the marginalisation of all women workers in the area of OHS. This problem was exacerbated in the 1990s by the ascendancy of enterprise bargaining in the labour market and became institutionalised in the Liberal Federal Government's drastic changes to Australia's industrial relations laws in 2006. According to Jenny Macklin, the Labor Deputy Opposition Leader, 'We already have a situation in Australia where women are paid less than men. When it comes to individual contracts, women are even more disadvantaged than men on individual contracts . . . The vast majority of women working casual or part-time don't have a strong position of negotiation' (Macklin 2005).[6]

In addition to a lack of bargaining power for women, Australia's highly sex segregated workforce further limits women's ability to have their right to workplace equality recognised. This applies specifically to the legalised prostitution industry, where women make up 90 per cent of the labour force (Banach and Metzenrath 2000, p. 16). Historically occupational segregation has seen a lack of priority given to women's workplace health and safety issues (see Forastieri 2000; Musolino 2001). The female workforce in the past was concentrated in a narrow band of generally low paid occupations in light manufacturing (such as food processing and the making of clothes), clerical and other office work, retailing, and other service areas such as nursing. OHS research and policy debate, however, has been fixed on industry, that is on male-dominated occupations, with OHS identified hazards 'based on male populations and injuries reflecting their work experiences' (Quinlan 1991, p. 107). Legal

---

6. As I have suggested previously the historic illegality and the ongoing fragmentation of the prostitution trade means that prostituted women have no collective power. In addition most women do not see prostitution as a viable career option.

academic, Victor Gleeson, says that this bias has meant that traditional style of OHS legislation was:

> Directed mainly to guarding employees against equipment that cuts, crushes and burns . . . [and covered] other matters relating to OHS such as ventilation and safe methods of exit that can have relevance to the industry (1992, p. 2).

In this context women's work was either not acknowledged or it was considered to be hazard free.

Feminist influence on OHS legislation

This marginalisation of women's health and safety issues has been critically debated by Australian feminists for over two decades. The 1990 Australian National Health Safety Commission, which formulated a national approach to women's OHS, found women workers 'identified as particularly disadvantaged by out-moded workforce structures, workplace arrangements and attitudes' (1990, pp. 1–2). Jenni Nearie is a former director of Worksafe Australia, a national coordinating body for the various administrative arms of work related statutory bodies like the VWA. In her report on the Commission's work, Nearie stated that women workers still 'tended to be employed in small businesses in areas with limited or no award coverage . . . or jobs not subject to regulation such as piecework and outwork' (1990, p. 3). Other critics of legal regulation of the workplace found that where women were employed in larger industries they were in all-female or female dominated workplaces and therefore had difficulty having work-related harms recognised as OHS issues (Hunter 1995, p. 233).

As a response to the array of ongoing concerns about the Australian workplace's failure to address women's OHS needs, Worksafe Australia established a Women's Advisory Committee as well as setting up a national inquiry into Equal Opportunity and Equal Status for Women in Australia. These initiatives attempted to place risks to women's health resulting from workplace conditions as pivotal to OHS discourse (Blackmur et al. 1993, pp. 3–5). However at the beginning of the twenty-first century, Renata Musolino, the OHS Information Officer of the Victorian Trades Hall Council (VTHC), stressed that women's health and safety was still not being adequately addressed in female-dominated workplaces. Musolino, in an address to the VTHC Occupational Health and Safety Representatives Conference in Melbourne in 2002, disclosed that still 'Very little is known about the effects of work on women's health and safety specifically. This is despite the fact that about half of the workforce in Australia is made up of women' (2002, p. 27).

A further problem with trying to address the health and safety concerns of the female labour force is that introducing women's concerns into dialogues around OHS does not necessarily benefit women. As contemporary feminist critiques of OHS policy have pointed out, work-related health issues were frequently viewed as being related to the specificity of being a woman rather than to working practices or a work environment. The work of Karen Messing, Katherine Lippel, Diane Demers and Donna Mergler (2000), for example, support this view. In their research which focused on physical job demands, occupational illness and sex differences in the workforce, they found that the common official approaches to women's work-related health issues were based on the biomedical model. As the authors explain, 'Although research shows that the sexual division of labour is determined by multiple social, economic, and political forces, day-to-day struggles of women for safe and equal integration in the workplace confront discourse on biological differences' (2000, p. 32). This narrow approach has meant that there is reluctance by employers to adapt the workplace to women's needs or compensate them for their workplace injury.

In the international sphere these limitations to creating a safe and healthy work environment for women are being acknowledged and replaced with comprehensive strategies that take account of the full dimensions of work-related health issues. Valentina Forastieri, an ILO spokesperson on gender issues, promotes the importance of this reappraisal of women's OHS needs in relation to Safe Work, a global program on safety, health and work. Forastieri calls for a re-evaluation of the traditional bio-medical model, which she maintains, in a similar vein to Messing and her colleagues, 'concentrates it[s] attention on . . . trying to determine the causes of the pathology on an individual basis, and using curative methods to control it' (2000, p. 15). Forastieri's main criticism of the approach is that 'little attention is given to prevention and to those environmental and social factors that interact with the biological causes of the ill-health of groups or populations' (2000, p. 15). Safe Work, in contrast, aims to promote 'an integrated multi-disciplinary approach which takes into account the physical, mental and social well-being of men and women workers' (2000, p. 1).

Among workers who should be given a special focus in the development of national preventative action programmes, Forastieri includes those:

> [W]ho may be in a vulnerable situation due to gender or age (such as women workers and elder workers); or who lack fundamental social and health protection. This latter group takes in informal sector workers, agricultural workers, migrant workers and child labourers' (2000, p. 1).

In theory prostituted women in the legal system fit within these categories as both women and as 'workers' in the informal sector, and often as migrants. However one of the more groundbreaking aspects of Safe Work's program is that it stresses that working conditions and the working environment should be adapted to fit the physical and mental capacity of all workers. This contrasts with the traditional approach, demanding that workers modify their behaviour while dangerous work practices remain intact. This last point is critical when evaluating whether the application of health and safety can ameliorate the harms of prostitution. In practice, as I later demonstrate, OHS codes for the prostitution industry make clear that prostituted women must adapt their behaviour, for example, to minimise the violence in prostitution as such violence is acknowledged as an occupational health risk within the prostitution work environment. This adaptive approach is inevitable as prostitution work practices and the prostitution work environment are inherently harmful, thus risks to women's health and safety cannot be eliminated.

Self-regulation versus government control

In general the VWA, by the mid-1990s, considered that OHS regulations, as determined through the 1985 OHS Act and its subsequent amendments, should be designed to move beyond the traditional industry-based OHS approaches in the workplace.[7] The VWA argues that the most relevant clauses within the OHS Act are the provision for research into occupational health and safety issues (*Occupational Health and Safety Act 1985*, s. 8[1])[j]); the function of health and safety representatives and their committees, for example, reviewing information related to the health of employees (1985, s. 32[2][a][ii]); and in general duties imposed by the Act, for example, for employers to monitor the health of employees (1985, s. 21[4][a]). Thus the Authority's intention is that regulation should reflect a more worker-orientated understanding of workplace harm. This more inclusive

---

7. This interpretation takes account of the amendments to the original *Occupational Health and Safety Act 1985* and *Industrial Relations Act 1996* which brought together the various consultative bodies that administered the Act into one body, the VWA.

conceptualisation of OHS inevitably has created a degree of legitimacy to ongoing demands by prostitutes' rights organisations for safe and healthy workplaces.

By 1990 the Prostitutes' Collective of Victoria (PCV) was promoting itself as a vehicle through which 'people who worked in the sex industry [could] have a say in their working environment and have the opportunity to make unsafe work unnecessary' (Prostitutes' Collective of Victoria 1990a, p. 15). The PCV's Women's Project for 1990 exemplified this commitment. Its aim was to educate prostituted women on the adoption of practical measures to achieve their work entitlements. They believed that 'attaining rights . . . as a sex worker may be as simple as accessing a non-discriminatory health service (or complaining about bad treatment) or as complex as working on the Code of Practice for health and safety standards in parlours' (1990a, p. 15). Its submission to the Health Department's Code of Practice's Working Party, responsible for formulating the first code of practice for licensed brothels – *The Health (Brothel) Regulations 1990* – was among its early initiatives to have 'workplace harm' laws reflect the experience of those within the industry. The PCV's submission, for example, stressed the need to move beyond traditional notions of OHS, and examine the 'psychological and emotional aspects of working [in prostitution] which needed to be brought to the attention of brothel managers' (1990a, p. 15).

The PCV throughout the 1990s, continued in its attempt to provide input into the formulation of codes for the legal prostitution sector. It criticised the 1990 regulations for its failure to acknowledge harms that were specific to the industry. In its *Hussies Handbook* (c.1995), a self-help health and safety booklet, it provided a list of various abuses that women had identified as 'workplace' harms. These included mandatory health checks, abusive communication, intimidation or bullying, sexual harassment and stalking, rape and sexual assault, pregnancy from rape, and mental stress (Prostitutes' Collective of Victoria c.1995, p. 4). This supposed failure of the Government to respond to the OHS requirements of those in the industry provided the PCV with grounds to argue for self-regulation. However the Government has responded by claiming that as the prostitution industry consists of a myriad of legal and illegal activities, no one organisation has the capacity to coordinate OHS at such a broad level.

When the Government released its 2001 *Regulatory Impact Statement* on new brothel health regulations, it defended its position as the major regulator of the State's prostitution industry. It began by highlighting how the industry's workforce was now highly segmented consisting of both legal and illegal sectors and that it took in brothel workers, escort workers, tabletop dancers, bondage and discipline centres and street workers (Victoria 2001a, p. 64). Subsequently it had little problem arguing that as 'there is no strong association in the sex worker industry that could deal with issues of sex worker health and brothel cleanliness as well as provide information on STIs, this [self-regulation] is not an appropriate option' (2001, p. 64).

The Prostitutes' Collective's failure to unionise in the mid-1990s undoubtedly strengthened the Government's position. The reality was that most of the women involved in prostitution did not want to categorise themselves as 'sex workers' as many saw themselves as transient 'workers' or were involved in illicit drug use. There was the further problem that as most brothel owners classified prostituted women as independent contractors it was difficult for those within the industry to present a united front in demanding appropriate working conditions.[8] More importantly prostituted women still had to establish a legitimate

---

8. I have discussed these problems more extensively in Chapter Four.

employer-employee relationship before industrial rights could become the employer's responsibility.

Inevitably the fragmented nature of the prostitution trade meant that there were few avenues for the development of ethical codes for the trade or mechanisms to encourage compliance.[9] By default the State became the principle creator of OHS standards for the prostitution industry. As suggested previously the State's priorities and their methods of ensuring compliance offers minimal protection for prostituted women.

Victoria's OHS prostitution strategies

The Health (Brothel) Regulations 1990 were produced as part of the Government's legislative response to Victoria's 1985 *Inquiry into Prostitution* which provided the foundations for the State's contemporary prostitution legislation (Victoria 2001a, p. 54). While the Inquiry's focus was on the workability, or otherwise, of existing legislation and town planning practices, the Government's mandate to address the 'social, legal and health aspects of prostitution – in all its forms' (Victoria 1985a, p. 11) meant that the State's lawmakers were to consider the health and safety of prostituted women.

The 1994 *Prostitution Control Act*, the existing institutional framework regulating Victoria's prostitution industry, exhibits a similar concern for the health and safety of prostituted women, although clearly within a harm minimisation framework. The main objectives of the Act included maximising 'the protection of prostitutes and their clients from health risks' (*Prostitution Control Act 1994*, s. 1[b]) and, as suggested above, 'the protection of prostitutes from violence and exploitation' (idem, s. 4[g]). Under the auspices of the Act the Prostitution Control Board is given an educative role to provide information about the dangers

---

9. For further analyses of problems related to the industrial aspects of the prostitution industry from a legal perspective see Gleeson 1992, pp. 183–189.

inherent in prostitution which covered risks to women's health (Victoria 1994a, p. 1455). The *Prostitution Control (Amendment) Act 1999* extended the objects of the original 1994 Act, to specifically include the promotion of 'the welfare and occupational health and safety of prostitutes' and 'to ensure that brothels are accessible to inspectors, law enforcement officers, health workers and service providers' (*Prostitution Control Act 1994*, s. 4[g] amended by No. 44/1999, s. 6[2]).

In a similar way to mainstream work environments, OHS for the prostitution industry is implemented through specific regulations, codes and guidelines. As I indicated, these are produced solely by the State and monitored by Victorian health authorities. The Victorian Department of Human Services' *Health (Infectious Diseases) Regulations 2001*, which incorporates the 1990 *Health (Brothels) Regulations*, are the main standards adopted by State agencies to implement the various requirements of Victoria's prostitution legislation. While the Department listed the PCV among its 'peak [consulting] bodies' (Victoria 2001a, p. 67), the regulations reveal that public policy on health and safety for the industry is unambiguously designed to create a safe sex culture for the general public by minimising the danger from sexually transmitted infections (STIs). This raises the question of whether Victorian lawmakers have ever been overly concerned with the health and safety of women in prostitution.

STIs, AIDS and public health

STIs are infectious diseases spread from person to person through direct body contact or contact with infected body fluids. The term is used to describe any disease acquired primarily through sexual contact. Sexually transmitted infections include syphilis, human papillomavirus, chlamydia, genital warts, gonorrhoea, trichomoniasis, hepatitis B, herpes and HIV. Safe sex is about reducing the risks of transmission of such diseases.

The Victorian 2001 brothel regulations inevitably address such potential risks as the use and storage of condoms; the right of prostituted women to refuse service to men suspected of STIs; inappropriate use of medical evidence of STIs provision of information for safe sex in brothels; cleanliness and inspection and interviews by health officers and local government officers (2001, div. 4).

As I showed in my analysis of the role of the Prostitutes' Collective of Victoria in containing HIV/AIDS, the link between the prostitution industry, sexually transmitted infections and public health is a continuing theme in the public debate around the AIDS crisis and associated treatises on STIs. The impact of STIs for women in prostitution is acknowledged in this context, but dialogue is firmly biased towards the role of prostituted women in containing what increasingly came to be perceived as a public health emergency. This influence was apparent at a Government level as well as stemming from prostitutes' rights and AIDS organisations.

The 1991 Legal Working Party of the Intergovernmental Party on AIDS was critical in establishing a role for State Governments to minimise the spread of STIs and HIV within the prostitution industry. The Working Party maintained that prostitution businesses were a high-risk area for HIV infections (Intergovernmental Committee on AIDS 1991, p. 49). In its analysis of how or whether the law should regulate the industry to contain the spread of HIV, it made the case that laws regulating and/or penalising prostitution impeded public health programs by driving people at risk of infection underground. The Working Party's alternative recommendation was that legally binding rules for safe sex practices should be 'enacted at a state and territory level . . . for premises where sex workers are employed' (1991, p. 49). Managers would be required 'to supply free condoms and sexual health educational material including, where appropriate, translations which related to the predominant ethnicity of clients and workers' (1991, p. 49).

This link between containing STIs among prostituted women and protecting the public's sexual health is more immediately apparent in the State's 2001 *Health (Infectious Diseases) Regulations*. The sole purpose of the regulations is to 'protect public health by containing the spread of infectious diseases, particularly STIs in brothels' (Victoria 2001a, p. 56). The Government impact statement prepared prior to the 2001 regulations clearly made the point that the reworking of the 1990 laws is a direct response to 'the high level of public concern regarding infectious disease control'. Clauses relating to brothels merely represent 'one part of the total package to prevent and minimise the spread of infectious diseases in various settings', (2001a, p. 1) thus meeting the Government's legislative responsibility to contain STIs. Six of the nine health regulations relating to prostitution deal exclusively with brothel owners' responsibilities to ensure safe sex is practised on their premises and standards of cleanliness are maintained.

In addition to institutional controls, health promotions have given prominence for funding for the prostitution industry to safe sex practices.[10] In keeping with Victoria's harm minimisation approach, grants are provided mainly for industry sponsored health promotions that circulate information on the supply and use of condoms, dental dams[11] and gloves. The PCV in its *Hussies Handbook*, for example, maintains that 'Responsible safe sex practices by sex workers has helped to keep the rate of STDs in the sex industry low compared with the rest of the community' (Prostitutes' Collective of Victoria c.1995, p. 15).

---

10. See Chapter Three for more detail of these grants.
11. Dental dams are small sheets of latex that are placed over the anus or other genitalia to form a barrier against infection spreading between these parts of the body and the mouth.

In a similar way the OHS strategies developed by Resourcing Health and Education for the Sex Industry (RHED), the PCV's successor, are concentrated on narrow concerns like 'blood borne viruses such as HIV and Hepatitis' and 'sexual health screening'. RHED also promotes the fact that it is a primary provider of free needles and syringes, condoms and lubricants (RHED 2003, p. 1).

The Victorian Government's safe sex agenda for prostitution has gained credibility with reported high success rates in containing the spread of STIs within the State's legal prostitution industry. The Government's 2001 health regulations impact statement emphasised that the prostitution industry's promotion of 100 per cent condom use, accounts for Australia's very low rates of infection with HIV, and the AIDS virus, compared with many other parts of the world (Victoria 2001a, p. 56). The impact statement draws on research conducted by Victoria's La Trobe University's Centre for Sexual Health. Pyett et al. for example, argue that in Victoria's legal brothels prostituted women engaged in sexual practices that involved little risk of AIDS or other STIs. The researchers found that 'The relative lack of organizational obstacles to safe practices for prostitutes working in legalized brothels in Victoria . . . favours consistent condom use with clients and discourages anal sex' (Pyett et al. 1996a, p. 92). Included among the factors they saw as contributing to this positive result were:

> State funding and support for a sex worker organization which promotes safer sexual practices; brothel managers allowing the sex worker organization to conduct education programmes in the brothels; brothel managers providing condoms and lubricant for workers; and legislation which exempts prostitutes working in legal brothels from legal sanctions (1996a, p. 92).

The extent to which such research should justify the Government's emphasis on safe sex should be challenged. In their study, Pyett et al. reveal that, at a minimum, 20 per cent of women working in Victoria's legal brothels acknowledge having STIs while in prostitution (Pyett et al. 1996a, p. 89 and p. 91). Moreover the researchers also pointed out the limitations of analysis that is based solely on voluntary reporting. A major problem they note is the social stigma that is attached to AIDS being associated with prostitution, which can lead to some distortions that include the 'over-reporting of safe sex practices such as the frequency of condom use, and underreporting of the more negative aspects of prostitution like STIs' (1996a, p. 87).

Despite the limitations of current research on the prevalence of STIs among prostituted women, the Victorian Government in its 2006 Regulatory Impact Statement on the *Proposed Prostitution Control Regulations* continues to stress the importance of regulation of the industry to protect public health (2006, pp. 3, 16). Contradictorily it did put the caveat that the evidence upon which its position was based was 'not necessarily conclusive' (2006, p. 16). The Government does maintain that 'a sexually transmitted infection is greater in an unregulated environment than an environment where specific STD controls exist' (2006, p. 20). This fact, however, does not negate the reality that the health risk for both prostituted women and the wider public remains considerable. The serious flaws in the harm minimisation approach become obvious in the case of mandatory testing, which I discuss below.

The safe sex focus is likely to continue to dominate OHS policy around Victoria's prostitution industry because it has significant encouragement at a regional as well as at an international level as suggested in Chapter One. At the Sixth International Congress on AIDS in Asia and the Pacific (ICAAP) held in Melbourne in 2001, Sharon Burrow, President of the

Australian Council of Trade Unions (ACTU), stressed the connection between the fight against HIV and AIDS in the Asia-Pacific region with the struggle for human rights and workers' rights, which she maintained must include those 'working' in prostitution (Sahdev 2002, p. 1). The Conference especially sought participation from prostitutes' rights organisations in the region. 'It is vital', Burrow said, 'that these women are seen as being engaged in work and therefore have the same rights as other workers to organise and expect that their right to health and safety at work are respected' (2002, p. 1). The point ignored in these dialogues is that it is the male buyers who are the main transmitters of STIs, not prostituted women. Any strategy that pretends to address the harms of prostitution but does not take account of this reality will ultimately fail to protect women.

Men's invisibility in safe sex agendas

There are an increasing number of critics who challenge the assumption that public health programs are beneficial to prostituted women. Psychologist Melissa Farley, in collaboration with Vanessa Kelly, undertook a thorough analysis of the topic. Their chief finding was that 'Although at first glance, the public health attention to the risk of HIV infection includes the prostituted woman herself; on closer inspection, it becomes apparent that the overarching concern is for the health of the customer to decrease his exposure to disease' (2000, p. 2). In critically reviewing the medical and social sciences around prostitution, Farley and Kelly thus exposed the over emphasis on HIV/AIDS while minimal attention was given to the intrinsic harm of prostitution. As they found:

> Much of what has been written about in prostitution in the medical and social sciences fails to address the sexual violence and psychological harm, which both precede and are intrinsic to pros-

titution . . . instead there has been an almost exclusive focus on sexually transmitted disease (STD), especially the immuno-deficiency virus (HIV) . . . Although HIV has certainly created a public health crisis, the violence and human rights violations in prostitution have also resulted in health crises for those prostituted (2000, p. 2).

Farley and Kelly's discourse becomes immediately relevant when evaluating the various procedures put in place for creating a safe sex culture within Victoria's prostitution industry. The Victorian experience demonstrates that in practice safe sex strategies, whether facilitated through an institutional framework or educative processes normalise prostitution by categorising it as work rather than violence, albeit at times hazardous work. Further, the Government's safe sex model ignores the male user in prostitution by placing the responsibility for safe sex on the prostituted woman, thus blaming the victim.

Imagine a worker whose employer is not responsible for harms and accidents in the workplace. Nurses receive compensation and often counselling if a patient passes on an illness whether intentionally or unintentionally. The Australian Medical Association stipulates that 'Appropriate insurance cover must be available to all health care professionals, in both the public and private sectors, who are at risk of exposure to these infections. Adequate compensation and counselling must be provided for those who may contract such infections in the course of their work' (2004, p. 6). As I will explain further, the most disconcerting aspect of the Government's targeting of prostituted women as 'purveyors of disease' is that male 'customers' are among the highest risk group for and STIs.

A further problem with the Government's approach to OHS for the prostitution industry is that it equally ignores the power imbalance that exists between the prostituted woman and buyer. It assumes prostituted women are able to dictate how sex with a buyer will be conducted, which is a falsehood. Finally although STIs and HIV/AIDS are categorised as high OHS hazards within the prostitution industry, established injury management procedures for STIs are frequently as debilitating and life threatening as the contagion itself.

Mandatory testing: leaving men's sexual rights unchallenged

Mandatory testing of women in prostitution which is presumed within Victoria's prostitution legislation fundamentally penalises women and leaves unchallenged men's 'natural' right to sex. Offences under the *Prostitution Control Act 1994* provide for the registration of prostituted women and compulsory medical testing: quarterly blood tests for HIV and monthly genital swabs for STIs (1994, s. 20[2][a] i and ii). The Government ensures compliance by penalising 'prostitution service providers' who knowingly allow a woman to be prostituted, whether in a brothel or in escort work, while infected with STIs (1994, s. 19[1][a] and [b]). The prostituted person who works knowing they have an STI is penalised (1994, s. 20[1]). Both operators and the women involved can offer a defence against the charge if they can show that the woman has undergone regular health checks.

Clearly these legal strictures place the responsibility for safe sex on women, as there is no requirement for men who use women in prostitution to undergo similar testing. Moreover the underlying message is that prostituted women are the purveyors of disease: that they are 'infected' women who are a danger 'to public health', a perspective as I have suggested previously is constructed around the whore stigma.[12] Hadden Storey, a Victorian State Liberal Minister, revealed this bias, paradoxically when defending his Government's position on mandatory testing. As he put it:

---

12. I examined discourses on the 'whore' stigma in Chapter One.

The dangers to public health are significant when prostitutes infected with sexually transmissible diseases continue to work. It will be a simple matter for precautions to be taken to avoid committing this offence. As long as prostitutes receive fortnightly medical checks which show that they are free of infection, they cannot be convicted (Victoria 1994d, p. 962).

Labor parliamentarian, Donato Nardella, offers a similar view. Speaking during the passage of the *Prostitution Control (Amendment) Act 1997*, he made the point that 'We should never lose sight of the health implications [of prostitution] and the need to regulate the industry in the interests of the broader community' (Victoria 1997a, p. 1143). He justified his stance by suggesting that 'Experience in Africa, Thailand, New York City and the Caribbean shows that prostitution is a very important method of transmitting HIV/AIDS' (1997a, p. 1143).

Critics of mandatory testing

International human rights discourses on AIDS have been particularly vocal in highlighting the discriminatory and ineffective character of mandatory testing. The UN guidelines regarding HIV/AIDS and human rights have prohibited 'Coercive measures, such as mandatory screening, lack of confidentiality and segregation' as these tactics 'drive people away from preventative education and health-care services and subvert this process of behavioural change' (United Nations Programme on HIV/AIDS 1998, p. 3). Taking a similar position, the ILO, in its Code of Practice on HIV/AIDS and work, has called for 'broader legal and public policy' that is responsive to 'infected and affected' peoples (ILOAIDS 2001). But it is prostitutes' rights groups together with AIDS organisations who have been the most unyielding in their opposition to mandatory testing, a stance that I suggest however, is inconsistent with their overall promotion of a safe sex culture. Their objection to such testing is that it stigmatises prostituted women as 'diseased' and 'irresponsible' and isolates 'workers' as vectors of disease rather than their 'clients' who actually are a critical risk group (Banach and Metzenrath 2000, p. 6).

There is extensive documented evidence that HIV/AIDS is overwhelmingly transmitted via male-to-female vaginal and anal intercourse, not vice versa (Farley and Kelly 2000, p. 4). One Melbourne-based study of 4000 men who use prostituted women determined that 'clients represent a multiple risk population with respect to HIV and other STIs [and] clients are twice as likely to have had unsafe sex with twice as many people as non-client men' (Moore 1999, p. 32). Thus the spread of STIs occurs through buyers who transmit disease from one prostituted woman to another and then go back into the wider community to their wives and female/male partners. According to a 1998 study – 'Project Client Call' – 50 per cent of men who used women in prostitution in Victoria were married or in a de facto relationship (Louie et al. 1998, p. 7). However the bias that underpins Victoria's laws on mandatory testing is particularly difficult to understand in circumstances where the Victorian Government itself acknowledges this discrepancy between practice and logic. Its 2001 *Brothel Regulations Impact Statement* admits that while people in prostitution have been seen to be the 'cause of the spread of STIs . . . this is not the case' (Victoria 2001a, p. 54).

In addition to the clear discrimination that underpins mandatory testing, the process itself is ineffectual in containing STIs including AIDS. Compulsory testing for STIs ignores the three-month dormancy window for various infections (Banach and Metzenrath 2000, p. 6). So although a woman may test negatively on a particular date, and on this basis continue to be prostituted, she may still be infected with an STI or HIV/AIDS. There is the further problem of realistically policing women in prostitution to determine whether or not they are 'working' while infected.

During the passage of the *Prostitution Control (Amendment) Act 1999* through parliament, the Labor member Robert Hulls, questioned the ability of the then Liberal Government to provide 'appropriate resources to ensure that inspectors carry out inspections' (Victoria 1999a, p. 1192). Essentially there were very few inspectors to carry out AIDS and STI tests in brothels (and presumably conduct follow-ups on escort workers), and most of these worked on a part-time base. However subsequently testing has become even less frequent because the 2000 *Brothel Health Regulations* reduced the State's responsibility to inspect brothels from once every three months to once a year (Victoria 2001a, p. 53). These circumstances mean that safe sex is put back on the employer and his responsibility to provide a general duty of care towards employees and to maintain a safe working environment.

The obvious question is, if mandatory testing represents an abuse of prostituted women's human rights and fails as a means of protecting public health, what is the Victorian Government's motivation in maintaining it as a legal requirement? I would argue that mandatory testing creates the semblance that the State Government is responsive to the perceived public health crisis related to STIs and HIV/AIDS, while keeping intact men's right to use and abuse women in prostitution. As Janice Raymond maintains 'medicalization, which is rightly viewed as a consumer protection act for men rather than as a real protection for women, ultimately protects neither men nor women' (Raymond 1998b, p. 5). The issue then is do the limitations of the Victorian legislative model for OHS change if we shift our attention away from mandatory testing to educative, peer-based approaches to health and safety for prostituted women?

Peer-based approaches to safe sex

The compliance of prostitutes' rights organisations with Government initiated safe sex strategies implies a consensus that STIs represent a significant health risk for the sex industry. In contrast to the State Government's reliance on mandatory testing, these groups, together with anti-HIV/AIDS advocates, view peer-based education around safe sex as the most feasible means of achieving a positive outcome in negating the spread of sexual diseases. They argue that peer-based approaches based on education strategies have the advantage of reaching prostituted women, providing accurate information about the most effective ways of preventing workplace health risks and supporting them in their efforts to utilise these measures consistently (Cohen, Alexander, Wofsky 1988). The Scarlet Alliance, together with the Australian Federation of AIDS, indeed have stressed that Governments should 'recognise the expertise of peer-based approaches delivered through prostitutes' rights community organisations and adequately fund them to continue and expand their work' (Banach and Metzenrath c.2000, p. 21). Thus they want self-regulation of OHS as opposed to Government regulation for the industry.

In order to evaluate the applicability of peer-based approaches in managing OHS for the Victorian industry it is useful to examine the range of possible options that exist within the Australian context. These include State, Territory and National OHS strategies that have been developed by prostitutes' rights organisations. New South Wales (NSW) and Queensland are the only States that have so far created OHS guidelines specifically for the prostitution industry.

Contemporary models for OHS strategies

WorkCover NSW's *Health and Safety Guidelines for Brothels* (2001), produced in collaboration with the State's Health Department, were unique in that they were the first regulatory standards to treat prostitution as no different from mainstream workplaces. Prostitutes' rights organisations were directly involved in creating the guidelines which are meant to complement these groups' own OHS literature or codes of practice. The guidelines specify that brothel owners have the same OHS and human resource obligations as any other proprietor in that 'brothel owners have certain duties with regard to employees, subcontractors and visitors to the workplace as defined by the State's OHS legislation' (2001, p. 3). Mirroring normative standards of Australian industrial rights, the NSW guidelines make specific provision for workplace consultation requiring employers to 'consult with their employees to enable those employees to contribute to making of decisions affecting their health, safety and welfare at work' (2001, Clause 2[1]).

The avenue for peer consultation in NSW was well established as by the late 1990s, WorkCover NSW, the State's Health Department, and the Sex Workers Outreach Project (SWOP),[13] had set up training programs for those 'working' in the State's legal brothel sector. WorkCover introduced the programs which were designed to educate both employers and 'workers' about best practice under its Injury Prevention, Education and Research Grant Scheme. One of the outcomes of the initiative was 'Getting on Top of Health and Safety', an OHS resource developed by SWOP to be used in combination with the 2001 *Brothel Guidelines* (Tucker 1999, p. 3). A similar but more extensive resource is *A Guide to Best Practice: Occupational health and safety in the Australian sex industry*[14] (c.2000) developed by the Scarlet Alliance. It claims that *Best Practice* is the most representative

---

13. SWOP is the Australian branch of the international Network of Sexwork Organisations.

14. *A Guide to Best Practice* (Elder c.2000) was produced by the Scarlet Alliance's OHS working group and the Australian Federation of AIDS.

OHS document for prostituted women, as the national body has drawn on its State and Territory members in formulating the code of practice. The new element in both these materials are the breadth and diversity of health risks that are recognised as resulting from the prostitution 'work' experience.

In contrast to Victoria's approach to OHS for the prostitution industry, this new style peer-based strategy goes far beyond the containment of STIs. *Best Practice*, for example, covers building safety and cleanliness, client screening procedures, violence in the workplace, alarm systems and bedroom lighting, repetitive strain injuries and drugs in the workplace (Elder c.2000, pp. 20–21). Other identified risks are generic to many workplaces. These include inappropriate storage and handling of chemicals, smoking in the vicinity of chemicals, no formal emergency exits, unsafe egress from spas, unsafe storage of chemicals (c.2000, p. 29). Although the inclusion of more generic problem areas indicates the extent to which prostitutes' rights organisations are able to normalise prostitution as no different from other businesses, the inclusion of 'violence' and 'drugs' as workplace risks suggests the guidelines are intended to reflect the harms of prostitution that are specific to the industry. But despite attempts to identify the way various 'work' practices and the 'work' environment impact on the health and safety of those within the industry, STIs remains a central concern. The Scarlet Alliance's *Guide to Best Practice*, indeed stresses that 'the practice of safe sex must be the basis on which workplaces operate' (2000, p. 16).

Still one of the most distinctive features of the NSW approach is that it situates safe sex practices outside of public health discourses. When evaluating the peer-based approach as a possible option for Victoria, Kevin Jones from Workplace Safety Services Victoria argued that STIs can and should be considered as occupational diseases. His view was that 'the "illegitimacy" and unlawfulness of the sex industry keeps regulatory attention on the public health arena rather than accessing the resources in work-place safety' (Jones 2000, p. 2). STIs, Jones says, must be treated 'in a similar fashion to silicosis, asbestosis and chemical sensitivity' (2000, p. 2). This is unlikely to occur because as we have seen brothel owners deny the employer-employee relationship. They argue that most prostituted women are contractors and thus they have no legal obligation to their 'workers' to implement OHS workplace safety education, for example. Most sex business operators do not have workers compensation coverage. Between 1990 and 2000 there were only five work compensation claims lodged with the Victorian WorkCover Authority for the industry (Jones 2000, p. 1). However even if there was a commitment by sex business management to take responsibility for peer-based OHS programs this would not protect prostituted women's health and safety. A focus on education around safe sex is in effect as flawed as the Victorian Government's primary reliance on mandatory testing.

STIs and prostituted women

The NSW WorkCover brothel guidelines operate in parallel with other Commonwealth and State health and safety practices for ensuring workplace safety. This means that employers must apply risk management to their place of work. In the prostitution work environment, employers are required to treat any work practices and procedures that have the potential to harm the health and safety of those within the industry as an OHS issue (New South Wales WorkCover Authority 2001, p. 3). *Getting on Top* lays out specific risk management procedures for the prosti-tution 'workplace' that involves a risk identification process, systematic risk assessment, risk control measures and moni-toring and review (Sex Workers Outreach Project 1996, p. 14). The guidelines therefore offer alternatives to mandatory testing although they are still concerned with safe sex. *Best Practice* reinforces the role of brothel owners and managers in supplying safe sex resource information and equipment to the extent that 'Employers should ensure that all employees are well informed of the need to use condoms, dams, and water-based lubricants, and that ongoing access to information and training regarding safe sex practice is provided' (Elder c.2000, p. 20).

Practical advice given to sex business operators on how they can best meet their responsibility may include providing the means to allow prostituted women to examine the buyers for STIs, which according to *Best Practice* is an 'appropriate control measure to eliminate or reduce risk'. Risk management procedures listed suggest that employers provide a '100-watt lamp for employees to perform thorough examinations of their clients' (c.2000, p. 65). In the case of outcalls, prostituted women should 'carry a small torch'. The procedure begins with the prostituted woman 'visually inspect[ing] the client' followed by 'gently squeez[ing] along the shaft of the client's penis to see if discharges emerge' (c.2000, p. 56). While a woman theoretically has the right to refuse service if she suspects the buyer is infected, the examination process itself is flawed as a means of controlling, eliminating or reducing the risk of STIs. It places an impossible responsibility on the woman involved. She is supposed to carry out inspections with a torch alone with a man who might threaten or assault her. Moreover the prostituted woman's role in carrying out STIs inspections is based on a supposed expertise in identifying these diseases.

The Commonwealth-sponsored *STD Handbook* lists under 'quick reference' a minimum of 23 STDs that women in prostitution must identify to reduce risks to their sexual health. In addition to the improbability of women without either medical or nursing qualifications gaining such expertise, both Government sources and prostitutes' rights organisations have acknowledged that many STIs cannot be identified visually. The

STD Handbook, states for instance, that Hepatitis A, B, and C frequently have no symptoms in the initial stages, although the consequences may lead to death through cirrhosis (Snow 1998, pp. 37–38). WISE, an ACT-based prostitutes' rights group, believes there is 'no sure way to tell if your client is free of STDs including HIV/AIDS'. At best 'a visual check . . . is one way to find some of the more obvious symptoms of STDs' (1997, p. 11). The inadequateness of inspection for STIs as a means of protecting prostituted women means that women are encouraged to fall back on using condoms and other personal protection equipment (PPE).

Best Practice promotes the fact that most prostituted women are skilled at using condoms (Elder c.2000, p. 17), a view that is supported by some international research (see Plumridge and Abel 2001, p. 82). In addition the guidelines provide employers with a list of methods for quality control to ensure that the personal protection equipment they are using are kept in optimal conditions to guard against deterioration (Elder c.2000, p. 24). However skilled use of condoms and other personal protective equipment has only limited benefit. The immediate drawback of using PPEs is that they fail to fully protect against all types of STIs. Herpes is a typical infection, which may be transmitted irrespective of a person using condoms or dental dams. The Commonwealth's STIs reference states that the virus normally occurs on a man's balls, while a condom only protects what it covers, that is the shaft of the penis (Snow 1998, p. 34). Herpes is an occupational risk that 'cannot be avoided no matter how careful [the prostituted women] may be' (Snow 1998, p. 34). This would also be the case with human papilloma virus (a strain of herpes) which transmits risk for cervical cancer to women. Nearly all cervical cancers (97.7 per cent) are directly linked to previous infection with one or more of the oncogenic (cancer-inducing) types of HPV (McIntosh 2003, p. 1).

However, even if condoms offer some protection against a woman contracting other STIs, skilled use of condoms and other personal protective equipment cannot counteract the high-risk of condom breakage and slippage that is inevitable in prostitution. One former prostituted woman, Lyn Shelton, told the Queensland's Crime and Misconduct Commission's prostitution review committee, that '3–4 condoms out of a box of 24 would break, even though they were of good quality' (Queensland 2004, p. 59).

Condom breakage and slippage

Getting on Top lists condom breakage and slippage as a severe health risk, which can cause death or disability. Its probability is 'anytime' and the need for a contingency plan is 'immediate' (Sex Workers Outreach Project 1996, p. 22). The resulting harm is both physical and psychological. SWOP's fact sheet, 'Condom Breakage and Slippage' indeed declares the experience to be 'one of the most stressful' occupational risks for those within the industry (Sex Workers Outreach Project c.1996, p. 1). The words 'You want it all OUT. Immediately' are highlighted across the introductory page.

The application of OHS to the prostitution industry implies that the 'work place' can be made safe. Subsequently prostitutes' rights organisations must continually rework their risk management procedures for STIs as each former strategy is shown to have critical flaws. *Best Practice* has two main strategies for treating condom breakage and slippage. The first focuses on STIs in general, the other relates exclusively to HIV/AIDS. An evaluation of treatment for condom failure during vaginal sex is sufficient to illustrate the harmful effect of such treatments on women. Under the heading 'Action to be taken in the event of condom breakage and/or slippage', the woman at risk is advised to remove excess semen 'by squatting and squeezing it out using vaginal muscle exertion' (Elder c.2000, p. 43). Follow-up procedures involve using fingers 'to scoop out any remaining excess semen, though care must be taken to avoid scratching the lining of the vagina with fingernails' (Elder c.2000, p. 43). This action is intended to be preparatory to some form of scouring or flushing, mainly douching or spermicides.

Ironically *Best Practice* and the Commonwealth's *STD Handbook* both caution against resorting to either douching or flushing in the event of condom breakage or slippage (Elder c.2000, p. 67; Snow 1998, p. 21). Douching is considered to be hazardous because 'the vagina is susceptible to infections by getting rid of naturally occurring bacteria' (Elder c.2000, p. 67). Further the process can push semen up the vagina towards the cervix, causing pelvic inflammatory disease (PID) and ectopic pregnancy. Spermicides such as Nonoxynol–9 may be beneficial against STIs as they kill sperm and infections in the vaginal tract. Their detrimental effects are genital irritation, vaginal and cervical ulcers and recurring yeast infections. *Best Practice* emphasises that Nonoxynol–9, for example, when used 'can result in a greater risk of STIs taking place' (Elder c.2000, p. 67).

For all these reasons, the option that remains for prostituted women in attempting to counter the inevitable risk of STIs is to have a health check as soon as possible after an 'accident', a procedure that differs little from mandatory testing. Moreover as SWOP makes clear, 'this may give [the prostituted woman] inaccurate results due to the different window periods it takes to reveal STIs' (Sex Workers Outreach Project c.1996, p. 1). As well women face the onerous experience of constant testing – 'straight away after condom breakage for gonorrhoea . . . two weeks [afterwards] . . . for a swab for chlamydia', as well as HIV and syphilis tests, to be tested again within three months (c.1996, p. 1).

The psychological harm that results from the process wherein prostituted women are compelled to undergo constant testing is highlighted well by the PCV. As Keith Gilbert from the Collective suggests, 'In the case of HIV – a potentially life-threatening organism – concerns are exaggerated by the asymptomatic and unpredictable nature of the virus itself, and by the fact that you must wait at least three months after transmission-risk activity until you can receive an accurate HIV-antibody test result' (Gilbert 1992, p. 9). Ultimately, knowledge that one has contracted an STI is simply a precursor to treatment, neither a cure nor good health.

HIV/AIDS treatment for women who are at risk due to condom breakage or slippage is post-exposure prophylaxis (PEP). The term is used to describe giving HIV antiviral drugs to a person following high-risk potential exposure to HIV. In a work-related environment, PEP is a normal procedure for health care workers who have been at risk of contacting HIV/AIDS. *Best Practice* maintains that this should apply to people engaged in prostitution 'where a condom has broken during penetrative sex or where a worker has been forced to have vaginal or anal sex with a client [without a condom]' (Elder c.2000, p. 25). This, however, does not occur.

In 2006 New South Wales is the only State or Territory where PEP is available under the Pharmaceutical Benefits Scheme to those within the industry. Thus in Victoria, prostituted women must still bear the cost if they decide to take drugs to prevent HIV. However even if PEP were to become more cost effective, the drugs' benefit for prostituted women is limited. According to *Best Practice* success rates for the drugs are still unproven. Inevitably the advice offered is that 'Because of the difficulties associated with accessing PEP, and with maintaining the necessary treatment program as well as the uncertainty regarding its effectiveness, choosing to commence PEP is a difficult decision to make' (Elder c.2000, p. 25).

Queensland's more recent 2002 *Health and Safety Guidelines for Brothels* may have been expected to overcome some of the limitations of the NSW model and the related prostitutes' right OHS literature. However, the Queensland guidelines draw heavily on NSW's WorkCover and the State's OHS Brothel Guidelines (Prostitution Licensing Authority 2002, p. 3). There is the same emphasis on 'good lighting for physical examination of clients' and 'observing safe sex practices'. In addition a licensee is expected to 'provide an adequate supply of PPE [personal protection equipment] and ensure it is adequately maintained' (2002, p. 5). Most significantly the Queensland Government promotes mandatory testing. As its guidelines state: 'approved managers and sex workers all commit an offence if a sex worker is permitted to work at a brothel during any period in which the sex worker is known to be infective with an STI' (2002, p. 6).

It can be argued that any measure that may minimise or at least decrease the harm of prostitution is beneficial. However as I illustrated previously, contemporary OHS research and policy is increasingly developed within a human rights framework. This has meant that OHS standards must reflect the rights of all workers to a safe and healthy work environment based on the assumption that the workplace is not inherently harmful. When it was established that the use of asbestos in buildings lead to asbestosis, authorities recognised that workplaces where asbestos existed could not be made hazard free. As a result its further use was banned. OHS strategies must not expect workers to modify their behaviour so that dangerous work practices can continue. What other categories of workers have to accept STIs as an 'inevitable' rather than an accidental consequence of simply going to work? Defining STIs as an occupational health hazard does nothing to ameliorate the physical and psychological harm they cause to prostituted women.

Conclusion

Undoubtedly locating prostituted women as legitimate workers allowed for women in prostitution to demand the same industrial rights as all other participants in the Australian labour force. The industrial rights system, as understood within the broader spectrum of human rights, appeared to offer the potential for eliminating the harms of prostitution. OHS is seen as critical to achieving this end. Feminists' analyses of the secondary status of women in the workforce helped formulate contemporary OHS policy in Australia to meet the specific needs of women, especially prostituted women, who could be categorised as part of a segregated, female workforce. These OHS codes provided a unique resource for analysing the power relations involved in prostitution.

As became apparent Victoria's legislators and the State's health authorities have constructed OHS policy for the prostitution industry primarily as a means of protecting the public's sexual health. OHS standards and their implementation are focused on 'safe sex' and the containment of STIs a strategy in effect aimed at protecting the health of male consumers and the general community. Women's health and safety is considered only when it can be fitted into this public health framework. But this narrow focus on safe sex has diminished prostituted women's right to be safe and healthy, while ensuring that the right of men to purchase women for their sexual gratification remains unchallenged.

The more recent OHS guidelines created by prostitutes' rights organisations have sought to widen the public health focus of more traditional approaches to OHS for the industry. Their potential for ameliorating the harms of prostitution derives from the participatory approach taken by these groups in the formulation of regulations and guidelines. They successfully gained the support of the New South Wales Government and WorkCover authorities, developing a model that could be adopted in the future by other States and Territories including the Victorian Government. Queensland has already followed suit. Nonetheless, the focus remains on the containment of STIs. The newer model ostensibly is more beneficial for prostituted women as by treating STIs as a legitimate occupational risk, it works to destigmatise those within the industry as 'purveyors of disease'. But changing nomenclature does not eliminate the harm to women from STIs. Moreover the risk management procedures adopted to minimise the inevitable harm to women's health and safety are inadequate, and often more debilitating than the initial infection.

The basic principle that the work environment must not be inherently harmful to workers, simply cannot be applied to prostituted women. However in those Australian States and Territories where prostitution is legitimised as 'sex work', such as Victoria, OHS strategies must fall back on making it incumbent on the workers to wear protective equipment and be prepared to handle occasional emergencies. This is the only alternative option to mandatory testing that is available to women working in a legalised prostitution system. In my view it fails them profoundly.

CHAPTER SEVEN

Rape and Violence as Occupational Hazards

Clearly violence is the norm for women in prostitution. Incest, sexual harassment, verbal abuse, stalking, rape, battering, and torture – are points on a continuum of violence, all of which occur regularly in prostitution. In fact prostitution itself is a form of sexual violence that results in economic profit for those who sell women, men and children. Though often denied or minimized, other types of gender violence (while epidemic) are not sources of revenue.

FARLEY ET AL. (2003, P. 60).

Introduction

As I have discussed in the previous chapter, Victoria's Occupational Health and Safety agenda for the prostitution industry neither protects public health nor adequately treats the harms of STIs and HIV/AIDS for women in the industry. Moreover it does not seriously address the full spectrum of harms to women that result from their experience of being prostituted. But do the more comprehensive OHS codes of practice and literature developed by Australian prostitutes' rights organisations including the Prostitutes' Collective of Victoria (PCV) offer any further protection for prostituted women? Prostitution is dissimilar to other forms of work as it involves the use of a woman's body by the buyer for his sexual gratification. No other workplace has to cover the range of health and safety issues that ensue from this sexual and economic exchange. In my view OHS's preventative strategies to change harmful 'work' practices or the prostitution 'work' environment must ultimately prove ineffectual as sexual exploitation and violence are inherent in the prostitution contract.

We must question firstly who controls the prostitution act. Are women in prostitution in a position to negotiate how the prostitution act will be conducted? And if they are not in control, how does the inequality between the 'buyer' and the 'bought' impact on OHS outcomes? Does not the buyer's perception of women in prostitution as sexed bodies, recreate conditions in which acts of violence such as sexual harassment and rape are not only perceivable, but are an expected part of the prostitution transaction? Sexual violence perpetrated against women in the prostitution industry is not a consequence of aberrant male behaviour; rather it is an inherent part of prostitution. The critical point of this chapter is to expose how the 'normal' acts of prostitution cannot be construed as other than sexual exploitation and violence against women.

Who controls the prostitution act?

Feminist psychologist Melissa Farley and colleagues recently produced a comprehensive analysis of the extreme and pervasive forms of trauma experienced by women in prostitution.[1] As they put it clearly:

> In prostitution, there is always a power imbalance, where the john has the social and economic power to hire her/him to act like a sexualized puppet. Prostitution excludes any mutuality of privilege or pleasure. Its goal is to ensure than one person does not use her personal desire to determine which sexual acts do and do not

---

1. Farley et al.'s excellent collection has drawn on the work of psychologists, psychiatrists, lawyers, and anti-violence advocates.

occur – while the other person acts on the basis of this personal desire (2003, p. 34).

Australian prostitutes' rights organisations take a different position. They maintain that many women 'choose' prostitution as a legitimate form of employment. Their perspective is that prostituted women are not victims but negotiators involved in business transactions. In contrast to Farley and others, they put the unsustainable position that gender power relations are not intrinsic to the prostitution act and thus the harms of prostitution can be eliminated or minimised through the application of OHS to the industry.

This concept of prostitution as a transaction between two equal parties was well established in the advocacy work of prostitutes' rights organisations in the early 1990s. The idea was central to the PCV's 1992 submission to the Law Reform Commission of Victoria on *Regarding Sentencing Practices in Rape Cases* (Gilbert 1992). The PCV maintained that violence against prostituted women resulted from a few aberrant 'clients' and buyers in general should not be stigmatised as violent. Indeed it made the point that 'Sexual acts within commercial sexual transactions are, commonly, more clearly negotiated than other sexual acts [as] the role of a client of a sex worker is clear within commercial sexual transactions' (1992, p. 4). It is interesting that critics from the left have stressed that the shift towards individual contracts under the new Australian Workplace Agreements System reinforces the already inequitable relationship between the employer and the employee, particularly for women and other marginal workers. However when it comes to prostitution and the sexual exploitation of women and girls we are all supposed to take the opposite position. I maintain that the idea that prostituted women have considerable leverage when negotiating with men who demand unsafe sex ignores the power differentiation between the buyer and the bought created through male sexual dominance and economic and racial inequalities.

Radical feminists have always found the notion of consent problematic between two parties with unequal access to power. As Susan Hawthorne argues, 'consent is a method by which one party is granted permission to carry out particular actions that have an impact on the other party. Legally speaking, it changes the act from one of violation to one that is acceptable' (2002, p. 382). She makes the further point that 'consent is also used by the state and the powerful to make the powerless feel as though they have some control over their lives'. But as she concludes, 'it is a false sense of control, and one that fools the powerless into colluding with those in power' (2002, p. 356). Sheila Jeffreys makes a similar argument. As she sees it 'Oppression cannot effectively be gauged according to the degree of "consent", since even in slavery there was some consent if consent is defined as inability to see, or feel entitled to, any alternative' (1997, p. 135). Given such arguments Janice Raymond proposes that the word 'compliance' more accurately reflects the relationship between the powerful and the powerless as 'compliance is required by the very fact of having to adapt to conditions of inequality (1995, p. 7). However given that prostitutes' rights organisations operate under the pretence that prostituted women can indeed negotiate an equitable sexual contract with a client their OHS literature generally promotes 'worker' responsibility in minimising prostitution harms. In response to the limitations of current safe sex policy Sex Workers Outreach Project (SWOP) suggests that 'Workers can minimise condom breakage by being prepared' (c.1996, p. 1). Their information sheet on condom breakage and slippage advises women to:

> Have a number of different sizes of condoms in supply . . . **Do not let the client put the condom on** [SWOP's emphasis]. It is best

you do this, as you are aware of the possible damage to the condom and feel confident that it is properly on (c.1996, p. 1).

The assumption that prostituted women can themselves minimise the harms of prostitution in relation to safe sex presupposes a willingness by the buyers to agree to a safe sex agenda.

Male power and male perceptions

There is a growing body of evidence to indicate that men who use prostitution take no responsibility for safe sex and many demand the opposite. A 1997 New Zealand pilot health study of buyers' behaviour by sociologists, Chetwynd and Reed, revealed that male users took no initiatives towards safe sex and the use of condoms (cited in Plumridge and Abel 2001, p. 79). These findings are similar to the results of a 1998 Victorian study carried out by the MacFarlane Burnett Centre for Medical Research. It concluded that buyers revealed an ongoing reluctance to use condoms and that one in five men have unsafe sex (Louie et al. 1998, p. 23). Thus the educative role that prostituted women might have around safe sex is immediately compromised by the buyers' perception that their purchasing power entitles them to demand any type of sex they want. This heightens the risk of STIs and HIV to an unacceptable level.

Several studies have confirmed that the power relationship between the prostituted woman and the buyer is a crucial factor in the safety of commercial prostitution encounters. One New Zealand survey found that, 'More than half the women (58 per cent) in the study reported that they had felt pressure to accept a client when they did not want to (53 per cent of street workers and 59 per cent indoors)' (in Plumridge and Abel 2001, p. 79). Significantly there is also evidence that brothel owners and buyers in Australia's legalised prostitution environment coerce women into performing unwanted sex.

In 2001 the Federal Occupational Health and Safety Commissioner, Jocelyn Plovits, revealed that in the Australian Capital Territory women were pressured to have full sex without condoms in unhygienic and often unsafe conditions (Clack 2002, p. 10). The Victorian Government's *Infectious Diseases Health Regulations 2001 Impact Statement* similarly confirmed that male buyers 'found condoms unacceptable' and, when refused sex without condoms they 'would seek other avenues for unsafe sex' (Victoria 2001a, p. 61). As one respondent to a PCV question-naire explains, buyers were not deterred by legal regulations: 'When someone has attacked a worker on the street . . . there's a fair chance they're going to be accessing sex workers in other sectors of the industry' (Chambers 1995, p. 21).

Priscilla Pyett and Deborah Warr's sociological study of women in prostitution in Victoria demonstrated that 'client resistance, whether in the form of threats or enticements, was a continual obstacle to be overcome by negotiation in the sexual encounter' (1999, p. 186). The authors believed that women in street prostitution were more vulnerable to physical coercion to perform sex without condoms. Their crucial finding, however, was that in the State's licensed brothels 'management did not insist on condom use for all services, [and] women experienced competition from other workers and considerable pressure from clients' to perform unsafe sex (1999, p. 186).

Women's 'consent'

Women in prostitution comply to men's demands for sex with-out condoms for diverse reasons. Melissa Farley, in her work with Vanessa Kelly, lists these as extending from economic vulner-ability to homelessness, drug abuse, or because women are 'seasoned' to accept male demands through childhood sexual abuse and as women in prostitution (2000, pp. 11–14). As early as 1992 Sarah Keogh, in a report for the Prostitutes' Collective of Victoria on 'The Effects of the Prostitution Regulation Act' drew attention to the economic uncertainty for women working in Victoria's legal brothels. One interviewee was reported as saying:

> There are a lot of women who don't get picked all night; you sit around for eight hours, or you may even do a double shift and be in the one place for sixteen hours, and you earn $40. And that is really hard (Keogh 1992, p. 20).

Sarah Priesley, who worked for six years in illegal and legal brothel prostitution in the Australian states of Queensland, New South Wales and Victoria, has also highlighted how the buyer's economic power means that he determines how the sexual act will be played out. When describing one of her first experiences of brothel prostitution she says how the 'service' involved her straddling the buyer's body after which she says she 'sucked his cock, which tasted of cold flesh and cheap soap' (1997, p. 25). Inexperienced at disassociating from her feelings, she started to cry:

> Tears spilt onto his balls as he prodded his fingers into my vagina. He didn't seem to notice anything was wrong and just carried on . . . Doing this was taking my dignity away and I couldn't believe that I had sunk this low, to let a stranger use my body for his pleasure with only money as recompense (1997, p. 25).

Six years later in Melbourne, Priesley found that her circumstances had changed little. She speaks of one regular, Mike, who liked her to act like a young girl:

> He would spank my arse quite hard and push my head down to suck his cock. He was about sixty . . . At the end of the booking he liked to fuck me face down so he could ram his cock into me, as if he was raping me. I would moan softly like a young girl . . . He made me sick and I hated him, but the booking only went for twenty minutes, and he paid me one hundred and seventy dollars for that (1997, p. 160).

Priesley says she was often compelled to perform anal sex because she 'could get so much more money for it' (1997, p. 91). Thus prostituted women comply with having their bodies violated to economically survive, a 'choice' they would refuse in other circumstances. Most prostituted women face low paying jobs or unemployment. Moreover many who have a history of prostitution fear disclosure when seeking employment. In addition as a Norwegian study by Hoigard and Finstad found:

> Through their own experiences and cultural milieu [prostituted women] acquired a view of their personal value and their bodies that make prostitution an alternative to other forms of support. It is this combination of self-image and an oppressed position in class society that can be fateful (1992, p. 76).

Drug addiction and 'choice'

Substance addiction is a further reason why women concede to male demands for unsafe sex. Graaf et al.'s research (1995) into the impact of drug and alcohol use on prostitution behaviour established that condom usage decreased when women needed money for drugs. Graaf and his colleagues argued that the economic incentive to support a drug habit meant that prostituted women would be induced to accept demands for unsafe sex. They believe that the increased vulnerability of prostituted women because of substance addiction could be overcome if the women were put on a methadone program in addition to them changing their 'distinctively negative work-attitude' (in Farley and Kelly 2000, pp. 32–39). Farley and Kelly, in their critique of the Graaf study highlighted how the authors had adopted a 'blaming the victim' mentality to address the problem. However they considered that one of the major oversights in Graaf and his colleagues' work is that it ignores that substance addiction is commonly a coping mechanism for women to deal with their experience of being prostituted. Women use drugs to survive prostitution.

Existing literature on violence and prostitution has demonstrated that prostituted women use drugs as a pivotal defence mechanism to survive in prostitution (Farley and Kelly 2000, pp. 39–41). Pyett and Warr (1999) found that in 'only a few cases did heavy drug use preceding [*sic*] the woman becoming involved in sex work' (1999, p. 539). Farley and Kelly in the same way exposed that 'a significant percentage of women enter prostitution with no previous drug or alcohol abuse' (2000, p. 11). According to these authors women 'initiated or increased drug or alcohol use to anaesthetize the pain of physical injuries and verbal abuse inflicted on them in prostitution' (2000, p. 11).

In the Victorian context a Melbourne-based Legal Centre and Advocacy Program for Women in Prison offers support for Farley and Kelly's findings. In their submission to a 2003 Senate Inquiry into poverty, the group concluded that from their experience of working with women in the State's prison system, 'Many women use drugs to anaesthetise the pain, grief and anger of sexual abuse in their lives, whether that abuse is ongoing or perpetrated during their childhood' (Darebin Community Legal Centre and the Advocacy Program for Women in Prison 2003, p. 9). As they reported:

> Women who work in prostitution talk about the use of drugs to 'get them through it'. A cycle of forced dependence is created. Drug use at first functions to dull the pain of sexual abuse, women then prostitute in order to support their drug use and drug use increases in order to make the experience of prostitution bearable (2003, p. 9).

Thus prostituted women use substance abuse as a means to dissociate in order to survive prostitution which itself is often a consequence of a history of sexual abuse.

Few studies have been undertaken on substance addiction among prostituted women in Victoria post-legalisation. Even so the precise incidence of substance addiction in the State's legal sector is likely to be difficult to determine. As Pyett, Haste et al. point out, because the law does not tolerate drug or alcohol use in the State's licensed brothels the official statistics are likely to be significantly underestimated (1996a, pp. 87–89). A 1994 Australian study determined that the number of those within the industry using intravenous drugs was five to seven times more than the non-prostituted population. The study canvassed both legal and illegal industry sectors (Sharp 1994, p. 226). Pyett and Warr's 1999 research similarly suggests that drug use is not limited to the unregulated sector. They found that in Victoria, 'Almost all the street workers and half of the brothel workers reported current or recent injecting drug use' (1995, p. 5). The Scarlet Alliance in its publication *Best Practice OHS for the Sex Industry*, support Pyett and Warr's evaluation suggesting that 'all brothels, at one time or another, have employed users of alcohol and other drugs' (Elder c.2000, p. 62).

Despite pro-legalisation advocates' continued promotion of the belief that substance abuse does not occur in legal brothel prostitution, the NSW *Health and Safety Guidelines for Brothels* (2001), which continues to be the main OHS model for the Australian prostitution industry, does recognise drug abuse as a health risk within the legal sex industry (New South Wales Work-Cover Authority 2001, p. 8).[2] Risk management practices for safe drug usage adopted in the guidelines, as well as by Scarlet Alliance in its *Best Practice* (c.2000), promote the use of 'sharps containers'[3]

---

2. The more recent Queensland reference to drug and alcohol abuse limits its reference to brothel owners' responsibility to refuse entry to affected 'workers' or 'clients' (Prostitution Licensing Authority 2002, p. 8).

3. A sharps container is a receptacle for disposal of used hypodermic needles and other drug delivery instruments.

and drug rehabilitation programs for workers. The Scarlet Alliance's 'sex industry workplace drug and alcohol policy', indeed stresses that workers should be offered rehabilitation and support, and not be dismissed (Elder c.2000, p. 63). However as I previously made clear OHS policy that promotes the right of women who are substance abusers to remain in prostitution, does not consider that such abuse may be a direct consequence of abuse and debasement experienced by women as a result of their being prostituted.

Women's 'choice' to be prostituted is at best a 'constrained decision' based on economic and social inequalities between themselves and buyers. Even when coercion is not overt women in the prostitution industry remain disempowered. A prostituted woman must appear to agree to any sexual acts a buyer demands to obtain a booking. She then is later forced to attempt to renegotiate the way the sexual act will be performed when the booking has commenced and she is alone with the buyer. Ingrid Barclay's study, which looked at the experience of four women in one of Melbourne's legal brothels, substantiates this point well (2001). One woman said:

> I'm always having to say that I will do something in the booking that I don't want to, that is normally outside the service that I like to provide. It's hard because if the client has asked me, I know that he will ask everyone. If you want to get booked you have to do these things (2001, p. 32).

Another interviewee reported that 'To get regulars you have to conduct the booking all about him. You have to indulge in his type of conversation, his type of sex' (2001, p. 32).

Rape as coercion

As all these examples demonstrate prostituted women have no autonomous control over the prostitution act. However any pretence they may have, is totally negated by the act of rape. Australian feminist lawyer, Jocelynne Scutt, has argued that 'prostitutes by their very trade . . . are subject to the crime of rape and indeed murder . . . and they have little legal redress when they suggest they have been raped' (in Guymer and Klein 1999). The extent of rape of prostituted women is difficult to determine because the social stigma attached to prostituted women means that they do not generally report rape (Sullivan 2003). What I intend to make clear, however, is that the normalisation of violence and rape as work means that women in prostitution struggle to define what is in fact rape and what is supposed to be 'work'.

Most of the evidence relating to men's rape of women in prostitution is anecdotal. The PCV's *Hussies Handbook*, a self-help manual for prostituted women, upfront identifies rape as an occupational hazard. It states clearly that 'Sex workers can be, and are, raped' (c.1995, p. 19). *Best Practice* in a similar way acknowledges that 'workers are forced by clients to have sex without a condom against their will' (Elder c.2000, p. 22). Some prostituted women report that their main fear of men not using condoms is that their abusers might have AIDS (Keogh 1992, p. 20). However prostitutes' rights organisations, in accepting prostitution as legitimate work, have little recourse but to attempt to minimise the incidence of rape experienced by women in prostitution, an effort in which their strategies fail.

Training in communication and negotiation skills is highly recommended in OHS guides for the prostitution industry as a means to protect women against rape. The Commonwealth sponsored *STD Handbook* says: 'It is important that you and your client clearly understand your boundaries and expectations of the service. You need to take control of the situation, tactfully, politely and yet firmly' (Snow 1998, p. 9). Disturbingly the idea of 'worker' control in rape is now mainstreamed in OHS literature, a ploy that takes accountability for the abuse away from the buyer.

Women in prostitution must adapt to an identified life-threatening work-related harm. Such harm cannot be eliminated, as male violence is an intrinsic part of women's experience of being prostituted.

Teaching prostituted women to negotiate their safety

The Professional, the industry magazine produced by Sex Workers Outreach Project (SWOP), reflects the tendency among prostitutes' rights organisations to promote the importance of prostituted women themselves minimising the risk of rape. 'Negotiating condom use' (1995, p. 4), for example, emphasises the positive advantage of women attaining skills that help her work collaboratively with her rapist. Women are told to 'Be prepared to be a health educator and share knowledge'. SWOP further suggests that 'dealing with stubbornness and ignorance will also build confidence and strength'. SWOP, however, does caution women that they must 'Be careful and suss the client out, as you can be much more vulnerable without clothes on' (1995, p. 7). What SWOP clearly fails to provide is just how does a woman 'suss the client out', or what she is to do if she is threatened with violence.

Some specialist groups are emerging which purport to offer programs on self-defence and conflict resolution for the prostitution industry that potentially provide some avenue of defence against the violence of prostitution. The services of Pacific Martial Arts are a typical example. The company offers industry employers a short course in which prostituted women are taught to handle threatening situations. Excerpts from the company's promotional material explains how its course '[A]llows employees in the sex industry to react to threatening situations in a number of ways' (Brental c.1998 p. 1). It promises to teach women how to adopt 'submissive but protective postures' and 'how to create a *common vision* [my italics] with an aggressor, which can often lead to a compromise of initial harmful intentions'). Other advertising catch phrases include 'controlling self-violation, that pre-empts negative outcomes'; 'creating a common vision that shares an empathetic rapport with the violator'; 'de-escalation negotiation'; 'maintaining "first strike" advantage' (c.1998, p. 1). This program is suggestive of crisis management for hostage situations. In what other non-military profession can hostage negotiations be deemed necessary to cope with the normal workday?

Sheila Jeffreys in *The Idea of Prostitution* (1997, p. 137) has made the point that:

> [I]t is surprising that prostituted women are seen to have such power. In other situations in which women find themselves alone with unknown men who expect to use them sexually, they are more likely to feel vulnerable. Payment does not make a difference . . . employment, marriage and prostitution create social relations of subordination, not equality.

OHS strategies, in treating prostitution as no different from other forms of work, operate as if this power differential is irrelevant.

The acceptability of placing the responsibility for her safety on the woman who is abused by a buyer is nonetheless increasing. While Victoria's primary approach to dealing with the health and safety of prostituted women is through regulatory procedures, Resourcing Health and Education for the Sex Industry (RHED), which is responsible for augmenting sexual health programs for the industry, has developed guidelines supposedly aimed at assisting prostituted women to deal with violence. Their rhetoric mirrors that of Pacific Martial Arts. According to RHED's web page, women must 'take control from the start and keep it' (2006a, p. 6). The point is to, 'Build a façade, construct a screen, as long as you put yourself across in a way that . . . the client knows not to screw you around!'. There is a caveat, however. Women are told 'Don't relax after the job's done – that can be the time he'll assault you.'

It is perhaps inevitable that when all other strategies fail to protect women from violence, duplicity becomes an acceptable work skill that women in prostitution must acquire to remain safe. SWOP's safe sex guidelines instruct that when dealing with men's unwillingness to engage in safe sex, women should suggest to the buyer that they want 'to change positions'. 'Certain positions', SWOP says, will 'allow [a woman] to check the condom discreetly, for example if you are doing it from behind, you can reach underneath and check the condom without the client noticing' (c.1998, p. 1). Apart from the unknown consequences for the woman if the man discovers the deception, no other work environment demands fraudulence as essential to being able to conduct work and avoid assault.

The most critical problem with negotiation and duplicity as a means of diffusing a potentially violent situation is that such methods may, in fact, exacerbate the harm done to women by the buyer. Farley and Kelly have found that women were at a higher risk of physical violence when they attempted to insist on condom use with buyers whose violence already contributed to their relative powerlessness. They argue:

> It would be more appropriate, to view all prostituted women at risk, as it has been established that women were unable to prevent johns' demands for unsafe sex, and were often physically assaulted when they requested condoms (2000, p. 39).

If OHS authorities are serious about preventing the spread of STIs and HIV/AIDs among prostituted women, rape must be recognised as a high risk in contracting these diseases. Clearly there are serious, indeed fundamental, contradictions in the current Australian OHS priorities whether emanating from Governments or from prostitutes' rights organisations. This is true irrespective of whether the issue of safe sex is managed from a regulatory perspective or whether it is about peer-based education. OHS guidelines can suggest and encourage condom use, for example, but cannot enforce their use, and neither can the prostituted women. It is the buyer who controls the prostitution interaction.

Collusion between management and the buyer

The expectation that prostituted women's bodies become available to the buyer for him to use at his will is sustained by similar expectations held by many brothel owners and managers. Despite the principal OHS requirement that employers must maintain a safe and healthy environment for workers, there is evidence that brothel owners and managers collude with buyers in maintaining women's unequal position in the prostitution transaction. Sarah Keogh's research on Victoria's legalised prostitution system provided some disturbing insights about the role of brothel and escort management. One interviewee reported that her 'option' to reject a client, whom she was seriously uncomfortable about servicing, had to be weighed against pressure from her workplace and her own financial needs. She explains how her agency would have fined her A$300, if she had refused bookings with a man who was 'abusive', 'drunk' and 'always threatened physical violence'. Although she found him 'really horrible' and 'didn't want to be there' the agency kept sending her to the buyer because he demanded that she service him (Keogh 1992, p. 22).

The above account exposes that legalisation and its promise to protect the health and safety of women in prostitution has in effect exacerbated the lack of choice for prostituted women. As another interviewee testifies:

> The legal system has done nothing for the women in terms of improving their working conditions, in fact, it has done the opposite . . . There is definitely far more competition, the clients are

extremely demanding, the control over what the women will and won't do is often taken out of their hands . . . We're put in a position where the type of service we offer is stipulated to us . . . There is a range of fantasy line work you can do, but for women who have just started working, this can be a somewhat daunting prospect (Keogh 1992, p. 7).

Alison Arnot-Bradshaw, as PCV project manager under Victoria's legalised prostitution system, believes that men have become more demanding in the type of services they want. The demand for oral sex, for instance, has been replaced by the demand for anal sex (Sullivan 1999a). The Melbourne-based legal advocacy group for women in prison similarly drew attention to the fact that, 'Despite claims that brothels provide safer working environments, many women report . . . that they *prefer to risk violence at the hands of clients* [my italics] than be subjected to violence by both clients and brothel staff and security' (Darebin Community Legal Centre and the Advocacy Program for Women in Prison 2003, p. 8).

The Ugly Mugs program perhaps best illustrates the continuous threat of violence that is part of the experience of being prostituted irrespective of legalisation. The program, which is organised by various prostitutes' rights organisations, involves the setting up of a database on violent buyers from all sectors of the industry, both legal and illegal. The reports are then distributed to police, social workers and those in the industry. The urgency of some kind of reporting to protect women is suggested by the following statement, given to the PCV by one victim of an 'ugly mug'. As the woman said 'no one told me what to do and what not to do, I had to work that out for myself . . . if you end up with [an ugly mug] what's going to be the best way to get out of this?' (Chambers 1995, p. 22). The reality is that prostituted women struggle to avoid 'ugly mugs' because an 'ugly mug' and a 'client' are one and the same person.

Risking women's reproductive health

That prostituted women have minimal power to negotiate the prostitution act has extensive implications for women's health and safety. In addition to the potential for women to contract STIs and HIV/AIDS, women's reproductive health is at risk through either condom slippage and breakage, or rape. Reproductive health is recognised as an OHS issue under the International Labour Organisation's *Resolution on Equal Opportunities and Treatment* (1989, p. 7). The Resolution proposes that governments should introduce measures to extend special protection to women and men for those types of work, which have proved to be harmful to them, chiefly concerning their reproductive function.

In New South Wales women's reproductive health is protected under the current WorkCover NSW *Health and Safety Guidelines for Brothels*. Regulation 2.8 stipulates that employers must ensure protection to minimise harm to pregnant women and their foetus (2001, p. 9). *Best Practice* suggests that employers can carry out their 'duty of care' in relation to women's reproductive health through placing a limitation on the amount of shift work pregnant workers engage in, requirements for longer breaks between buyers, and exemptions from performing certain duties such as heavy lifting (Elder c.2000, p. 33). However neither WorkCover nor the Scarlet Alliance adequately addresses unwanted pregnancy as an inherent occupational health and safety risk for women in prostitution.

The risk of unwanted pregnancy

The Scarlet Alliance's *Best Practice* states that 'The sex industry stands apart from other industries in that it is the only industry where unwanted pregnancy could be an occupational hazard' (c.2000, p. 34). As an unwanted pregnancy is a probable and direct result of women's experience of being prostituted, OHS guidelines can only seek to minimise the risk. Disturbingly risk management procedures to deal with the problem of pregnancy are as hazardous to the health of prostituted women as were the procedures to deal with potential STIs discussed in the previous chapter.

Best Practice attempts to counteract the harm to a woman's reproductive health in the section 'Preventing pregnancy after condom breakage or slippage'. The guidelines suggest the most appropriate action is the 'morning after' pill (c.2000, p. 69). The morning after pill is defined by Public Health Association of Australia (PHAA) as 'emergency contraception'. According to the Association 'the most commonly used method is a high dose of oestrogen and progestogen taken within 72 hours of unprotected sex (UPS) or the insertion of a intrauterine device (IUD) up to 5 days post UPS' (Public Health Association of Australia 1999).

In 2004 Postinor–2, a new form of emergency contraceptive, became available over the counter (that is without a medical prescription), in Australia. Postinor–2 is designed to be taken within 72 hours of unprotected sex. It comprises two tablets each comprising levonorgestrel, a synthetic hormone derived from progesterone, and requires the second tablet to be taken exactly 12 hours after the first dose (Australian Prescription Products Guide 2004). Postinor–2 is a very poor contraceptive, with pregnancy being prevented in only 85 per cent of cases. Even this is misleading. Trials on the drug show the efficiency rate drops to 58 per cent after the first 48 hours. It is also highly dangerous, particularly if the woman is already pregnant, or is taking medicines like barbiturates (sleeping tablets) or insulin (for diabetes). Very common side effects include nausea (50.5 per cent), fatigue (28.5 per cent), vomiting (18.8 per cent), and abdominal pain (20.9 per cent). Of greater concern is that the incidence of vaginal haemorrhaging, which is life-threatening, is 4.2 per cent (Australian Prescription Products Guide 2004).

Queensland's Self Health for Queensland Workers in the Sex Industry (SQWISI) does acknowledge that the morning after pill is 'not recommended or suitable for use on a regular basis' (1997, p. 17). An additional problem that it notes is that women at risk 'may need to be seen 4 weeks later to ensure pregnancy has not proceeded'. But other options promoted by prostitutes' rights organisations and OHS literature to reduce the risk of pregnancy are equally harmful to women's health.

Besides advocating condom use, prostitutes' rights organisations generally promote most forms of contraception as feasible means of safeguarding against unwanted pregnancies. SQWISI provides some of the more comprehensive information on the range of contraceptive methods currently available in Australia (1997, p. 17). Nonetheless the complications associated with various contraceptive methods described mean that women are advised to use them only in association with condoms. In addition to the problems with the morning after pill explained above, SQWISI notes that the oral contraceptive pills may cause spotting between periods while 'spermicides may irritate the vagina' and diaphragms are 'unreliable'. SQWISI believes that Depo Provera, the three-month injectable hormonal contraceptive is the exception. According to its literature the drug's 'safety is well established'. Moreover, it is promoted as being particularly suitable 'for workers in the sex industry [because] the drug commonly leads to no periods at all' (1997, p. 17). But an examination of the use and effects of Depo Provera reveals that its use as part of an OHS policy is an abuse of women in prostitution, both as 'workers' and as women.

Depo Provera has historically been coupled with social control in the context of the global population crisis. Eco feminist, Asoka Bandarage, who analysed the potential harm of the contraceptive to women's health and welfare, writes how the drug 'was tested and used on minority women in the US and thousands of poor women in the Third World' (1997, p. 83). Bandarage cites a report by the Canadian Women's Committee on Reproduction, Population and Development. She exposes how Canadian doctors prescribed it when they considered the benefits outweighed the risks of unwanted pregnancy although it was generally not available in the country. The groups targeted were 'Aboriginal women, women with disabilities, teenagers, women of color, women living in poverty, and substance abusers' (1997, p. 83).

In addition to the clear racist and classist associations with Depo Provera's use, the drug also has a range of incapacitating and life-threatening side effects. Bandarage lists among these:

> Risk of birth defects due to women taking the drug during pregnancy; negative impact on infant development due to ingestion of hormones in breast milk; breast cancer, endometrial cancer and cervical cancer (1997, p. 84).

Among the most common side effects are 'menstrual disorders, skin disorders, fatigue, headaches, nausea, depression, hair loss, delayed return to fertility, weight change and loss of libido (1997, p. 84). Women in prostitution are thus faced with the option of unwanted pregnancies, or risk management procedures, which again are proven to be debilitating and life-threatening.

Undoubtedly once the abortion pill RU486 becomes available in Australia it too will be suggested as an option to terminate early pregnancies for women in prostitution. Klein, Raymond and Dumble's *RU486: Misconceptions, Myths and Morals* (1992) is the most comprehensive analysis of the contradictions associated with its use. Renate Klein and Janice Raymond, founding members of the Feminist International Network of Resistance to Reproductive and Genetic Engineering (FINRRAGE), examined the contradictions inherent in RU486 as part of an ongoing critique of multinational pharmaceutical companies. The authors argue that the pharmaceutical companies created a reproductive technology market which is largely untested and harmful to millions of women. The market also takes in the contraceptive pill, the Dalkon Shield, Norplant and Depo Provera.

The debate on the safety of the use of RU486 resurfaced in Australia during the Commonwealth Inquiry on Therapeutic Goods Amendment (Repeal of Ministerial responsibility for approval of RU486) Bill 2005.[4] In her submission to the inquiry, Klein, a biologist and social scientist who has been an academic and activist in women's health over the past 20 years, produced extensive evidence of the debilitating and life-threatening side-effects of administering the contraceptive to women to procure an abortion. Adverse effects include deaths (from sepsis, blood loss, heart problems), the need for blood transfusions, incomplete abortions, severe pain, vomiting and diarrhoea (Klein 2006, p. 10).

Klein adopts the term 'chemical' abortion as opposed to 'medical' abortion as she notes women are being given a 'drug cocktail of two powerful chemicals, RU486 and a prostaglandin – which is inherently unpredictable' (2006, p. 2). She explains how as RU486 only works in 40–60 per cent of women, 48 hours after its administration the second drug, a prostaglandin must be taken. 'Severe and painful contractions' can result in 'irreversible damage' and uncontrollable blood loss. Klein further notes that as 'the RU486/prostaglandin abortion is incomplete in up to 10 per cent of women, the remains of the pregnancy must be removed by dilation and curettage (D&C)'.

There is a further possibility that women may die from bacterial infection as RU486 also blocks glucocorticoid receptors, which leads to a weakened immune system (Klein 2006, p. 2).

---

4. The Bill was passed in April 2006 handing responsibility for the approval of the drug to the Therapeutic Goods and Drugs Administration.

That such a violent drug is considered a safe means of dealing with an unwanted pregnancy is unacceptable. That it is likely to be considered as a risk prevention strategy within OHS policy for the prostitution industry is a human rights violation.

Pregnancy and STIs as an industrial disease

Australian prostitutes' rights organisations reject the knowledge that many of the risks to the health and safety of women in prostitution are endemic to the industry. To recognise such life-threatening and psychologically damaging risks as inherent in prostitution is clearly counterproductive to their goals of normal-ising prostitution as work. Thus such groups continue to create options that are intended to minimise the harm to prostituted women resulting from their everyday 'working' lives. However a significant problem with adopting a harm minimisation approach to STIs is that from the Australian Government's perspective, STIs are considered to be a risk to public health. Most prosti-tution and OHS legislation, as we have seen, prohibits women who have contracted a disease from continuing to work. In such circumstances prostitutes' rights organisations have come up with an initiative, albeit a particularly dangerous one for prostituted women, which they believe allows women with STIs to continue to 'work'.

The Scarlet Alliance has made a case that STIs must be recognised as an industrial disease, since women contract these infections as a consequence of prostitution work practices. Its position is that, '[I]f the STI is contracted through sex work STIs should be seen as industrial diseases and workers retrained to perform other work' (Elder c.2000, p. 35).[5] Increasingly Australian prostitutes' rights organisations suggest that one of

---

5. These views were already expressed a decade earlier by the PCV; see for example, Prostitutes' Collective of Victoria, 'Towards a Code of Practice' (1990) in *Working Girl* 10, p. 15.

the ways around the problem of women working with STIs is for these women to offer sado-masochism and bondage and discipline services (S&M/B&D). SWOP promotes S&M/B&D as beneficial to women in prostitution as it allows them to continue to work if they have contracted an STI. In addition S&M/B&D is marketed as a highly attractive form of work, as it is promoted as involving a range of consensual activities that transcends the sexual experience by breaking through pain barriers (Sex Worker Outreach Project 1997, p. 1).

Is sadomasochism safe sex?

The Scarlet Alliance supports the idea of S&M/B&D as a viable work option for those in the industry who have contracted STIs because its practices do not involve the exchange of bodily fluids, and thus the transmission of STIs. However S&M/B&D is violence and recreates the dominant-submissive power relations of prostitution. Indeed as I will discuss, much of the OHS literature on S&M/B&D substantiates that it is harmful to women, despite prostitutes' rights organisations' promotion of the practice as safe sex.

S&M/B&D is frequently referred to as esoteric work. Within the industry it is generally considered as high risk for Repetition Strain Injury (RSI) (Elder c.2000, p. 36). The Scarlet Alliance insists that the employer's responsibility should cover a comprehensive training program in the safe use of S&M/B&D equipment. This it argues is imperative 'for the safety of both employees and clients (c.2000, p. 39). SWOP also 'strongly recommends . . . full training and experience before attempting to service any client' (1997, p. 2). According to its OHS literature S&M/B&D requires 'a high level of concentration [and] can be more physically demanding than straight sex work'. Equipment includes branding irons, whips and canes, hot wax and piercing instruments (1997, pp. 2–3).

Some Australian states have already supported prostitutes' rights organisations in their efforts to normalise S&M/B&D as an acceptable OHS program. The ACT's Workers in Self Employment (WISE), conducts S&M/B&D training workshops, which have been advertised as a legitimate business expense for brothel owners or for an individual, and thus a valid tax deduction (1997, p. 1). SWOP's training sessions suggest that 'Etiquette'; that is the use of 'safety words', and the setting of limits and scenes before a session commences, purportedly minimises the risks of excesses during the session that would be harmful to the recipient's health (1997, p. 3). As such S&M/B&D training programs can be considered as no different from training programs for legitimate industries. However again the crucial question arises: Can a prostitution practice that is inherently harmful be made safe?

Body fluids and infectious organisms

SWOP's OHS booklet, *Sadomasochism, bondage and discipline* (1997), was produced specifically to deal with occupational risks associated with the practice. It begins with the presumption that 'Responsible S&M/B&D has always been about safety' (1997, p. 3). SWOP's detailed lists of S&M/B&D health risks and the ineffective measures it proposes to deal with the consequences of such harms, however, completely invalidates such a statement, as does other OHS S&M/B&D literature.

S&M/B&D practices commonly bring participants in contact with bodily fluids. These may include blood, vomit, urine, faeces, saliva and semen, which according to SWOP 'may contain infectious organisms'. Women are exposed to these harmful organisms through skin cuts, grazes, rashes and piercings (SWOP 1997, p. 3). The Scarlet Alliance cautions practitioners that 'special care' must be taken 'in cleaning up spills of these fluids to avoid transmission of viruses such as Hepatitis A, B, or C and others' (Elder c.2000, p. 47). Thus while prostitutes' rights organisations promote S&M/B&D and suggest it may have a low risk factor for contracting HIV, they equally recognise it may be high risk in other ways.

SWOP's risk management procedures for S&M/B&D provides extensive information on health risks involved in the more common practices – whipping, fisting, water sports, scat, rimming, branding, bondage, shaving, hot wax, electrical torture, spanking and piercing (1997, p. 4). A focus on just four of these activities exemplifies that such practices are intrinsically harmful to a woman's health. SWOP explains how during whipping 'breaks in the skin may occur' while 'bull whips and canes are likely to cause marks and bruises, if not cuts'. Fisting is considered particularly dangerous because as 'Fists are big things, [they] can create more serious tears than other sexual activities [and] if the person fisting has cuts or sores' there is the risk of HIV. Latex gloves are recommended as a precaution against the spread of infection. However, as with all prophylactics, there is no guarantee that breakages will not occur. SWOP notes how 'Latex gloves are particularly susceptible to tearing from fingernails' (1997, p. 4).

Water sports, which involve one person urinating on another, are further S&M/B&D activities that are extremely harmful to women in prostitution. SWOP identifies these activities as 'a low risk activity for HIV on the outside of the body *as long as* [SWOP's emphasis] there are no cuts or breaks in the skin or mouth'. The pamphlet also alerts practitioners to 'Never let anyone piss in your arse' although it is more ambiguous about 'pissing in your mouth', concluding that it is a 'low-risk activity for HIV, but high risk for Hepatitis' (1997, p. 5). Branding is also stated to be extremely hazardous. Individuals who engage in branding may be protected from HIV/AIDS, because the high temperatures of branding implements kill the virus. However, they generate 'problems with blistering and fluid arising' (1997, p. 6).

No OHS prevention strategy can eliminate the transmission of bodily fluids that may contain dangerous organisms when S&M/B&D practices, by their very nature, involve blood, vomit, urine, faeces and saliva. In addition no OHS strategies can deal with all the health risks resulting from S&M/B&D practices as is the case with prostitution *per se* when what a 'service' entails is limited only by the mind of the buyer. Still identifying something as prostitution, does nothing to eliminate the harm to women of abusive and violent practices.

The power dynamics of S&M/B&D

In S&M/B&D, economics and the need of prostituted women to compete for a buyer remain paramount in the negotiation between the buyer and the bought. Rates are negotiated according to the content of the session and the role the prostituted woman is to take in that session. As SWOP explains, 'Dominants (masters/mistresses) and submissives are paid according to the severity of the session, but a submissive usually receives a lot more than a dominant' (1997, p. 6). Sarah Priesley, after having worked in brothel prostitution for six years, believes that most women in prostitution 'specialize in something . . . for extra money' (1997, p. 91). She describes one 'submissive booking', where the woman involved 'was tied up and gagged in the room'. The buyers (two men) then 'whipped her badly and burnt her with cigarette butts'. But in a legalised system no crime has been committed. As Priesley reflects 'No-one could blame the client since she'd agreed to do the booking, and that is what he wanted to do'. She says, it was irrelevant that the woman left the booking 'screaming' (1997, pp. 92–93). It obviously was also irrelevant that the woman was being tortured which in all other contexts but prostitution is illegal.

S&M/B&D OHS guidelines do not deal with specific hazards that a prostituted woman incurs from taking the role of a submissive. This is not surprising as no OHS strategy could eliminate the harms from being a recipient of violence, whether in the form of branding, whipping, cutting or other forms of violence, or as seen above, anything else that might yet be envisaged by the buyer.

Potential and actual violence is as pervasive a feature in S&M/B&D as with straight commercial sex. OHS information sheets caution women involved in S&M/B&D 'to always take precautions with unknown clients, especially when working alone'; 'to never work alone' or, if no other choice is possible, 'to get a friend or partner to call after the session to check on you' (Sex Workers Outreach Project 1997, p. 5). In these circumstances violence inherent in S&M/B&D practices is aggravated by the buyer acting out other forms of violent behaviour against prostituted women.

One might assume that women who reverse the role and act as a dominatrix can reverse the power dynamics that are normally at play in S&M/B&D. However acting as a dominatrix does not equate to equal power between the woman and the buyer. Toby Summer (pseudonym) expands this point in 'Women, Lesbians and Prostitution: A Working-class Dyke Speaks Out Against Buying Women for Sex' (2001). As she explains:

> The prostitute who performs as a female sadist, a dominatrix, does not reverse the dynamic of dominance and submission. It may be true that she has 'complete power' over the male masochist's body for those moments that she is paid to do what she is told to do by him . . . but it is also true that the power of male supremacy is so great that a man can feel very safe even while he chooses to toy with 'submission' momentarily (in MacKinnon 2001, p. 1438).

Thus while women may take on the mantle of dominance for a specified period, it does not alter the social structure and power relations under a male supremacist society. As Summer concludes, if 'the dominatrix *used* that "power" that she has during this singular moment in history – in the way that men use their power over women – she'd be either in jail or dead' (in MacKinnon 2001, p. 1438).

Sadomasochism as torture

A further disturbing element of the prostitution industry's promotion of S&M/B&D is that it normalises the practice of torture within society. Susan Hawthorne in her research into the contemporary torture of lesbians exposes the way in which consensual S&M/B&D creates an acceptance of political torture, 'by the eroticization of torture as just another sexual thrill' (2005/2006, p. 35). As she says, 'domination, an integral part of male sex right practices, is the model for lesbian sadomasochism' (2005/2006, p. 40). Pat Califia (now Patrick), one of the major proponents of the practice, exemplifies this point well. In *The Lesbian S/M Safety Manual* (1988) Califia illustrates how domination is central to the sadomasochistic practices. As 'he' says:

> One way to keep bondage erotic is to ask yourself the question 'Why is this person being tied up?' Is it because you want to make them helpless for torture? Make their sex completely accessible . . . as a pain trip, or as sensory deprivation? (in Hawthorne 2005/2006, pp. 35–36).

Throughout her work Hawthorne has documented the horrific treatment of lesbians who are tortured in families, in prisons and in mental asylums, explaining how in many countries being lesbian still carries an immediate jail sentence. She is thus particularly disturbed about what Califia has to say about sexual excitement:

> By reviving the notion that sex is dirty, naughty, and disgusting, you can profoundly thrill some lucky, jaded lesbian by transforming

her into a public toilet or bitch in heat (in Hawthorne 2005/2006, p. 39).

Califia and her followers attempt to distance themselves from their legitimisation of torture by categorising sadomasochistic practices as simply 'play' and 'performance'. It is 'consensual, non-consent play'.

This performance aspect is pushed also by Margot Weiss (2005). To her the Abu Ghraib photographs of American soldiers torturing Iraqi prisoners are 'merely a scene, a spectacle'. 'Play torture' which parodies the actors in this performance, she says, 'serves as a critique, as it disrupts how people understand the world'. Thus the scenes 'become a creative re-enactment about powerlessness over the war' (in Hawthorne 2005/2006, p. 41). Hawthorne counters this explanation arguing that torture is not performative but real. 'It is more than just "powerlessness"; it is subjugation, degradation, abandonment, and dehumanization, a person does not know if they will live or die' (2005/2006, p. 41). She makes the important analogy that:

> In a similar way to that in which Western culture has appropriated the cultures of indigenous and non-Western peoples, the practi-tioners of S/M are appropriating the experiences of oppressed peoples who have been tortured by dictatorial governments or who have been slaves under racist regimes or the lesbians who are tortured by fundamentalist and militarized regimes (2005/2006, p. 43).

Califia's understanding of 'humiliation' in sadomasochism 'performance' leaves no doubt that Hawthorne is correct. From Califia's perspective:

> [Humiliation] . . . is the deliberate lowering of the bottom's status to an eroticized, yet stigmatized, identity. This may include turning the bottom into: (1) an object or a machine, (2) an animal, (3) a child or baby, (4) a member of the opposite sex, (5) a sexual object

or genital, (6) a servant or slave. Humiliation can also involve treating the bottom as a member of a racial or ethnic group, sexual orientation or socioeconomic class which the top pretends to resent, dislike etc. (in Hawthorne 2005/2006, p. 43).

What Califia describes as a consumer experience is an act that is ultimately full of contempt for others. As Hawthorne makes clear, like prostitution 'the promotion of sadomasochism . . . contributes to the escalation of violence and social acceptance of violence under the guise of "free choice"' (2005/2006, p. 40).

Violence: aberrant male behaviour or part of the job?

Campaigns by prostitutes' rights organisations to have OHS codes of practice adopted within the prostitution workplace are formulated on the assumption that violence is not intrinsic to sadomasochism or prostitution *per se*. The PCV position is that male buyers who perpetrate violence against women in prostitution are not 'clients' but 'pose as clients' (Gilbert 1992, p. 6). But as I have suggested throughout this book, I strongly believe that the harm prostitution causes is inherent in prostitution work practices *per se* and the idea that prostitution can be negotiated as a contract between two equal consenting adults, is wishful thinking.

Feminists working in the area of violence against women, together with prostitutes' rights organisations, have identified many forms of violence that women in prostitution routinely experience (see Chapter One). This violence may be physical, psychological, social or sexual, although most frequently the violence that women in prostitution encounter combines most of these features. Acts of violence include abusive communication, intimidation or bullying as well as physical abuse that may range from punching to choking to the use of weapons and murder (Sex Workers Outreach Project 1996, p. 5). SWOP extends the definition of violence to the threat of physical violence, which frequently manifests as death threats (Bridgett 1997, p. 5).

The form of violence that women in prostitution are at particular risk of is sexual violence. Sexual violence is behaviour of a sexual nature, which is unwanted, or occurs without consent, and ranges from sexual harassment and stalking to sexual abuse and rape. Despite efforts to normalise prostitution as work, various prostitutes' rights organisations have acknowledged that prostituted women experience sexual violence through penetration of the vagina, mouth or anus with a penis, tongue, fingers or other body parts or objects; being made to look at or pose for pornographic photos, videos or magazines; oral or genital contact, touching, fondling, kissing or being forced to touch the offender (Elder c.2000, p. 36; Prostitutes' Collective of Victoria c.1995, p. 19).

There is extensive anecdotal evidence that violence remains a pervasive feature of Victoria's model prostitution system. The PCV's 1992 submission to the Law Reform Commission Victoria, regarding sentencing practices in rape cases, reported that 'Sex workers (women, men and transsexuals) have been and continue to be targets of rape and other violent acts', irrespective of Victoria having then already experienced nearly a decade of partial legalisation of the State's prostitution industry (Gilbert 1992, p. 32). Keith Gilbert, who authored the submission, estimated that the PCV was receiving 'an average of 20 reports of violence against sex workers each week'. This figure, he believed however, was in fact 'an under representation of the level and incidence of violence against sex workers' (1992, p. 32).

The PCV's reports, newsletters, magazines and OHS material also provide extensive information on the level of violence experienced by those within the Victorian industry. The excerpt below relates the experience of a rape victim working privately in Victoria. It was published in the August 1999 edition of the

PCV's coverage of its *Ugly Mugs*. Clearly, from the victim's perspective, what follows had not been negotiated:

> He was standing at the side of the bed, gently stroking the worker's hair and kissing her, then he changed rapidly and pushed the worker down on the bed, and then raped her vaginally and then flipped the worker over and raped her anally . . . he came twice during the period he was raping her. The more the worker struggled the more the client got off on it, so the worker lay still, terrified if she continued to struggle that he would be even more violent. He then got off her body and said 'that was the best fuck I ever had' (Prostitutes' Collective of Victoria 1999, p. 17).

In reply to the buyer's query if he had given her enough money, the woman replied 'for what you have done no amount of money would be enough'. What is particularly disturbing in this account is the PCV's continued use of the term 'worker' rather than the more factual idiom of woman and rape victim.

For the buyers it is apparent that making prostitution work allows them to perpetuate violence that in any other area of work would constitute a crime. One woman interviewed by PCV's Sarah Keogh said how one buyer told her at the end of a brutal session, 'Well honey, you've chosen to work here, these are the bad sides, and you're earning all this money so you should be ready for it' (1992, p. 21). While treating prostitution as no different to other occupations allows such behaviour to be accepted as just part of the job, the environment in which prostitution takes place undoubtedly encourages male aggression.

In addition to rape, pornography is one of the more easily identifiable forms of violence that prostituted women are confronted with in their 'working' environment. Under the heading 'STD Potential Videos' published in *Working Girl* (Prostitutes' Collective of Victoria 1991), a woman employed in a legal brothel tells how 'porno videos . . . [are played] continually'. This, she says, results in giving 'clients a false impression of what services are provided'. The woman also considers that the pornography becomes an obstacle to safe sex. From her perspective it was hard 'to convince the client to use condoms after seeing these videos' (PCV 1991, p. 6). In Melbourne's legal brothels prostitution thus becomes, what radical feminist Kathleen Barry defines as 'the enacted version of pornography, where graphic representation of the subordination of women comes to life' (1995, p. 57).

The scene discussed above has parallels to those described by D. A. Clarke in her exploration of connections between the sex trade and neoliberal dogma (2004). In one instance she tells how public humiliations are now part of regular talkshows in the US. In particular she describes how one 'shock-jock, Howard Stern' convinced a woman to strip in the studio and then eat dog food from a bowl. In return Stern would give air time to music recorded by her friend. However there is in theory no victim here. As Clarke stresses, 'The pseudo-Smithian ideology of "choice" and the rest of the market-populist mumbo-jumbo, would of course emphasise this woman's "choice" to endure such a scene, rather than questioning the ethics of Stern, the radio station, or the advertisers and the listeners' (2004, p. 170).

In prostitution it is difficult to question the demand side of the transaction. As Clarke goes on to say:

> The religion of the Market rests on a fundamental assumption that all desires and appetites [including the consumption of pornography and prostitution] are valid, and that to criticise any 'customer preference' is to become that dreadful thing, a judgmental or Puritanical person – committing the cardinal sin of Interfering with the Free Market (2004, p. 187).

Thus we can blame the prostituted woman for the violence perpetrated against her but never the buyer.

Violence as an OHS risk

The inclusion of violence as an OHS risk for the prostitution industry seemingly provides some measures of protection for the women who are victims of such abuse. This is whether perpetrated by sex business operators or buyers. The NSW OHS brothel guidelines and the Queensland regulations both focus on eliminating violence through an employer's 'duty of care . . . to create a workplace where the risk of violence is minimised' (New South Wales WorkCover Authority 2001, p. 8; Prostitution Licensing Authority 2002, p. 8). In practice this means implementing procedures to eliminate potentially 'abusive situations, violence or intimidation from their workplace – regardless of the source' (New South Wales WorkCover Authority 2001, p. 8). As is common practice, the actual procedure for implementing OHS employer responsibility for the industry is dealt with in the codes of practice developed by worker groups, in this instance Australian prostitutes' rights organisations.

The Scarlet Alliance's *Best Practice* (Elder c.2000) deals with employer responsibility, which it sees mainly in terms of providing security. In addition to in-house responses that may include installing safety devices (panic/alarm buttons) in workrooms and video surveillance to screen clients, it also recommends that the employers provide safety information to 'workers'. These should entail 'how the employees should safely extricate themselves from the client's pressure' and 'what measures to take to alert others to the situation' (Elder c.2000, p. 37). But the guidelines offer no practical measures on how women may 'safely extricate' themselves from the buyer. They equally ignore the disparity that exists between a man and a woman within the prostitution transaction when as suggested earlier, a woman's demonstration of assertiveness towards a buyer is frequently a precursor to violence.

In addition to providing security, OHS literature encourages employers to offer appropriate training to non-prostituted staff that take bookings, staff phones or are at reception. Most risk prevention training is limited to offering advice on 'how the receptionist is expected to act in the situation', 'how other staff should respond' and 'the circumstances in which police must be called' (Sex Workers Outreach Project 1996, p. 37). The specific skills that receptionists need to develop are an ability to identify a 'dangerous client' during 'the booking stage' and during 'liaison with client'. Employers must instruct staff to respond to 'clients who exhibit verbally or physically threatening or abusive behaviour' (1996, p. 38). Again the guidelines are ambiguous about what such training would involve. For example how does a receptionist distinguish between a 'dangerous client' and a non-dangerous buyer?

Safety procedures of escort work

Risk management procedures for escort workers require even stronger security precautions. One of the proposals put forward by the Scarlet Alliance is for the receptionist to identify a potentially dangerous job prior to her taking a booking. How a receptionist is supposed to elicit this information through telephone communication remains of course unclear. Follow-up procedures involve contacting Call Directory Assistance to verify whether the caller is legitimate, an action that is potentially an invasion of privacy and therefore illegal. The next part of the process is to check the *Ugly Mugs* report. As the booking is normally arranged by telephone a photograph or verbal description of a male abuser would not assist in identification. A final strategy is to ascertain on the telephone whether the client is alone or has omitted mentioning how many men are on the premises (Elder c.2000, p. 71). The complete impracticality of this last task highlights the ludicrousness of the whole OHS employer responsibility approach to violence in the prostitution 'workplace'. Moreover it assumes a body of men organising a gang rape will admit to their crime prior to it occurring.

The impracticalities of the present approach offered by OHS codes and guidelines, however, are not limited to the booking process. Once a booking for an escort worker has been made, a whole range of other protective strategies are to become operational. *Best Practice* stipulates that an employer in carrying out his or her 'duty of care' should supply escort workers with a mobile phone, a personal alarm and a 'trained' driver. The expectation is that the driver will assist a woman if she encounters danger once she arrives at the buyer's premises. A driver's brief should include 'driving skills, not [to be] intoxicated, and [to treat the] woman respectably' (Elder c.2000, p. 72). Again how these job skills qualify a driver to act as a bodyguard as suggested above is not mentioned. There is the further problem of the illegality of a non-authorised person entering private premises without the owner's permission.

Accommodating violence: prostituted women's OHS responsibilities

Perhaps in recognition of the unworkability of relying on employer responsibility to eliminate violence in the prostitution 'workplace', OHS literature has progressively focused on 'worker control'. SWOP's *9 Lives: surviving sexual assault in the sex industry* (Bridgett 1997) demonstrates well how prostitutes' rights organisations place more and more of the responsibility for risk management on women working in brothels or as escorts. The NSW occupational health and safety authorities offer the booklet as an essential resource for those in the industry as does the Scarlet Alliance and most State and Territory prostitutes' rights organisations.

9 Lives (the title says it all) deals with risk prevention strategies for minimising violence that occurs as part of the everyday experience of women in prostitution. In addition it offers advice on coping with the health and safety repercussions for victims. Women are encouraged to use their intuition to identify a 'dangerous' client before entering. 'Sussing out the client' and 'gut instinct' are common expressions used throughout the booklet (Bridgett 1997, pp. 3–5). The information is often presented in cartoon form, accessible and concise, but dilutes the seriousness of the topic. 'Selina', a central cartoon character, for example, takes the form of a cat. She promotes 'Pussy Power' and admonishes prostituted women not to 'leave home without [their] intuition' along with their 'personal alarms' or 'deadly stilettos' (Bridgett 1997, pp. 3–5). The booklet, in a similar way to other OHS literature for the industry, offers no guidelines for developing 'intuition' or even a pro-forma checklist on how the 'violent criminal' may be readily identified.

SWOP's precautionary tactics for escort workers include 'Avoid working alone', 'Pretend you are not working alone' or 'Try and see one client at a time [and] make sure there is no-one hiding at the job'. Women are also warned to 'Keep your client on your turf so you know how to escape'; 'Code Red: Be prepared for any emergencies – set up a safety code system with your co-workers, manager or receptionist' (Bridgett 1997, pp. 3–5).

While Victoria's primary approach to dealing with the health and safety of prostituted women is through regulatory procedures, RHED which offers sexual health programs for the State's prostitution businesses, has developed some guidelines to assist prostituted women to deal with violence. It offers a similar range of suggestions to women working alone as other OHS literature for the industry. In the same way they are told to 'develop strategies to reduce your isolation . . . Have your mobile phone . . . have your buddies, spotters, backups and "trusted others" in place and [lastly] have your self-esteem in place' (RHED 2006a, p. 5). The women are also advised that 'pens, screech whistles and breath sprays can make good weapons, and may allow you the opportunity to get away' (RHED 2006b, p. 1).

These risk prevention strategies that are considered normal safety procedures for women whether working in brothels or as escorts only too readily illustrate how the prostitution work environment is unquestionably a place of extreme and constant violence when compared to other workplaces. Ironically although RHED argues that male violence against prostituted women is aberrant behaviour, they are explicit about the fact that 'most Ugly Mugs look and act like ordinary men, come from all social classes, income levels, races and age groups' (2006a, p. 6). As they say, 'they fit nicely into normal society, have nice girl-friends/boyfriends, nice wives, nice mates, nice jobs and nice hobbies'.

'Have I been raped?'

Supporters of legalisation have argued that once prostitution was legitimised as work, women who experienced violence would more readily seek assistance from police and health workers. A critical problem with recognising the violence of prostitution is that, in a legalised prostitution system, the boundaries between what constitutes work and what constitutes violence is blurred for the prostituted woman. Feminists have successfully used 'consciousness raising' and 'naming' to allow women to identify child sexual abuse, rape in marriage, and sexual harassment as violence against women (see Jeffreys 1997, p. 253). In a similar way SWOP promotes 'consciousness raising' to assist prostituted women to see dominant interpretations of prostitution abuse as 'just sex'. In 9 Lives prostituted women are told that, 'Learning to recognise violence is the first step we can take in protecting ourselves' (Bridgett 1997, p. 2). This feminist-based strategy for dealing with the violence of prostitution potentially is a more positive means of addressing violence than the strategies emanating from the more mainstream OHS literature for the prostitution industry. Yet *9 Lives* also acknowledges that '[I]t can sometimes be difficult to immediately tell the difference between when a client has "gone too far" and when a sexual assault has occurred'. Prostituted women are advised to speak 'to co-workers and people they trust so that sexual assault can be more easily recognised' (1997, p. 5).

The reality is that most women in prostitution may find it difficult to define rape and sexual abuse. As Melissa Farley has concluded in her work with survivors of prostitution:

> If rape is defined as any unwanted sex act, then prostitution has an extremely high rate of rape because many survivors view prostitution as almost entirely consisting of unwanted sex acts or even, in one person's words, paid rape (2003, p. 100).

Making prostitution legal does not change these facts.

The harms of prostitution

The violence of prostitution affects the physical and mental health of all women in the industry. Farley and Kelly have pointed out that in addition to the harm associated with contracting STIs and chronic hepatitis, 'the consequences of sexual and physical violence begin with murder and expand to encompass a range of other harms'. These 'other harms', commonly include joint pain, cardiovascular symptoms, neurological problems and respiratory symptoms (2000, pp. 48–51).

Sarah Priesley's account of her involvement in prostitution in Australia suggests how such damage to women's health is normalised within the prostitution environment. She tells how some women she knew 'had worked for so long [in prostitution] that they'd lost control of their bladders, and they'd wet themselves . . . without even knowing' (1997, p. 92). Priesley also wrote about a young Chinese girl, Mimi, with whom she worked. The woman had worked for six months to save 50 thousand dollars. To achieve this:

> [S]he'd worked seven days a week . . . sometimes she would see sixteen clients in a day and night. Now she only did part service because she was bleeding from a period that wouldn't stop (1997, p. 146).

For many women in prostitution the injury to their health is ongoing and can affect them whether they remain in prostitution or not. The literature on the health consequences of sexual violence suggests that prostituted women may suffer irreparable harm through the abuse of prostitution. Sue Orsillo who works with the US National Centre of Post-Traumatic Stress Disorder describes how women may experience physical, psychological or behavioural damage as a result of being sexually violated. This long term damage manifests itself as depression, fear, anxiety, lack of trust, withdrawal, shame, self-blame, guilt, humiliation, anger or rage headaches, muscle tension, gastro-intestinal upset and genital or urinary complaints, suicidal actions, anorexia, alcohol and drug addiction, isolation, eating disorders, sleeping problems, phobias or nightmares (Orsillo 2006).

Indeed, sexual violence produces intense feelings of violation in victims because of the very intrusive nature of these crimes.

Dissociation and post-traumatic stress disorder

Violation and post-traumatic stress are the inevitable consequences of the violence of prostitution. SWOP's analyses of the effects of the violence of prostitution found that in general, most prostituted women experience feelings of numbness, shock, fear, flashbacks, loss of control, nightmares, depression, anger, desensitisation, shame and guilt (Bridgett 1997, p. 16). The

PCV's submission *Regarding Sentencing Practices* (1992) similarly highlighted how women who came in contact with the Collective reported that they experienced trauma after being raped by buyers (Gilbert 1992, p. 11). In other interviews, women expressed their sense of violation and powerlessness to PCV workers adopting phrases such as 'I feel so helpless', 'Will I ever be in control again?' or 'Why am I so calm? Why can't I cry?' (Prostitutes' Collective of Victoria 1994a, p. 26). In contrast some women deny to both others and themselves that they have been assaulted. They ask themselves 'Was it really sexual assault?' or say 'I'm O.K. I'll be all right'.

Priesley says when at 19 she first became involved in prostitution, she was told that 'the only way to stop yourself from getting hurt [emotionally] . . . was to distance yourself during the booking'. In practice, however, dissociation was not always possible:

> I tried to switch off [from a drunk john who ridiculed the size of her breasts and then bit them]. Every move he made on my body hurt and every smart comment rang in my ears and hurt as well. I didn't really know how to distance myself from bad clients. How could you? (1997, p. 37).

Melissa Farley, through her work with medical professional Colin Ross and psychotherapist Harvey Schwartz, has defined dissociation as a means of psychological survival. As they explain:

> Dissociation is an elaborate escape and avoidance strategy in which overwhelming human cruelty results in fragmentation of the mind into different parts of the self that observe, experience, react, as well as those that do not know about the harm. Given the burden of a lifetime trauma experienced by women in prostitution, the extended use of dissociation is easy to understand (Ross, Farley and Schwartz 2003, p. 205).

The problem with dissociation, as these authors argue, is that it can perpetuate women's experience of violence.

Paradoxically, although the dissociative adaptation protects the person from the emotional impact of trauma, it increases the risk of further victimization since the survivor tends to dissociate in response to actual danger cues that are similar to the original trauma (2003, p. 205).

Thus prostituted women may know that a buyer will be violent towards them. However, a pattern of dissociation developed to protect them from emotional trauma resulting from the violence of prostitution may then prevent them from mobilising 'other, healthier defensive strategies'.

Ross, Farley and Schwartz established that women from across the spectrum of the prostitution industry were found to have dissociative disorders. This was irrespective of whether women were prostituted in brothels, on the streets, or in strip clubs. Dissociative disorders were in turn associated with 'post-traumatic stress disorder, depression and substance abuse' (2003, p. 199). These findings build on earlier analysis undertaken by Farley and Kelly, wherein they concluded that 'The constant humiliation, the social indignity and misogyny result in personality changes' which we now know 'as complex post-traumatic stress disorder' (2000, p. 48). This obliteration of prostituted women's emotional well-being has led Farley and Kelly, together with other anti-violence feminists, to identify prostitution *per se* as a form of sexual violence.[6]

Prostitutes' rights organisations despite their pro-prostitution position have also acknowledged that dissociation is an inevitable consequence of prostitution. There is a tendency, however, for some to ignore the long-term outcomes for women who must

---

6. I have discussed anti-violence analyses of prostitution as sexual violence in Chapter One.

resort to it in order to survive. One piece published in *Working Girl* suggests that the mind/body split employed by women in the industry is little more than creating fantasy or performance. As Sophie Kennedy writes:

> Brothels just ooze with popular culture's notion of femininity. I don't wear make-up in my private life and I very rarely dress up to go out. But when I go to work, I take great pride in putting on my costume. Layer upon layer of foundation, powder, blusher, eye-liner; hair tied back in a ponytail and then concealed under a wig and some stunning garment of clothing I wouldn't dare to go out in . . . women all revert to children playing dress up . . . it is a world of fantasy and play-acting. Once dressed, we sit and wait, the greatest, the greatest of all feminine traits being passivity. We wait for men to choose us above other women and they choose us according to our appearance (Prostitutes' Collective of Victoria 1994b, p. 10).

An alternative and more realistic view of how playing a variety of sex-roles impacts negatively on a woman's well-being is presented in SWOP's industry magazine, *The Professional*:

> At the end of a busy day, week or month it can be easy to lose a sense of yourself with all the energy around, especially if you've been spending time playing a variety of sex-roles for others. There are often warning signals that can help us to realise that we need to take a bit of time out to slow down, sit or lie down and turn back into ourselves. A classic feeling like you couldn't face another client right now. Where there is a feeling like you're losing control. Is it getting hard to maintain personal or working boundaries? (Tantra Man [pseudonym] 1994, p. 23).

However acknowledging the problem of dissociation that comes from 'the unique sort of pressures' that are faced by women in prostitution does not alleviate the problem. OHS literature can offer women suffering from dissociative disorders nothing but the rather meagre suggestion that they adjust to the situation. Ultimately women are advised that emotional healing for the rape, violence and depersonalisation that prostituted women experience daily can be achieved through taking time out to play some calming, soothing music, take a long hot bath, and for the victim to say to herself 'remember I'm beautiful' (1994, p. 23).

Such healing strategies mirror those put forward in *9 Lives*. Here women are told:

> Even though you may feel fearful for some time after a sexual assault do not show it to clients as they may take advantage . . . stand loud and proud at work with your clients . . . Visualise a royal warrior princess and copy her pose [and] . . . Adopt a position of assertiveness and practice being in control with your clients (Bridgett 1997, p. 18).

The themes here are the same as I have identified previously in this chapter. And they have all the same limitations: It is the responsibility of the victim to ensure her own health and safety, the same with negotiation skills, the same with demands to take control. The buyer and the violence remain invisible.

Conclusion

In this chapter I have outlined the contradictions underpinning peer-based approaches to OHS. As suggested, prostitutes' rights organisations attempt to deal with the harms of prostitution as aberrant parts of the prostitution industry. Thus the violence of prostitution becomes an aspect of the prostitution industry, which, it is claimed can be eliminated, or at least minimised through OHS.

Conversely I argue that the application of OHS in the prostitution industry cannot be in the interests of prostituted women. The experience of legalisation in Victoria and the types of OHS legislation and policy available within Australia as a whole succinctly demonstrate that public policy supports the idea of health and safety for prostituted women only to the extent that it correlates with the interests of the male consumer and the state's public health strategies. The supposedly more responsive OHS codes developed by prostitutes' rights organisations contain equal contradictions. These leave unchallenged the prostitution behaviour of the 'normal client' and continue to promote the erroneous idea that violence is located outside the prostitution work environment.

The best that can be offered to ameliorate the harm of prostitution is a set of wholly inadequate techniques that, in some cases, are themselves life-threatening. The following are among the skills demanded in order to avoid such 'occupational hazards' as contracting life-debilitating infections, assault, rape or even death:

- Proficiency in sexual health education
- Ability to make medical diagnosis of a minimum of 25 STIs
- Handling of personal protective equipment
- Deception and duplicity
- Thorough understanding of highly complex and dangerous contraceptive methods
- Hostage negotiating
- De-escalating violent situations
- Highly developed intuitive skills to differentiate between rapists and other 'clients'
- Self-defence against rape
- Disassociation, or ability to perform a mind-body split.

In any other workplace these abuses of women's human rights, which we call 'occupational risks', have nothing to do with labour regulations. They are considered a criminal offence. As such I maintain that prostitution can never be an occupation comparable to other forms of legitimate work. It is at its core a manifestation of male violence against women. Indeed the application of OHS to Victoria's prostitution industry helps maintain the invisibility of the real harm of prostitution. It in fact reifies the intrinsically violent nature of the industry.

CHAPTER EIGHT

Making Men's Demand Visible

The issue where we initially had problems identifying its relevance to a congress on working life concerned the sex trade or commercial sex work as it is sometimes called to describe an activity which for many women in the world is the only opportunity available to earn a living . . . We would like to state categorically that prostitution should never be seen as an alternative to normal work. Trafficking is a crime and those who carry it out are criminals. However, the women who suffer this form of exploitation should never be treated as criminals themselves, but rather as victims in need of support. We are convinced that there is only one humane way to go: all women, regardless of where in the world they live, must be given the opportunity to find a way of earning a living other than through prostitution or as a victim of trafficking.

OHLSSON, KNOCKE AND GRADIN 2002.[1]

The disturbing worldwide trend to accept the sexual exploitation of women and girls as a legitimate activity called 'work' within the mainstream economy is undoubtedly profitable for sex businesses and governments alike. It similarly profits organised crime, which remains entrenched in the prostitution industry,

---

1. Inger Ohlsson is the Director-General of the Swedish National Institute for Working Life, Wuokke Knocke is Associate Professor at the Swedish National Institute for Working Life, and Anita Gradin is a former Swedish Minister and a European Union Commissioner.

whether or not prostitution operates within a regulatory system. The Australian State of Victoria, which is now in an advanced stage of the industrialisation of prostitution, demonstrates only to clearly what happens when prostitution is normalised and protected by the State. Its experience is crucial to debates among international feminists, human rights activists, ethicists, policy makers and those individuals concerned with creating a democratic society, on whether prostitution should be considered 'work' and an issue of 'choice' – or whether it is sexual exploitation and violence and denies women their right to equality and safety. I believe that Victoria's legalisation of prostitution must be recognised as a failed experiment, both from the point of view of the State's objectives and also, importantly, for the women (and men) who are prostituted. Having studied the developments in Victoria over two decades I have come to the conclusion that legalised prostitution is government-sanctioned abuse of women and an attack on their human rights and labour rights.

Victoria's legalised prostitution system is constructed around a belief in what Carole Pateman (1988) identifies as the fundamental social contract – a man's innate right to women's bodies for sex. When women are not available, or not prepared to fulfil this need for free, a 'surrogate class of women' – prostituted women – meet this demand. When looking at the process of how prostitution became normalised as work in the State of Victoria, it was apparent that the Government, supported by pro-prostitution advocates, accepted in principle the inevitability of prostitution based on men's 'natural' demand for sex. The forces propelling Victoria's shift from treating prostitution as an illegal and deviant activity to legitimate work, concentrated on establishing the right of individuals to be free from State interference in their private lives. This libertarian perspective allowed prostitution to be reframed as a sexual activity taking place in the private sphere between two consenting adults. Pro-prostitution advocates argued that this purported liberty did not alter because money changed hands. Ironically however, the exchange of money for sex meant that prostitution was not just a private matter but also a business activity that had to meet the same regulatory standards that apply to other industries.

A further influence feeding into Victoria's liberalisation of the State's prostitution law was neo-liberal economic beliefs, which encouraged the freeing up of the market place. Supporters of legalisation drew on this philosophy to justify that market forces must be allowed to determine the supply of, and demand for, prostitution services, a system in which women are no different than commodities of market exchange.

As Victoria attempted to bring the prostitution industry under regulatory control, it became obvious that prostitution cannot be regulated in a similar way to other commercial practices and legitimate work. Successive Victorian Governments found that the legal industry must be subject to specific regulations that relate to local zoning laws, health inspections, as well as some form of licensing to eliminate the criminal element. There was also the reality that in practice the Government has no control over most of the industry, which continues to operate illegally or unregulated under its 'model' system. Essentially as a consequence, Victoria has ended up with a two-tier system, composed of legal and illegal sectors.

Australian feminists who have attempted since the late 1970s to introduce feminist theory and practice into the ongoing debates on Victoria's prostitution law reform were divided in their support of making prostitution 'work'. The appeal for socialist and liberal feminists was that reframing prostitution as a labour issue would potentially end the criminalisation and stigmatisation of women in the prostitution industry. Although socialist feminists in particular, saw a contradiction in supporting the idea of prostitution as work – as they recognised it as sexual exploitation – they sought a compromise by focusing on prostituted women's rights as workers. This strategy was underpinned by a belief that once prostitution was no longer treated as a criminal activity, women in prostitution would be entitled to the same industrial rights as all other workers. Ultimately they could become sufficiently empowered economically to escape their exploitation.

Feminist campaigns in support of prostitution as work also took up liberal ideas about sexual and economic autonomy – the right to choose and the right to sexual freedom and expression. These liberal ideologies supported the notion of prostitution as work and women's rights were juxtaposed with women's rights to sexual autonomy. In contrast to these socialist and liberal orientated positions, radical feminists, from the outset, were opposed to legitimising prostitution as work. They considered prostitution as sexual exploitation and argued that no solution which ignored the male demand for this kind of sex, would eliminate the oppression of women in the prostitution industry. Radical feminists unequivocally challenged the essentialist biological model (men 'need' sex), which legitimised male sex rights. But these ideas were marginalised in Victoria's legal restructuring of the prostitution industry, as the State was only prepared to engage with feminist views that could be assimilated into its pro-prostitution agenda.

The Prostitutes' Collective of Victoria (PCV), whose origins were in the Women's Liberation Movement, was also only successful to the extent that its goals fitted in with the State Government's priorities. While initially the Collective was closely allied with socialist feminists, its growth and legitimacy became dependent on its cooption by the State. This organisational shift saw the PCV relinquish its advocacy for the rights of prostituted women as women's human rights, in favour of becoming a sexual health service provider for the prostitution industry in general –

'workers', sex business interests and buyers. Eventually the PCV became an arm of the State's regulatory system working to contain the spread of HIV/AIDS and other STIs. These changes were accompanied by the transformation of the Collective's ideological perspective. The PCV increasingly promoted prostitutes' rights as sexual rights portraying prostituted women as just one of many sexual minorities oppressed by legal and social stigma. This shift in thinking was largely determined by the AIDS crisis and the increasing influence of queer politics within the PCV. However reframing prostitution as an expression of sexual freedom also led to eliminating the boundaries between the PCV's initial constituency – prostituted women – and the buyers. What disappeared here was the reality that the State's prostitution industry is a service that fulfils the sexual demands of men and it was they – the consumers – whom the system protected.

One of the immediate consequences of Victoria's legalisation of prostitution was the unprecedented demand for prostitution and the expansion of the industry. Victorians whether they have agreed with this development or not, are now daily exposed to the State's prostitution culture. While moral concerns still impose some restrictions on the extent to which prostitution is accepted and made visible in Victoria, the Government's recognition of prostitution as a legitimate commercial practice has meant that municipal councils face difficulties in contesting the establishment of brothels in their city. As offering sexual services now qualifies as a lawful use of land, they have minimal grounds to oppose their establishment. The only exception is where prostitution is recognised by the State as causing a measurable harm. The Government considers prostitution as unproblematic as long as it does not take place in a locality frequented by children, for instance. The liberal individualism that underpins the State's prostitution laws thus overrides community rights and sanctions the inroads made by prostitution on public space, or, from a feminist perspective, the rights of women as a social group to be free of sexual exploitation.

Inevitably the normalisation of prostitution as legitimate commercial activity has also meant that the economic and political power of sex entrepreneurs has been significantly increased. There are few restrictions to the open marketing and selling of women for sex except some restrictions of the form and content of advertising. The Victorian Government has linked up with other vested interests, including some of Australia's mainstream financial institutions, to encourage the prostitution industry, either openly, through tax incentives or by providing loans, or indirectly, by creating an environment in which prostitution tourism can flourish unrestricted. The industry is free to utilise the media and lobbying activities to further normalise the trade in women. One of the most overt illustrations of just how the prostitution industry has been allowed to promote itself is the annual staging of Sexpo since 1997 at the State's Convention Centre in Melbourne (see Chapter Four for in-depth discussion).

This normalisation and mainstreaming of prostitution as a legitimate commercial activity had provided the major rationale for the mobilisation of a female 'workforce' for the prostitution industry. As argued by Melbourne-based Legal Centre and Advocacy Program for Women in Prison, 'Women, simply by being women, are automatically employable as prostitutes' (Darebin Community Legal Centre and the Advocacy Program for Women in Prison 2003, p. 8). As a result, 'This makes prostitution among the most accessible jobs for economically disadvantaged women' (2003, p. 8). Over the last two decades more and more women have been drawn into the industry. Most women still resort to prostitution because of hardship. They experience violence at the hands of buyers and brothels owners, contempt, low pay and drug addiction. They remain part of the secondary workforce, identified as either casuals or contractors, with minimal industrial rights. Moreover the 'work' of prostitution ensures that women are not in a position to develop skills that would make them more widely employable. The Government offers no assistance or retraining programs to enable the high percentage of women who wish to exit the industry to do so. Women's right to equality in the workplace is thus denied to those women entrapped in a life cycle of prostitution.

The option for prostituted women to gain proprietorship of their working lives is restricted further under Victoria's legalised prostitution regime as the State's prostitution law facilitates the dominance of the industry by sex entrepreneurs. However the liberal language of 'choice' and 'agency' works to hide prostituted women's inability to achieve workplace equality. The Victorian Government, in facilitating this 'choice', indeed perpetuates the economic disempowerment of women.

An even more overt demonstration of Victoria's failed experiment with legalised prostitution is that the vast majority of the State's industry operates either on the margins of the legal sector or in a totally illegal environment. Victoria's lawmakers are confronted with the challenge of regulating an industry whose boundaries are constantly changing and expanding. The Government's attempt to introduce catch-up legislation has proved ineffective at achieving these goals. No Government has been able to adequately address the range of sexually exploitative practices that sex entrepreneurs will invent to circumvent the law to maximise their profits. This is an inherent weakness of a system that legalises certain prostitution acts under certain conditions hoping that other forms of sexual exploitation will simply disappear. Tabletop dancing is but one example of prostitution-like activities that continue to operate relatively unregulated at the margins of Victoria's legal prostitution sector. The Government also appears to have no solution to the State's numerous sex businesses which operate illegally.

Women have been drawn into the illegal prostitution sector in an attempt to gain some economic independence or because of substance addiction, age discrimination or outright coercion. The illegal industry is characterised by sexual and economic exploitation, continuing criminal involvement in the trade and sex trafficking. There is also evidence of child prostitution. However taken together, as we have seen, the boundaries between the legal and clandestine market are often illusory in terms of exploitation of women, and criminal ownership and practices.

In the face of ongoing evidence that legalisation fails to achieve any of its objectives, the Government remains committed to a policy that accepts the inevitability of prostitution. As one of its significant beneficiaries, it has little option but to continue to attempt to use piecemeal legislation to try to address the worst aspects of the industry. The State's *Justice Legislation (Sexual Offences and Bail) Act 2004*, for example, will not end the cycle of sex trafficking as it only focuses on the traffickers and not the men who are gratified by prostitution. Similarly street prostitution continues to increase although associated prostitution activities remain illegal. Without effective exit programs and a determination by the State Government to prohibit male use of women on the street, street prostitution will remain an insoluble problem. While it is a fundamental duty of government to protect those in society most at risk, the State Government policies merely aim to hide street prostitution. This does nothing to help those who are vulnerable through histories of child sexual abuse, poverty, homelessness, and substance abuse.

The pro-prostitution, pro-legalisation position becomes totally unstuck, however, when the health and safety of prostituted women is not protected even where prostitution operates under supposedly optimal conditions. That is where prostitution takes place within licensed sex businesses. One of the strongest feminist arguments in support of making prostitution work was that women in prostitution would receive the same industrial rights as all other workers. But occupational health and safety regulations have largely been driven by discourses on public health. Such regulations continue to victimise women in prostitution and endanger·their health. The Government's safe sex agenda aims to prioritise the health and safety of the wider community over that of women in prostitution. But by ignoring male behaviour and men's dominance in the prostitution transaction, the Victorian Government protects neither women nor public health.

Looking beyond this public health focus, both the nature of prostitution and the work environment are inherently characterised by constant and extreme violence and sexual harassment. These have major adverse effects on women's physical and reproductive health and have harmful short, and long, term psychological consequences for women. Many prostituted women live in a state of constant trauma. Programs developed by prostitutes' rights organisations (currently supported by the States of New South Wales and Queensland OHS regulation), are based on the assumption that the harms in prostitution are mainly aberrant to the prostitution industry and can therefore be eliminated or exceedingly minimised. The actual prostitution act is taken to be a consensual act between two equal participants in a commercial transaction. But what became apparent in looking at the history of prostitution in Victoria is that those women who work in Victoria's legalised brothels or for licensed escort agencies are seldom in a position to negotiate on an equal basis with the buyer. Male economic and social power and their understanding that their money is buying a simple commodity, negate any such suggestion.

If we accept the pro-prostitution argument that prostitution is work, and that the escalation in the global trafficking of people for sex is a labour and migration issue, we must also concede that there exists a class of women for whom sexual stereotyping, sexual abuse and harassment in the workplace are illegal and a violation of their human rights, and another class, where these same violations are deemed to be a mere commercial transaction without any consequences. The pro-prostitution stance on prostitution as work reinstates the age-old dichotomy between Madonna and whore.

Despite a decisive movement towards legalisation of prostitution worldwide, many countries are seeking alternative and more effective strategies to combat the expansion of the global sex trade. Prohibition harms women and girls caught up in systems of sexual exploitation while legitimising prostitution creates a boon to sex exploiters. The way forward from both a radical feminist perspective and a human rights perspective is to differentiate between decriminalisation for women in prostitution and the normalisation and legitimisation of the prostitution industry and the institutionalisation of men's right to women's bodies. As I outlined in the introductory chapter this is the model adopted by the Swedish Government in 1999 which provides a viable alternative to the Victorian legalisation model. Sweden recognises that prostitution exists because of male demand and women's poverty, aggravated by economic and social disparity between countries, races and classes and by women's histories of sexual violence and abuse. It also does not differentiate between sex trafficking and prostitution but understands that the latter is a precursor for such trafficking. It prosecutes men who buy women (and men) for sex.

Pro-prostitution advocates have predicted that the Swedish Act relating to the purchase of sexual services would result in an upsurge in illegal prostitution driving the practice underground. On the contrary there are measurable indications that the legislation has both reduced prostitution generally and curtailed sex trafficking. Gunilla Ekberg, Sweden's Special Advisor on issues of prostitution and trafficking has analysed the effect of

337

Sweden's no tolerance stance on sexual exploitation after six years of operation. Drawing on data from police, social service providers and people with experience of prostitution, Ekberg found that across the country street prostitution had fallen by at least 30 to 50 per cent and the recruitment of new women has come to a halt. Sweden which has a population of nine million people has no more than 500 women in the street trade (2004, p. 1193). As I highlighted in Chapter Five, St Kilda, the hub of Victoria's street prostitution, alone has between 300 and 350 people continually involved in prostitution on the streets. These numbers represent an increase of between 100 to 150 per cent since the Victorian Government legalised prostitution (Attorney-General's Street Prostitution Advisory Group 2002, p. 44).

Sweden's success in creating a legislative framework which reduces prostitution and sex trafficking is further suggested by the decline in the number of prostituted women exploited in the country overall. Within a two-year period (1999–2002) the number fell from 2,500 to around 1,500. Significantly the number of buyers also decreased by 75 to 80 per cent (Ekberg 2004, pp. 1193–1194). The Swedish National Criminal Investigation Department (NCID) believes that Sweden's law has indeed acted as a deterrent against purchasing commercial sex across the spectrum of prostitution activities. This includes 'men who use women in apartment brothels, at porn and striptease clubs, and through agencies' (in Ekberg 2004, p. 1209). Again the comparison with Victoria is stark. As I have exposed throughout this book, the State's legalised regime has resulted in the massive expansion and diversification of both the legal and illegal prostitution industry with more and more women and girls drawn into, and then entrapped in, this system of sexual exploitation (see in particular Chapters Four and Five).

Sweden's anti-prostitution legislation has equally proven to be an effective barrier to the wider problem of sex trafficking. While the numbers of those trafficked into the country for prostitution has remained relatively constant since the new prostitution laws were passed, neighbouring Scandinavian countries have witnessed a dramatic increase. The NCID estimates that between 400 and 600 women are trafficked into Sweden every year mainly from Eastern European countries. In comparison Denmark where 5,500 to 7,800 women are prostituted every year, 50 per cent are victims of trafficking (Ekberg 2004, p. 1194). Similarly in Finland up to 15,000 women are prostituted annually mainly from Russia and the three Baltic republics of Estonia, Latvia and Lithuania (Finland Adopts Legislation on Assistance to Victims of Trafficking 2006).

The NCID, utilising police reports from the Baltic States, has confirmed that criminals no longer consider Sweden a good market for their trafficking activities (NCID 2002, p. 20). Some prostituted women involved in Sweden's trafficking investigations have told police that Denmark, Germany, Holland and Spain are now more attractive to criminals (NCID 2002, p. 34). Such countries either tolerate or have legalised prostitution. As Ekberg says, 'Traffickers and pimps are businessmen who calculate profits, marketing factors, and risks of getting caught when deciding in which countries they will sell women into prostitution' (Ekberg 2004, p. 1200).

Increasingly other countries are beginning to appreciate the soundness of the Swedish legislation as an alternative and effective model for combating prostitution and sex trafficking. In 2002 the majority of members of the Nordic Council, a regional body of Parliamentarians from Iceland, Norway, Denmark, Sweden and Finland, issued a statement that future anti-trafficking strategies must focus on the root cause, the demand for women and children for prostitution. In the following year the Baltic countries of Estonia, Latvia and Lithuania also adopted a resolution against the trafficking of women and children that focused on criminalising the purchasing of sexual services (Ekberg 2004, p. 1208). The UN Commission on the Status of Women followed suit at its 49th session (Beijing + 10) held in New York in March 2005. Among five new resolutions the Commission adopted was the commitment towards 'Eliminating the Demand for Trafficked Women and Girls for All Forms of Exploitation' (UN Non Government Liaison Services 2005, p. 4).

Finland is the first European country apart from Sweden to pass legislation that addresses the demand side of the prostitution equation. In June 2006 the Finnish Government passed law making the purchasing of sexual services a crime in circumstances involving the procuring or trade in human beings (Finland Passes Law on Criminalisation on the Purchase of Sexual Services of Victims of Trafficking 2006, p. 1).

Outside of Europe, several Asian countries have introduced progressive anti-prostitution legislation. In 2003 the Philippines Government enacted its landmark *Anti-Trafficking in Persons Act (Republic Act 9208)* which established strong institutional mechanisms to protect and support victims of trafficking, as well as criminalising all perpetrators of trafficking, which includes bride traffickers and organisers of sex tourism. The most groundbreaking piece of the Philippines' legislation is that it criminalises those who buy trafficked women, such as members of the military.[2]

In 2004 South Korea became the second country in the world to criminalise all purchases of sexual services. South Korea's *Act on the Prevention of Prostitution and Protection of Victims Thereof (APPPVT) 2004* and the *Act on the Punishment for Procuring Prostitution and Associated Acts (APPPAA) 2004* are both part of its wider program to reduce prostitution and sex trafficking.

---

2. Under the Act the penalty for a first offence is six months community service and a fine of P50,000 (A$1269) and for a second offence one year imprisonment and a P100,000 (A$2539) fine (s. 11 [a] [b]).

The new anti-prostitution laws impose strong penalties on brothel owners, while simultaneously protecting women who are deemed to be victims of prostitution. The stipulation within the APPPAA requiring the confiscation of all profits or assets resulting from prostitution activities creates a strong economic disincentive for pimps and traffickers. Moreover Article 21 of the Act which penalises buyers is a clear statement that the South Korean Government recognises the critical role that demand plays in the sexual exploitation of women and girls.

After the law was enacted the Prostitution Prevention Comprehensive Plan was announced, providing a comprehensive system encompassing survivors' care, self-sufficiency and protection. Thus, the Government became responsible for every step of support for survivors of sexual exploitation. In 2004, for the first three months under the Plan, as much as US$6.9 million of the national budget was funnelled into measures to assist survivors of sexual exploitation. It rose to US$22.2 million in 2005 in the first full year of implementation and US$20.4 million is budgeted in 2006 (Song 2006, p. 1). While this represents a highly progressive strategy, there is also an assumption that some women choose prostitution and thus should be subject to criminal charges. Feminist activists Dorchen Leidholdt and Hilary Sung-hee Seo make the essential point that 'In implementing the new law, however, it will be critically important for criminal justice authorities in Korea to understand that few prostituted women enter the industry voluntarily' (2004, p. 1).

While neither the Philippines, Korea or Finland have gone as far as Sweden in full decriminalisation of prostitution for women (in the case of Korea) or criminalising all buyers of prostitution irrespective of whether the women have been trafficked for sexual purposes (Philippines and Finland), these countries' approach to prostitution are a critical step towards ending the sexual exploitation of women and children globally. While the law alone is not sufficient to create a democratic society where women can live free of all forms of male violence, as Gunilla Ekberg explains:

> As with all laws, the Law has a normative function. It is a concrete and tangible expression of the belief that Sweden's women and children are not for sale. It effectively dispels men's self-assumed right to buy women and children for prostitution purposes and questions the idea that men should be able to express their sexuality in any form and at any time (2004, p. 1205).

Sweden's law is grounded in the belief that prostitution and the trafficking of women and girls for sexual exploitation is an anathema in a democratic society where full gender equality is an accepted principal. What does this mean for Australia and Victoria in particular, where it is increasingly acceptable for men to visit brothels, strip clubs and sex trade shows? I believe that the Victorian Government through its legalisation of prostitution has facilitated the creation of a prostitution culture which normalises the view that there exists a class of women who exist for men's use and for their sexual gratification, commodities that can be bought and sold. However men's prostitution behaviour affects not just women in prostitution but all women. Equality between men and women cannot exist if men feel free to exploit and perpetrate violence against any woman. Prostitution teaches men and boys that women are sex objects put there for their use. The increasing numbers of men who purchase sex, many with wives and partners, means that prostitution sex is becoming a major paradigm for all heterosexual relations whether this is among intimate partners or within the workplace.

As became obvious throughout this book, the critical problem for the State of Victoria and other States and countries who replicate its legislative approach is that once men's 'right' to buy women and girls is legitimised in a society, any government's ability to contain the industry or end the sexual and economic exploitation of prostituted women and girls, is seriously diminished.

Glossary

buyer. I use the term buyer throughout this book to refer to a person (normally a man) who purchases women and children for sex. The term 'buyer' is a more realistic term than 'client' which is a neutral and euphemistic expression that implies that the man is the recipient of a service a woman wants to provide. Buyer reflects the reality that the man is an active agent in the prostitution transaction.

Coalition Against Trafficking in Women (CATW). CATW is a non-governmental organisation that promotes women's human rights by working internationally to combat sexual exploitation in all its forms. It was the first NGO to focus on trafficking in persons and is particularly strong in making connections between human trafficking and prostitution. CATW, which was formed in the US in 1989, has Category II Consultative Status with the United Nations Economic and Social Council and has established affiliated groups in the Asia-Pacific, Latin America, Africa, North America, Europe and Australia.

commercial sexual exploitation. Commercial sexual exploitation is the marketing and selling of women and children for sex or products that exploit their sexuality for profit.

consent. Consent underpins Victoria's legalised prostitution system. Prostitution is taken to be a consensual act between two equal parties where the prostituted woman 'consents' to be used sexually by the male buyer. Legally consent means to agree with another's action and assumes that the person consenting understands the full implications of the action that they have agreed to. This legal interpretation takes for granted that the conditions under which men consent to sex in the prostitution transaction are the same as those for women. Catharine MacKinnon puts it well when she explains that the law presents consent 'as a free exercise of sexual choice under conditions of power without exposing the underlying structure of constraint and disparity' (1989, p. 168). If women are denied economic independence, access to work which would allow them to develop skills so they could economically survive, they have nothing to fall back on but to sell their bodies. In reality the power differentiation between women without other resources, who are forced to rely on their bodies for a livelihood, and the male buyer, means that women's ability to negotiate sex is nullified. Women's need to comply is simply taken as consent.

Consent is only required when people are vulnerable in some way: legally, medically, emotionally, sexually, as research objects. Consent legitimises the actions of the powerful, and from a legal perspective, turns an act of violation into something acceptable. However consent does work to create the illusion that the powerless have some control and allows them to collude with the powerful (see Hawthorne 2002, pp. 382–383 for an expansion of this argument).

criminalising prostitution. Criminalising prostitution means prostitution and related activities are designated an illegal and criminal act, punishable by some form of sanction, either fines or imprisonment. In reality most countries tolerate some form of prostitution and adopt a policy of control and containment rather than complete prohibition. Often prostitution itself is not illegal, but related activities such as soliciting, advertising, brothel keeping, living off the earnings, and prostituting minors, are all criminal offences.

decriminalising prostitution. Decriminalising prostitution involves states legitimising what was previously an illegal activity as part of the mainstream economic sector. Decriminalisation permits prostitution to be recognised as legitimate work and pimps and brothel owners as legitimate business operators.

forced-free distinction. The forced-free distinction within prostitution is promoted by pro-prostitution advocates who suggest that many women 'choose' prostitution freely. They believe that women are subjected to exploitation and abuse which are similar in nature to that experienced by others working in low status jobs in the informal sector such as the garment industry or agricultural labour. Thus prostitution is only a problem when it involves 'forced labour' or 'forced migration'. Discourses which promote the forced-free distinction take no account of the gender power dynamic that is intrinsic to prostitution. The concept of choice is nullified for prostituted women because their social and economic status ensures submission and compliance (see consent).

globalisation. Globalisation refers to the current opening up of a global market associated with increasing mobility of goods, services, labour and capital across national borders. It is underpinned by *laissez-faire* capitalism and ideas of free trade which promote the privatisation of countries' economies and weakening trade regulations. Political manoeuvres, using economic pressure, diplomacy or military intervention are all justified by the ceaseless quest to ensure the continuous unlocking of foreign markets. Moral or ethical concerns are dismissed as irrelevant to the overall goal of high profits and market efficiency. This globalisation of the world economy overwhelmingly benefits the rich countries of the world, including the transnational sectors, leaving many peoples vulnerable and open to exploitation. It has led to the destruction of jobs, the wearing away of labour rights, reduced public expenditure, higher consumer costs, land enclosures, environmental devastation, the breakdown of indigenous cultures and escalating poverty. The globalisation of the economy has also seen the globalisation of the prostitution industry with women and girls just another tradable commodity in the marketplace. The poverty resulting from the reign of this free-market ideology of course makes women and girls especially vulnerable to sexual exploitation (see neo-liberalism).

harm minimisation. Harm minimisation is a strategy based on the assumption that some people will always engage in behaviours which are considered by most members within a society as unacceptable, dangerous or carrying risks. Proponents of harm minimisation attempt to reduce harms related to the activity rather than prevent the behaviour itself. Victoria's harm minimisation approach to prostitution thus accepts the inevitability of prosti-tution and seeks to reduce the worst aspects of the trade in women and girls.

legalising prostitution. Legalisation removes criminal charges from a current illegal activity but laws and regulations still apply to how, where, and under what circumstances, the activity is allowed. In the instance of prostitution the Victorian Government recognises some forms of prostitution as a lawful activity (brothel/escort prostitution), while others (street prostitution) continue to be included in the criminal code. Specific planning and health regulations apply to the industry.

liberal individualism. Liberal individualism is a system of beliefs that promotes the importance and independence of the individual. Liberalism advocates that people have certain innate rights and believes that these must be protected by the state together with individual property rights. Conversely liberalism argues for constitutional limitations on government to safeguard personal liberty. Liberals generally agree that society should have very limited interests in the private behaviour of its citizens, chiefly in the areas of free speech, personal conscience or religious principles, political associations, and private sexual relations. Essentially liberalism is about the right of people to define and seek their own happiness unrestricted. When talking about prostitution, feminists who support its legitimisation as work utilise the language of liberal individualism to promote prostitutes' rights campaigns as a struggle for self-determination and economic and sexual freedom.

male sex right. Carole Pateman (1988) defines the male sex right as the fundamental social contract – a man's innate right to women's bodies for sex. The idea of male sexual privilege pervades such mainstream institutions as the medical and health professions and the law which judges sexual relations as healthy from the male perspective. It is also upheld by traditions and culture. The male sex right is justified by the essentialist biological belief that sexuality is simply a 'natural' instinct or drive that exists independent of the social context in which male and female relations are played out. As radical human rights activist John Stoltenberg says, 'To have sex with someone and simultaneously to be "a real man" is necessarily and subjectively to *have* that person, to *take* that person, to *possess* that person' (2004, p. 402). Today men have unlimited access to women through pornography and prostitution.

neo-liberalism. Neo-liberalism as both a philosophy and a practice is concerned with the marketplace and the pure force of commerce to order all human relations. Economic individualists, or to use the more popular term 'economic rationalists', eschew state intervention in favour of individualism and a *laissez-faire* economic environment and call for the deregulation of the market. Indeed all other economic actors bar the market, whether governments or individuals, are considered subordinate to the pure force of commerce. Every form of socialism, collective responsibility or ideas of social good or humane public policy is diminished in this context (see globalisation).

normalisation. Normalisation is a process whereby actions, behaviours or beliefs are accepted in society through repetition or through propaganda to the extent that they are never questioned but are considered by most people within a society as natural.

objectification. I use the term objectification to describe the process where a person or a group make another person into an object. When one person objectifies another person and regards them as any other object, which exists only for their use or personal pleasure, they deny the other's humanity. Once we set others up as objects and not subjects there is no avenue for mutuality or reciprocity. What follows is inequality, cruelty, injustice, oppression, injury, unkindness, atrocity and savagery (see Fox 1999, pp. 211–214; 221). The market morality that now dominates world societies with its unquestionable belief that all desires should and can be met, makes it increasingly acceptable for women and children to be commodified as sexual objects for male use.

power. Power is the ability to act. The concept of power, however, is dualistic involving both restraint and enablement. The first relates to power over another person or group to carry out one's will even against resistance. Power may involve either overt force, that is violence and physical power, or the ability to impose one's will through having authority over another, that is political, social or economic power. Power in this sense is essentially the abuse of another's vulnerability. Traditionally, and in many circumstances today, men have power over women. In contrast power as enablement relates to a person's ability to perform or to exercise agency to bring about significant change in their lives.

prostituted woman. Throughout the book I use the term prostituted woman/girl, the term adopted by survivors of prostitution or 'survivor groups'. In contrast the expression 'sex work' implies vocational choice and the acceptance of what in any other context would be described as sexual harassment, sexual exploitation, or sexual abuse. Survivors of prostitution therefore reject the object/ noun 'prostitute'. In the same way that women who experience sexual violence have had something done to them (normally by a man), prostituted women also have had violence perpetrated against them by another person (normally a man).

I use the term woman/girl because prostitution is gender specific. While some men and boys are exploited in prostitution (about 10 per cent) they are not abused because they are men and boys, they are abused because they are less powerful, that is, oppressed because of class and/or race, unlike women and girls who are raped because we are female (see Ekberg 2004, p. 1120).

prostitution industry. I define the prostitution industry as including all forms of commercial sexual exploitation, whether legal or illegal. It is important to see prostitution as an industry because this makes clear that prostitution is not about sex but about the commodification of women and girls for men's sexual gratification and for profit. I include within the industry organised prostitution in brothels, massage parlours and escort services, street prostitution, the mass pornography trade, internet prostitution, strip clubs, telephone sex, sex trade shows and bride trafficking. I also include third party beneficiaries such as the media, airlines, hotel chains, tourist industries, international communication networks and banks who all benefit from the commercial sexual exploitation of women and girls. My main focus in this book has been Victoria's brothel, escort and street prostitution trade, industry lobbyists, as well as some of third party beneficiaries such as the State's financial institutions.

sexual exploitation. Sexual exploitation is an abuse of a position of vulnerability, differential power, or trust for sexual purposes. It involves the sexual violation of a person's human dignity, equality, and physical and mental integrity. It is a practice by which some people (primarily men) achieve power and domination over others (primarily women and children) for the purposes of sexual gratification, financial gain, and/or advancement (Coalition Against Trafficking in Women 1995, p. 3).

sexual liberalism. Sexual liberalism derives from liberal individualism. Sexual liberals see the sexual as a dimension of the individual, a natural force that exists prior to and restrained by the structures of society. They therefore advocate more sexual freedom and freedom of sexual expression. In the contemporary climate 'restricted sexual activities' have expanded to encompass sadomasochism, the making and consumption of pornography, cross-generational sex or what is understood as child sexual abuse and the selling of sex as a commodity. Sexual liberalism gives license to treat the other as a sexual object which only exists in relation to an individual's desire. The other is identified solely as their body, or fragmented or fetishised as parts rather than an individual complex person (see objectification). In this context sexual freedom and sexual exploitation become undifferentiated.

sex-gender system. The sex-gender system refers to the institutionalised system by which society transforms biological sex into culturally defined gender roles. Patriarchal society uses certain facts about male and female physiology as the basis for constructing a set of 'masculine' and 'feminine' emotional and psychological characteristics and then uses these 'constructed' differences and behaviours to justify the established inequitable relations between men and women.

violence against women. Violence against women is a chosen violent act against a woman or girl child simply because of her gender, simply because she is female. Violence against women cuts across race, religion, income, class and culture. It is deeply embedded in all cultures, so much so that for millions of women it is normalised as just part of their daily existence. Violence against women refers to many kinds of discrimination and physical acts of violence including but not limited to rape, beatings, domestic violence and murder, which are considered personal. This includes female infanticide, or in its more benign guise, the screening of foetuses to determine the sex which has resulted in the aborting of millions of female foetuses worldwide. Violence against women also takes in such institutionalised processes as sterilisation and forced abortion or alternatively forcing women to bear children, as well as prostitution and sexual slavery. Violence against women is one of the most obvious means by which patriarchal power is expressed and maintained.

Abbreviations

AAEI	Australian Adult Entertainment Industry Awards
ACT	Australian Capital Territory
ACTU	Australian Council of Trade Unions
AEP	Adult Entertainment Permit
AFAO	Australian Federal AIDS Organisation
AGSPAG	Attorney General's Street Prostitution Advisory Group
AIRC	Australian Industrial Relations Commission
ALHMWU	Australian Liquor, Hospitality and Miscellaneous Workers Union
ANCA	Australian National Council on AIDS
ANZSIC	Australian and New Zealand Standard Industrial Classification
APC	Australian Prostitutes' Collective
APPPAA	*Act on the Punishment for Procuring Prostitution and Associated Acts*
APPPVT	*Act on the Prevention of Prostitution and Protection of Victims Thereof*
ASX	Australian Stock Exchange
ACT	Australian Capital Territory
AWA	Australian Workplace Agreements
BLA	Business Licensing Authority
CEDAW	*Convention on the Elimination of All Forms of Discrimination against Women* 1979
COYOTE	Call Off Your Old Tired Ethics

DIMIA	Department of Immigration and Multiculturalism and Indigenous Affairs
ECP	English Collective of Prostitutes
ECPAT	End Child Prostitution and Trafficking (extension of acronym: End Child Prostitution, Child Pornography, Child Sex Tourism and Trafficking in Children for sexual purposes)
GAATW	Global Alliance Against Traffic in Women
ICPR	International Committee of Prostitutes' Rights
ILO	International Labour Organisation
ISCHA	Inner South Community Health Service
LHMU	Liquor, Hospitality and Miscellaneous Union
LLC	Liquor Licensing Commission
MAV	Municipal Association of Victoria
NACAIDS	National Advisory Committee on AIDS
NAEA	National Adult Entertainment Association
NCID	National Criminal Investigation Department (Sweden)
NESB	Non-English Speaking Background
NGO	Non-government Organisation
NSW	New South Wales
NVE	Non-violent erotica
OHCHR	Office of the High Commissioner for Human Rights
OHS	Occupational Health and Safety
PAG	Prostitutes' Action Group
PCV	Prostitutes' Collective of Victoria
PJC	Parliamentary Joint Committee on the Australian Crimes Commission
QLD	Queensland
RHED	Resourcing Health and Education for the Sex Industry
RMIT	Royal Melbourne Institute of Technology
SAGE	Standing Against Global Exploitation
SDA	Shop Distributors and Allied Employees Association

STD	Sexually Transmitted Disease
STI	Sexually Transmitted Infection
SWAIDS	Social Workers and AIDS
SWOP	Sex Workers Outreach Project
SIERA	Sex Industry Employees Rights Association
UN	United Nations
UNAIDS	United Nations Programme on HIV/AIDS
UNODC	United Nations Office on Drugs and Crime
UNIFEM	United Nations Development Fund for Women
VAAC	Victorian AIDS Action Committee
VCAT	Victorian Civil and Administration Tribunal
VWA	Victorian WorkCover Authority
WEL	Women's Electoral Lobby
WHO	World Health Organisation
WISE	Workers in Self Employment

Table of Legislation

Acts

Vagrancy Act 1966 (Victoria)
Workplace Relations Act 1996 (Commonwealth)
Workplace Relations Act 1997 (Victoria)

Regulations

Health (Brothel) Regulations 1990 (Victoria)
Health (Infectious Diseases) Regulations 2001 (Victoria)
Prostitution Control Regulations 1995 (Victoria)

Parliamentary Debates

Victoria, 1978, *Parliamentary Debates,* Assembly, 14 November:
2353

Victoria, 1980, *Parliamentary Debates,* Assembly, 6 November:
2274–2278

Victoria, 1980, *Parliamentary Debates,* Assembly, 28 April: 76–78

Victoria, 1982, *Parliamentary Debates,* Council, 22 May: 355

Victoria, 1984, *Parliamentary Debates,* Council, 1 May: 2527–2587

Victoria, 1984b, *Parliamentary Debates,* Council, 18 April: 2304

Victoria, 1985, *Parliamentary Debates,* Assembly, 3 October: 1053

Victoria, 1987, *Parliamentary Debates,* Council, 7 October: 726–741

Victoria, 1994, *Parliamentary Debates,* Council, 4 October:
105–107

Victoria, 1994a, *Parliamentary Debates,* Assembly, 21 October:
1453–1458

Victoria, 1994b, *Parliamentary Debates,* Assembly, 16 November:
1851–1884

Victoria, 1994c, *Parliamentary Debates,* Council, 7 December:
1263–1278

Victoria, 1994d, *Parliamentary Debates,* Council, 29 November:
962–966

Victoria, 1997, *Parliamentary Debates,* Assembly, 22 May:
1612–1626

Victoria, 1997a, *Parliamentary Debates,* Council, 27 May:
1143–1151

Victoria, 1999, *Parliamentary Debates,* Assembly, 6 May: 810–881

Victoria, 1999a, *Parliamentary Debates,* Assembly, 25 May: 1191–1211

Victoria, 1999b, *Parliamentary Debates,* Council, 1 June: 960–968

Victoria, 2000, *Parliamentary Debates,* Council, 15 March: 291–305

Victoria, 2000a, *Parliamentary Debates,* Assembly, 11 April: 849–867

Victoria, 2001, *Parliamentary Debates,* Assembly, 4 April: 637–645

Victoria, 2003, 'Assembly' *Parliamentary Debates (Hansard),* (7 May): 1507

Victoria, 2004, *Parliamentary Debates,* Assembly, 21 April: 712–718

Victoria, 2004a, *Parliamentary Debates,* Council, 6 May: 638–640

Victoria, 2004b, *Parliamentary Debates,* Assembly, 9 May: 925–936

Victoria, 2004c, *Parliamentary Debates,* Council, 11 May: 750–759

Victoria, 2004d, *Parliamentary Debates,* Council, 14 October: 914–915

Bibliography

Accsex/Access Plus. (2001). *Information Sheet*. Melbourne. ClubXSexpo Trades Exhibition (8–11 November). Melbourne Convention Centre, Victoria.

Adkins, L. (1995). *Gendered Work, Sexuality, Family and Labour Market*. Buckingham UK: Buckingham Open University Press.

Adkins, L. and V. Merchant (eds). (1996). *Sexualising the Social: Power and the Organisation*. Basingstoke and Houndsmill: MacMillan.

Aghatise, E. (2004). *Trafficking for Prostitution of Women from West Africa to Europe*. International Research and Action Conference: Innovations in Understanding Violence Against Women (25–28 April). Wellesley MA: Wellesley Centres for Women.

AIDS Conference. (2005). *AIDS Conference Calls for Renewed Response*. (July 28). Rio de Janeiro.
http://www.ndtv.com/template/template.asp?

Aitkin, J. (1978). *The Prostitute as Worker*. Paper presented at the Women and Labour Conference. Sydney: Macquarie University.

Alderson, P. (1999). *Legal Dictionary*. Roseville, New South Wales: McGraw-Hill Book Company Australia Pty Ltd.

Alexander, P. (1988). 'Prostitution A Difficult Issue for Feminists.' In F. Delacoste and P. Alexander (eds). *Sex Work: Writings by women in the sex industry*. Pittsburgh: Cleis Press.

Altman, D. (2001). *Global Sex*. Chicago: The University of Chicago; Sydney: Allen and Unwin.

Almodovar, N. J. (1999) 'For Their Own Good: The Results of the Prostitution Laws as Enforced by Cops, Politicians and Judges.' *Hastings Women's Law Journal*. 10: 101–115.

Altink, S. (1995). *Stolen Lives: Trading Women into Sex and Slavery*. London: Scarlet Press.

America's Debate Inc. (2004). 'Should We Legalize Prostitution?' *American Debate – Lifestyle Issues.* 5 July. America's Debate Inc: http://www.americasdebate.com/forums/index.php?showtopic=7094

Anker, R. (1998). *Gender and Jobs.* Geneva: International Labour Office.

Arnot-Bradshaw, A. (1999). *Sex Work and the Law.* The Department of Criminology, Seminar. (14 May). Melbourne: The University of Melbourne.

Arnot, A. (2002). Legalisation of the Sex Industry in the State of Victoria, Australia: the impact of prostitution law reform on the working and private lives of women in the legal Victorian sex industry. (M.A. Thesis). University of Melbourne, Department of Criminology.

Arnot, M. (1988). 'The Oldest Profession in a New Britannia.' In V. Burgmann and J. Lee (eds). *Constructing a Culture: A People's Identity of Australia.* Melbourne: McPhee Gribble: 42–62.

Asia Acts. (2003). *Anti-Trafficking Laws Philippines.* (September 30). http://www.stopchildtrafficking.info/index.php

Attorney-General's Street Prostitution Advisory Group. (2002). *Final Report.* Melbourne: Victorian Department of Justice and Legal Policy.

Australian Associated Press Ralph Wragg Equities News. (2003) 'Ferret's Float: Daily Planet.' (6 January). *AAP Information Services Pty Ltd.*

Australian Associated Press. (2004). 'NSW: Four people to stand trial for sex slavery.' (14 October). *AAP Information Services Pty Ltd.*

Australian Broadcasting Corporation. (2006). 'Police officer trafficked drugs, court told.' *ABC News Online.* 6 October. http://www.abc.net.au/news/newsitems/200610/s1757576.htm

Australian Bureau of Statistics. (2004). *Sexual Assault in Australia: A Statistical Overview.* cat. no. 4523.0. Canberra: ABS.

Australian Council of Trade Unions. (1995). *Working Women's Policy.* Melbourne: Australian Council of Trade Unions, ACTU House.

Australian Council of Trade Unions. (2004). http://www.actu.asn.au/public/about/

Australian Democrats. (2001). http://www.democrats.org.au/policies

Australian Government. (2006). *Workchoices: A new workplace relations system.* https://www.workchoices.gov.au/ourplan/

Australian Greens. (2006). 'Policies: Women.' *Australian Greens Online.* http://greens.org.au/policies/careforpeople/women

Australian Law Reform Commission. (2003). *Film and Literature Censorship Procedure*. Report No 55:
http://www.austlii.edu.au/au/other/alrc/publications/reports/55/

Australian Medical Association. (2004). *Blood Borne Viral Infections*. Position Statement:
http://www.ama.com.au/web.nsf/doc/WEEN-5XK8TE/$file/Blood%20Borne%20Viral%20Infections%20-%20March%202004.doc

Australian Prescription Products Guide (2004). *APP Guide Online*:
http://www.appco.com.au/appguide/

Australian Prostitutes' Collective. (1985). *Facts on Aids for Working Girls*. Information Sheet. St. Kilda, Melbourne: Prostitutes' Collective of Victoria, Archives.

Australian Prostitutes' Collective. (1987). *Australian Prostitutes' Collective Membership Application*. St Kilda, Melbourne: Prostitutes' Collective of Victoria Archives.

Bacon, J. (1976/1977). 'The Real Estate Industry in Women.' *Vashti*. 17: 5–8.

Bae-Sook, Cho. (2006). *Now Is Time to Kick Off Anti-Prostitution Campaign*. Seoul: Centre for Women's Human Rights:
http://www.stop.or.kr/english/index.php

Banach, L. (1999). *Unjust and Counterproductive: The Failure of governments to protect sex workers from discrimination*. Sydney: Scarlet Alliance and Australian Federation of AIDS Organisations

Banach, L. and S. Metzenrath. (c.2000). *Principles for Model Sex Industry Legislation*. Sydney. A joint project of the Scarlet Alliance and the Australian Federation of AIDS organisations:
http://www.scarletalliance.org.au/pub/

Bandarage, A. (1997). *Women, Population and Global Crisis*. London and New Jersey: Zed Books.

Barclay, I. (2001). Practices of Negotiating Between Sex Work and their Clients (Honours Thesis). The Department of Political Science. Melbourne: The University of Melbourne.

Barry, K. (1979). *Female Sexual Slavery*. Englewood Cliffs, New Jersey: Prentice-Hall.

Barry, K. (1995). *The Prostitution of Sexuality: The Global Exploitation of Women*. New York: New York University Press.

Bartlet R. (2003). 'Call for Immigration Action on Sex Trafficking.' J. Highfield. Producer. *The World Today.* (3 April). Sydney: Australian Broadcasting Commission.

Bastow, K. (1996). 'Prostitution and HIV/AIDS.' *Canadian HIV/AIDS Policy & Law Newsletter.* 2(2): 13–15.

Bell, S. (1994). *Reading, Writing and Rewriting the Prostitute Body.* Bloomington, Indiana: Indiana University Press.

Belsar, P. (2005). *Forced Labor and Human Trafficking: Estimating the Profits.* Special Action Program to Combat Forced Labour. DECLARATION/WP/42/2005. Geneva: International Labour Office.

Benbow, H. (2001) 'Lighten up – sexual exploitation is fun.' *The Paper.* (14 November) Melbourne: 6.

Benjamin, H. and R. E. L. Masters. (1965). *Prostitution and Morality.* London: Souvenir Press.

Bennett, B. (1992). 'Prostitution in Victoria: The Role of Local Government – An Inner City Perspective.' In S. Gerull and B. Halstead (eds). *Sex Industry and Public Policy: Proceedings of Conference Australian Institute of Criminology.* (6–8 May 1991). Canberra: Australian Institute of Criminology: 190–199.

Biles, A. (1979). 'Propositions on Prostitution.' *Scarlet Woman.* 10: 18–22.

Bindel, J. (2004). 'Streets Apart.' *The Guardian.* (15 May): http://www.guardian.co.uk/weekend/story/01215900,00.html

Bindel, J. and L. Kelly (2004). *A Critical Examination of Responses to Prostitution in Four Countries: Victoria, Australia; Ireland; the Netherlands; and Sweden.* Local Government and Transport Committee. Evidence Received for Prostitution Tolerance Zones (Scotland). Bill Stage 1. London: Metropolitan University.

Bindman, J. (1997). *Redefining Prostitution as Sex Work on the International Agenda.* Vancouver: Network of Sex Work Projects. http://www.walnet.org/csis/papers/redefining.html

Binnie C. (2004). 'Sex Slave Ring Smashed.' *Herald Sun.* (25 May). Melbourne: 6.

Birnbauer, W. (2003). 'Red light blue.' *The Age.* (9 December). Melbourne: 4.

Blackhurst, C. and A. Gatton (2002). 'A gangland killing, lap dancers who are said to sell sex.' *The Independent.* (16 September). London:

http://findarticles.com/p/articles/mi_qn4153/is_20020916/ai_n120 21092

Blackmur, D., D. Fingleton and D. Akers (eds). (1993). *Women's Occupational Health and Safety: The Unmet Needs*. Brisbane, Queensland: Women's Consultative Council: School of Management, Human Resources and Industrial Relations.

Blakey, S. (1991). 'Co-ordinators Letter.' *Working Girl*. 11: 4.

Bland, L. and F. Mort (1997). 'Thinking Sex Historically.' In L. Segal (ed). *New Sexual Agendas*. Basingstoke; Hampshire; Houndsmill and London: MacMillan Press: 17–31.

Blume, J. (2005). 'Prostitution Gives Me Power.' *Marie Claire*. July: 108–111.

Bone, I. (2002). 'The Business of Pleasure.' *City Weekly* (Victoria). (22 November): 8.

Boseley, S. and S. Goldenberg. (2005). 'U.S.-Based Aid Groups Receive Ultimatum: Pledge Your Opposition to Prostitution and Sex Trafficking or Do Without Federal Funds.' *Policy and Advocacy.* (July): http://www.siecus.org/policy/PUpdates/pdate0192.html

Bottom, B. (1985). 'Walker's Law: A licence for Mr Big to make a killing in brothels.' *The Age – Good Weekend*. (5 October): 38–39.

Bottom, B. (1991). *Inside Victoria: A Chronicle of Scandal*. Chippendale, NSW: Pan MacMillan.

Bottom, B. (2004). 'Gang War: Hits and Misses.' *The Bulletin*. (26 April). 122 (16): http://global.factiva.com.mate.lib.unimelb.edu.au/en/eSrch/ss_hl.asp

Bottom, B. (2004a). 'Deadly Consolidation Grips the Underworld.' *Sunday Age*. (20 June). Melbourne: 14

Bottom, B. and J. Medew. (2004) 'The Unfair Fight: Why Corruption's Unchecked.' *Sunday Age*. (23 May): 8.

Bourdieu, P. (1998). *The Essence of Neo-Liberalism*. Le Monde: College de France.

Brady, N. (1998). 'Uni Union to Advise Sex Work Students.' *The Age*. (10 June): 3.

Brental, S. (c.1998). *Dealing with Menacing and Violent Behaviour in the Sex Industry*. Canberra: Eros Foundation Publications and Archives, Flinders University, Adelaide, South Australia.

Bridgett, M. (1997). *9 Lives: Surviving Sex Assault in the Sex Industry.* Darlinghurst, NSW: Sex Workers Outreach Project.

Bristow, E. (1977). *Vice and Vigilance.* Dublin: Gill and MacMillan.

Brock, D. (1989). 'Prostitutes Are Scapegoats in the AIDS Panic.' *Resources for Feminist Research.* 18: 213–16.

Bronitt, S. (2004). Two Visions of the Human Rights Act 2004 (ACT): *A 'Clayton's' Bill of Rights or the New Magna Carta?* Paper presented at Australia's First Bill of Rights: A Forum on the National Implications of the ACT Human Rights Act, 1 July. Canberra: The Australian National University.

Bronitt S. (1995). 'The Right to Sexual Privacy, Sado-masochism and the Human Rights (Sexual Conduct) Act (Cth).' *Australian Journal of Human Rights.* 2 (1): 59–73.

Bronte (pseudonym). (1999). 'The Working Mother To Be.' *Working Girl/Working Boy.* 28: 16–21.

Bugge, Axel. 2005. 'Brazil spurns US AIDS cash over prostitution issue.' *Reuters.* 4 May 2005: 1

Business Licensing Authority (2004). *Prostitution Service Providers*: http://www.consumer.vic.gov.au/bla/blasite.nsf/pages/bla_prostitution

Business Licensing Authority (2004a). Personal Correspondence. Melbourne.

Business Licensing Authority (2006). *Prostitution Service Providers*: http://www.consumer.vic.gov.au/bla/blasite.nsf/pages/bla_prostitution

Butcher, S. (2004). 'Illegal Brothel fines $45,000 after sting.' *The Age.* (16 July): 3.

Capital Women. (1997). 'What the World Sees Now: The Australian Report to CEDAW.' *Capital Women Newsletter* (Canberra). 38: 1–12.

Carbonell R. (2003). 'Sex Slavery Arrests in Australia.' M. Colvin Producer. *PM.* (11 July). Australian Broadcasting Commission.

Carr, A. (1992). 'When We Were Very Young: The early years of the HIV/AIDS epidemic in Victoria.' *National AIDS Bulletin.* 5: 15–17.

Carrick, D. Producer. (2000). 'Human Trafficking.' *Law Report.* (15 November). Presenter Chris Richards. Radio National. Australian Broadcasting Corporation: http://www.abc.net.au/rn/talks/8.30/lawrpt/stories/s212435.htm

Carrington, K. (2003). *Trafficking and the sex industry: from impunity to protection*, Current Issues Brief 28 (2002–03). Canberra: Parliament of Australia, Parliamentary Library.

Castle, S. (2006). 'Trafficking forces clampdown in Amsterdam's red-light area.' *The Independent.* (15 December): 1: http://news.independent.co.uk/europe/article2032667.ece

Catanzariti, J. and M. Baragwanath. (1997). *The Workplace Relations Act.* Manly, New South Wales: Newsletter Information Services.

Chambers, C. (1995). *Who Cares for Whores? An Evaluation of Ugly Mugs: A Self-Help Approach Used by Prostitutes to Make their Work Safer.* St Kilda, Melbourne: Prostitutes' Collective of Victoria.

Chapkis, W. (2000). 'Power and Control in the Commercial Sex Trade.' In R. Weitzer (ed). *Sex for Sale: Prostitution, Pornography and the Sex Trade.* New York: Routledge and Kegan Paul: 181–201.

Charles, M. (2003). 'Daily Planet Sees Red.' *Herald Sun* (Melbourne). (2 September): 35.

Charlesworth, H. and C. Chinkin. (2000). *The boundaries of international law.* Manchester, UK: Manchester University Press.

City of Stonnington. (2003). *Council Minutes.* (24 July): http://www.stonnington.vic.gov.au/files/file3f4]199701e945.htm

Clack, P. (2002). 'Brothels fail health, safety test.' *The Canberra Times.* (5 May): 10.

Clack, p. (2004). 'Jane Errey: The Democrats' best hope for Canberra'. *City News.* (14 April). Canberra: 6: http://www.citynews.com.au/news/Article.asp?id=2102

Clarke, D. A. (2004). 'Prostitution for everyone: Feminism, globalisation and the "sex" industry.' In C. Stark and R. Whisnant (eds). *Not For Sale: Feminists Resisting Prostitution and Pornography.* Melbourne: Spinifex Press: 149–205.

ClubXSexpo (2002). *Club X–Sexpo – Health, Sexuality & Lifestyle Expo.* http://www.sexpo.com.au

ClubXSexpo (2004). *Club X–Sexpo – Health, Sexuality & Lifestyle Expo.* http://www.sexpo.com.au

ClubXSexpo (2004a). *Club X–Sexpo – Health, Sexuality & Lifestyle Expo.* http://www.sexpo.com.au/testimonials.cgi?page+other&topic+page&id+20041111&testid+20000641131

ClubXSexpo (2004b). *Club X–Sexpo – Health, Sexuality & Lifestyle Expo.*

http://www.sexpo.com.au/media.cgi?story=200411051721&page+m ain&id=20041111

ClubXSexpo (2004c). *Club X–Sexpo – Health, Sexuality & Lifestyle Expo.* http://www.sexpo.com.au/media.cgi?story=200411051723&page+m ain&id=20041111

ClubXSexpo (2005). *Club X–Sexpo – Health, Sexuality & Lifestyle Expo.* http://www.sexpo.com.au

ClubXSexpo (2006). *Club X–Sexpo – Health, Sexuality & Lifestyle Expo.* http://www.sexpo.com.au

Coalition Against Trafficking in Women (1995). *Proposed Convention Against Sexual Exploitation.* (Revised Edition, January 1995). N. Amherst, MA: Coalition Against Trafficking in Women.

Coalition Against Trafficking in Women. (2001). *Written Statement to the United Nations Commission on Human Rights 57th Session.* (15 June). http:action.web.ca/home/catw/readingroom.shtml?x+16042

Coalition Against Trafficking in Women. (2006). http//www.catwinternational.org/

Cohen, J., P. Alexander and C. Wofsky. (1988). 'Prostitutes and AIDS: Public Policy Issues.' In M. Blumburg (ed). *From AIDS: The Impact on the Criminial Justice System.* Columbus, Ohio: Merrill Publishing Co.: pp. 91–100.

Collier, M. (2002). *Contraception: healthy choices.* Marrickville, NSW: Choice Books.

Comfort, A. (1979). *The Joy of Sex.* London: Quartet.

Committee on Women's Rights and Equal Opportunities. (2004). *Draft Report on the Consequences of the Sex Industry in the European Union.* Provisional, E2003/2107(INI) 9 January. European Parliament.

Commonwealth of Australia. (2000). *Tomorrow's Children: Australia's National Plan of Action against the Commercial Sexual Exploitation of Children.* Canberra, ACT. Department of Family and Community Services.

Commonwealth of Australia. (2003). *Trafficking in Women for Sexual Servitude.* Joint Committee on the Australian Crimes Commission. Melbourne (18 November).

Commonwealth of Australia. (2004). *Trafficking in Women for Sexual Servitude.* Joint Committee on the Australian Crimes Commission. Canberra (26 February).

Connelly, M. (1980). *The Responses to Prostitution in the Progressive Era.* Chapel Hill, North Carolina: University of North Carolina Press.

Conrad, P. (1997). 'Second Couple Fight Sexpo Ban on Baby Entry.' *The Age.* (23 September): 5.

'Controlling Street Prostitution in Victoria.' (2004). *Legal Outcomes.* John Wiley and Sons Australia Ltd.
http://www.jaconline.com.au/legaloutcomes/hot-topics/008-prostitution/index.html

Coomaraswamy, R. (1997). *Report of the Special Rapporteur on violence against women, its causes and consequences.* Commission on Human Rights resolution 1997/44 GE.00-11334 (E). Geneva: United Nations Economic and Social Council.

Coomaraswamy, R. (2000). *Integration of the Human Rights of Women and the Gender Perspective.* E/CN.4/2000/68. Commission on Human Rights. Fifty-sixth session. (29 February). Geneva: United Nations Economic and Social Council.

Coomaraswamy, R. and L. M. Kois. (1999). 'Violence Against Women.' In K. Askin and D. Koenig (eds). New York. *Women and International Human Rights Law. Vol. 1.* Ardsley: Translational Publishers Inc.

Cooper, A. (2004). 'Interview with Robyn Flynn.' *360 Degrees.* CNN Radio broadcast (July 5):
http://www.cnn.com/TRANSCRIPTS/0407/05/acd.00.html

Consumer Affairs Victoria. (2006). *Regulatory Impact Statement Proposed Prostitution Control Regulations 2006.* Melbourne: Department of Justice.

'Council Will Curb Massage Parlours.' (1978). *Southern Cross.* (Melbourne: St Kilda Edition). (18 October). 1.

Coveney, L., M. Jackson, et al. (eds). (1984). *The Sexuality Papers.* London; Melbourne; Sydney; Auckland and Johannesburg: Hutchinson in association with The Explorations in Feminism Collective.

Crawford, A. (2001). 'The Move towards Sexual Liberation.' *The Age.* (14 March). Melbourne: 3.

Crime and Misconduct Commission. 2004. *Regulating Prostitution: An Evaluation of the Prostitution Control Act 1999 (QLD).* Queensland.

'Curbing Crime in the Sex Industry.' (1999). *The Age.* (7 May). Melbourne: 18.

Dabscheck, B. (1995). *The Struggle for Australian Industrial Relations.* Melbourne: Oxford University Press.

Dabscheck, B. (1998). 'Human Rights and Industrial Relations.' *Australian Journal of Human Rights.* 4 (2): 16–32.

Dagobert, D. R. (1975). *Dictionary of Philosophy.* Totowa, New Jersey: Littlefield, Adams and Co.

Daily Planet. (2003). http://dailyplanet.com.au/content2/index.html

Dana (pseudonym). (1990). 'Letter to the Editor.' *Working Girl.* 9: 16.

Daniels, K. (1984). *So Much Hard Work: Women and Prostitution in Australian History.* Sydney: Fontana; Collins.

Darebin Community Legal Centre and the Advocacy Program for Women in Prison (2003). *Joint Submission of Darebin Community Legal Centre and the Advocacy Program for Women in Prison.* Melbourne: DCLCAPW.

Dargan, F. (1998). 'Sex in the Suburbs.' *Sunday Herald Sun.* (26 April). Melbourne: 18.

Das, S. (1997). 'Table-top Dancing Denigrates Women: Kennett.' *The Age.* (19 September). Melbourne: 6.

Davies, S. (1995). 'Captives of their Bodies: Women, law and punishment 1880s–1990s.' In D. Kirkby (ed). *Sex Power and Justice: Historical Perspectives of the Law in Australia.* Melbourne: Oxford University Press: 99–117.

de Stoop, C. (2000). *Contraception: the hidden truth.* Castle Hill, NSW: C. de Stoop.

Deery, S. J. and D.H. Plowman. (1991). *Australian Industrial Relations.* Roseville, NSW: McGraw Hill Book Company.

Delacoste, F. and P. Alexander (eds). (1988). *Sex Work: Writings by Women in the Sex Industry.* London: Virago.

DeMaere, K. (2005). 'Decriminalisation as Partnership: An overview of Australia's Sex Industry Law Reform Model.' *Sex Work and Law Enforcement Research for Sex Work.* No. 8 (June).

Department of Education, Science and Training (2002) 'Higher Education Report for the 2002–2004 Triennium.' Commonwealth of Australia: http://www.dest.gov.au/archive/highered/he_report/2002_2004/html/contents.htm

Department of Family and Community Services. (2000). *Tomorrow's children: Australia's national plan of action against the commercial sexual exploitation of children.* Canberra: Department of Family and Community Services.

Department of Tourism and Trading (2002). 'Licenses Should Now Be Aware of the New Adult Entertainment Permits.' *Update 7.* (June). Melbourne: Liquor Licensing Division.

Deuk-kyoung, Yoon. (2006). *Korea's Legal Effort for Ending Sexual Exploitation.* Seoul: Centre for Women's Human Rights: http://www.stop.or.kr/english/index.php

Dhar, S. (2005). 'Kolkata sex workers oppose US bill.' *Hindustan Times.* (27 May): http://www.hindustantimes.com/2005/Dec/07/7170_0,0006000100 01.htm

Dobinson, S. (1992). 'Victorian Situation with Legalisation.' In S. Gerull and B. Halstead (eds). *Sex Industry and Public Policy Proceedings of Conference Australian Institute of Criminology.* (6–8 May 1991). Canberra: Australian Institute of Criminology: 117–121.

Doezema J. (1998). 'International Activism: Jo Doezema Interviews NWSP Coordinator, Cheryl Overs.' In Kempadoo and J. Doezema (eds). *Global Sex Workers Rights, Resistance, and Redefinition.* New York and London: Routledge and Kegan Paul: 204–209.

Duelli-Klein, R. (1983). 'Hegwig Dohm: Passionate Theorist.' In D. Spender (ed). *Feminist Theorists: Three Centuries of Women's Intellectual Traditions.* London: The Women's Press: 165–183.

Dufty N. F. and Fells R. E. (1989). *Dynamics of Industrial Relations in Australia.* Sydney: Prentice Hall.

Dunn M. (2001). 'Illegal Brothels Spread In Suburbia'. *Herald Sun.* (7 September). Melbourne: 7.

Dunstan, K. (1979). 'Melbourne Massage Industry'. *The Bulletin* (16 August): 28–29.

Dworkin, A. (1992). 'Prostitution and Male Supremacy.' Speech presented at a symposium on Prostitution: From Academia to Activism. *Michigan Journal of Gender and Law.* (31 October): http://www.nostatusquo.com/ACLU/dworkin/MichLawJourI.html.

Dworkin, A. (1997). *Life and Death.* New York: The Free Press.

Economic and Social Commission for Asia and the Pacific. (2005). 'Violence against and Trafficking in Women as Symptoms of

Discrimination: The Potential of CEDAW as an Antidote.' *Gender and Development Discussion Paper.* Series No. 17

ECPAT (1998) *Youth for Sale: ECPAT Australia's National Inquiry into the Commercial Exploitation of Children and Young People in Australia.* Collingwood, Victoria: ECPAT Australia Inc.

ECPAT (2004). *Facts and Figures: Australia.* http://www.globalmarch.org/worstformsreport/world/links/australia. htm#cs1.

'Eight sentenced in Finland's first sex trafficking trial.' (2006). *The Peninsula.* (21 July). http://www.thepeninsulaqatar.com/Display_news.asp?section=world _news&month=july2006&file=world_news20060721114956.xml.

Ekberg, G. (2004). 'The Swedish Law That Prohibits the Purchase of Sexual Services: Best Practices for Prevention of Prostitution and Trafficking in Human Beings.' *Violence against Women.* 10: 1187–1218.

Elder, D. (compiler). (2000). *A Guide to Best Practice Occupational Health and Safety in the Australian Sex Industry.* Sydney: Scarlet Alliance and the Australian Federation of AIDS Organisations.

Ellis, H. H. (1946). *Sex in Relation to Society.* London: W.M. Heinemann (First published 1937).

English Collective of Prostitutes (1977). *Vickers in the House of Lords.* London: Fawcett Library Archives.

English Collective of Prostitutes. (2006). http://www.allwomencount.net/EWC%20Sex%20Workers/SexWork Index.htm

Eriksson, M. (2004). *Draft Report on the consequences of the sex industry in the European Union.* Committee on Women's Rights and Equal Opportunity, European Union (9 January): http://action.web.ca/home/catw/attach/ErikssonDraftReportJan2004 .pdf

Eros Foundation. (1993). *Eros Committee Meeting Notes.* (6 May). Canberra: Eros Foundation Publications and Archives, Flinders University, Adelaide, South Australia.

Eros Foundation. (1993a). *Eros Foundation – General Meeting Victoria.* Canberra: Eros Foundation Publications and Archives, Flinders University, Adelaide, South Australia.

Eros Foundation. (1994). *New Brothel Set to Educate Federal Parliamentarians – First Sex Industry Budget Brought Down.* Press Release. Canberra: Eros Foundation Publications and Archives, Flinders University, Adelaide, South Australia.

Eros Foundation. (1995). 'Sexpo.' *The Eros Journal: Logical Perspectives of Love and Sex.* January/February: 8.

Eros Foundation. (1997). *Memos to Network.* Canberra: Eros Foundation Publications and Archives, Flinders University. Adelaide, South Australia.

Eros Foundation. (1997a). *Laughter and Light: Inside the Australian Sex Industry.* Canberra: the Eros Foundation.

Eros Foundation. (1998a). 'Melbourne Club X–Sexpo.' *Adult Industry Review.* 11(5): 21.

Eros Foundation. (c.1998). *The Eros Foundation: Seeking Logical Perspective on Love and Sex.* Canberra: Eros Foundation.

Exhibition and Event Association of Australia. (2002). *Announcing the 2002 Melbourne Club X Sexpo.* Promotional Leaflet Sent to Melbourne Traders. Melbourne: Exhibition and Event Association of Australia.

Expert Group Meeting on Sexual Exploitation, Violence and Prostitution. (1991). *The Penn State Report.* Pennsylvania, USA: UNESCO Division of Human Rights and Coalition Against Trafficking in Women.

Farley, M., I. Baral, M. Kiremire & U. Sezgin (1998). 'Prostitution in Five Countries: Violence and Posttraumatic Stress Disorder.' *Feminism and Psychology. 8* (4): 405–426.

Farley, M. & H. Barkan (1998a). 'Prostitution, Violence Against Women, and Posttraumatic Stress Disorder.' *Women and Health. 27* (3): 37–49.

Farley, M. & V. Kelly. (2000). 'Prostitution: a critical review of the medical and social sciences literature.' *Women and Criminal Justice. 11* (4): 29–64.

Farley et al. (2003). 'Prostitution and Trafficking in Nine Countries: An Update on Violence and Posttraumatic Stress Disorder.' In M. Farley (ed). *Prostitution, Trafficking and Traumatic Stress.* Binghamton, NY: Haworth: 33–74.

Farley M. (2004). '"Bad for the Body, Bad for the Heart" Prostitution Harms Women Even if Legalized or Decriminalized.' *Violence Against Women.* (October 2004): 1087–1125.

Farley, M. (ed). (2004a). *Prostitution, Trafficking and Traumatic Stress.* Binghamton, NY: Haworth.

Farley, M. (2005). *Unequal.* Coalition Against Trafficking in Women: http://action.web.ca/home/catw/readingroom.shtml?x=81265&AA_EX_Session=3650b7072c7c1e2f309be1894a85d590.

Federal Capital Press of Australia Limited. (2003). 'Australia: Sex Slavery Crack Down.' (6 November). The Federal Capital Press of Australia Limited.

'Finland Adopts Legislation on Assistance to Victims of Trafficking.' (2006). *Legislation Online.* OSCE Office for Democratic Institutions and Human Rights. (27 June): http://www.legislationline.org//news.php?tid=1&jid=17.

'Finland Passes Law on Criminalisation on the Purchase of Sexual Services of Victims of Trafficking' (2006). *Legislation Online.* OSCE Office for Democratic Institutions and Human Rights. (21 June): http://www.legislationline.org//news.php?tid=1&jid=17.

'Fins pass anti-prostitution law' (2006). BBC News (21 June). UK: http://news.bbc.co.uk/2/hi/europe/5103132.htm.

Forastieri, V. (2000). *Information Note of Women Workers and Gender Issues on Occupational Health and Safety.* Geneva: International Labour Office. http://www.ilo.org/public/english/protection/safework/gender/womenwk.htm.

Forbes, M. (1999). 'Thai Women Tell Of Unpaid Brothel Work.' *The Age.* (1 December). Melbourne: 3.

Forbes, M. (1999a). 'The Sex Business: New sex laws to tackle prostitution at table-top dancing clubs.' *The Age.* (3 March). Melbourne: 3.

Forbes, M. (1999b). 'Prostitution Law Needs Overhaul.' *The Age.* (2 March). Melbourne: 12.

Forbes, M. (1999c). 'Sex Boom Fuels Super Brothels Bid.' *Sunday Age.* (28 February). Melbourne: 1.

Forbes, M. (1999d). 'Police Brothel Alarm.' *The Age.* (1 March). Melbourne: 1.

Forbes, M. and M. Marino. (1999). 'Prostitution Scheme Slammed.' *The Age.* (3 December): 6.

371

Forbes, M. and R. Millar (1997). 'Council Calls For Curbs On City Sex Clubs.' *Sunday Age.* (8 June). Melbourne: 5.

Forbes, M. and T. Hemmings. (2000). 'Prostitution Sentence Provokes Outcry.' *The Age.* (2 December). Melbourne: 10.

Ford, M. (2001). *Sex Slaves and Legal Loopholes: Exploring the legal framework and legislative responses to the trafficking of Thai 'contract girls' for sexual exploitation to Melbourne, Australia.* Melbourne: Victoria College.

Ford, R. (2006). 'Mini-brothel plan to take sex off the streets and into suburbs.' *The Times.* (January 18): http://www.timesonline.co.uk/article/0,,2-1991111,00.html.

Forell, C. (1994). 'More Enlightened Laws Needed to Tackle Prostitution. *The Age.* (7 November). Melbourne: 13.

Fox, M. (1999). *Sins of the Spirit, Blessings of the Flesh.* New York: Three Rivers Press.

Freedom, E. (1998). *Reader's Companion to U.S. Women's History.* Geneva: Houghton Mifflin.

García-Moreno, C. and Watts C. (2000) 'Violence against women: its links with HIV/AIDS prevention.' *AIDS.* 14 5000–8000.

Gatton, A. and C. Blackhurst. (2002). 'A gangland killing, lap dancers who are said to sell sex.' *The Independent.* (16 September). London: http://findarticles.com/p/articles/mi_qn4153/is_20020916/ai_n120 21092

Gatton, A. and P. Lashmar. (2002). 'Spearmint Rhino: lap-dancing club boss is convicted fraudster.' *Evening Standard.* (17 February). London: http://www. independent.co.uk/>Independent.

Gerull, S. and B. Halstead (eds). (1992). *Sex Industry and Public Policy Proceedings of Conference Australian Institute of Criminology.* (6–8 May 1991). Canberra: Australian Institute of Criminology.

Gilbert, K. (1992). *Submission to the Law Reform Commission in Victoria Regarding Sentencing Practices in Rape Cases.* Melbourne: The Prostitutes' Collective of Victoria: 1–16.

Giobbe, E. (1991). 'Prostitution: Buying the Right to Rape.' In A. Wolpert Burgess (ed). *Rape and Sexual Assault III. A Research Handbook.* New York: Garland Publishing.

Gleeson V. (1992). 'Industrial Aspects of the Sex Industry.' In S. Gerull and B. Halstead (eds). (1992). *Sex Industry and Public Policy:*

Proceedings of Conference Australian Institute of Criminology. (6–8 May 1991). Canberra: Australian Institute of Criminology: 183–189.

Global Alliance Against Traffic in Women. (2004).
http://gaatw.net/component/option,com_frontpage/Itemid,1/

Global Coalition on Women and AIDS. (2004). *Epidemic Update.* (December) http://womenandaids.unaids.org/.

Global Programme on AIDS and Programme of STD (1989). *Consensus Statement from the Consultation on HIV Epidemiology and Prostitution.* Geneva: World Health Organization.

Goldman, E. (ed). (1911/1969). *The Traffick in Women.* New York: Dover.

Gorjanicyn, K. (1992). 'Legislation Social Reform: Guns, Grog and Prostitution.' In M. Considine and B. Costar (eds). *Trials in Power: Cain, Kirner and Victoria 1982–1992.* Melbourne: Melbourne University Press.

Goward, P. (1996). 'The Happy Hooker User.' *The Sydney Morning Herald.* (26 July): 18.

Graaf, R. et al. (1995). 'Alcohol and drug use in heterosexual and homosexual prostitution, and its relation to protection behaviour.' *AIDS Care.* 7(1): 35–47.

Gravesen, L. (2005). 'Taxpayers foot bill for disabled Danes' visits to prostitutes.' *Telegraph* (UK). (2 October):
http://www.telegraph.co.uk/news/main.jhtml;jsessionid=H1QT4NB IIPMCRQFIQMFSFFOAVCBQ0IV0?xml=/news/2005/10/02/wda ne02.xml

Gray D. (2003). 'Special Court to Deal with Street Prostitution.' *The Age.* (30 October). Melbourne: 7.

'Groups Seek Government Action.' (1978). *Southern Cross.* (Melbourne, St Kilda Edition). (1 November): 7.

Guymer, L. (1998). 'Anti-Pregnancy "Vaccines" a Stab in the Dark.' *Birth Issues.* (Brisbane). 7: 87–91.

Guymer, L. and R. Klein. (1999). *Steps to Theorizing: Prostitution and the Sex Industry.* Geelong, Victoria: Deakin University.

Hancock, L. (1992). 'Legal Regulation of Prostitution: What or who is being controlled.' In S. Gerull and B. Halstead (eds). *Sex Industry and Public Policy: Proceedings of Conference Australian Institute of Criminology.* (6–8 May 1991). Canberra: Australian Institute of Criminology: 165–171.

Hansen, M. (2002). 'Presentation by the Director General.' *Infocus Program on Promoting Declaration* [ILO Declaration on Fundamental Principles and Rights at Work]. (October). Geneva, International Labour Organisation.
http.www.ilo.org/public/english/standards/declaration/background/index.htm

Hanuschack, D. (1997). 'The Reality of Sex Work.' Lecture given by representative of the Prostitutes' Collective of Victoria. Human Sexuality Study Group 8. (14 May). Melbourne: The University of Melbourne.

Hawthorne, S. (2002). *Wild Politics: Feminism, Globalisation and Bio/Diversity.* Melbourne: Spinifex Press.

Hawthorne, S. (2005/2006). 'Ancient Hatred and Its Contemporary Manifestation: The Torture of Lesbians.' *Hate Studies.* 4 (1): 33–58.

Hoigard, C. and L. Finstad (1992). *Backstreets: Prostitution, Money and Love.* Cambridge, UK: Polity Press.

Holland, S. (2003). 'Prostitution in Victoria.' *Stats Flash.* Melbourne: Department of Justice (Victoria):
http://www.justice.vic.gov.au/CA256902000FE154/Justice_Statistics_Stats_Flash_Index/$file/Stats_Flash_Index.pdf

Holli, A. (2004). *Debating Prostitution/Trafficking in Sweden and Finland.* Paper presented at the Second Pan-European Conference – Standing Group on EU Politics held in Bologna, 24–26 June.

Holsopple, K. (1998). 'Stripclubs According to Strippers.' In D. Hughes and C. Roche (eds). *Making the Harm Visible: Global Exploitation of Women and Girls.* Kingston, Rhode Island: Coalition Against Trafficking in Women: 252–276.

Home Office. (2004). *Paying the Price: A Consultation Paper on Prostitution.* London: HMSO.

Horin, A. (1991). 'Prostitutes Win A Special Flat-Tax Deal.' *Sydney Morning Herald.* (4 May). Sydney: 1.

'Howard's Workplace Revolution.' (2006). Editorial. *The Australian.* (27 March): 2.

Hughes, D. (1996). 'Sex Tours via the Internet.' *Agenda: Empowering Women for Gender Equity.* 28: 71–76.

Hulls R. (2002). 'Realistic Response.' *Herald Sun.* (24 June). Melbourne: 19.

Human Rights Watch. (2005). *United States: U.S. Backs Down on Prostitution Pledge.* Press Release. (May 4).
http://www.hrw.org/update/2005/06/#us

Hunter, A. (1991). 'Scarlet Update.' *Working Girl.* 11: 31.

Hunter, A. (1992). 'The Development of Theoretical Approaches to Sex-Work In Australian Sex-Work Organisations.' In S. Gerull and B. Halstead (eds). *Sex Industry and Public Policy: Proceedings of Conference Australian Institute of Criminology.* (6–8 May 1991). Canberra: Australian Institute of Criminology: 109–114.

Hunter, R. (1995). 'Women Workers and the Liberal State: Legal regulation of the workplace, 1880s–1980s.' In D. Kirkby (ed). *Sex Power and Justice.* Melbourne; Oxford; Auckland and New York: Oxford University Press: 219–236.

Hynes, P. (1999). 'Taking Population out of the Equation: Reformulating I = PAT.' In J. Silliman and Y. Kings (eds). *Dangerous Intersections: Feminist Perspectives on population, Environment and Development.* Cambridge, MA: South End Press: 39–73.

IBIS Business Information Pty. Ltd (1998–October 2005). *Q9529 Personal Services nec in Australia.* IBISWorld:
http://www.ibisworld.com.au/Industry/definition.asp?Industry_id=6 78.

IBISWorld. (2006). Q9528 *Sexual Services in Australia.* (May): IBISWorld Pty Ltd.

ILOAIDS. (2001). *The ILO Code of Practice on HIV/AIDS and work.* Geneva: International Labor Office:
http://www.ilo.org/public/english/protection/trav/aids/publ/code.htm

ILOAIDS. (2004). 'Women, Girls, HIV/AIDS and the World of Work.' *ILOAIDS Brief.* (December). Geneva: International Labour Organization Programme on HIV/AIDS and the World of Work. http://www.ilo.org/public/english/protection/trav/aids/publ/women-iloaids-brief.pdf

Inform Victoria (2001). *Inner South Community Health Service.* http://www.inform.webcentral.com.au/t_pcv.htm

Inglis, J. (1984). 'Working Towards a Collective of Prostitutes.' *Scarlet Woman.* 18: 16–19.

Intergovernmental Committee on AIDS Legal Working Party. (1991). *Recommendations of the Legal Working Party of the Intergovernmental*

Committee on AIDS. Canberra: Department of Health, Housing and Community Services.

International Committee for Prostitutes' Rights. (1985). *World Charter for Prostitutes' Rights*. First World Whores' Conference, Amsterdam: Prostitutes' Collective of Victoria, Archives.

International Labour Organization. (1989). *Resolution on Equal Opportunities and Treatment: Special protective measures for women and equality of opportunity and treatment*. DOC(MEPMW/1989/7). Geneva: International Labour Office: http://www.ilo.org/public/english/employment/gems/eeo/ilo/intro2. htm

International Labour Organization. (1996). *List of Ratifications of International Labour Conventions: Australia*. Geneva: International Labour Office. http://webfusion.ilo.org/public/db/standards/normes/appl/index.cfm ?lang=EN

International Labour Organization. (1996). *Declaration on Fundamental Principles and Right to Work*. Developed at the Ministerial Conference of the World Trade Organization 1996 and accepted ILO 86th Session, Geneva, June 1998. http://www.ilo.org/dyn/declaris/DECLARATIONWEB.static_jump ?var_language=EN&var_pagename=DECLARATIONTEXT

International Labour Organization. (2002). *Infocus: Program on Promoting Declaration*. Geneva: International Labour Office: http://www.ilo.org/public/english/standards/decl/declaration/faq/ind ex.htmv

International Labour Organization. (2004). *Towards a Fair Deal for Migrant workers in the Global Economy*. Report VI. Geneva: Internal Labour Conference, 92nd Session.

International Network Against Child Prostitution and Sexual Abuse. (1998). *Use of children for prostitution and a Congressional hearing in the State of Paraiba*. Brazil: NGOAEs/International Network Against Child Prostitution and Sexual Abuse (6 April).

Jacaranda Online. (2004). *Controlling Street Prostitution in Victoria*. Brisbane, Australia: John Wiley and Sons: html://www.studyon.com.au/vic/legal3-4/print/hot-topics/008-prostitution/grace-ilardi.html

Jackson, M. (1984). 'Sexology and the Universalization of Male Sexuality (From Ellis to Kinsey, and Masters and Johnson).' In L. Coveney and M. Jackson, et al (eds). *The Sexuality Papers*. London; Melbourne; Sydney; Auckland and Johannesburg: Hutchinson in association with The Explorations in Feminism Collective.

Jackson, S. and D. Otto. (1979). 'Prostitution: from delicacy to dilemma.' *Scarlet Woman*. 8: 11–18.

Jackson, S. and S. Scott (eds). (1996). *Feminism and Sexuality: A reader*. Edinburgh: Edinburgh University Press.

Jaget, C. (1980). *Prostitutes Our Life*. Bristol: Falling Wall Press.

Jeffreys, S. (1997). *The Idea of Prostitution*. Melbourne: Spinifex Press.

Jeffreys, S. (2000). 'Australia and the Traffic of Women into Sexual Exploitation.' *Arena Magazine*. (April): http://www.arena.org.au/Archives/Mag%20Archive/Issue%2058/feat ures_58.

Jeffreys, S. (2003). *Unpacking Queer Politics*. Cambridge: Polity Press; Malden, MA: Blackwell Publishers Inc.

Jeffreys, S. (2005). *Beauty and Misogyny*. London: Routledge.

Jeness, V. (1993). *Making it Work: The Prostitutes' Rights Movement in Perspective*. New York: Aldine de Gruyter.

Jennings, M. (2001). 'Australia's Child Sex Industry Growing: A report.' *PM*. M. Colvin. Producer. (10 December). National Radio. Australian Broadcasting Commission.

Johnson, D. (1984). 'St. Kilda Voices.' In K. Daniels (ed). *So Much Hard*. Sydney: Fontana.

Johnson, P. (1994). 'Brothel manager jailed over hire of schoolgirls.' *The Age*. (25 February). Melbourne: 3.

Jones, K. (2000). 'Workplace safety services safe sex industry.' *Occupational Health and Safety Magazine*. (February). Melbourne: CCH Australia: http://www.worksafety.com.au/Safe-Sex-Industry.html

Justine (pseudonym) (1997). 'From Stripper to Whore.' *Working Girl/ Working Boy*. 24: 14–16.

Kaiser Daily HIV/AIDS Report. (2005). *US Requirement That AIDS Groups Sign Pledge Against Commercial Sex Work 'Harms' AIDS Work*. (2 September): http://kaisernetwork.org/daily_reports/rep_index.cfm?DR_ID=32372

Kantola, J. and J. Squires. (2002). *Discourses Surrounding Prostitution Policy in the UK.* A paper presented in the PSA Annual Conference, Aberdeen, 5–7 April. Bristol, UK: Department of Politics, University of Bristol.

Kappeler, S. (1990). 'Liberals, Libertarianism, and the Liberal Arts Establishment.' In D. Leidholdt and J. Raymond (eds). *The Sexual Liberals and The Attack On Feminism.* New York: Pergamon Press: 175–183.

Kappeler, S. (1995). *The Will to Violence.* Melbourne: Spinifex Press.

Kappeler, S. (1996). 'Subjects, Objects and Equal Opportunities.' In S. Jackson and S. Scott (eds). *Feminism and Sexuality: A reader.* Edinburgh: Edinburgh University Press: 342–347.

KaiserNetwork.org. (2005). 'U.S Requirement That Aids Groups Sign Pledge Against Commercial Sex Work "Harms" AIDS Work' (2005). *The Henry J. Kaiser Family Foundation: Kaiser Daily HIV/AIDS Report.* (2 September):
http://kaisernetwork.org/daily_reports/rep_index.cfm?DR_ID=32372

Kelly J. and F. Burstin (2002). 'Sex Uproar: Taxes to Pay for Sex Zones.' *Herald Sun.* (20 June). Melbourne: 1.

Kelly, L. (1996). 'Surviving Sexual Violence.' In S. Jackson and S. Scott (eds). *Feminism and Sexuality: A reader.* Edinburgh, Edinburgh University Press: 194–197.

Kelly, L. and L. Regan (2000). *Stop Traffic: Exploring the extent of, and responses to, trafficking in women for sexual exploitation in the UK.* London: Policing and Reducing Crime Unit, Research, Development and Statistics Director, Home Office.

Kempadoo, K. and J. Doezema (eds). (1998). *Global Sex Workers: Rights, Resistance and Redefinition.* London and New York: Routledge.

Keogh, S. (1992). *The Effects of the Prostitution Regulation Act on Victorian Sex Workers.* Melbourne: Prostitutes' Collective of Victoria.

Kirkby, D. (1997). *Barmaids: a history of women's work in pubs.* Cambridge and Melbourne: Cambridge University Press.

Klein, R. (1996). '(Dead) Bodies Floating in Cyberspace: Postmodernism and the Dismemberment of Women.' In D. Bell and R. Klein (eds). *Radically Speaking: Feminism Reclaimed.* Melbourne: Spinifex Press: 346–358.

Klein, R., J. Raymond and L. Dumble (eds). (1991). *RU486: Misconceptions, Myths and Morals.* Melbourne: Spinifex Press.

Klein, R. (2006). *Submission to the Senate Community Affairs Legislation Committee for the Inquiry into the Therapeutic Goods Amendment (Repeal of Ministerial responsibility for approval of RU486) Bill 2005.* (15 January).

Konkes, C. (2002). 'Green Light for Safer Sex Work.' *The Australian.* (22 January). Sydney: 3.

Koval, R. (1997). Interview with Mark Selange. *Ramona Koval.* (6. October). Radio broadcast. 2RN (Sydney).

Lacy, C. (1996). 'Fairer Side of the Sex Industry.' *Herald Sun.* (13 August). Melbourne: 43.

Lantz S. (2003). *Sex work and study: students, identities and work in the 21st century.* (PhD Thesis). Department of Education, Policy and Management. Melbourne: The University of Melbourne.

Lap-Chew, L. (1999). 'Global Trafficking in Women: Some Issues and Strategies.' *Women's Studies Quarterly* XXVII (1 and 2, Spring–Summer): pp.11–18.

Lauder, S. (2006). 'Sex Slavery Laws used in sentencing for the first time.' *PM.* (9 June). Producer Mark Covin: Australian National Broadcasting:
http://www.abc.net.au/pm/content/2006/s1659778.htm

Leary, V. (1995). 'Lessons from the Experience of the International Labour Office.' In A. P. Clerendon (ed). *Rights: A Critical Appraisal.* Oxford: Oxford University Press: 580–619.

Leidholdt, D. (1990). 'When Women Defend Pornography.' In D. Leidholdt and J. Raymond (eds). *The Sexual Liberals and the Attack on Feminism.* New York: Pergamon Press: 125–131.

Leidholdt, D. (1999). 'Prostitution a Form of Modern Slavery.' In D. Hughes and C. Roche (eds). *Making the Harm Visible: The Global Sexual Exploitation of Women and Girls.* Kingston, Rhode Island: Coalition Against Trafficking: 49–55.

Leidholdt, D. (1999a). 'Position Paper for the Coalition Against Trafficking in Women.' *Coalition Against Trafficking in Women*: (www.uri.edu1artsci/wms/hughes/catw/posit2.htm

Leidholdt, D. (2003). 'Demand and the Debate.' *Coalition Against Trafficking in Women.* 16 October 2003:

http://action.web.ca/home/catw/readingroom.shtml?x=53793&AA_
EX_Session=96bc5f2586cd698425ce35d5b41417f2

Leidholdt, D. and Hilary Sung-hee Seo. (2004). 'Korea on Right Path to Fight Sex Trade. Sweden Spearheads Public Education Campaign.' *The Korean Times.* (26 October):
http://times.hankooki.com/lpage/special/200410/kt2004102619312
245250.htm

Lim, Lin Lean. (1998). *The Sex Sector: The Economic and Social Bases of Prostitution in Southeast Asia.* Geneva: International Labour Office.

Longo, E. (1997). 'New Energy Around Casino Attracts Brothel.' *The Age.* (6 May). Melbourne: 3.

Lopez-Jones, N. and English Collective of Prostitutes (eds). (1993 [first published 1988]). *Prostitute Women and AIDS: Resisting the Virus of Repression.* London: Crossroads.

Louie R. et al. (1998). *Project Client Call.* Melbourne: Macfarlane Burnett Centre for Medical Research.

Lumby, K. (1998). *Bad Girls: the media, sex and feminism in the 90s.* Sydney: Allen and Unwin.

MacDonald, A. (1992). 'Supreme Court Recognizes FDA's Sound Judgment In Banning RU 486 – A Dangerous Drug.' *PR Newswire.* (20 July): 1.

MacKinnon, C. (1979). *Sexual Harassment of Working Women: a case of sex discrimination.* New Haven, CT: Yale University Press.

MacKinnon, C. (1987). *Feminist Unmodified.* Cambridge and Massachusetts: Harvard University Press.

MacKinnon, C. (1989). *Towards a Feminist Theory on the State.* Massachusetts: Harvard University Press.

MacKinnon, C. (1992). *Sexual Harassment as Sex Discrimination. Sexual harassment: confrontations and decisions.* Buffalo, N.Y: Prometheus Books.

MacKinnon, C. (1993). 'Prostitution and Civil Rights.' *Michigan Journal of Gender and Law. 1*: 13–31.

MacKinnon, C. (1996/1982). 'Feminism, Marxism, method and the state: An agenda for theory.' In S. Jackson. and S. Scott (eds). *Feminism and Sexuality: A reader.* Edinburgh: Edinburgh University Press: 182–90. First published in *Signs. 7* (3) 1982: 515–544.

MacKinnon, C. (2001). *Sex Equality.* New York: Foundation Press.

Macklin, J. (2002). *Students Poverty: Time for the Facts.* Media Release (July). Australian Labor Party.
http://www.alp.org.au/media/0702/20001657.html

Macklin, J. (2005). *Impact of Howard Government industrial relations agenda on women/attack on student services.* Australian Labor Party.
http://www.alp.org.au/media/0705/dsiedu210.php

Mahoney, K. (1993). 'Destruction of Women's Rights through Mass Media Proliferation of Pornography.' In P. Mahoney and K. Mahoney (eds). *Human Rights in the Twenty-first Century: A Global Challenge.* Boston: Dordrecht; London: Martinus Nijhoff.

Makkai, T. (2003). 'Thematic Discussion on Trafficking in Human Beings.' *Workshop On Trafficking In Human Beings, Especially Women And Children.* Australian Institute of Criminology. Convenor. 12th Session of the Commission on Crime Prevention and Criminal Justice (15 May). Vienna.

Maman, S. et al. (2000). 'The Intersections of HIV and violence: directions for future research and interventions.' *Social Science and Medicine. 50*: 459–478.

Marensky, M. (2003). 'Stripping.' *Street Stories.* (31 May). Australian Broadcasting Commission.

Marino, M. (2003). 'Sex In Our City: Plenty Apparently.' *Sunday Age.* (8 June). Melbourne: 5.

Masterson, A. (1998) 'Sex Circus: Sensuality Slides As Sales Soar.' *Sunday Age.* (22 November). Melbourne: 2

'Mayor Calls for Brothel Laws.' (1978). *Southern Cross.* (Melbourne, St Kilda Edition). (15 November): 1.

Mayson, D. (1995). 'A Workers' Guide to Fantasy.' *Working Girl/ Working Boy.* 18: 28.

McIntosh, N. (2003). 'Human Papillomavirus and Cervical Cancer.' *Reproductive Health Online.* JHPIEGO, an affiliate of Johns Hopkins University:
http://www.reproline.jhu.edu/English/3cc/3refman/cxca_hpv1.htm

McKinney, I. (2001). *Trafficking in Women for Prostitution,* [public forum]. (21 November). Melbourne: The University of Melbourne.

McLeod, E. (1982). *Women Working: Prostitution Now.* London and Canberra: Croom Helm.

McMillan, B. (1988). 'Letters.' *Working Girl.* 3: 13.

Medew, J. (2006). 'Policeman faces 80 drug charges.' *The Age*. (7 October): p. 3.

Medical News Today. (2005). 'Over 100 Groups Urge President to Enforce Anti-Prostitution Policy to Aid Sexually Exploited Women and Children.' Press Release. (10 August).
http://www.medicalnewstoday.com/

Melbourne City Council/Melbourne Metropolitan Planning Scheme (2000). 'Melbourne Planning Scheme, Local Planning Policies.' *Strategy for a Safe City 2000–2002*. Melbourne: Department of Planning and Environment (Victoria).

Messing, K., K. Lippel, D. Demers and D. Mergler (2000). 'Equality and Difference in the Workplace: Physical Job Demands, Occupational Illness and Sex Differences.' *National Women's Studies Association Journal. 12*(3): 21–49.

Millett, K. (1971). *Sexual Politics*. New York: Avon Books.

Millett, K. (1975). *The Prostitution Papers*. Frogmore, St Albans: Herts, Paladin Books.

Milovanovic, S. (2003). 'Strip Club Dancers Raped, Court Told.' *The Age*. (21 February): 4.

Minchin, L. (2003). 'Australia's Sex Trade Thriving: Expert.' *The Age*. (21 October). Melbourne: 3.

Minchin, L. (2003a). 'A Red Light on Trafficking.' *The Age*. (25 October). Melbourne: 5.

Mitchell, G. (2000). *From Exclusion to Community and Connectedness*. Melbourne: 'Sacred Heart Mission St Kilda.

Mitchell, J. (1974). *Psychoanalysis and Feminism*. New York: Pantheon Books.

Monash City Council. (2003). *Monash Council Welcomes Government Talks on Illegal Brothels*. Media release. (4 September):
www.monash.vic.gov.au/news/media3903.htm

Monzini, P. (2005). *Sex Traffic Prostitution, Crime and Exploitation (Global Issues)*. London and New York: Zed Books. Translated by Patrick Camiller.

Moor, K. (2004). 'Crown Accused Over Prostitutes.' *Associated Press*. (30 June):
http:www.com.au/common/story/pag),45057,9995904%255E2879 3,00.html

Moore, S. (1999) 'Characteristics, Attitudes, Behaviour of Australian Men Who Visit Female Sex Workers.' *Venereology, the International Journal of Sexual Health, 12* (1): 29–35.

Morgan, R. and M. Russell (1978). 'Prostitution and the Law: The politics of being on the game.' *Vashti 4*: 16–17.

Moschetti, C. (2006). *Conjugal Wrongs Don't Make Rights: International Feminist Activism, Child Marriage and Sexual Relativism.* (PhD Thesis). Melbourne: The University of Melbourne.

Murphy, C. (2003). 'Making Sex Pay.' *BBC Online.* (17 July): htpp:/www. BBC NEWS Europe Making sex pay.htm

Murphy, P. (2002). 'Brothel Probes Go Too Far.' *The Age.* (1 June). Melbourne: 1.

Murphy, P. (2002a). 'Top-End American Franchise Muscle In To A Bare Market.' *The Age.* (21 September). Melbourne: 3.

Murphy, P. (2002b). 'Licensed brothels call for blitz on illegal sex shops.' *The Age.* (3 June). Melbourne: 3.

Murphy, P. (2003). 'New Squad to Police Sex-trade Boom.' *The Age.* (22 May). Melbourne: 2.

Murphy, P. (2003a) 'Police/Council' at loggerheads about who is responsible.' *The Age.* (12 August). Melbourne: 5.

Murphy, P. (2003b). 'Agony for Sex Slaves as State's Illegal Brothels Flourish.' *The Age.* (14 July): 1.

Murray, K. (2001). Sex Work as Work: Labour Regulation in the Legal Sex Industry in Victoria. (Masters Thesis). Faculty of Law. Melbourne: University of Melbourne.

Musolino, R. (2002). 'Recent Developments in Unions and OHS Issues.' *Women and Occupational Health and Safety.* Melbourne Trades Hall Council:
http://www.ohsrep.org.au/campaigns/womenbckgrnd.html

Nagle, J. (1997). *Whores and Other Feminists.* New York: Routledge and Kegan Paul.

Naidoo, M. (1996). 'Official-sex comes second to a good flutter.' *The Age.* (24 July). Melbourne: 1.

National Adult Entertainment Industry. (1996). 'Sexpo 96 Success.' *Sex Files: The Newsletter of the National Adult Entertainment Industry 1*: 1.

National Board of Health and Welfare. (2003). *Prostitution in Sweden: Knowledge, Beliefs and Attitudes of Key Informants.* Situation Description. Stockholm: Socialstyrelsen.

National Criminal Investigation Department. (2002). *Trafficking in Women.* Situation report no. 5 (1 January–31 December). Stockholm: NCID, National Criminal Intelligence Service, Illegal Immigration Unit.

National Criminal Investigation Department. (2003). *Trafficking in human beings for sexual purposes.* Situation report no. 6 (1 January–31 December). Stockholm: NCID, National Criminal Intelligence Service, Illegal Immigration Unit.

National Health and Safety Commission Australia. (1990). *National Approach to Women's Occupational Health and Safety.* Canberra: AGPS.

Nead, L. (1999). 'Stigmatization of Prostitutes.' In R. Nye (ed). *Sexuality.* Oxford: Oxford University Press: 131–132.

Nearie, J. (1990). 'Danger: Women at Work.' *Worksafe Australia.* (May) 5: 1.

Neave, M. (1988). 'The Failure of Prostitution Law Reform.' *Australian and New Zealand Journal of Criminology 21*: 202–211.

Neave, M. (1988a). 'Overview of National Legal Responses to Prostitution – Prostitution Laws – Strategies for the Future.' *Sex Industry and the AIDS Debate 88.* Report and Conference Papers. First National Sex Industry Conference (22–25 October). St Kilda, Melbourne: Prostitutes' Collective of Victoria.

Neave, M. (1994). 'Prostitution Laws in Australia: Past and Current Trends.' In R. Perkins, G. Prestage, R. Garrett and F. Lovejoy (eds). *Sex Work and Sex Workers in Australia.* Sydney: University of New South Wales Press: 67–99.

Nengeh, M., D. Allman, et al. (2000). *HIV/AIDS and Prostitution: The Top 25 Resources.* Health Canada: Canadian HIV/AIDS Legal Network: http://pubs.cpha.ca/PDF/P3/17998.pdf

Newton, J. (1997). Sex: It's A Seller's Market. *The Financial Review.* (7 March). Sydney: 3–4.

Norberry, J. (2005). *Criminal Code Amendment (Trafficking in Persons Offences) 2004.* (4 February). Canberra: Parliament of Australia. Department of Parliamentary Services.

Nordic Baltic Campaign Against Trafficking in Women. (2002). *Final Report*. Coordinator, Gunilla Ekberg. Oslo and Stockholm: Nordic Council of Ministries.

Noske, H. and Deacon S. (1996). *Off Our Backs: A Report into the Exit and Retraining Needs of Victorian Sex Workers*. St. Kilda, Melbourne: Prostitutes' Collective of Victoria.

Nussbaum, M. (1999). *Sex and Social Justice*. Oxford: Oxford University Press.

O'Brien, N. (2003). 'Officials impotent on sex slave trade.' *The Australian*. (29 March): 15.

Occupational Safety and Health Convention, 1981. (No. 155). Geneva: The United Nations International Labour Organisation.

O'Connell Davison, J. (1998). *Prostitution, Power and Freedom*. Cambridge: Polity Press.

Office of the Attorney-General. (1999). *Targeting Illegal Brothels*. Press Release (6 May).

Office to Monitor and Combat Trafficking in Persons (2004). *Trafficking in Persons Report*. (14 June).The United States Department of State. http://www.state.gov/g/tip/rls/tiprpt/2004/

Office to Monitor and Combat Trafficking in Persons. (2005). *Trafficking in Human Beings*. (26 June). The United States Department of State. http://www.state.gov/g/tip/rls/tiprpt/2005/

Office to Monitor and Combat Trafficking in Persons. (2005). *UN Commission on the Status of Women Adopts US Human Trafficking Resolution*. Fact Sheet. (March 18). The United States Department of State. http://www.state.gov/g/tip/rls/fs/2005/43630.htm

Office to Monitor and Combat Trafficking in Persons (2006). *Trafficking in Persons Report* (14 June). The United States Department of State. http://www.state.gov/g/tip/rls/tiprpt/2006/65983.htm

OHCHR. (2006). *Special Rapporteur on violence against women, its causes and consquences*. United Nations: Office of the High Commission of Human Rights:
http://www.ohchr.org/english/issues/women/rapporteur/

O'Neill, M. (1996). 'Researching Prostitution and Violence: Towards a Feminist Praxis.' In M. Hester, L. Kelly and J. Radford (eds). *Women, Violence and Male Power: Feminist Research, Activism and Practice*. Buckingham and Philadelphia: Open University Press.

Orsillo, S. (2006). *Sexual Assault Against Females.* National Centre for PTSD
http://www.ncptsd.va.gov/facts/specific/fs_female_sex_assault.html

Osotimehin, B. (2005). 'The Other Half.' *New York Times.* (19 August):
http://www.nytimes.com/2005/08/19/opinion/19osotimehin.html?e
x=1282104000&en=f4f7e9e505940ade&ei=5088&partner=rssnyt&
emc=rss

O'Toole, L. (1998). *Pornocopia: Porn, Sex, Technology and Desire.* London: Serpent's Tail.

Overall, C. (1992). 'What's Wrong with Prostitution.' *Signs. 17*(4): 705–724.

Overs, C. (1988). *Sex Industry and the Aids Debate.* Report and Conference Papers First National Sex Industry Conference. (22–25 October). St Kilda, Melbourne: Prostitutes' Collective of Victoria: 108–17.

Overs, C. (1988a). 'First National Conference.' *Working Girl. 6*: 2–3.

Overs, C. (1989). 'The Vth International Conference on AIDS.' *Working Girl. 7*: 4–7.

Overs, C. (1991). *National Consultation on the Issues and Needs of HIV Positive Sex Workers.* Canberra: Scarlet Alliance.

Overs, C. and P. Longo (1997). *Making Sex Work Safe.* London: Network of Sex Work Projects and Russell Press Ltd.

Outshoorn, J. (ed). (2004). *The Politics of Prostitution: Women's Movements, Democratic States and the Globalisation of Sex Commerce,* Cambridge: Cambridge University Press.

Pateman, C. (1988). *The Sexual Contract.* Cambridge: Polity Press.

Patten, F. (1994). *President's Report The Eros Foundation – 1994.* Canberra: The Eros Foundation Publications and Archives, Flinders University, Adelaide, South Australia.

Paul, S. (2002) 'Brothels Want To Seduce Investors: Sex Sells, And Australian Regulators See No Reason Why A Popular Bordello Can't Go Public.' *Reuters.* (23 July): D3.

Paul, S. (2003). 'Investors Pounce on Brothel Shares.' *Reuters News.* (1 May): 16, 41.

Peetz, D. (2005). *The Impact of Australian Workplace Agreements and the Abolition of the 'No Disadvantage Test.'* Griffith, Queensland:

Department of Industrial Relations, Griffith Business School, Griffiths University.

Petzall, S., N. Timo, et al. (2002). *Australian Industrial Relations in a South East Asian Context.* Emerald, Victoria: Eruditions Publishing.

Perkins, R. and G. Bennet (1985). *Being a Prostitute.* Sydney: Allen and Unwin.

Perkins, R. (1991). 'The Prostitutes' Response.' *Working Girls: Prostitutes, Their Life and Social Control.* Canberra: Australian Institute of Criminology: http://www.aic.gov.au/publications/lcj/working/ch5.html

Perkins, R. and G. Gareth. (1994). *Sex Work and Sex Workers in Australia.* Sydney: University of New South Wales Press.

Pheterson, G. (ed). (1989). *A Vindication of the Rights of Whores.* Seattle: Seattle Press.

Pheterson, G. (1993). 'The Whore Stigma – Female Dishonour and Male Unworthiness.' *Social Text.* Winter Edition: 39–63.

Pheterson, G. (1996). *The Prostitution Prism.* Amsterdam: Amsterdam University Press.

Phillippe, R. (1994). City Brothel, escort agency owners find a new voice.' *Truth National.* Melbourne: 43.

Pink Palace. (2003). *Melbourne Brothel "The Pink Palace" – Opens Australia's First Disabled Access Room.* Media Release. Melbourne: Eros Foundation Publications and Archives, Flinders University, Adelaide, South Australia.

Pinto, S., A. Scandia and P. Wilson. (1990). 'Prostitution Laws in Australia.' *Trends and Issues in Crime and Criminal Justice. 22*: 1–7.

Planet Platinum (2004). http://www.planetplatinum.com/au

Plumridge, L. (2001). 'Rhetoric, Reality and Risk Outcomes in Sex Work.' *Health, Risk and Society. 3*(2): 199–215.

Plumridge, L. and G. Abel (2001). 'A "segmented" sex industry in New Zealand: sexual and personal safety of female sex workers.' *Australian and New Zealand Journal of Public Health. 25* (1): 77–83.

Police vs. Gary Glazner and Paul Donato Mariono (1999). p.48.

Priesley, S. (1997). *The Prostitution Trap.* Smithfield, NSW: Gary Allen.

Pringle, R. (1988). *Secretaries Talk: Sexuality, power and work.* Sydney: Allen and Unwin.

Project Respect. (2006). *About Trafficking*:
http://www.projectrespect.org.au/faq.html

Prostitutes' Collective of Victoria. (1985). 'Facts on Aids for Working Girls.' St Kilda, Melbourne: Prostitutes' Collective of Victoria Archives.

Prostitutes' Collective of Victoria. (1987). 'Tax Seminar.' *Working Girl.* 4: 2.

Prostitutes' Collective of Victoria. (1989). *Working Girl* (Video Recording). St Kilda, Melbourne: Prostitutes' Collective of Victoria.

Prostitutes' Collective of Victoria. (1990). 'The History of the PCV (Part 1).' *Working Girl.* 8: 1–3.

Prostitutes' Collective of Victoria. (1990a). 'History of the PCV (Part 2).' *Working Girl.* 9: 15.

Prostitutes' Collective of Victoria. (1990b). 'Towards a Code of Practice: Occupational Health and Safety.' *Working Girl.* 10: 17.

Prostitutes' Collective of Victoria. (1990c). 'WorkCare.' *Working Girl.* 9: 17–18.

Prostitutes' Collective of Victoria. (1990d). 'Mister Please, Please, Fantasy Work: extras ain't what they used to be.' *Working Girl.* 9: 16.

Prostitutes' Collective of Victoria. (1990e). 'Fantasy work.' *Working Girl/Working Boy.* 10: 12.

Prostitutes' Collective of Victoria. (1991). 'STD Potential Videos.' *Working Girl.* 11: 13.

Prostitutes' Collective of Victoria. (1992). 'Two-faced.' *Working Girl/ Working Boy.* 13.

Prostitutes' Collective of Victoria. (1992a). *Working Girl/Working Boy.* 13.

Prostitutes' Collective of Victoria. (1992b). 'Fantasy and Bondage and Discipline Workshop.' *Working Girl/Working Boy.* 13: 2–3.

Prostitutes' Collective of Victoria (1992–1993). *Annual General Report.* St Kilda, Melbourne: Prostitutes' Collective of Victoria.

Prostitutes' Collective of Victoria (1993). 'Current Affairs.' *Working Girl/Working Boy.* 14: 5.

Prostitutes' Collective of Victoria (1993a). 'Client's Corner.' *Working Girl/Working Boy.* 14: 14.

Prostitutes' Collective of Victoria (1994). 'Dancing on the Tables is Allowed.' *Working Girl/Working Boy. 15*: 7.

Prostitutes' Collective of Victoria. (1994a). 'Fear loathing shame and anger – Rape.' *Working Girl/Working Boy. 15*: 26.

Prostitutes' Collective of Victoria. (1994b). 'Licked groped ravished.' *Working Girl/Working Boy. 15*: 10.

Prostitutes' Collective of Victoria. (1994c). 'Diary of a Male Street Worker.' *Working Girl/Working Boy. 15*: 6.

Prostitutes' Collective of Victoria. (1994d). 'Handy Hints for Transsexuals.' *Working Girl/Working Boy. 15*: 45.

Prostitutes' Collective of Victoria (c.1994). *Ten Point Plan for Decriminalisation*. St Kilda, Melbourne, Prostitutes' Collective of Victoria Archives.

Prostitutes' Collective of Victoria. (c.1995). *Hussies Handbook*. St Kilda, Melbourne: Prostitutes' Collective of Victoria Archives.

Prostitutes' Collective of Victoria. (1996). *Prostitutes' Collective of Victoria Annual General Report*. St Kilda, Melbourne: Prostitutes' Collective of Victoria Archives.

Prostitutes' Collective of Victoria. (c.1996). www.arts.unimelb.edu.au/amu/ucr/student/1996/m.dwyer/pcvhome. html

Prostitutes' Collective of Victoria. (1998). 'Needle Works.' *Working Girl/Working Boy. 25*: 17.

Prostitutes' Collective of Victoria. (1998). *Annual General Report*. St Kilda, Melbourne: Prostitutes' Collective of Victoria Archives.

Prostitutes' Collective of Victoria. (1999). 'Ugly Mugs.' *Working Girl/ Working Boy. 26*: 16–17.

Prostitution Licensing Authority. (2002). *Health and Safety Guidelines for Brothels*. Brisbane: The State of Queensland.

Public Affairs Branch for the Office of Major Projects (1996). 'Agenda 21.' *Agenda 21 Quarterly 2*. Melbourne: Projects Department of Infrastructure.

Public Health Association of Australia (PHAA). (1999). *Policy Statement – Emergency Contraception*. Adopted at the 1999 AGM of the PHA and revised in September 2002.

Purdie, D., M. Dunne, et al. (2002). 'Health and Demographic Characteristics of Respondents in An Australian National Sexuality

Survey: Comparison and population norms.' *Epidemiology and Community Health*. *56*: 748–753. Photocopy. Eros Foundation Publications and Archives, The University of Flinders, South Australia.

Pyett, P., B. Haste, et al. (1996a). 'Risk Practices for HIV Infection and Other STDs Amongst Female Prostitutes Working in Legal Brothels.' *AIDS Care. 8* (1): 85–94.

Pyett, P., B. Haste, et al. (1996b). 'Who Works in the Sex Industry? A profile of female prostitutes in Victoria.' *Australian Journal of Public Health 20* (3): 431–433.

Pyett, P. and D. Warr (1996). *When 'Gut Instinct' Is Not Enough: Women at Risk in Sex Work: Report to the Community.* Melbourne: Centre for the Study of Sexually Transmissible Diseases, La Trobe University.

Pyett, P. and D. Warr (1999). 'Women at Risk in Sex Work: Strategies for Survival.' *Journal of Sociology 35* (2): 183–259.

Pyett, P., D. Warr and J. Pope (1999). *It Goes With the Territory: Street sex work is risky business.* Melbourne: Australian Research Centre in Sex, Health and Society, Faculty of Health Sciences, La Trobe University.

Queen v Glazner, Gary. (2000). Transcript of trial proceedings, vols 1 and 2. Available from the Office of Public Prosecutions, Melbourne.

Queen v Tang, Wei. (2006). VCC637. Melbourne.

Queensland. (1989). *Report of the Commission of Inquiry into Possible Illegal Activities and Associated Police Misconduct.* (Chairperson G.E. Fitzgerald QC). Brisbane: Government Printer.

Queensland. (2004). *Regulating Prostitution: An Evaluation of the Prostitution Control Act 1999. Crime and Misconduct Commission.* Queensland.

Quinlan, M. (1993). 'Women's Occupational Health and Safety: a conceptual framework.' In S. Blackmur, D. Fingleton and D. Akers (eds). *Women's Occupational Health and Safety: The Unmet Needs.* Brisbane: Queensland Women's Consultative Council: School of Management, Human Resources and Industrial Relations.

Quinlan, M. and P. Bohle. (1991). *Managing Occupational Health and Safety in Australia.* South Melbourne: MacMillan Education

Ray, G. (2003). 'The Youngest Profession.' *Newcastle Herald Weekender* (28 June): 67

Raymond, J. (1995). *Women As Wombs: Reproductive technologies and the battle over women's freedom.* Melbourne: Spinifex Press.

Raymond, J. (1998). *Legitimating Prostitution as Sex Work: UN Labour Organization (ILO) Calls for Recognition of the Sex Industry.* N. Amherst, MA: Coalition Against Trafficking in Women.

Raymond, J. (1998a). 'Prostitution as Violence Against Women: NGO Stonewalling in Beijing and Elsewhere.' *Women's Studies International. 21*(1): 1–9.

Raymond, J. (1998b). *The Health Effects of Prostitution.* N. Amherst, MA: Coalition Against Trafficking in Women.

Raymond, J. (2001). *Guide to the New UN Trafficking Protocol.* N. Amherst, MA: Coalition Against Trafficking in Women in association with the European Women's Lobby, MAPP and the Association Des Femmes De L'Europe Meridionale.

Raymond, J. (2003). *The Ongoing Tragedy of International Slavery and Human Trafficking.* Testimony on October 29, 2003, before the Subcommittee on Human Rights and Wellness of the Committee on Government Reform, House of Representatives, United States': Coalition Against Trafficking in Women (29 October): (http://action.web.ca/home/catw/readingroom.shtml?AA_EX_Session=8a2fc95a86690a245221978c1eb48376&x=53794

Raymond, J. (ed). (2004). *Violence Against Women.* October. US: Sage Publications.

Raymond, J. (2004a). 'Ten Reasons for Not Legalizing Prostitution and a Legal Response to the Demand for Prostitution.' In M. Farley (ed). *Prostitution, Trafficking and Traumatic Stress.* New York: Haworth Press: 315–332.

Reid, A. (1978). Labor Group's Shock Report on Marriage and Prostitution (9 July). *Bulletin.* Melbourne: 20–21.

Repetto T. (2003). *American Mafia: A history of its Rise to Power.* New York: Holt.

Resourcing Health and Education in the Sex Industry. (2000). *Sex Industry Health Service.* http://www.ischs.org.au/rhed2.htm

Resourcing Health and Education in the Sex Industry. (2001). *Red: magazine for the sex industry.* (2). St Kilda, Melbourne: Resourcing Health and Education in the Sex Industry.

Resourcing Health and Education in the Sex Industry. (2003). *Sex Industry Health Service.* http://www.ischs.org.au/rhed2.htm

Resourcing Health and Education in the Sex Industry. (2006) 'Sex in the City' *Health Information*: http://www.sexworker.org.au/healthinfo/

Resourcing Health and Education in the Sex Industry. (2006a). 'Power.' http://www.sexworker.org.au/uploads/documents/RHED_power.pdf

Resourcing Health and Education in the Sex Industry. (2006b). 'Safety tips for escort workers' http://www.sexworker.org.au/uploads/documents/Safety_Tips_for_E scort_Workers.pdf

Retschlag, C. (1999). '"Business-like" male sex workers deny industry myth.' *Courier Mail*. (2 March) Brisbane: 5.

Richardson, D. (1997). 'Sexuality and Feminism.' In V. Robinson and D. Richardson (eds). *Introducing Women's Studies: Feminist Theory and Practice*. London: Macmillan Press.

Richters, J. and C. Rissel. (2005). *Doing it down under: The sexual lives of Australians*. Sydney: Allen & Unwin.

RMITunion (RMITU). (2004). *'Students and Sex Work.' Your Rights as Workers*. Melbourne: RMITU: http://www.rmit.edu.au/browse;ID=ybbrnrb7uxj61;STATUS=A?QR Y=SEX%20WORK&STYPE=ENTIRE

Roberts, N. (1992). *Whores in History: Prostitution in Western Society*. London: Harper Collins.

Roberts, N. (1994). 'The whore, her stigma, the punter and his wife.' *New Internationalist*. 252 (February): www.newint.org/issue252/whore.htm

Robinson, P. (1993). 'Melbourne's Shy and Retiring Moguls of Porn.' *Sunday Age*. (17 January). Melbourne: 9.

Rollins, A. (1995). 'Illegal Brothels Will Survive, Say Police.' *Sunday Age*. (27 May). Melbourne: 11.

Rose, M. (2003). 'Illegal Brothels Rife In Residential Areas.' *Herald Sun*. (18 August). Melbourne: 1, 4.

Ross, C. A., M. Farley and H. Schwartz. (2003). 'Dissociation Among Women in Prostitution.' In M. Farley (ed). *Prostitution, Trafficking and Traumatic Stress*. Binghamton, NY: The Hawthorn Maltreatment and Trauma Press: 199–212.

Rowland, R. and R. Klein. (1996). 'Radical Feminism: History, Politics, Action.' In D. Bell and R. Klein (eds). *Radically Speaking: Feminism Reclaimed*. Melbourne: Spinifex Press: 9–36.

Royal Commission on Human Relationships. (1977). *Final Report.* (Chairman, E. A. Evatt), vol. 5. Australian Government Publishing Service. Canberra.

Rubin, G. (1993). 'Thinking Sex: The Limits of Feminism.' In H. Abelove, M. Aina Barale and D. Halperin (eds). *The Lesbian and Gay Studies Reader.* New York: Routledge: 27–34.

Sahdev, D. (2002). 'Not Just A Medical Issue – social and economic factors are a part of the AIDS pandemic.' Sixth International Conference on AIDS (8–11 October). Melbourne: http://www.earthtimes.org/

Salmons, R. (2003). 'Brisk Trade Sends Daily Planet Scrip into Orbit.' *The Age.* (3 May). Melbourne: 2.

Santos, A. (1999). 'Globalization, Human Rights and Sexual Exploitation.' In D. Hughes and C. Roche (eds). *Making the Harm Visible: Gobal Sexual Exploitation of Women and Girls.* Kingston, Rhode Island: Coalition Against Trafficking in Women: 33–41.

Satz, D. (1995). 'Markets in Women's Sexual Labor.' *Ethics. 106*: 63–85.

Saunders, K. (1995). 'Controlling (Hetero) Sexuality: The implementation and operation of contagious diseases legislation in Australia, 1968–1945.' In D. Kirkby (ed). *Sex, Power and Justice.* Melbourne; Oxford; Auckland and New York: Oxford University Press: 2–15.

Scarlet Alliance (c.2000). *Scarlet Alliance History.* http://www.scarletalliance.org.au/who/history

Scrambler, G. and A. Scrambler (eds). (1997). *Rethinking Prostitution: Purchasing Sex in the 1990s.* London; New York: Routledge.

Scutt, J. (1977). 'The Economics of Sex: Women in Service.' *Australian Quarterly. 15*: 32–46.

Segal, L. (ed). (1997). *New Sexual Agendas.* Houndsmill; Basingstoke; Hampshire and London: MacMillan Press.

Self Health for Queensland Workers in the Sex Industry (SQWISI). (1997). 'Condom Breakage and Slippage.' *Respect. 13*: 15.

Sendziuk, P. (2003). 'Denying the Grim Reaper, Govt Response to Aids.' *Eureka Street.* October: http://eurekastreet.com.au/articles/0310sendziuk.html

Sex Workers Outreach Project. (1995). 'Negotiating Condom Use.' *The Professional. 15* (June/August): 4.

Sex Workers Outreach Project. (1996). *Getting on Top of Health and Safety in the NSW Sex Industry.* Sydney, Sex Workers Outreach. Project funded under the New South Wales Industry Prevention Education and Research Grants Scheme.

Sex Workers Outreach Project. (c.1996). *Condom Breakage and Slippage.* Fact Sheet. Northern Territory: Sex Worker Outreach Project (SWOP), Eros Foundation Publications and Archives, Flinders University, Adelaide, South Australia.

Sex Workers Outreach Project. (1997). *Sadomasochism, Bondage and Discipline.* Sydney: Sex Workers Outreach Project (SWOP), Eros Foundation Publications and Archives, Flinders University, Adelaide, South Australia.

Sex Workers Outreach Project. (c.1998). *Commercial Sex Menu.* Sydney: Eros Publications, Eros Foundation Publications and Archives, Flinders University, Adelaide, South Australia.

Shamsullah, A. (1992). 'Politics in Victoria: Parliament, Cabinet and the Political Parties.' In M. Considine and B. Costar (eds). *Trials in Power: Cain, Kirner and Victoria 1982–1992.* Melbourne: Melbourne University Press: 11–24.

Sharp, R. (1994). 'Female Sex Work and Injecting Drug Use: What more do we need to Know.' In R. Perkins and G. Gareth (eds). *Sex Work and Sex Workers in Australia.* Sydney: Sydney University Press.

Sherwin, S. (1998). *The Politics of Women's Health: Exploring agency and autonomy.* Philadelphia: Temple University Press.

Silkstone D. (2004). 'Fines for St Kilda "sex tourists".' *The Age.* (29 May). Melbourne: 5.

Silvester, J. et al. (2003). 'Double Execution Linked To Sex Underworld.' *The Age.* (21 October). Melbourne: 1.

Silvester, J. and I. Munro (2004). 'Crime Groups Thriving.' *The Age.* (25 August). Melbourne: 1

Snow, J. (ed). (1998). *STD Handbook.* Canberra: Commonwealth Department of Human Services and Health, Education Section of the AIDS/STD Unit.

Social Questions Committee (Victoria) (1984). *Points Overlooked in the Recommendations for Legal Brothels.* Project funded by the Catholic Archdiocese of Melbourne on Social Issues. Melbourne: Catholic Women's Association Archives.

Social Questions Committee (Victoria) (1987). *Prostitution Regulation Act and the Government's Refusal to Proclaim It.* Project funded by the Catholic Archdiocese of Melbourne on Social Issues. Melbourne: Catholic Women's Association Archives.

Social Questions Committee (Victoria) (1990). *Participation in the Prostitution Debate in Victoria.* Project Funded by the Catholic Archdiocese of Melbourne on Social Issues May 1990. Melbourne: Catholic Women's Association Archives.

Social Security Network (1998). 'Brazil spends $1.7 ml on helping child prostitutes.' *Reuters.* (12 June). In F. Miko. (2003). *Trafficking in Women and Children: The US and international response.* CSR Report for US Congress. (10 July 2003): 7.

Song, Kyung Sook (2006). *Consistent, integrated efforts are urgently needed to help survivors start a new life.* Special Report. Seoul: Centre for Women's Human Rights:
http://www.stop.or.kr/english/index.php

South Australia (1998). *Parliamentary Debates.* Council, 22 July: 910.

Spearmint Rhino Online (2002). 'About Spearmint Rhino.' *Spearmint Rhino – Gentlemen's Clubs*:
http://www.spearmintrhino.com/about2.htm

Spender, D. (1980). *Man Made Language.* Boston: Routledge and Kegan Paul.

St Kilda Women's Liberation Group No. 5 (c.1975). *The Alternative to Illegal Prostitution was not Legal Prostitution.* Susan Hawthorne Files Melbourne.

Standing Against Global Exploitation (SAGE) (2005). 'Issues, Briefs and Articles' SAGE Information Centre:
http://www.sagesf.org/html/info_briefs_questions_sage.htm

Stark, C. and R. Whisnant (eds). (2004). *Not For Sale: Feminists Resisting Prostitution and Pornography.* Melbourne: Spinifex Press.

Stewart, S. (2003). 'Australian Brothels Hit the Market.' *Globe and Mail.* (29 November): 4.

Stoltenberg, J. (2004). 'Pornography and international human rights.' In C. Stark and R. Whisnant (eds). *Not For Sale: Feminists Resisting Prostitution and Pornography.* Melbourne: Spinifex Press: 400–409.

Strudevant, S. and P. Stolzfus (eds). (1992). *Let the Good Times Roll: Prostitution and the US Military in Asia.* New York: The New Press.

Stuteville, S. and A. Stonehill (2006). 'Sex Workers in the City of Joy.' *The Independent* (New York City). 89 (29 June): http://www.indypendent.org/?p=313

Sullivan, B. (1992). 'Feminist Approaches to the Sex Industry.' In. S. Gerull and B. Halstead (eds). *Sex Industry and Public Policy: Proceedings of Conference Australian Institute of Criminology.* (6–8 May 1991). Canberra: Australian Institute of Criminology: 7–12.

Sullivan, B. (1995). 'Rethinking Prostitution.' In B. Caine and R. Pringle (eds). *Transitions: New Australian Feminisms.* Sydney: Allen and Unwin.

Sullivan, B. (1997). *The Politics of Sex: Prostitution and Pornography in Australia since 1945.* Melbourne: Cambridge University Press.

Sullivan, B. (2003). *Can a Prostitute Be Raped? Sex Workers, Women and the Politics of Rape Law Reform.* Paper presented at the Australian Political Studies Association Conference. University of Tasmania, Hobart. 29 September–1 October 2003.

Sullivan, B. (2004). 'The Women's Movement and Prostitution Politics in Australia.' In J. Outshoorn (ed). *The Politics of Prostitution: Women's Movements, Democratic States and the Globalisation of Sex Commerce.* Cambridge: Cambridge University Press: 240–252.

Sullivan, M. (1998). 'Marketing Women's Sexual Exploitation in Australia.' In D. Hughes and C. Roche (eds). *Making the Harm Visible: Global Exploitation of Women and Girls.* Kingston, Rhode Island: Coalition Against Trafficking in Women: 181–187.

Sullivan, M. (1999–2000). "Victorian Values." *Trouble and Strife – the radical feminist magazine.* 40 (Winter). 59–64.

Sullivan, M. (1999a). Interview with Alison Arnot-Bradshaw. Project Worker for the Prostitutes' Collective of Victoria (15 June). Melbourne.

Sullivan, M. (1999b). Interview with Pauline Burgess. Industrial Relations and Women's Officer for the Shop Distributors and Allied Employees Association (20 October). Melbourne.

Sullivan, M. (1999c). Interview with Jocelyn Snow. Project Manager for the Prostitutes' Collective of Victoria (15 May). Melbourne.

Sullivan, M. (2004). *Making Sex Work: The experience of legalised prostitution in Victoria, Australia.* (PhD Thesis). The Department of Political Science. Melbourne: The University of Melbourne.

Sullivan, M. (2004a). 'Can Prostitution be safe? Applying occupational health and safety codes to Australia's legalised brothel prostitution.' In C. Stark and R. Whisnant (eds). *Not For Sale: Feminists Resisting Prostitution and Pornography.* Melbourne: Spinifex Press: 252–268.

Sullivan, M. (2006). *What Happens When Prostitution Becomes Work: An update on legalisation in Australia.* N. Amherst, MA: Coalition Against Trafficking in Women (CATW).

Sutton, C., S. Crittle and M. Forbes. (1999). 'Women for Sale at $40,000.' *Sun Herald* (22 August): 6–7.

Swan, R. (2003). 'Eros Challenges Government on Visa Plan.' *Eros Foundation.* (9 May):
http://www.eros.com.au/pressrelease.php?id+28.

Swedish Government Offices. (2001). *Follow-Up of the Violence Against Women Reform.*
http://www.naring.regeringen.se/inenglish/areas_of/equality.htm

Tailby, R. (2001). 'Organised Crime and People Smuggling/Trafficking to Australia.' Australian Institute of Criminology: *Trends And Issues In Crime And Criminal Justice*, 208: 1–6.

Tantra Man (pseudonym). (1999). 'Sexual Whirlpools and Setting the Limits.' *The Professional. 36*: 23.

Taylor, K. (2001). 'Organisers of sex servitude "let off".' *The Age.* (18 June). Melbourne: 6.

The Korean Legislator. (2006). *Act on Punishing of Procuring Prostitution and Associated Acts.* Seoul: Centre for Women's Human Rights:
http://www.stop.or.kr/english/index.php

The White House. (2003). *Bush Signs National Security Directive Against Human Trafficking.* Department of State Washington File Fact. Office of the Press Secretary (25 February):
http://www.uspolicy.be/Article.asp?ID=C4DC94E4-3C01-4760-9591-FB8518394E4A

Thomas, A. and C. Kitzinger (eds). (1997). *Sexual Harassment: Contemporary feminist perspectives.* Buckingham, UK; Bristol, PA, US: 1 Open University Press.

Thompson, S. (2000). 'Prostitution – A Choice Ignored.' *Women's Rights Law Report. 21*: 217–243.

'Time for a rethink on street soliciting' (2004). Editorial. *The Age.* (27 July). Melbourne.

Truong, Than-Dan (1996). 'Serving the Tourist Market: Female Labour in International Tourism.' In S. Jackson and S. Scott (eds). *Feminism and Sexuality: A reader.* Edinburgh: Edinburgh University Press.

Trussell J. et al. (1998). 'New Estimates of the effectiveness of the Yuzpe regimen of emergency contraception.' *Contraception. 57*: 363–369.

Tucker, S. (1999). 'Prostitutes to get on to of safety issues.' *The Newcastle Herald* (New South Wales). (4 November): 3

Tuttle, L. (1986). *Encyclopaedia of Feminism.* London: Arrow Books.

United Nations (1949). *The Convention for the Suppression of the Traffic in Persons and of the Exploitation of Others.*
http://www.unhchr.ch/html/menu3/33.htm.

United Nations (1981). *The Convention on the Elimination of All Forms of Discrimination Against Women.*
http://www.unhchr.ch/html/menu3/b/elcedaw.htm

United Nations (1995). *Beijing Declaration and Platform for Action.* Fourth World Conference on Women. (15 September). A/CONF.177/20. Geneva.

United Nations (1995a). *Report of the Fourth World Conference Beijing.* 4–15 September. Geneva: United Nations Publication.

United Nations (2000). *Protocol to Prevent, Suppress and Punish Trafficking in Persons, Especially Women and Children, Supplementing the United Nations Convention Against Transnational Organized Crime:* http://untreaty.un.org/English/notpubl/18-12-a.E.doc

United Nations. (2005). *Millennium Development Goals Report.* World Summit United Nations Headquarters. New York.

United Nations High Commissioner for Refugees (2002). 'Refugee Women.' *Global Consultations on International Protections.* (25 April). EC/GC/02/8:
http://www.unhcr.org/cgi-bin/texis/vtx/protect/opendoc.pdf?tbl=PROTECTION&id=3cd154b64

United Nations International Children's Emergency Fund (2004). *UNICEF at a Glance.* UNICEF. Geneva.
http://www.unicef.org/publications/index_19020.html

United Nations Non Government Liaison Services. (2005). 'Beijing + 10: 49th Session of the Commission on the Status of Women.' *Roundup:* http://www.un-ngls.org/documents/pdf/roundup/RU122-Commission-Status-Women.pdf

United Nations Office on Drugs and Crime (2004). *The Protocol to Prevent, Suppress and Punish Trafficking in Persons: Summary*: http://www.unodc.org/unodc/en/trafficking_protocol.html

United Nations Office on Drugs and Crime (2006). *Trafficking in Persons Global Patterns*. (April).
http://www.unodc.org/unodc/en/trafficking_human_beings.html

United Nations Programme on HIV/AIDS and Office of the United Nations High Commission (1998/2003). *HIV/AIDS and Human Right: International Guidelines*. Geneva; New York: United Nations Publications.

United States Deparment of Health and Human Services. (2006). 'HHS Fights to Stem Human Trafficking.' *Press Release*. (15 August). Health and Human Services Press Office.

Vance, C. (ed). (1984). *Pleasure and Danger: Exploring Female Sexuality*. London: Routledge & Kegan Paul.

Vanwesenbeeck, I. (1994). *Prostitutes' Well-Being and Risk*. Amsterdam: VU University Press.

Vicqua, J. H. (1994). 'Lesbians Light Up the Love Industry: A brief history of lesbian and prostitute sisterhood.' *Working Girl/Working Boy. 15*: 36.

Victoria (1978). *Parliamentary Debates*, Assembly, 14 November: 2353.

Victoria (1980). *Parliamentary Debates*, Assembly, 28 April: 76–78.

Victoria (1980a). *Parliamentary Debates*, Assembly, 6 November: 2274–2278.

Victoria (1982). *Parliamentary Debates*, Council, 22 May: 355.

Victoria (1984). *Parliamentary Debates*, Council, 1 May: 2527–2587.

Victoria (1984b). *Parliamentary Debates*, Council, 18 April: 2304.

Victoria (1985). *Parliamentary Debates*, Assembly, 3 October: 1053.

Victoria (1985a). *Inquiry into Prostitution: Final Report* (Chairperson M. Neave). Melbourne: Government Printer.

Victoria (1987). *Parliamentary Debates*, Council, 7 October: 726–741.

Victoria (1994). *Parliamentary Debates*, Council, 4 October 1994: 105–107.

Victoria (1994a). *Parliamentary Debates*, Assembly, 21 October: 1453–1458.

Victoria (1994b). *Parliamentary Debates*, Assembly, 16 November: 1851–1884.

Victoria (1994c). *Parliamentary Debates* Council, 7 December: 1263–1278.

Victoria (1994d). *Parliamentary Debates*, Council, 29 November: 962–966.

Victoria (1997). *Parliamentary Debates*, Assembly, 22 May: 1612–1626.

Victoria (1997a). *Parliamentary Debates*, Council, 27 May: 1143–1151.

Victoria (1997b). *Prostitution Control Act Advisory Committee Final Report*. Melbourne: Department of Attorney-General.

Victoria (1999). *Parliamentary Debates*, Assembly, 6 May: 810–881.

Victoria (1999a). *Parliamentary Debates*, Assembly, 25 May: 1191–1211.

Victoria (1999b). *Parliamentary Debates*, Council, 1 June: 960–968

Victoria (2000). *Parliamentary Debates*, Council, 15 March: 291–305

Victoria (2000a). *Parliamentary Debates*, Assembly, 11 April: 849–867

Victoria (2001). *Parliamentary Debates*, Assembly, 4 April: 637–645

Victoria (2001a). *Proposed Health (Infectious Diseases) Regulations 2001: Regulatory Impact Statement*. Melbourne: Public Health Division, Victorian Government Department of Human Services.

Victoria (2003). *Parliamentary Debates*, Assembly, 7 May: 1507.

Victoria (2004). *Parliamentary Debates*, Assembly, 21 April: 712–718

Victoria (2004a). *Parliamentary Debates*, Council, 6 May: 638–640

Victoria (2004b). *Parliamentary Debates*, Assembly, 9 May: 925–936

Victoria (2004c). *Parliamentary Debates*, Council, 11 May: 750–759

Victoria (2004d). *Parliamentary Debates*, Council, 14 October: 914–915

Victoria (2006). *Proposed Prostitution Regulation: Regulatory Impact Statement*. Melbourne: Consumer Affairs Victoria, Department of Justice.

Victorian WorkCover Authority (1996). *A Guide to Occupational Health and Safety Act, 1985*. Seventh revised edition. (September 1996). Melbourne: VWA.

Victorian WorkCover Authority (2006). 'Occupational Health & Safety Act – Working Together for Safer, Healthier Workplaces.' *WorkSafe*: http://www.workcover.vic.gov.au/vwa/home.nsf/pages/ohsact

Victorian WorkCover Authority (2006a) 'Workplace Consultation.' *WorkSafe*: http://www.workcover.vic.gov.au/vwa/home.nsf/pages/consultation

von Doussa, J. (2004). *Statement Delivered by The Hon. John von Doussa Australian Human Rights and Equal Opportunity Commission*. National Human Rights Institutions. Agenda Item 18(b) at the 60th Session of the UN Commission on Human Rights (14 April). http://www.hreoc.gov.au/about_the_commission/speeches_president /60th_Session.htlm.

Walkovitz, J. (1996). *Prostitution in Victorian Society*. Cambridge and New York: Cambridge University Press.

Walkowitz, J. (1996a). 'The Politics of Prostitution.' In S. Jackson and S. Scott (eds). *Feminism and Sexuality: A reader*. Edinburgh: Edinburgh University Press: 288–296

Walkovitz, J. (1999). 'Stigmatization and the Contagious Diseases Act.' In R. Nye (ed). *Sexuality*. Oxford: Oxford University Press: 28–30.

Walsh, J. (1996). 'The World's First Prostitutes Union.' *Marie Claire*. January: 48–51.

Webb, C. (2003) 'Daily Planet Looks for Some "singergies".' *The Age*. (2 September): 4.

Willis. J., K. Peterson, et al. (2004). *Sex Work and the Accumulation of Risk: Male sex work as cultural practice*. Melbourne: Australian Research Centre in Sex, Health and Society. La Trobe University, Faculty of Health and Science.

Winberg, M. (2002). Speech at the Seminar on the effects of Legalization of Prostitution Activities; A Critical Analysis organized by the Swedish Government.

Winter, B., D. Thompson and S. Jeffreys (2002). 'The UN Approach to Harmful Traditional Practices: Some conceptual problems.' *International Feminist Journal of Politics*. 4: 72–94.

WISE (1994). 'Sex and Disability.' *Working Girl/Working Boy. 15*: 8–19.

WISE (1997). *B&D Workshop Flyer*. Fyshwick, Canberra: Eros Foundation Publications and Archives, Flinders University, Adelaide, South Australia.

WorkCover NSW. (2001). *Health and Safety Guidelines for Brothels.* Sydney: New South Wales Department of Health.

Working Party to the Minister for Planning and Environment (1983). *Report on Location of Massage Parlours.* Melbourne: Government Printer.

World Health Organisation (1992). *Women's Health: Across Age and Frontier.* Geneva: World Health Organisation.

World Health Organization (1998). *Report on the global HIV/AIDS Epidemic.* (1998):
http://whqlibdoc.who.int/unaids/1998/a62410.pdf

Wynhausen, E. and N. O'Brien (2005) 'Sex Slave informant to be deported from Australia.' (23 January). *The Australian.*

Index

OTHER BOOKS BY SPINIFEX PRESS

NOT FOR SALE:
FEMINISTS RESISTING PROSTITUTION AND PORNOGRAPHY

Christine Stark and Rebecca Whisnant (eds)

This international anthology brings together research, heart-breaking personal stories from survivors of the sex industry, and theory from over thirty women and men – activists, survivors, academics and journalists. *Not For Sale* is groundbreaking in its breadth, analysis and honesty.

> Loving and militant, practical and prophetic, this book collects the least compromised writing on a most crucial problem of our time – even the bottom line issue of all time.
>
> – CATHARINE A. MACKINNON

ISBN 1 876756 49 7
ISBN 9 781876 756499

THE IDEA OF PROSTITUTION

Sheila Jeffreys

Sheila Jeffreys explores the sharply contrasting views of prostitution. She examines the changing concept of prostitution from White Slave Traffic of the nineteenth century to its present status as legal. This book includes discussion of the varieties of prostitution such as: the experience of male prostituters; the uses of women in pornography; and the role of military brothels compared with slavery and rape in marriage. Sheila Jeffreys explodes the distinction between 'forced' and 'free' prostitution, and documents the expanding international traffic in women. She examines the claims of the prostitutes' rights movement and the sex industry, while supporting prostituted women. Her argument is threefold: the sex of prostitution is not just sex; the work of prostitution is not ordinary work; and prostitution is a 'choice' not for the prostituted women, but for the men who abuse them.

ISBN 1 875559 65 5
ISBN 9 781875 559657

THE WILL TO VIOLENCE:
THE POLITICS OF PERSONAL BEHAVIOUR

Susanne Kappeler

Sexual violence, racial violence, and the hatred of foreigners: how should we understand these and other forms of violent human behaviour? A brilliantly original analysis of violence in its many forms. Susanne Kappeler argues that violence is not just a social phenomenon which can be analysed scientifically: rather, it is a type of action which individuals 'will' or choose to perform. Kappeler maintains that contemporary culture is one where no one is any longer held responsible for their actions and where the conception of universal responsibility becomes the equivalent of universal acquittal.

The Will to Violence is a powerful critique of the structural forces that control our relationships. Eloquent and passionate it exposes a number of assumptions considered fundamental to western philosophical discourse. It contains an important critique of psychoanalysis, discussions of the discourse of racism and the democratisation of violence.

ISBN 1 875559 45 0 (hb)   **ISBN 9 781875 559268 (hb)**
ISBN 1 875559 46 9 (pb)   **ISBN 9 781875 559466 (pb)**

HONOUR: CRIMES, PARADIGMS, AND VIOLENCE AGAINST WOMEN

Lynn Welchman and Sara Hossain (Eds)

Norma Khouri brought the issue of honour killings into the news in Australia. Whatever one thinks of Khouri, the story she had to tell was based on the reality of many women's lives, not only in Jordan but also in Italy, Kurdistan, Latin America, the UK, South Asian and Nordic countries.

The purpose of this book is to support human rights activists, policymakers and lawyers by explaining what constitutes honour crimes and how they vary across different country contexts. It develops a human rights framework as an alternative to a cultural relativist approach. It urges the reform of many national legal systems which enable men to rely on the pretext of 'honour crimes' in order to get a reduced sentence. Like other acts of violence against women, they have no justification.

In the Australian context, the provocation rule could be considered a descendant of the 'honour' defence. This rule has enabled men to claim provocation – an insult to their honour – as an excuse for murdering wives, girlfriends and former partners.

The book includes writers from the UK, Pakistan, USA, Brazil, Caribbean, Israel, Lebanon, Jordan, Sri Lanka, India, Egypt, Norway, Bangladesh, Italy and Kurdistan.

ISBN 1 876756 61 6
ISBN 9 781876 756611

ENOUGH

Patricia Hughes

In this powerful narrative, Patricia Hughes, author of the best-selling *Daughters of Nazareth*, tells how she stayed in an abusive relationship, until finally she said: ENOUGH.

Patricia Hughes' experience of domestic violence is not rare.

Domestic violence is the single most common source of injury among women between the ages of fifteen and forty-four, more common than car accidents, mugging and rape by a stranger combined, and accounts for approximately twenty to twenty-five per cent of visits by women to emergency rooms.

There's no easy fix… History often carries with it the presumption that things change for the better, that somehow the passage of time will bring improvements. This doesn't help the women of today. With so much stacked up against those who don't leave abusive men, help of some sort is more important than ever. But no-one ever seems to be there to tell actually how to do it.

Hopefully, that's where I can help. 'I know the pitfalls and the signs…'

Enough is an important and heartfelt personal guide for women in abusive relationships and for friends and family who want to understand and help.

Enough includes practical guidelines – seven identifiable steps to freedom from domestic violence – and a National Help, Support and Referral guide.

ISBN 1 876756 40 3
ISBN 9 781876 756406

HELP! I'M LIVING WITH A ~~MAN~~ BOY

Betty McLellan

AN INTERNATIONAL BESTSELLER

Are you tired of finding towels on the bathroom floor?

Have you ever walked through a supermarket with a thirty-five-year-old child who wants only the most expensive things on the shelves?

How do you go about making men understand the difference between helping out with the housework and doing it?

And what about violence?

Help! I'm Living with a ~~Man~~ Boy has forty-one practical scenarios that many women will identify with immediately plus suggestions for dealing with these situations. This book is about relationships. Its overall aim is to encourage women and men to look more honestly at the way they relate to each other, and to strive for a personal maturity that will allow each of them to enter into the give and take that constitutes relationships based on genuine love, respect and equality. The focus is on men's emotional maturity and the harmful and destructive behaviour which usually accompanies such immaturity. Betty McLellan is careful to point out, that this does not describe all men. Some men have achieved maturity and are contributing in a mature way to their relationships. Others, she admits have a long way to go.

ISBN 1 876756 62 4
ISBN 9 781876 756628

Notes

*If you would like to know more about Spinifex Press
write for a free catalogue or visit our website*

SPINIFEX PRESS
PO Box 212 North Melbourne
Victoria 3051 Australia
http://www.spinifexpress.com.au